Living Legends and Full Agency

Implications of Repealing the Combat Exclusion Policy

PUBLIC ADMINISTRATION AND PUBLIC POLICY
A Comprehensive Publication Program

EDITOR-IN-CHIEF

DAVID H. ROSENBLOOM

Distinguished Professor of Public Administration
American University, Washington, DC

Founding Editor

JACK RABIN

RECENTLY PUBLISHED BOOKS

Living Legends and Full Agency: Implications of Repealing the Combat Exclusion Policy, G.L.A. Harris

Politics of Preference: India, United States, and South Africa, Krishna K. Tummala

Crisis and Emergency Management: Theory and Practice, Second Edition, Ali Farazmand

Labor Relations in the Public Sector, Fifth Edition, Richard C. Kearney and Patrice M. Mareschal

Democracy and Public Administration in Pakistan, Amna Imam and Eazaz A. Dar

The Economic Viability of Micropolitan America, Gerald L. Gordon

Personnel Management in Government: Politics and Process, Seventh Edition, Katherine C. Naff, Norma M. Riccucci, and Siegrun Fox Freyss

Public Administration in South Asia: India, Bangladesh, and Pakistan, edited by Meghna Sabharwal and Evan M. Berman

Making Multilevel Public Management Work: Stories of Success and Failure from Europe and North America, edited by Denita Cepiku, David K. Jesuit, and Ian Roberge

Public Administration in Africa: Performance and Challenges, edited by Shikha Vyas-Doorgapersad, Lukamba-Muhiya. Tshombe, and Ernest Peprah Ababio

Public Administration in Post-Communist Countries: Former Soviet Union, Central and Eastern Europe, and Mongolia, Saltanat Liebert, Stephen E. Condrey, and Dmitry Goncharov

Hazardous Materials Compliance for Public Research Organizations: A Case Study, Second Edition, Nicolas A. Valcik

Logics of Legitimacy: Three Traditions of Public Administration Praxis, Margaret Stout

The Politics–Administration Dichotomy: Toward a Constitutional Perspective, Second Edition, Patrick Overeem

Available Electronically
PublicADMINISTRATION*net*BASE
http://www.crcnetbase.com/page/public_administration_ebooks

Living Legends and Full Agency

Implications of Repealing the Combat Exclusion Policy

G.L.A. Harris

CRC Press is an imprint of the
Taylor & Francis Group, an **informa** business

CRC Press
Taylor & Francis Group
6000 Broken Sound Parkway NW, Suite 300
Boca Raton, FL 33487-2742

© 2015 by Taylor & Francis Group, LLC
CRC Press is an imprint of Taylor & Francis Group, an Informa business

No claim to original U.S. Government works

Printed on acid-free paper
Version Date: 20140819

International Standard Book Number-13: 978-1-4665-1378-5 (Hardback)

This book contains information obtained from authentic and highly regarded sources. Reasonable efforts have been made to publish reliable data and information, but the author and publisher cannot assume responsibility for the validity of all materials or the consequences of their use. The authors and publishers have attempted to trace the copyright holders of all material reproduced in this publication and apologize to copyright holders if permission to publish in this form has not been obtained. If any copyright material has not been acknowledged please write and let us know so we may rectify in any future reprint.

Except as permitted under U.S. Copyright Law, no part of this book may be reprinted, reproduced, transmitted, or utilized in any form by any electronic, mechanical, or other means, now known or hereafter invented, including photocopying, microfilming, and recording, or in any information storage or retrieval system, without written permission from the publishers.

For permission to photocopy or use material electronically from this work, please access www.copyright.com (http://www.copyright.com/) or contact the Copyright Clearance Center, Inc. (CCC), 222 Rosewood Drive, Danvers, MA 01923, 978-750-8400. CCC is a not-for-profit organization that provides licenses and registration for a variety of users. For organizations that have been granted a photocopy license by the CCC, a separate system of payment has been arranged.

Trademark Notice: Product or corporate names may be trademarks or registered trademarks, and are used only for identification and explanation without intent to infringe.

Visit the Taylor & Francis Web site at
http://www.taylorandfrancis.com

and the CRC Press Web site at
http://www.crcpress.com

For all that I am and ever will be, I owe to my Mother,
Catherine "Kitty" Anita Brown Pickney.

Contents

Foreword xi
Preface xiii
Author xvii

SECTION I WOMEN AND WAR

1 Introduction: Women and the Military 5
　　The Opponents 12
　　The Proponents 15
　　Note 20
　　Appendix 1 20

2 Warriors to the Core 27

3 The Beginning of the Revolution: The American Experience 37
　　World War I 53
　　World War II 53
　　The Korean Conflict 54
　　The Vietnam Conflict 54
　　Operations Urgent Fury and Just Cause 54
　　Operations Desert Shield/Storm 55
　　Operation Enduring Freedom 55
　　Operation Iraqi Freedom 55
　　Operation New Dawn 56

4 Marginalized, Yet Accountable: The Irrationality of the Combat Exclusion Policy 57

5 The Enemy Within: Sex Crimes and the Evils of Asymmetry 87

SECTION II WOMEN IN WAR—LIVING LEGENDS: SISTERS-IN-ARMS UNDER COMBAT EXCLUSION

6 Taking Command: The Generals 137
    Major General Marcelite J. Harris, U.S. Air Force, Retired 137
    Brigadier General Wilma L. Vaught, U.S. Air Force, Retired 144

7 Commanding the Air: The Aviators 151
    Mrs. Anna Flynn Monkiewicz, Women Airforce Service Pilots (WASP) 151
    Colonel Pamela Rodriguez, Army National Guard, Retired 155
    Dr. Rita F. Sumner, U.S. Air Force 160
    Chief Warrant Officer 5, Trish Thompson, U.S. Army, Retired 163
    Master Sergeant Judith Hatch, Air National Guard (ANG), Retired 168
    Sharron Frontiero Cohen, U.S. Air Force 173

8 Commanding the Sea: The Mariners 179
    Dr. Darlene Iskra, U.S. Navy, Retired 179
    Maria "Zoe" Dunning, U.S. Navy, Retired 183
    Ms. Rose Marie Jackson, Commander, U.S. Navy, Retired 192
    Ms. Yona Owens, U.S. Navy 196

9 Commanding the Land: The Soldiers 203
    Colonel Beverly "Sam" Stipe, U.S. Army, Retired 203
    Command Sergeant Major Cynthia Pritchett, U.S. Army, Retired 207
    Ms. Sandra Intorre, U.S. Army, Retired 211
    Mrs. Tiffany Kravec-Kelly, U.S. Army Reserve 216
    Sergeant Michelle Wilmot, U.S. Army Reserve 223

SECTION III WOMEN AT WAR: TOWARD FULL AGENCY

10 On Gender and Citizenship 243
    On Gender 243
    On Citizenship 250

11 Repealing the Combat Exclusion Policy: Prospects for Implementation 257
    Army 259
    Air Force 261
    Navy 261
        Decision Point 1 261
        Decision Point 2 262
        Decision Point 3 262

  Decision Point 4 262
  Decision Point 5 262
 Marine Corps 263
 U.S. Special Operations Command 265

12 Impact of the Combat Exclusion Policy on the Recruitment, Promotion, and Retention of Women in the Military 267

13 Women in a Post-Combat Exclusion Environment: The Promise for Full Agency 277

SECTION IV WOMEN, WAR, THE MILITARY, AND BEYOND

14 In Conclusion: The Revolution Continues! 293

Bibliography 299

Index 331

Foreword

Honor. Courage. Commitment.

I didn't want to be "one of the boys," just part of the team. I wanted to serve my country with honor, courage, and commitment, just as my brothers-at-arms were doing.

Women have served in every conflict that has taken place on American soil. Some even disguised as men so they could fight. Although they were answering the call of their nation, and in many instances "freeing a man to fight," women still endured unfair and biased treatment.

The Women Airforce Service Pilots (WASPs) tested and ferried planes that were badly needed to replace the battle-wounded fleet overseas along with freeing male pilots for combat service and duties. One of their duties was even towing targets behind their plane that was being shot at with live ammo by male pilots in training. Even though these women served in World War II, they weren't recognized as veterans until 1977. This meant that for years, among other things, they could not receive treatment through the VA system and weren't even allowed to be buried in any of our national cemeteries.

When I first enlisted in the United States Army Reserve in 1993, women were not allowed to engage in direct combat or be a part of or attached to combat units. Our "herstory" is in the creation stages as we speak. Women are being placed in combat units, serving on submarines and even being evaluated for being in the infantry. The AH-1W Super Cobra Attack helicopter didn't know I was a woman. With the right training, I have no doubt that we will be just as prepared, qualified, and effective as the men we have been serving beside.

Although this body of work and research was initially started as a case study for repealing the combat exclusion law for women, G.L.A. Harris, PhD, does an excellent job cataloging our journey and giving specific examples of where we have been and where we have yet to go. Her work more than highlights the necessity for equal access and exposure being key to recruitment, retention, and promotion of women in today's military if we are to have the same chance for promotion and opportunities as our male counterparts. The dedication and commitment she placed into birthing this work is evident. It should be mandatory reading for the leadership in our country.

As the collective mindset continues to shift in our country, women will continue to move forward as the leaders we were born to be and in new capacities every day. It was an honor to serve as a United States marine; as we say in the Corps, *semper fidelis*, which means "always faithful." May we continue to push forward and, as a country, come together to support our men and women in uniform with honor, courage, and commitment. Our country depends on it.

Vernice "FlyGirl" Armour
Author, Speaker, Entrepreneur
America's First African American Female Combat Pilot

Preface

The seeds for the idea of this book began germinating following the publication of my first article about women in the military and during a time when I was feverishly preparing my portfolio in my bid for promotion and tenure. A senior colleague in my department approached me with a Call for Proposals grant flyer for junior faculty from a notable foundation and encouraged me to apply. While I was unsuccessful in securing this sizable grant, the idea for my book percolated as to its groundbreaking promise. Undaunted, I took the idea to another level by applying, this time, for an even larger grant, to the National Science Foundation (NSF) to fund my research and book. The feedback from the grant's reviewers was largely positive. However, the message conveyed was that I had not yet fully developed the idea to warrant funding. Moreover, as one reviewer claimed, the repeal of the combat exclusion policy was only a matter of time. The reviewer was right. But, fortunately, while the theme of my research and book proposal was to provide the evidence to justify the overdue repeal of the combat exclusion policy, more importantly, I believed then would be the emphasis on the personal stories of triumph in the face of adversity in living within a combat exclusion policy environment by those whom I envisioned were to be interviewed as part of the research. As well, unlike the many books that have been written before about the subject, to me, my research and book were more than just about the combat exclusion policy. In fact, in keeping with the theme of my first publication about women in the military, in this book I planned to address the unforeseen possibilities of equality for women, not only in the military, but in American society at large. I was determined at that point that my book would tackle the need for using the policy's then-potential repeal as a proxy for establishing full agency for women, particularly within a democratic society. As I recall, some of the NSF reviewers also suggested that I forge a possible partnership with like-minded scholars who conducted similar research. While this was an interesting and welcomed thought that I seriously contemplated, in the end, I decided against it. However, I pondered, how was I going to finance this project in light of its scope?

I was successful in securing promotion with tenure the following year but vowed it a priority to follow through with the completion of several manuscripts

I had in the queue for publication consideration. It was not until the following year or during the latter part of 2011 when I revisited the idea for my book and during my sabbatical at the University of Washington. Among my many priorities, the highest priority was to develop my book proposal for marketing on the publisher circuit. Prior to my sabbatical, though, I had consulted with a senior colleague with multiple books to his credit, who encouraged me to exercise a little creativity for he believed that my venture could be self-financed. During the second and final term of my sabbatical the following year, I secured a publishing contract with Taylor & Francis Group and immediately went about the business of seeking the approval for the human subjects' application through the institutional review board at my home institution. Following a record of four revisions, the research for the book was finally approved. The overriding concern of the board, and rightly so, was the vulnerability of the population of my proposed research. The review process therefore took much longer than anticipated. Nevertheless, on a shoestring budget—my own, that is—I proceeded to set in motion what eventually became the most enlightening journey of my life to date, both personally and professionally, that has culminated in this endeavor. Further, it was the urging of an attorney friend, Sharon Brown, which was subsequently echoed by my editor, Lara Zoble at Taylor and Francis Group, that eventually led to the chronicling of my own experience in writing this book.

My limited finances did indeed force me to become creative yet in the process succeeded in exposing me to experiences that otherwise I would not have had. I immediately contacted several women veterans organizations, most notably, the Alliance for National Defense and the Women in Military Service for America (WIMSA) Memorial Foundation, by making personal appeals to the organizations' respective former and current presidents, namely, Brigadier General Pat Foote and Brigadier General Wilma Vaught, two stalwarts in promoting the issues of women in the military. Almost immediately, with communiqués from Brigadier General Foote, an avalanche of women contacted me to volunteer for the research, and I was taken aback by the sheer volume of the response. Additionally, contacts through WIMSA followed suit; while the job of selecting those women who would best meet the criteria of the research was rendered more challenging as a result, the overwhelming response to the project was both a pleasant surprise and an affirmation of the importance of the topic of my research. And, while I had initially planned to select 25 women for the project, cost considerations moved me to be more realistic in my assessment. So, immediately before and following my military reserve duty during the summer of 2012, I traveled the northeastern, southern, western, and northwestern regions of the United States to interview the 17 former military women who were eventually selected to participate in this research and book. Some of these interviews were conducted using videoconferencing applications and others over telephone, while the majority of the interviews were in-person meetings. Some of these meetings resulted in my lodging in some rather questionable establishments, despite their seemingly intact national reputation, which varied from hotel to hotel and location to location, given the franchise. And a modestly priced all-inclusive package of hotel, airfare, and rental car service was no guarantee of a quality product. In some cases, given the venue of the interviews, I found myself apologizing profusely to the interviewees for the unconventional setting but in every case, they were most gracious and understanding. Again, it is important to note that these cost-containment measures were a condition of financing and were not to be attributed to the interviewees in any way. Fortunately, and particularly in the Northeast, I was able to secure quality accommodations at reasonable rates at various military installations. I visited retirement homes, private homes, and in one instance, prematurely ended the interview in a private home because the interviewee was suffering from congestive heart failure that required summoning an ambulance to the rescue. In this case, I asked the medical personnel if I could follow the emergency vehicle, with blaring sirens and all, to the hospital. Little did I know, however, that following an ambulance—given my unfamiliarity with the locale—meant giving chase through the streets of this rural town in a rental car and with high beam lights flashing following as closely as it was possible to the ambulance to convey the sense of urgency to fellow motorists and onlookers. In the chase, though, I lost track of the ambulance but managed to make it—without the aid of GPS, I might add—to the emergency room of the hospital where the interviewee had been admitted. I waited at the hospital until the interviewee's relative arrived and was also able to speak with her before leaving since the immediate danger had passed.

Most exciting though was the degree to which all of the women interviewed were not only exceptionally accommodating but yearned and were eternally grateful for the opportunity to have their stories told. Many repeatedly thanked me before and after the interviews for taking the time to record what they have always known to be important but which they believed few, if any, had taken the time or interest to explore. I, in turn, have been humbled by these genuine expressions of gratitude, particularly as a fellow veteran and sisters-in-arms, and I am deeply honored that I became the vehicle through which such stories are being chronicled, to give voice to women in the military. Still, it was the process of completing the transcription of the 17 interviews that helped me realize the magnitude of this research on multiple levels, which I had not realized when I first conceived of the project. For this purpose and throughout the book, I will utilize words that are uncommon in the English vernacular, and specifically as they relate to women such as *sheroes* instead of heroes; *sheroic*, not heroic; *ourstory* in place of history; and *ourstorical* for historical. This is an intentional effort to recast language as I so often do in the classroom, not from what might be interpreted as a feminist perspective but simply from a human perspective. By reframing how we think, speak, and portray women, in this case through a powerful medium like language, we attribute to women their value and worth to life itself and the undeniably pivotal role that they have played since the beginning of time in continually shaping society and, indeed, the world.

Thus, the 17 sheroes have become symbols of the varying degrees of hardships that women in the military endured within the combat exclusion policy environment, of the strategies that they cleverly devised for compliance in gaining acceptance while simultaneously deviating in other ways in an attempt to level the playing field, and of women who simply challenged the system head on. In all, these women are success stories in their own right. Even more significant is that their stories will forever be indelibly etched into our legacy as profiles in courage and American ourstory.

Author

Jamaican-born and raised but American-adopted, G.L.A. Harris is an associate professor in the Mark O. Hatfield School of Government at Portland State University, Oregon. She received her PhD in public administration with concentration in public management from Rutgers University. Her research examines the recruiting and retention patterns of the military, particularly those surrounding gender and race as well as other similar issues affecting military veteran populations including health-care disparities, civil rights, social justice and gender equity, organizational performance, and unionization, to name a few. She has published widely in journals such as *Public Administration Review, Journal of Public Affairs Education, Administration & Society, Review of Public Personnel Administration, Journal of Health and Human Services Administration, Public Integrity, Journal of Military Studies, Journal of Public Management and Social Policy, International Journal of Public Administration, Public Performance and Management Review*, and the *Encyclopedia of Public Administration and Public Policy*.

With Richard Greggory Johnson, III, Dr. Harris is the coeditor of the acclaimed book *Women of Color in Leadership: Taking Their Rightful Place*. She serves on a number of journal editorial boards such as the *Journal of Public Management and Social Policy, Journal of Health and Human Services Administration*, and *Open Journal of Political Science*. Dr. Harris is also a commissioned officer in the U.S. Air Force Reserve and formerly served on active duty with the U.S. Air Force.

WOMEN AND WAR 1

To say that women and war are incompatible elements of society, as the naysayers suggest, is to conveniently ignore women's past and present performance as a collective and as inherent parts of the milieu. Since the beginning of time and throughout ourstory, women have always fought alongside their brethren in battle to such a degree that DePauw (1998) considers women and war to be inextricable. Yet, modern-day rhetoric, at least within the United States, would have us believe that even with the recent repeal of the combat exclusion policy, the notion of women fighting in war is not only at best culturally unacceptable but at worst reckless. As Mazur (1998) puts it, war then always becomes this novel act in which women partake, even if they have done so repeatedly, time and time again. In the United States, women have served as a convenient resource for the military each time the nation has been called to arms. But, it is also important to note that ourstory is forever being filtered through the lens of the victor, not the so-called victim since to the victor goes the spoils of war. Further, memories become conveniently short and selective in recollection. However, despite the attempt to extricate any credit from the record and/or to couch the verbiage in such ways as to cast doubt about their presence and participation, leaving it to speculation at best, ourstory is incontrovertible and still abounds with innumerable examples to the contrary, that in effect, and for *ad infinitum*, women have always and continue to assume integral roles in war.

But this absence of women's voices as part of the discourse about war should not be surprising. For example, take the American military's philosophy, values, and beliefs about war, given its faithful adaptation of the Prussian thinker Karl von Clausewitz's philosophies espoused in *On War*. Little is known though that it was his wife Marie von Clausewitz, not Karl von Clausewitz, who crafted the preface of his now famous work for which she received no credit (Elshtain 1987). Further, at the time of his death, it was Marie who published his works, although at the time she dared to give herself a morsel of credit by framing her role as that of a sympathetic companion who was only supporting her husband. Yet, despite her need to remain silent and in the background, Marie subtly and somewhat with a tease intimated that she played more of an active role than was first conceived. She said about her husband's works, following his death and in her zeal to publish them, "Nevertheless, their publication called for a good deal of work, arranging of material, and consultation and I am profoundly grateful to several loyal friends for their assistance in these tasks" (Marie von Clausewitz, preface to *On War*, pp. 65–67, as cited by Elshtain 1987). In turn, Elshtain (1987) raises the question, though, that, in light of an otherwise happy marriage, are we as readers to believe that Marie von Clausewitz did not write much of her husband's work, if not all of it? It appears that as the dutiful wife, she recognized her place in society at the time and was content, at least publicly, not to receive recognition for her husband's writings, even if she did indeed craft those writings. DePauw (1998) skillfully resurrected works of a gone-by era or before Christ (BC) to deliver a treasure trove of facts that without this detailed data mining about women's roles in war, these data would probably have more or less remained dormant, if ever resurrected, or more importantly, reported. More documented works about women and war were recorded by the Greeks (i.e., Goldstein 2003; Jones 1997), while DePauw's (1998) and Jones's (1997) works begin with unearthing the Africans, who predated the Greeks and whom Jones (1997) acknowledges as the "Mother of Nations" (p. 81), where the now-famous female Amazons, or women of war, were discovered. This journey continues into what DePauw (1998) calls European warfare; the Age of Revolution, including the American Revolution; nineteenth-century wars including the American Civil War; WWs I and II through present-day wars; and to a visual documentary during the late twentieth and twenty-first centuries. These scenes are vivid depictions of women as both active participants and casualties of modern warfare around the world.

The succeeding section establishes women's irrefutable inclusion and leadership in changing the course toward war, if not themselves making wars for economic reasons as heads of states and/or for territory expansion to amass increasing power and influence. Thus, women's dominant roles in war during ancient times starkly contrasts with their reduced and largely tokenized roles during modern times. Specifically, women's role within the American military is particularly troublesome in the sense that their participation has been typified as one of close control, monitoring, and retrenchment, all laced with the practice of habitual selective amnesia by the civilian and military leadership during peacetime as to their abilities despite their consistent formidable performance during wartime. It is within this American context that women continue to serve as a convenient resource only to employed and deployed at will when the nation is called to arms or for like campaigns.

Chapter 1

Introduction: Women and the Military

On January 25, 2013, the then U.S. Secretary of Defense Leon Panetta announced that the long-standing policy in its various iterations, known in its last form as the combat exclusion policy that bars women from any jobs, occupations, and/or assignments that engage them in direct ground combat, will be repealed (Christensen 2013; Migdal 2013). According to the former secretary, full integration of women into all occupations in the military will be achieved by 2016 (Evans 2013) unless any branch of the military can demonstrate that there are certain roles for which women are either ill-equipped or simply not yet prepared to assume the roles (Sutton 2013). To that end, each military branch was asked to submit its plan for implementation by May 15, 2013 (Hlad and Shane 2013). Still, the news of the ban, albeit one that has been evolving over the years through a gradual chipping away of the policy, was palpable when it was announced as finally becoming a reality. Yet, I believe that it was the independent action and confluence of five events that provided the impetus for this unprecedented move in American ourstory (her/history).

First, two Army reservists legally challenged the unconstitutionality of the combat exclusion policy in a federal court in May 2012 (Tilghman 2013a). Second, in November 2012, the American Civil Liberties Union (ACLU), known for its reputation in successfully challenging the Department of Defense (DoD) and other entities over policies that it deems as unconstitutional, this time on behalf of four servicewomen against former Secretary of Defense Leon Panetta to rescind the ban on women serving in combat. This second lawsuit was joined by the Service Women's Action Network (SWAN), an advocacy organization for military women (Whitlock 2012).

In both lawsuits, the plaintiffs comprised women who have served in combatant roles and thus in dangerous positions that rendered them even more vulnerable to the risk of death because of the existence of the combat exclusion policy during Operations Enduring Freedom and Iraqi Freedom (Fox and Brown 2013; Tilghman 2013a). In fact, among the plaintiffs in the second lawsuit against the former Secretary of Defense, two of the four servicewomen, Army Staff Sergeant Jennifer Hunt and Major Mary Jennings Hegar of the California Air National Guard, are both Purple Heart medal recipients for wounds sustained in Iraq and Afghanistan, respectively, with Major Jennings Hegar also receiving the Distinguished Flying Cross with a Valor Device (Fox and Brown 2013; Hlad 2013; Whitlock 2012). But, coming on the heels of the repeal of the Don't Ask, Don't Tell, and Don't Pursue policy by President Obama on September 20, 2011 (Garamone 2011), a similar justification of unconstitutionality under the Fifth Amendment for equal protection (Tilghman 2013a) was cited for challenging the combat exclusion policy which was similarly filed in the U.S. District Court in San Francisco that has been customarily sympathetic to such claims.

Third, I also believe that, although conjecture at this point, in light of the unprecedented number of sexual assaults and sexually related cases reported that have dogged the military and despite the top to bottom review directed by then Secretary Panetta, the rate at which these incidences occur have largely gone unabated. Multiple lawsuits have been filed in federal court against former Secretaries of Defense Donald Rumsfeld, Robert Gates, and Leon Panetta; a former Secretary of the Navy (Ellison 2012; Moulton and Peterson 2012; Parker 2011); and two of the U.S. military academies: the Naval Academy and the U.S. Military Academy at West Point (Katz 2012). One of the class action lawsuits alleged that the Secretaries "ran institutions in which perpetrators were promoted and where military personnel openly mocked and flouted the modest Congressionally-mandated reforms" and where "it (the military) is an atmosphere of zero accountability in leadership, period" (Parker 2011). As Bernard (2013) declared, it is then ironic that the DoD should move to repeal the combat exclusion policy, yet the problems of sexual assault and the like, especially against military women, remain unaddressed. Hence, I believe that, notwithstanding the multiple lawsuits, the move to lift the combat exclusion policy may at least in part have been motivated by an assumption of how women in the military are being perceived by their male counterparts in the military given the presence of the policy. As a result, lifting the combat exclusion policy may have been promulgated in whole or in part in the hope of not only leveling the playing field for servicewomen, but by extension, improving how they are being perceived by their male peers in the military, which in turn, may serve over time to reduce the rate of sexual assault. *The Invisible War*, the highly acclaimed documentary film about the prevalence of sexual assault in the military, may only be the tip of the iceberg in successfully exposing the other war that women in the military are simultaneously forced to fight.

Fourth, and again purely speculation on my part, former Secretary Panetta's term in office has been rife with struggles on how to mitigate these gnawing and controversial issues. With the dual lawsuits as the backdrop and perhaps his legacy as an important consideration, the former Secretary can now leave office intact and with a record that may more likely be viewed in retrospect as favorable by ourstorians (her/historians).

Finally, there is no doubt that the Military Leadership Diversity Commission (MLDC) (2011) and the mainstay Defense Advisory Committee on Women in the Services (DACOWITS) (2012) had their hands in directing the administration's hammering of the final decisive nail to the coffin that led to the repeal of the combat exclusion policy. Neither for breaking its streak in reputation as the stalwart for consistently coming to the defense of military women nor for flinching on expressing its candor to lawmakers and military leaders alike about what have gone awry, DACOWITS not only hurled a blunt assessment and rebuke to the military for its handling of widespread sexual assault but dealt military leaders and commanders a stinging blow in making recommendations on how these deficiencies are to be remediated. These recommendations were contrary to the leaders' and commanders' major demands that they should not be held accountable for these assessments and these assessments should not become part of their performance evaluations by superiors. But, while current Secretary of Defense Chuck Hagel and the leadership in the military oppose this measure, as of late September 2013, the DACOWITS recommendation had gained steam in the form of a bill, sponsored by Senators Kirsten Gillibrand (D-NY) and Barbara Boxer (D-CA), which is slowly advancing its way through the Senate (Tilghman 2013b). Despite what seems to have become the customary partisanship and along party lines in Congress, the bipartisan support to date of 46 senators is being galvanized (Sohn 2013) even with such staunch conservatives like Senators Rand Paul (R-KY) and Ted Cruz (R-TX) (Delmore 2013). If passed, the bill would strip commanders of their discretionary authority on sexual assault cases and place them for prosecution in the hands of an independently formed office of high ranking military lawyers (Tilghman 2013b).

But, the military has traditionally stood as the vanguard for the advancement of many marginalized groups in American society, including African Americans, and specifically for this book, women as well. Although the initial premise behind this book was to make a compelling case for repealing the combat exclusion policy in light of the overwhelming evidence to date, it was during the initial stage of its writing that Secretary Panetta announced the long-awaited, unexpected, yet indeed overdue news. Now it is hoped that military women, like military men, will begin to enjoy an unprecedented level of equality for the good of the military and in the pursuit of their careers as never before experienced by any woman. And specifically for the combat exclusion policy, especially with regard to dangerous assignments and/or in combat zones, women will no longer be illegally placed into assignments at their peril nor will commanders be forced to needlessly consider their status as noncombatants in those assignments. Only women's requisite skills and capabilities as the sole determinants, as would be considered for all personnel in such assignments, will become the defining factors on where those skills and capabilities can be best utilized.

Through a thorough review of the extant literature, the collection of archival data and qualitative interviews with pioneering, prominent, and/or elite former military women, this research and book examine the roles of women in the military. I have operationalized pioneering, prominent, and/or elite former military women to encompass those categories of women whose service in the U.S. military has led them to assume precedent-setting roles as unique achievements, involvement in a series of firsts for women in still nontraditional occupations or critical assignments held, and/or those whose promotions have paved the path for other women in the military while serving under the combat exclusion policy. In essence, these are women whose remarkable contributions to the military meet the following criteria: former military women who are currently private citizens; have served on active duty, reserve, and/or National Guard; have assumed precedent-setting roles; have made unique achievements and have been in nontraditional occupations, critical assignments, and/or promotions held; and have served in both the enlisted and commissioned corps of the U.S. military. These women represent those who have blazed the trail and have been successful in their own right despite the presence of the combat exclusion policy; have set the stage for the achievement of equality for women in the military particularly given the recent repeal of the combat exclusion policy; and, as a result, have established the foundation for women as a prelude for achieving full agency in all walks of American life.

This book then attempts to satisfy the following questions. First, in light of the repeal of the combat exclusion policy, although not yet implemented, how can the success of women in the military serve as a benchmark for its repeal? Second, what will be the potential impact of repealing the policy on the recruitment, promotion, and retention of women in the military? And, finally, how can repealing the combat exclusion policy set women on the path to full agency and representation, not only in the military but beyond, that is, as full citizens in American society at large?

I propose that by portraying the lives of those former military women who a priori have successfully served during the combat exclusion policy becomes the basis for and a reliable predictor of things to come within a post–combat exclusion policy environment. This will form the centerpiece of the book. Seventeen former military women were interviewed as part of this research. The women represent a cross-section in age and thus generations, with the oldest at the age of 93 at the time of her interview in July 2012 who served prior to the build up to World War II (WWII) to the youngest in her late twenties during the latter half of 2012 who served during Operation Iraqi Freedom. These women pursued occupations in the military that were as diverse as those ranging from women who have repeatedly experienced and witnessed combat to women still in precedent-setting roles who have never knowingly experienced combat. Some of the women interviewed simply challenged what they deemed as unfair systems of exclusion based on gender and sexual orientation, for instance. Still others excelled in rank and only through sheer grit and determination did they succeed especially in those positions where they became accidental incumbents, given conditions on the ground during times of war. And, while incidental to this research, a modicum of racial and/or ethnic diversity was captured.

For this reason, this book has been purposefully divided into four distinct sections in order to address the multiple elements that I believe constitute and will best portray women's unique roles as active participants in war from the beginning of time. As such, Section I, entitled Women and War consisting of five chapters, presents the ourstory (her/history) of women's participation in war and subsequently in the U.S. military along with the rationales provided by opponents and proponents alike about women's participation in the American military. This timeline is punctuated by highlights of landmark periods for women in the U.S. military with each major military campaign. In addition, this section tackles the evolution of the combat exclusion policy and the seething underbelly of perhaps the unintended consequences of asymmetry, that is, through deliberate exclusion and thus the legal practice of gender discrimination in the U.S. military, what relegation to second-class citizenship can bring about for a segment of the military's population.

Section II, Women in War, with four chapters, marks the centerpiece of the book. Here, the stories about being in the military are brought to life by the 17 former military women (veterans) who are chronicled. These stories represent a rich panoply of experiences by those who served in both the enlisted and commissioned corps and in various occupations, including those who while as noncombatants were for all intents and purposes serving as combatants, yet devoid of both the benefit of the designation and the protection of combatants as their male counterparts. The women hail from those who rose to the rank of general officers to take command; took to the skies as aviators, including the first cohort of women to do so even before America's engagement in WWII; sailed the seas as mariners with the first woman taking command of a ship in the Navy and another serving as the first openly gay person in the military; and were part of the collective boots on the ground as soldiers including as one of the now famous all-female embedded teams during Operation Iraqi Freedom known as *Lioness*.

Section III, Women at War: Toward Full Agency, in four chapters, frames the discourse about how the recent repeal of the combat exclusion policy bodes well to ultimately serve as the catalyst to not only bring about full agency for women in the military but also for their civilian sisters in the larger American society.

Finally, Section IV, Women, War, the Military, and Beyond, in a single concluding chapter, discusses the potential demise for the military for failure to fully honor the conditions that brought about the repeal of the combat exclusion policy. I warn, however, that we, the citizenry, cannot sit upon our laurels by becoming complacent. For even in light of the successful integration of women throughout the military along with gains in parity for civilian women in the labor force in industries, occupations, and earnings, given ourstory, the journey toward full agency for women warrants that the revolution for such changes must continue.

Notwithstanding the recent lawsuits, and with the culmination of a series of events since 2008, it was only a matter of time that the combat exclusion policy would meet its demise. The release of the film *Lioness* highlighted for the first time the top secret insertion of women in direct ground combat by the DoD during Operation Iraqi Freedom (Alvarez 2009; McLagan and Sommers 2010; pbs.org/Lioness) along with the use of female engagement teams by the Marine Corps in Operation Enduring Freedom (DACOWITS 2009). The announcement by the U.S. Navy of its intentions to seriously revisit the issue of placing women aboard submarines (Bynum and Jelinek 2009) followed by the assignment of the first cohort of women who reported for submarine duty in Fall 2011 (Mount 2010; Weber 2010) was no less than monumental in its achievement of this formerly all-male domain.

But the push for this move, according to Iskra (2012) who is one of the women featured in this book, was twofold. One, there has been a precipitous fall in the number of male officers who have traditionally volunteered for these assignments. Apparently, the rate at which the Naval Academy graduates interested men has declined to 92 instead of the standard 120 men every four years. And, two, women, unlike men, are pursuing more technical degrees than in the past. So, the Navy's shift was not altogether altruistic, if at all. The move was driven primarily by the shortage of men coupled with the increasing number of women who are currently attaining more technical degrees for such career fields that essentially provided the justification for women's integration into this career field. And, during late 2012, the Navy graduated its first cohort of female submariners (Friedrich 2012). The promotion of Ann Dunwoody of the Army to the rank of four-star general served as another seminal event (Burnes 2008) as the first female in the military to be so recognized. In another milestone, Colonel Jeannie Leavitt, the first woman who was tapped for training to subsequently become the first female fighter pilot in the Air Force in 1993, was installed in mid-2012 as the first woman to command a combat fighter wing in the Air Force (Associated Press 2012). Leavitt has racked up more than 2500 hours on the Air Force's premier F-15E (Strike Eagle) fighter jet which includes flying 300 hours of combat during Operations Enduring Freedom and Iraqi Freedom.

Most recently, the Air Force saw fit to follow the Army by also promoting its first female four-star general, Janet Wolfenbarger, who ironically was in the first cohort of women to graduate in 1980 after the Air Force Academy first admitted women in 1976 (Coleman 2012; Dawley 2012). Nevertheless, another milestone was most recently reached for women in the military. Secretary of Defense Chuck Hagel announced the nomination of the first woman, Major General Michelle Johnson, for elevation to lead the 57-year-old institution, the youngest of the military academies, as its next Superintendent (Rodgers 2013). And, one of the multiple recommendations by the congressionally appointed MLDC (2011) that the military should remove the combat exclusion policy served as the final seminal but pivotal event to warrant the repeal of the combat exclusion policy. According to the MLDC, repealing the policy should include "removing barriers and inconsistencies, to create a level playing field for all qualified service members who meet the qualifications" (Summary, p. xvii). A concurrent and follow-up study by DACOWITS (2012) drew the same conclusion.

Originally enacted in 1948 as the Women's Armed Services Integration Act, the combat exclusion policy established specific parameters that restricted women to a targeted representation of the total military force (2%), the types of occupations in which women could serve and a limit in the rank that women could attain while serving in the military (U.S. General Accountability Office [GAO] 1987). Ironically, this period coincided with another landmark legislation; President Harry Truman's mandate for racial integration of the military (GAO 1998a, 1998b; Harrell and Miller 1997). Following the initial withdrawal of U.S. forces from Vietnam in 1973 (Keenan 2008) and the advent of the all-volunteer force, Congress authorized the increase in the number of women who could join the military yet imposed restrictions on where they could serve in what later came to be known as the combat exclusion policy. Then at 2.5% of the total military force in 1973, women were barred from serving on combat ships or Navy vessels outside of hospital ships or Navy transports (GAO 1987). With the expansion of women's roles, including the opening of the U.S. military academies to women (Harrell and Miller 1997), the DoD couched the combat exclusion policy as the risk rule to mean that women could not serve in positions, even in noncombat units, that were collocated with combat units, or with any units that placed them in direct harm's way (Keenan 2008). This new codified rule was designed to ensure that women remained as noncombatants.

However, women's unprecedented role and participation in Operation Desert Storm, at 7% of the total military force (GAO 1999; Harrell and Miller 1997; Harrell et al. 2002), forced Congress to reexamine the existing combat exclusion policy under the risk rule, and in so doing, resulted in the enactment of the National Defense Authorization Acts of 1992 and 1993, respectively. Both acts repealed the exclusion of women from combat aircraft as well as revoked the risk rule, given women's successful deployment during Operation Desert Storm (GAO 1998a; Harrell and Miller 1997; Harrell et al. 2002). A DoD-wide policy was subsequently crafted to more accurately reflect what positions constituted combat situations from which women were still excluded (GAO 1998a). As a consequence, more positions were opened to women than ever before (Harrell et al. 2002). In addition to flying combat aircraft, women could also serve on combat vessels. A new direct ground combat rule now delineated what assignments could exclude women. Additionally, a study commissioned by the then Secretary of Defense Les Aspin, ascertained that the performance of military units in terms of readiness, cohesion, and morale was negligibly impacted by the presence of female service members in those units (Harrell and Miller 1997). But, subsequent analyses by the GAO (1998b, 1999) determined that some female service members perceived that the new version of the combat exclusion policy unnecessarily restricted them from securing positions or assignments that rendered them competitive for career-enhancing assignments (GAO 1998b). The GAO (1998b, 1999) questioned whether or not some military branches were using the new interpretation of the combat exclusion policy as a pretext to exclude women from certain positions, thereby deliberately creating inequities in career opportunities between the male and female service members (Harrell et al. 2002). Further, as an earlier GAO (1998a) report noted in its summary, the outright move to integrate women into direct ground combat then could garner neither the congressional nor the public support needed to repeal the combat exclusion policy.

As of fiscal year (FY) 2011, women in the military comprised approximately 16.3% of the total military force (Population Representation in the Military Services, 2011; Pew Social Trends [Patten and Parker 2011]; Military OneSource Demographic Report 2011; Women in the Military Services of America [WIMSA]).[1] But, given the most recent iteration of the combat exclusion policy, while approximately 15%–20% of positions are still excluded to women (GAO 2005b; Titunik 2008), according to Parrish (2012), DoD will now open another 14,000 positions to women. As it currently stands, the Air Force remains the most female friendly of the services, with only 1% of its positions still closed to women; 66%, 68%, and 88% of positions in the Army, Marines, and Navy, respectively, are open to women (Parrish 2012). Operations in Afghanistan and Iraq have increasingly blurred the lines between what distinguishes positions in the theater of operations that are deemed to be in direct ground combat and those that are not. Titunik (2008) offers the role of the military police as one such example where military women were serving on the front lines of the insurgency and thus in direct ground combat as much as military men were. Likewise, women have made the ultimate sacrifice in Operations Enduring Freedom and Iraqi Freedom. Of the now 6640 military personnel killed in Operations Enduring Freedom, Iraqi Freedom, and New Dawn (post-Operation Iraqi Freedom), 152 have been women (Fischer 2013). Additionally, although this figure is nowhere near the recorded 90 women who were taken as prisoners of war during WWII, when a record 400,000 women were galvanized for the war effort, three military women were held as prisoners of war during Operation Iraqi Freedom (WIMSA, n.d). Therefore, women have increasingly served in direct ground combat whether or not they have been so sanctioned.

The Opponents

First, opponents to women in combat often provide the biological argument as evidence that women do not belong in combat (Jeffreys 2008; Maninger 2008; Simons 2000). I anticipate that the fervor and rhetoric associated with the recent repeal of the combat exclusion policy will no doubt ignite calls for its reconsideration by Congress, although surprisingly as of this writing, this has not been the case. Yet, Captain Kate Petronio, a Marine, who caused a firestorm of reactions based on her controversial article in the *Marine Gazette* entitled "Get Over

It: We Are Not Created Equal," does not dispute women's capabilities in combat at all. What appears to be the Captain's primary issue stems from her concern as to whether or not women can sustain the rigors of combat operations overtime (Petronio 2012). But, even Captain Petronio, who has accumulated an impressive number of missions in both Afghanistan and Iraq, including as a subject matter expert to commanders in an effort to expand the Team Lioness program beyond the search of women and children to the integration of female Marines into more combat operations, given her record to a great degree, may have only served to disprove her own trepidations about women in combat. And, this notion that women are biologically predisposed to certain limitations, while men are not, has been repeatedly refuted.

Supporters of women in combat say that the differences in physical capabilities are to be discounted for what should matter in the field is one's training (Miller 1998; DeCew 1995). According to former Congresswoman Patricia Schroeder (D-CO),

> The real issue is training. Some women can indeed carry as much weight, throw as far and run as fast as some men in physical strength and endurance. Such athletes as pitching ace Kathy Arendsen, who throws a softball 96 miles an hour underhand, and Florence Griffith Joyner, who runs the 100 meters faster than O.J. Simpson ever ran while competing for USC, would scoff at the "girls can't throw" argument. These women demonstrate that trained individuals can do anything. (1991, p. 73)

Further, as both DeCew (1995) and Segal (1982) contend, what about those men who lack upper body strength? Should they be excluded from combat? Additionally, as Segal (1982) noted, it is as unfair to exclude women as a group from combat because it is purported that these men lack upper body strength as it is to exclude men from the same career opportunities simply because they do. As for the second biological limitation presented by opponents to bar women from combat, some say that women's physical stature and frame make them unfit for this kind of duty (Maninger 2008). Yet, although studies by Hosek et al. (2001), Moore (2002), and Cohn (2000) point to a resentment on the part of male service members as well as the disproportionate number of females who are involuntarily separated from the military for lack of physical conditioning and medical injuries, other studies demonstrate that when properly trained, military women, like military men, can withstand the physical rigors of training (U.S. Army 2002; Wilson 1995). Similarly, a more recent report by DACOWITS (2012) indicated that women experience an inordinate rate of health maladies in the forms of hip, back, knee, and other pain and injuries, not because of any innate inability to endure the associated training for combat but simply because the equipment that women must don are designed for men, not women. The Committee recommended that the services collaborate on the testing, product development, and procurement of such equipment for more appropriate design for women.

The Army found that performance during training was not a matter of gender but based on each service member's commitment to the Army and confidence in their ability to succeed (U.S. Army 2002). The pregnancy rationale, which too has been proffered by opponents of women in combat (i.e., Maninger 2008), has been equally refuted by supporters of women in combat. Said Segal (1982) of the charge that only women get pregnant, this condition should not preclude all women from combat. Moreover, most women who become pregnant do so only during limited periods of their lifetime (DeCew 1995). And, as reported by Segal (1982), even men in combat are not in combat for most of their military lives. So, as Segal argued, because some people in a particular group contract the flu, doing so does not justify that all members of that group should be excluded for fear that others will also contract the flu. As Harrell and Miller (1997) and Hosek et al. (2001) found, pregnancy almost never becomes an issue in military units since women do all that they can to avoid even the perception that they are impeding or disrupting the mission. Given the above perceived limitations, according to the opponents of women in combat, unit performance will be adversely impacted, training standards in the military will be compromised (Jeffrey 2007; Maninger 2008; Simons 2000), and if women serve in the military, they will be relegated to only support functions.

There are also speculations by opponents that women will serve as distracters to men in battle (Sheppard 2007; Simons 2000; DeCew 1995) and women need to be protected (Nantais and Lee 1999) for they are the victims, caretakers, and nurturers of society (Kennedy-Pipe 2000). Jeffreys (2008), for instance, claims that because the military is a masculinized and dangerous institution of sexual domination, to bring women into this environment is to subject them not only to similar dangers as men but to becoming the sexual exploits of friends and foes alike. In essence, women are then in danger of becoming the spoils of war given their mere presence. Yet, as Titunik (2000, 2008) disputes, the military has been unfairly mischaracterized as macho. Others have argued that it is the cultural socialization that women do not belong in the military that reinforces such myths (Ellefson 1998; Goldstein 2003; Snyder 2003; DeCew 1995). Further, women, like men, are not born warriors; they must be socialized for warfare (Goldstein 2003; Snyder 2003). Still others have demystified the gendered military as no place for women, particularly in combat (Stiehm 1982, 1988; Kennedy-Pipe 2000), and dispelling the belief that men must serve as the protectors of women who as victims are in need of protection (Enloe 1983; Morris 1996; Segal 1993). But, according to Segal (1995), women's roles in the military and thus their participation have waxed and waned over time, for following any expansion of women's service, an inculcation of "a cultural amnesia" (p. 761) by society repeatedly takes root even though women's increased participation in the military has always been typified by marked increases in the nation's call to arms (DeCew 1995). Consequently, women's participation in the military has been defined as sporadic, not linear (Segal 1999).

The Proponents

Accordingly, war is a man's prerogative and by extension, so is direct ground combat. So, to continue the exclusion of women from combat would represent what still distinguishes men from women in the military and the coveted role of that separation is the opportunity to serve in combat. Serving in combat then, it is believed, is one way of achieving respect and earning the reward for valor (Kennedy-Pipe 2000). However, some also believe that this prize has been deliberately reserved for men and from which the military leadership is disproportionately drawn for this reason (Kennedy-Pipe 2000; Putko 2008b). Yet, in every respect, opponents of women in the military rationalize to maintain the combat exclusion policy even though with the passing of time the policy has experienced a loosening of its grip on what defines direct ground combat and has been repeatedly invalidated by the military's own research findings (Wilson 1995) resulting in its recent repeal. As in the film *Lioness*, the Army's decision to embed female soldiers, dubbed Team Lioness as combatants, played a critical role in not only helping to calm the fears of women and children but in doing so were able to conduct searches of Iraqi women without concerns about violating cultural norms or mores (Independent Lens 2008). More importantly, this cohort of soldiers successfully executed the mission under the same dangerous conditions as male soldiers and in the process demonstrated to the military, Congress, and the American public, for that matter, that women have already met and surpassed the arbitrary targets for what constitutes "direct ground combat." But, especially what the film *Lioness* demonstrated was the tremendous quandaries that were experienced by the women, not only to their military careers but once they were no longer engaged in such activities. For example, one problem that persists and unintentionally creates additional inequities for women veterans is that the DD Form 214 does not accurately reflect nonoccupationally related duties for women who have served in combat (Lioness Report 2012). Consequently, there is the increased likelihood that these women may never receive earned benefits for health care or otherwise because the nature of their work has not been documented or accurately documented.

According to Burrelli (2012) of the Congressional Research Service (CRS), the "nonlinear" and "irregular" nature of the battlefield in Operations Enduring Freedom and Iraqi Freedom have blurred the lines between what constituted direct ground combat and what did not along with the collocation of combat units with combat support units to which women were primarily assigned and the use of women in such programs as Team Lioness. The Army's own gender studies 10 years earlier showed that performance in training is higher in mixed-gender units than in single-gender units (U.S. Army 2002), thus supporting earlier findings by Harrell and Miller (1997). Proponents of women's increased integration in the military are for the most part unified, although Titunik (2008) distinguishes that each faction within this camp have different philosophies of what represents full integration of women in the military. Either way, and especially now that the combat exclusion policy has been repealed, the reasons for its repeal have already been borne out by women's continual and effective performance in the military together with an expansive body of research that contradicts the views of opponents of women in combat and the realities of war on the ground, particularly with regard to Operations Enduring Freedom and Iraqi Freedom.

A compendium of publications on women in combat from the Army's Strategic Studies Institute has overwhelmingly supported repealing the combat exclusion policy (Putko and Johnson 2008). What is noteworthy is that the calls for integrating women into combat roles and for repealing the combat exclusion policy have been coming from inside the military itself. The compendium's contributors included a complement of Army commanders who provided evidence from the theaters of operations that the time had then come for the military to repeal the combat exclusion policy (Grosskruger 2008; Twitchell 2008). They stated that women under their commands and in leadership positions have uniformly displayed the competence, will, and commitment to fight the enemy, wherever the enemy was present. A report by DACOWITS (2009) spoke to the level of confidence in the capabilities that commanders have in their female service members and the increasing number of deployments by women to Operations Enduring Freedom and Iraqi Freedom at 53% compared to men at 71%. And, while women continued to be disproportionately assigned to support occupations (i.e., health care and administration), they were increasingly being called upon to fill positions that directly placed them in the line of fire (i.e., infantry, gun crew, and seamanship), thus questioning their designation as noncombatants given their roles in combat.

Supporters of women in combat maintain that to deny women the right to combat is to reinforce the culture of exclusion to women in the military (Ellefson 1998; Harris 2009; Putko 2008b; Titunik 2000, 2008). So, many cite the state of affairs, most notably those in Operations Enduring Freedom and Iraqi Freedom, which marked contradictions between the policy and practice given conditions on the ground (Burnes 2008; Grosskruger 2008; Keenan 2008; Putko 2008a; Sheppard 2007; Titunik 2008; Twitchell 2008). And, as aforementioned, the calls for repealing the combat exclusion policy have emanated from those within the military as well as from leaders who have retired from the military including Major General Jeanne Holm, Brigadier General Pat Foote, and members of DACOWITS (Miller 1998). The evidence also demonstrates that a psychology of exclusion of women cadets begins as early as at the Army's U.S. Military Academy that is even before the women are commissioned as officers (Putko 2008b). The career fields with the highest honor—infantry and armor—are closed to women. The closest allied field to which women cadets could aspire is military police. Some scholars believe though that this combat experience for men is not only a mark of high honor but should the men seek political office, having combat experience is a prized qualification (Kennedy-Pipe 2000). As such, because for the most part the path to general officer is through combat arms, in a combat exclusion environment, women had no real incentive of aspiring to or securing Army leadership since these career opportunities were already closed to them (Putko 2008b).

Besides, the fallout of continuing the combat exclusion policy would be the adverse impact on an already overstressed military force (National Security Advisory Group 2006). With this in mind, there are still four interrelated themes which have been absent from the discourse about the combat exclusion policy and/or have not been discussed to the extent necessary to address the shortcomings now that the policy has been repealed, although more recently these issues were reported by the MLDC (2011). First, what will be the impact of the repeal on the recruitment, promotion, and retention of women in a post–combat exclusion policy environment? Enlisting "high quality recruits," or those who are college bound between the ages of 17 and 24, has more recently become a challenge for the military (Bachman et al. 2000; Lindon 2008; Population Representation in the Military Services 2011). These recruits have been specifically targeted by the military, for although they are the least likely to pursue the military as a career, should they enlist, they are the most likely to complete their terms of enlistment. Similarly, traditional groups like African Americans and even white males in the aforementioned age groups and young women are no longer turning to military service at traditional rates (Armour 1996; Baldor 2007; Regan 2005). Some military branches in years past have also not been as successful in meeting recruiting goals (National Security Advisory Group 2006), while others have only succeeded because of the imposition of the stop loss policy that involuntarily extends service members in the military (GAO 2005c), especially during Operation Iraqi Freedom. The MLDC (2011) also indicated the need for DoD to infuse more demographic diversity at lower ranks to build capacity over time from which to draw for diversity in leadership.

The high unemployment rate since 2008 has actually bode well for the military which according to its latest population report (Population Representation in the Military Services 2011) described its recruitment for the last three years as "excellent" (Executive Summary, p. 1). Moreover, the accessions to the military in terms of the quality of the recruits between ages 17 and 24 during this period has been its highest since the advent of the all-volunteer force in 1973 (Population Representation in the Military Services 2011). Yet, in the same vein, the report concedes to present and expected challenges ahead for the military in that when the economy improves, it will become increasingly difficult for it to sustain both the level and quality of recruitment. In addition, recruits in this age category are less likely than in the past to recommend the military as a viable option to others. To further compound these challenges, the civilian youth from which the military draws its recruits are plagued with such maladies as obesity, drug abuse, and other problems that render them medically unqualified for military service.

A second issue that was not being addressed even before the repeal of the combat exclusion policy is what impact will the repeal have on the retention of women in the military? The military has experienced the loss of junior personnel and personnel with critical skill sets (GAO 2005a, 2005b, 2005c, 2007; National Security Advisory Group 2006). Junior officers have also been leaving the military at unprecedented rates (Shanker 2006) as well as are some mid-career officers (French 2000). Another group to which the military has turned yet their attrition rates are faster than the military can retain them is white women (Harris 2009; Hosek et al. 2001; Park 1999). The attrition rates for white women are the highest for any group in the military. For instance, unlike other groups, white female officers are the least likely to remain in the military between retention cycles, and as a consequence, are less likely than their white male peers to be promoted (Hosek et al. 2001).

Women in the military on average are more likely than men in the military to be involved in dual military marriages (Joint Economic Committee 2007). For female officers, that rate is seven times higher than their male peers (Population Representation in the Military Services 2006). And, when women in the military experience conflict with career and family, they are far more likely than men to voluntarily terminate military service (DACOWITS 2003), especially in an era of increasing deployments (DACOWITS 2005; Joint Economic Committee 2007). Junior personnel and women are also less likely to complete a 20-year career in the military (DACOWITS 2003, 2006; GAO 2001). And because women in the military are less likely to view the military as a viable career option and more likely to prematurely leave the military as a result (DACOWITS 2012; MLDC 2011), these concerns led the MLDC (2011) to raise even greater concerns about the retention of women in the military in light of a drawdown of forces environment. As the MLDC (2011) indicated, the drawdown of forces in Iraq that began in 2011 and those in Afghanistan which began in 2012 are likely to create significant retention gaps for women in the military. More importantly, the MLDC was concerned that a drawdown of forces without such consideration would leave the military with a dearth of highly qualified women, so much so that it requested the assistance of DACOWITS (2012) for further investigation. DACOWITS recommended that the military continue to develop strategies by paying particular attention to those that seek to retain qualified women. And, like the MLDC (2011), DACOWITS (2012) recommended that women be fully integrated into combat ground units without regard to gender and through the further development of gender-neutral physical standards. In other words, DACOWITS (2012) reinforced this recommendation by affirming the conclusion of the MLDC (2011) that the way to stave off the attrition of women in the military is to repeal the combat exclusion policy.

Third, given the concerns of both the MLDC (2011) and DACOWITS (2012), the military faces the additional challenge of stabilizing promotion rates in light of the lack of availability of large enough pools of qualified females from which to promote. Most female officers, for example, are concentrated at the junior officer or company grades (0–1 to 0–3) where the attrition rates are the highest for this group (DoD 2004). As a consequence, the low numbers of qualified females available for promotion consideration, coupled with the disproportionate attrition within this group, principally white females, create confounding effects that discourage females at lower ranks to remain long enough to be promoted to higher ranks (0–4 to 0–5) (Evertson and Nesbitt 2004). The elevation of Ann Dunwoody to the rank of a four-star general and subsequently Janet Wolfenbarger of the Air Force is an anomaly of sorts in the sense that elite military women who have been so elevated do not have combat experience since at the time they were barred from combat. Additionally, for white women, unlike other groups, post-military earnings have shown that they are penalized for military service (Cooney et al. 2003; Mehay and Hirsch 1996; Segal and Segal 2004), although white women, more so than any other group, support gender equality in the military. In this case, white females, from which the military largely recruits, do not consider the military as a viable career option (Harris 2009).

Finally, the current discourse about the combat exclusion policy has been devoid of what the overall impact of repealing the policy will mean not only for women in the military but for women in American society at large. Mazur (1998) attempts to dispel the myth of the novelty effect that often plagues military women owing to their absence from certain venues such as combat that serves to reinforce their status as victims. Mazur argues that women are so portrayed because they lack full agency. Harris (2009) advanced Mazur's (1998) agency theory by developing a theory of attrition that suggests that, at least for white females, especially in light of their disproportionate and premature exodus from the military, once they join the institution, this signals a struggle for full agency. Thus, while white females' departure from the military is disquieting, doing so is simply one way in which they attempt to assume control to exercise full agency. This gap in the existing discourse about the combat exclusion policy fails to acknowledge that although the discourse is about the exclusion of women from combat, the larger issue lies in using the removal of the combat exclusion policy to advance the full agency of women in the military and in other domains of American life. In addition, failure to do so would be simply undemocratic, for Snyder (2003), Kennedy-Pipe (2000), and others (i.e., Segal 1982, 1993, 1995, 1999) have convincingly argued that the role of women in the military should not devolve into gender capability but that such performance should be based on military effectiveness. So to frame women's performance in terms of military effectiveness is to deemphasize the importance of gender and focus on the primacy of their contribution to the overall mission (Snyder 2003). For women in the military, like men in the military, service means the subordination of self to that of country (Baker 2006). However, women, like men, demand to be treated not as second-class citizens but as fully functioning members and citizens of a democratic society who have the right to bear arms.

20 ■ *Living Legends and Full Agency*

And, in an effort to meet the current and future demands of the military and to compete for the most talented in society, women have earned and must be given the right to full agency. According to Lindon (2008), it then behooves the military to open up more positions to women and one way of achieving this goal is through the recent repeal of the combat exclusion policy. As such, this research and book will also speak to this larger issue of what the repeal of the combat exclusion policy and thus a post–combat exclusion policy environment will mean for achieving full agency for women not only in the military but in the larger American society.

Note

1. Data differ and were reconciled among the four sources.

Appendix 1

The below tables (Tables A1.1 through A1.7) are schematic representations of women's participation in the American military. Table A1.1 shows the increasing participation rates of women in the military campaigns since the Civil War along with the number of women declared as prisoners of war (Department of Veterans Affairs 2011; Women in Military Service for America [WIMSA] Memorial Foundation, Inc., 2011). Table A1.2 is a breakdown by military branch of women's composition as a percentage of the total military force (WIMSA 2011). Table A1.3 represents the numbers of women who have paid the ultimate sacrifice, including those wounded in action, during each major military campaign beginning with the Civil War through present (Defense Manpower Data Center [DMDC]; as of October 30, 2013; Fischer 2013). Table A1.4 displays the occupations in which women in the active duty component of the enlisted corps are distributed (Population Representation of the Military Services FY 2011). Table A1.5 reflects similar data for enlisted women within the reserve components of the military (Reserve and National Guard; Population Representation of the Military Services FY 2011). Table A1.6 has similar data for women within the commissioned corps on active duty while Table A1.7 shows the same data where women officers are distributed within the various occupations according to military branch and component (Population Representation of the Military Services FY 2011). Note, however, that these data reflect information for FY 2011, or prior to the repeal of the combat exclusion policy. While there might have been minor movement afoot in terms of moving women into positions and assignments designated as combat and combat related, the data here might not have changed, if any, since they were collected for the FY 2011 report.

Table A1.1   Representation of Women That Served in Major Military Campaigns and Held as Prisoners of War

Military Campaign	Number Served	Prisoners of War (POWs)
Civil War	Unknown	1
Spanish-American War	1,500	Unknown
World War I	10,000+	Unknown
World War II	400,000	90
Korean Conflict	120,000	Unknown
Vietnam Conflict	7,000	Unknown
Operation Urgent Fury (Deployed)	170	–
Operation Just Cause	770	–
Operation Desert Storm	41,000	2
Operation Enduring Freedom/ Operation Iraqi Freedom	200,000+	3

Source: Department of Veterans Affairs, 2011; Women in Military Services for America (WIMSA) Memorial Foundation, Inc., 2011.

Table A1.2   Women's Representation as a Percentage of the Total Military Force (Includes the Coast Guard)

Military Branch	Active Duty	%	Reserve	%	Guard	%
Army	76,694	13.6	62,473	21.6	53,290	14.6
Marine Corps	13,677	6.8	5,704	5.7	–	–
Navy	53,385	16.4	20,549	19.9	–	–
Air force	63,552	19.1	28,463	26.6	19,500	18.5
Total DoD	207,308	14.5	117,189	19.6	72,790	15.5
Coast guard	6,790	15.7	1,592	16.7	–	–

Source: Women in Military Service for America (WIMSA) Memorial Foundation, Inc. 2011 (As of September 30).

Table A1.3 Representation of the Total Number of Women Who Have Made the Ultimate Sacrifice (Casualties) and Were Wounded in Action in Military Campaigns

Military Campaign	Deaths	Wounded in Action
Civil War	Unknown	Unknown
Spanish-American War	20+	Unknown
World War I	172	Unknown
Korean Conflict	2	Unknown
Vietnam Conflict	8	Unknown
Operation Desert Storm	15	Unknown
Operations Iraqi Freedom/New Dawn	110	637
Operation Enduring Freedom	49	358

Source: Defense Manpower Data Center (DMDC) (As of October 30, 2013), Fischer, H., U.S. Military Casualty Statistics: Operation New Dawn, Operation Iraqi Freedom, and Operation Enduring Freedom, Congressional Research Service (CRS). February 5, 2013, http://www.fas.org/sgp/crs/natsec/RS22452.pdf.

Table A1.4 Women Represented within Each Occupation as a Percentage of the Total Enlisted Active Force by Military Branch

	Occupation									
	Infantry/Gun Crews/ Seamanship[a]	Electronics	Communication	Medical	Other Technical	Administrators	Electrical	Craftsman	Supply	Nonoccupational[b]	% Women
Army	0.93	11.4	9.2	27.4	17.5	32.6	7.4	9.5	17.7	5.0	13
Navy	14.6	11.9	21.7	19.6	5.8	24.2	13.0	13.2	19.6	23.5	16.4
Marine Corps	0.54	4.9	8.3	—	8.0	18.7	4.7	5.7	8.9	7.6	6.9
Air force	7.2	9.3	22.2	49.3	15.2	36.0	5.9	6.3	17.1	18.4	19.1
Total DoD	2.7	10.2	14.2	30.5	13.6	30.1	8.5	9.3	16.5	15.0	14.2

Source: Population Representation of the Military Services FY 2011.

[a] Women do not currently serve in infantry but do serve in other positions as gun crews, air crews, and seaman specialties.
[b] Nonoccupational may include students, patients, and individuals with unassigned duties and unknowns.

Table A1.5 Women Represented within Each Occupation as a Percentage of the Total Enlisted Reserve Force by Military Branch

	Infantry/Gun Crews/ Seamanship[a]	Electronics	Communication	Medical	Other Technical	Administrators	Electrical	Craftsman	Supply	Nonoccupational[b]	% Women
Army National Guard	0.44	13.1	6.5	29.0	21.6	33.4	6.6	10.1	18.5	20.0	14.9
Army Reserve	1.5	17.2	16.5	36.2	23.6	36.1	11.2	11.1	19.7	23.1	22.9
Naval Reserve	17.5	15.6	26.2	27.2	10.3	36.4	12.1	12.6	21.9	18.4	21.1
Marine Corps Reserve	0.49	2.9	4.6	—	2.8	16.5	3.6	4.8	5.6	2.9	4.3
Air National Guard	8.9	7.8	21.5	50.4	15.0	40.0	6.4	6.5	17.5	21.2	18.6
Air Force Reserve	9.8	12.1	35.1	53.7	12.5	40.0	7.4	9.4	21.8	26.9	25.3
Total DoD	2.0	12.3	13.2	36.3	19.8	35.5	7.8	10.2	18.5	19.9	18.0

Source: Population Representation of the Military Services FY 2011.

[a] Women do not currently serve in infantry but do serve in other positions as gun crews, air crews, and seaman specialties.
[b] Nonoccupational may include students, patients, and individuals with unassigned duties and unknowns.

Table A1.6 Women Represented within Each Occupation as a Percentage of the Total Active Duty Commissioned Officer Corps Force by Military Branch

	General Officers[a]	Tactical Operations	Intelligence	Engineering and Maintenance	Scientists and Professionals	Health Care	Administration	Supply, Procurement, and Allied	Nonoccupational[b]	% Women
Army	5.9	2.8	18.8	16.0	12.8	37.3	28.7	20.7	9.3	17.5
Navy	8.4	8.0	15.6	5.9	19.2	37.5	22.2	13.8	15.4	16.4
Marine Corps	1.1	2.4	6.1	6.1	12.7	–	19.8	10.2	9.0	6.3
Air Force	8.8	7.2	25.7	12.9	19.8	43.9	31.3	20.6	10.4	18.8
Total DoD	6.05	5.10	16.55	7.73	16.13	39.57	25.50	16.33	11.03	14.75

Source: Population Representation of the Military Services FY 2011.

[a] Tables exclude the 980 individuals assigned as general/flag officers by the Defense Data Manpower Center (DMDC) (19 females in the Marine Corps and 19 in the Air Force).

[b] Nonoccupational may include students, patients, and individuals without assigned duties.

Table A1.7 Women Represented within Each Occupation as a Percentage of the Total Reserve Commissioned Officer Corps Force by Military Branch

	General Officers[a]	Tactical Operations	Intelligence	Engineering and Maintenance	Scientists and Professionals	Health Care	Administration	Supply, Procurement, and Allied	Nonoccupational[b]	% Women
Army National Guard	7.2	2.2	14.2	13.0	7.6	31.6	24.0	21.1	15.0	13.1
Army Reserve	10.3	3.2	19.5	16.8	11.3	43.9	33.3	21.5	20.3	25.3
Naval Reserve	20.0	6.9	14.0	7.8	13.3	43.7	28.0	16.0	17.3	17.2
Marine Corps Reserve	20.0	2.5	7.7	9.1	8.2	—	23.7	15.1	3.7	7.1
Air National Guard	8.6	6.5	23.2	10.9	14.4	37.1	33.2	18.0	16.0	17.7
Air Force Reserve	16.9	10.2	33.5	20.2	24.0	47.8	45.2	26.7	11.3	26.1
Total DoD	10.6	5	18.8	13.9	13.4	41.4	31.5	20.9	16.3	19.1

Source: Population Representation of the Military Services FY 2011.

[a] Tables exclude 715 individuals classified as general/flag officer by the Defense Manpower Data Center (DMDC), of which there are 27 females.
[b] Nonoccupational may include students, patients, and individuals with unassigned duties and unknowns.

Chapter 2

Warriors to the Core

The evidence of what today is called Sudan from approximately 6500 BC lies the burial ground of Jebel Sahaba, one of 20 women and some 20 men along with 7 unidentified adults as well as children in the first recorded scene of women in war (DePauw 1998). During biblical times or as described in the Old Testament, women strategically aided men in exchange for their families' safety, as in the case of Rahab, who assisted in hiding spies sought out by the King of Jericho; Deborah, in the Book of Judges, who was hailed for leading the Israelites during the twelfth century BC; Jael, who after providing food to Mon, caught him off guard by crushing his skull with a deadly blow to his head; and Judith, described as an Hebrew, who with the aid of a servant, decapitated the head of an Assyrian commander who had come to capture the town of Bethula. The head of the commander was handed to a demoralized army that was subsequently defeated by the Hebrews. Accordingly, though effeminate by today's standards, Ramses II of Egypt strikes a rather feminine pose during the thirteenth century BC as he charges into battle (Goldstein 2003). It is thus argued that although women must have participated in wars on horseback, for unknown reasons, they were missing in critical mass from any large-scale effort even though figures such as those of Ramses II contradict their absence. But, specifically, the presence of figures with such feminine poses on chariots during war resulted in Egypt's expansion in territory because from all indications, it appears that the degree to which these chariots were deployed was less dependent on gender than it was about the skills of the person to control the horse while riding to accurately strike the target (Goldstein 2003). Similarly, because chariots of the day were costly, it is speculated that the allocation of such resources would have also been dependent upon the skill of the person, again without regard to gender and for the purpose of empire expansion.

The Assyrian queen Shammuramat, or Semiramis, ruled during the ninth century BC, from 811 to 806 (DePauw 1998). She was known for leading expeditions, by first assault and capture of the Citadel, captured Babylonia, and most famously expanded her empire by invading India and today's Pakistan. And like her male predecessors, she memorialized her exploits in a bronze statue of herself donning a sword, inscribed with the following:

> Nature made me a woman yet I have raised myself to rival the greatest men. I swayed the scepter of Ninos: I extended my dominions to the river Hinamenes Eastward; to the Southward to the land of Frankincense and Myrrh; Northward to Saccae and the Scythians. No Assyrian before me had seen an ocean, but I have seen four. I have built dams and fertilized the barren land with my rivers. I have built impregnable walls and roads to far places and with iron cut passages through mountains where previously even wild animals could not pass. Various as were my deeds, I have yet found leisure hours to indulge myself with friends. (Herodotus 4.118, in DePauw 1998, pp. 41 and 42)

Goldstein's (2003) speculation about women's employment as skilled chariot drivers was confirmed by DePauw's (1998) writing about women who served as drivers in battle during Shammuramat's reign. And, Herodotus, "the father of history" or what I connote as ourstory throughout this book (DePauw, p. 40), documented that women in North Africa were routinely used as chariot drivers. Such Egyptian warrior queens, around 3000 BC, predated the Assyrians, like Maryet-Nit, Khentkawes, Neferusobek, Ahmose-Nofretari, and Ashotep, sometime between the twenty-fifth and sixteenth centuries BC. Queen Hatshepsut of Egypt, while more prone than her predecessors to concentrate on business opportunities of the time, nevertheless engaged in exploits for empire expansion. She was known to lead her troops into battle and was the first woman on record to use a false beard, a symbol of wisdom for pharaohs, and adorned herself with other male adornments.

While the recorded ourstory about the Egyptians is well intact, that of the Libyans and people in other parts of North Africa is etched in the African Sahara (DePauw 1998). Considered the first Amazons or female warriors, it was the Greek and Roman classical writers who subsequently published this information about them. DePauw (1998) chastises that today we seem to dilute this potent yet reviled piece of our past as myths and relegate them as "unicorns or centaurs" (p. 43) or as mythologized figures through such modern-day entertainment as the TV series *Xena: Warrior Princess* or via the early twentieth-century play starring Katharine Hepburn as Antiope (Goldstein 2003). But such roles, that is, as Amazons, are to be taken seriously (DePauw 1998) and not idealized as mere fiction. Another group, known as the Scythian Amazons or Sarmatians, as they were referred to by the Greeks, was particularly unique (DePauw 1998). Herodotus believed this unique group to be direct descendants of the African Amazons. These women mated with Scythian men in exchange for leaving their own tribes yet enjoyed the liberties of women in their own societies. Writings from Herodotus show that these Scythian women were "riding to the hunt on horseback, sometimes with, sometimes without their menfolk, taking part in war, and wearing the same sort of clothes as men" (Herodotus 4.117, in DePauw 1998, p. 47). Further, these steppes, or a nomadic people, were characterized by their powerful matriarchal societies (DePauw 1998; Goldstein 2003). Davis-Kimball (1997) reports a site where graves of women were discovered during the 1950s equipped with such war implements as swords, spears, arrowheads, daggers, and armor. Another interesting fact is that in seven graves of female warriors that were excavated, one grave contained the body of one with bowed legs, suggesting a life of riding on horseback, and with a bronze arrowhead in a leather pouch donned around her neck. Others were buried with bent arrowheads, attesting that they were killed in battle.

A succession of Ethiopian queens, whom the Greeks distinguished as Kentakes or Candace, reigned prior to 332 BC over Ethiopia, Sudan, and areas of Egypt, although it was only when Alexander the Great sought to conquer the kingdom did this record come to light (Jones 1997). In one famous prelude to a siege of Ethiopia, Alexander encountered the Black Queen Candace of Ethiopia, who calculated Alexander's advance and implemented a well-executed war plan designed to counter his forces. As Alexander approached, he could not help but be in awe of the queen's display of force and strength. He calculated that challenging her would deal his forces a fatal blow, so he retreated. Shanakdakhete is shown in regalia of armor handling a spear, in a relief dated around 170 BC. While she ruled neither as queen nor as queen mother, she ruled independently, although her husband and son constituted her cadre. Other warrior queens followed, including Amanirenas, Amanishakhete, Nawidemak, and Malegereabar. For instance, 150 years later, Petronius, Roman governor in Egypt, attempted once again to wage battle or capture the region, when he and his forces were overpowered by Queen Amanirenas. The queen and her forces not only succeeded in retaining her territory but captured parts of the enemy's in the process.

The Yoruba people of West Africa are renowned for their capacity for producing female sheroes (heroines) and armies (Jones 1997). The bordering Hausa women are similarly reputed as commanders. Centuries later, in 1536, Queen Arninatu controlled the Hausa empire, and following a succession of 17 queens, the eldest female child of Queen Bakwa Turunku, and queen of Zazzau, subsequently renamed the region Zaire, which is known today as the Democratic Republic of Congo. With an iron hand, she ruled her empire that comprised of seven states, for 34 years, eventually occupying regions of Central Africa. The queen forged trade route agreements across the Sahara to North Africa. Today, she is revered and credited, among many things, for bringing the kola nut to the region. Nigeria has also commemorated its queen with a statue in its National Theater in Lagos. The queen sits regally on a horse with a sword in her hand. There have been numerous queens in the motherland of Africa, too many to mention here, which include Queen Dahia "the sorceress" (Jones 1997, p. 85) of Carthage and Mauritania; Judith, queen of the Falashes (Jones 1997), who is infamous for the murder of the members of the family of

Solomon; the Queen of Sheba; and most notorious was Zinga Mbandi (Jones 1997), daughter of the King of Ndongo. When, in 1620, she tried to negotiate Ndongo's independence with the Portuguese governor, she found the governor seated on a large chair. But she and the governor's attendants were left to stand. Zinga immediately commanded one of the servants to the floor on his hands and knees. She then sat on the servant to enable her to maintain level eye-to-eye contact with the governor to formally introduce herself and to proceed with the negotiations.

The Greeks recorded their own ourstory of warrior women, who followed their African ancestors. King Harpalykos of Thrace acculturated his daughter Harpalyce with regular doses of warlike exercises, including throwing darts, racing, and using the bow and arrow (DePauw 1998). Following her father's defeat, Harpalyce marshaled the army's forces to liberate her father. Another famous Greek warrior woman, Atalanta, was known for her courage and military prowess. To further demonstrate that women, like men, were an integral part of war, Greek art, as engraved on the west side of the Parthenon, reflects scenes of women and men in battle (Goldstein 2003). Ironically, the naysayers, or those who find an inherent incompatibility between women and war, find the idea of Amazon and war to be nonexistent. And, as the myth goes, Amazons would cut off their breasts so as to make shooting the bow and arrow much easier for them (DePauw 1998; Goldstein 2003).

Roman author Justin suggested that the word *Amazon* means "without breasts," a definition that directly contradicts Greek art that shows women with breasts in the heat of battle (DePauw 1998). According to DePauw, for unknown reasons, this definition has erroneously taken traction and is regularly repeated as such today. But again, DePauw refutes this definition as myth, for, as she asserts, "mastectomy is not an effective way to increase the strength of chest muscles. That some women in some parts of the globe may have practiced ritual mutilation to prevent the development of a breast is possible—but the Amazons of the ancient world were not among them" (DePauw 1998, pp. 51 and 52).

DePauw affirms Justin's myth that the word *Amazon* is not of Greek origin but from Iran: *hamozyn*, which means "warrior" (p. 52), which is how the Libyans referred to themselves. Men were believed to have used such a term to represent the abnormal as one way of reaffirming their own patriarch as normal or in the mainstream (Goldstein 2003). While Goldstein concedes that even some women use the term, it has often conveyed mixed messages since men use the term to bolster their masculinity. Amazon women are often portrayed in modern genre as the femme fatale. It was believed that in Amazon societies, the roles were reversed (Crim 2000). Men simply functioned as breeders and servants, whereas women were the sources of power. The Greeks made it a point of defeating the Amazons in order to present a masculine society and thus patriarchy. And, despite this contradiction, Greek mythology still elevated the status of women, providing a direct connection between women and war. Athena was considered a goddess of wisdom and a warrior. Other indications of this connection are the strong relationship between Aphrodite, the Goddess of Love, and Ares, the God of War.

The record books show that the Romans believed that Africa and North Africa, or the region that is now famously referred to as the Middle East, promised much wealth and influence but was occupied by people they viewed as barbarians (DePauw 1998). It was during this time when Cleopatra VII of Egypt took reign but at that time part of Egypt had succumbed to Roman rule (Grant 1972; Ludwig 1937). But her father only served at the pleasure of the Romans. Cleopatra was politically astute and had a great deal of influence on Julius Caesar and Mark Antony, eventually convincing Antony to relinquish his wealth and land to her. However, Octavian, his brother-in-law, mounted an assault against Cleopatra, accusing her of machinating a Cleopatra–Anthony alliance as a plot for a new dynasty in Alexandria, not Rome. Yet, Antony continued to support her. Although Cleopatra lost the battle due to miscalculation on her part, she attempted to establish an agreement with Octavian, which he refused. Consequently, Queen Cleopatra took her own life rather than be captured and taken to Rome to signal Octavian's victory. Cleopatra has been vilified by Roman historians as a scheming seductress whose desire was to destroy Rome (Abbott 1941). While there have been many Egyptian queens who operated under Roman rule, unlike Cleopatra, the memory of Queen Septimia Zenobia has been held in high esteem. "Her face was dark and of a swarthy hue. Her eyes were black and powerful, her spirit genuinely great, and her beauty incredible … Her voice was clear and like that of a man. Her sternness, when necessity demanded, was that of a tyrant; her clemency when her sense of right called for it, that of a good emperor" (DePauw 1998, p. 103).

Queen Zenobia ruled Palmyra in Syria during the third century BC (Vaughan 1967). She resisted the invasion by Rome under Claudius, who was succeeded by Aurelian and who expanded the Roman Empire by capturing other lands.

At the time, Zenobia controlled what are now Saudi Arabia, Armenia, Persia, Egypt, and Syria (DePauw 1998). When Aurelian sought to retake the territories, he encountered stiff opposition from her army of 70,000. Although the Romans encircled the queen in Palmyra, Aurelian was concerned about possible defeat. He wrote,

> There are Romans who say that I am waging a war against a mere woman, but there is as great as an array before me as though I were fighting a man. I cannot tell you what a great store of arrows, spears and stones is here, what great preparation they have made. There is no section of the wall that is not held by two or three engines of war. Their machines even hurl fire (Newark 1989, p. 64).

Aurelian made attempts to negotiate with Zenobia and her army to surrender by notifying her by way of a letter (Newark 1989). But the queen took issue with the tone of Aurelian's letter and fired back with a fiery reply. Under the cover of night, Queen Zenobia escaped by using a female camel (DePauw 1998; Vaughan 1967), instead of a horse as it was faster. However, she was intercepted before she could cross into Persia and was captured. But, unlike Cleopatra, Zenobia did not commit suicide; when asked why she had not resisted to the end, she replied "You, I accept are an Emperor because you win victories. But your predecessors I have never regarded as worthy of Emperorship. I desired to become a partner in the royal power should there be enough land" (Newark 1989, p. 73). The Romans were known to give any excuse for a parade and Aurelian's victory was no exception (DePauw 1998). Zenobia spent the rest of her life remarried and in Rome. Her sons became well known and her daughter married into influential families. Perhaps the reason for Zenobia's positive regard by those who recorded Roman ourstory can now be well understood for even the victor, Aurelian, sang her praises, by saying, "… what manner of woman she is, how wise in counsel, how steadfast in plans, how firm toward soldiers, how generous when necessity calls, and how stern when discipline demands" (Newark 1989, p. 73).

The fall of the Roman Empire brought with it the introduction of Christianity to Europe. Alfred the Great defeated the Scandinavians and in AD 878 established an agreement with the Vikings to divide England up but engaged in other agreements to recover his lands once lost to the Vikings (DePauw 1998). His daughter, Aethelflaed, married to forge alliances with another Saxon royal family. After her father's death, she created other alliances with her brother to seal the family's holdings. She had one child with her old and ill husband but discontinued a sexual relationship with him by declaring that producing a child for the old man was already painful enough as a king's daughter, and it would have been inappropriate to continue such affairs just for the joy of it (DePauw 1998). Her discipline was so admired by Christian England that following her husband's death, she assumed power as Lady of the Mercians. Aethelflaed is described by William of Malmesbury as "a woman who protected men at home and intimidated them abroad" (Newark 1989, p. 94). She expanded her territory by building forts, convinced the Welsh to cede to her authority after capturing their king's wife and members of his court, and seized the Viking military center at Derby. When she died, her brother continued her conquest by capturing Danelaw, which her father had negotiated away.

Matilda of Italy was famous for her command of armies in Europe (Eads 1986; DePauw 1998). She was described as fierce, for in addition to being trained on the finer things of life such as embroidery, given her stature, her mother saw fit to have Matilda ensconced in learning how to ride with a lance, be a foot soldier, and use the sword and battle ax. There are numerous accounts of her going into combat on behalf of protecting the welfare of Pope Alexander II in 1061. According to the records,

> Now there appeared in Lombardy at the head of her numerous squadrons the young maid Matilda, armed like a warrior, and with such bravery, that she made known to the world that courage and valor in mankind is not indeed a matter of sex, but of heart and spirit (DePauw 1998, p. 85).

During feudal Europe, while kings increased their vast hoards of wealth at the expense of peasants and were succeeded by each other in the passing of the monarchy, their queens functioned more than just wives on the issues of the day, not to mention military matters such as war (Crim 2000). This inclination to include noblewomen in state affairs, which, it appears, should have been the sole purview of men, moved ourstorians to conclude that bloodline took precedence over gender. For this reason, it was also believed that many such women consciously became acculturated in the ways of knowing of men as a way to secure legitimacy for their authority.

Eleanor of Aquitaine is considered to be the most noteworthy Frenchwoman in the Middle Ages, who ruled her kingdom in southwestern France with an iron fist. Marriage to England's Henry II only increased her reach. As one Greek observer put it, as Eleanor and her then husband, King Louis VI of France, proceeded en route to Jerusalem:

> Females were among them, riding horseback in the manner of men, not … sidesaddle, but unashamedly astride, bearing lances and weapons as men do. Dressed in masculine garb, they conveyed a wholly martial appearance, more mannish than the Amazons. One [Eleanor] stood out from the rest … and from the embroidered gold which ran around the hem and fringes of her garments was called the Gold Foot. (Newark 1989, pp. 107 and 108)

Said Crim (2000), while many at the time resented Eleanor's influential role, she coalesced her power that endeared the loyalty of her subjects through her various exploits, including two strategic marriages. Another strong contender in Italy, like Matilda, was Christine de Pisan (1390–1429) (Crim 2000; DePauw 1998). However, de Pisan, unlike her predecessor, was known more for her literary acumen and desire to uplift the status of all women including noblewomen, the bourgeois, and lower class women (Crim 2000). Her great intellect on diplomacy, politics, and the like were sought after for consultation by the leaders of the day, and her writings by today's standards are considered unusual, as masculine topics.

Even more unusual and again by today's standards, de Pisan deliberately used her position of influence to impart counsel on politics with the military to women (Crim 2000). Her legacy, *Treasure of the City of Ladies*, set out to make as a matter of record women's impact on the important issues of the day, including warfare. She also developed a manual on the tactics of warfare entitled *Feats of Arms and Chivalry* using archival data and interviews with knights, in which she discussed the most desirous qualities for becoming a good soldier and commander (DePauw 1998). And, while she did not believe that women were equal to men, she was of the mindset that women should avoid taking up arms for the purpose of demonstrating their equality even as she counseled others on the strategies of warfare (Crim 2000), for

> [t]he proper role of a good, wise queen or princess is to maintain peace and concord and to avoid wars and their resulting disasters. Women particularly should concern themselves with peace because men by nature are more foolhardy and headstrong, and that overwhelming

desire to avenge themselves prevents them from foreseeing the resulting danger of terrors of war. But woman by nature is more gentle and circumspect. (Christine de Pisan as cited by Crim 2000, pp. 23 and 24)

Instead, de Pisan believed that women should take up martial arts. In the *Book of the Deeds of Arms and Chivalry* in 1410, de Pisan encouraged princes to dedicate themselves not for war itself, but for the benefits of the state (Crim 2000).

It was Pope Urban II who declared the First Crusade as a means of defending Christendom against the Moslems of the Middle East and Turkey (DePauw 1998). This period lasted from 1095 through the fifteenth century. During this time, despite being considered baggage by commanders and a moral inconvenience, women became equally inspired and accompanied soldiers for the trek to Jerusalem. Many donned men's clothing as soldiers, although they were clearly identified as women. It is worth noting here that it was this period, which witnessed a defense of Christianity, that introduced intolerance and hypermorality, especially regarding women who often accompanied these crusades as soldiers (DePauw 1998); however, the Greeks held contradictory views about women and their biological predispositions for war (Goldstein 2003), and the Romans believed that the presence of women and the comforts they provided soldiers made fighting men soft (DePauw 1998).

Prior to the birth of Islam, during the seventh century, women were a visible part of war in the Arab world (Fraser 1990). Maaria, a queen in Syria, conquered the territories of Phoenicia, Palestine, and Egypt, including the Roman legions. Another, Hind al-Hunud or the Hind, as she was called, was involved in the Battle of Badr with Mohammed. As well, she was a follower of the Cult of the Lady of Victory, whose members dedicated themselves to battle by deliberately placing themselves in danger to encourage their men to fight. Women who fought along with Mohammed include Salaym Bint Malhan, who fought while she was pregnant, pulling swords and daggers that were secured around her stomach (Miles 1988). Aishah, Mohammed's last wife, fought in the Battle of the Camels, while Khawlah Bint al-Azwar al-Kindlyyah and others fought at the Battle of Yermonks. Khawlah, who was a tall knight muffled in black and fighting with ferocious courage, when captured, shouted to her fellow female prisoners, "Do you accept these men as your masters? Are you willing for your children to be slaves? Where is your famed courage and skill that has become the talk of the Arab tribes as well as in the cities?" (Miles 1988, p. 66). The Islamic writer, I Made ad-Din, documented that both Christian and Moslem women who fought during the Crusades displayed great strength and were indistinguishable from the men except for the jewelry that adorned their feet. While he came to the conclusion that such behavior for women was peculiar, records consistently show this is not the case (Gibb 1973). During the Second Crusade in 1145, King Louis VII of France was accompanied by his wife Eleanor of Aquitaine on horseback and she and other noblewomen armed themselves with knives and battle axes (Kelly 1950). Similarly, during the Third

Crusade, England's King Henry II and Richard the Lionhearted, his son, enlisted lower-class women as laundresses who came to accompany troops on foot. France's Joan of Arc is unique in the sense that she remains a national figure today (Crim 2000). As the story goes, after receiving a vision from God, Joan of Arc finally convinced Charles VII to have her command the invasion against the British. She led France to victory by retaking all of the previously lost territory but her influence over Charles VII became suspect and she was betrayed to the British. Regrettably, Joan of Arc was branded a heretic for communicating with angels and burned at the stake as a result (Crim 2000).

Finally, Dahomey, modern-day Benin, was famous for its army of Amazon women (Alpern 1998; Goldstein 2003; DePauw 1998). The women were initially recruited as a tactic by King Agadja to swell the size of his army so it appeared larger than it actually was, with male soldiers populating the rear with female soldiers (Alpern 1998; Goldstein 2003); the tactic proved more successful than initially conceived. The corps originated in 1727 (Alpern 1998; Goldstein 2003; DePauw 1998). The women regularly trained together, were in peak physical condition and strength, and were reputed to be very fast. They were also reputed for their cruelty; while in some instances male soldiers were known to abandon their posts, especially in times of combat, there are no such reports about the women soldiers (Alpern 1998; DePauw 1998; Goldstein 2003). They remained fiercely loyal to the king, including those who were captured to serve but who refused to return to their homelands. In a famous battle with the French, the Dahomey women, using high-powered rifles, engaged in hand-to-hand combat with French troops in the trenches (Alpern 1998; DePauw 1998). Unfortunately, it proved to be a point of no return for the Dahomey troops. Like their predecessors, as the French advanced, the French heard a series of explosives as the Dahomey leveled their city rather than have it captured by the French. At the time, the total force had swelled to approximately 5000, during the mid-nineteenth century (Alpern 1998; DePauw 1998).

Chapter 3

The Beginning of the Revolution: The American Experience

Although there are countless more examples that serve as irrefutable evidence of women's direct involvement in war around the world, the American experience, though much more recent by Old World standards (i.e., Africa), is no less profound. While exceedingly slow to be realized and born out of necessity, the trajectory of women's progress in the American military has been one of ebbs and flows. As Segal (1995) noted, women's participation in the military increases and decreases before, during, and following times of major conflicts. However, in the same vein, she also bemoans that following each of these campaigns, amnesia sets in wherein society tends to conveniently forget about the sheroic lengths to which its women have uniformly performed and without whom the military's successes could not have been achieved. Unquestionably, women have always heeded the nation's calls to arms (DeCew 1995). Yet, their progress in the American military has not been defined by a unilinear evolution but to put it bluntly, one of convenience and who could be disposed of as easily during peacetime as they are found to be indispensable for the sake of patriotism during national crises (Francke 1997). And, women's exclusion from the military was designed by law from the start, although neither the absence nor the presence of law ever precluded or deterred women from serving in various capacities in the American military (Holm 1992, attributed to Henry Steele Commager and Richard Morris who attributed it to Martin in Spirit. See Holm 1992, p. 15).

During the war of 1812, Lucy Brewer received credit by the Marine Corps as the first known female marine to serve on the USS *Constitution* as George Baker for three years (Holm 1992). In 1846, Sarah Borginis, a striking figure of over six feet in height, impressed General Zachary Taylor; she put herself in danger to protect the troops during the Mexican bombardment of Fort Brown, and she was promoted to the commissioned rank of Colonel in the Army. The Civil War created a situation for the country that required massive levels of treasure, including human beings. Many restrictions, which included the use of women, were relaxed to galvanize support for the war. And, according to DePauw (1998), this war represented a departure in how war was being fought. Further, unlike previous wars, both sides were American. Yet, securing data that provided evidence of women's roles during the American Civil War was challenging to say the least because for some, their participation was more or less a matter of curiosity. While data are available, much of them have been held as part of private collections. Additionally, in combing through these available data, particularly with regard to camp followers, meant discerning whether or not those who served were men or women as many women disguised themselves as men while others made only passing reference to the existence of female soldiers. Still, it was common knowledge that women served in regiments with men that "her sex was notorious to all in the regiment, but no notice was taken of it so long as she conducted herself properly. They also said that she was not the only representative of the female sex in the ranks" (DePauw 1998, p. 149), unless, of course, the woman was with child and was going into labor (DePauw 1998). Reportedly, women were disguised as spies as their counterparts in Europe had done and established informal networks in order to hide their identities.

Women were commonly in this role (Holm 1992). One such example was a socialite named Rose O'Neal Greenhow who was incarcerated for passing intelligence to the Confederate Army that led to its victory at the First Battle of Bull Run. Likewise, Pauline Cushman, an actress, was a spy for the Union Army who narrowly escaped execution when she was saved by the Union Army. Some served as nurses, notably Clara Barton (Holm 1992), who later established the National Cemetery in Arlington, Virginia, as well as began and served as the first president of the American Red Cross and Sarah Emma Edmonds who also served as a spy for the Union Army (DePauw 1998) as Franklin Thompson (Goldstein 2003). A colorful Cuban named Loreta Janeta Velazquez served in the Confederate Army (DePauw 1998; Holm 1992) by donning the Confederate uniform and gluing on a mustache and beard to make her disguise more credible. She made repeated attempts to succeed in the military, including in the infantry and then as a cavalry officer but only succeeded in leading patrols and was revealed when she was wounded (Holm 1992). Many women who were wounded avoided going to the hospital for treatment to avoid detection (DePauw 1998). Though many joined the war effort out of patriotism by disguising themselves as men, others did their duty by remaining on the home front, though not willingly. As one Confederate woman lamented, "We who stay behind may find it harder than they who go. They will have new scenes and constant excitement to buoy them up and the consciousness of duty done" (Faust 1990, pp. 1204 and 1205). Another woman compared her state to that "like a pent up volcano. I wish I had a field of my energies … now that there is … real tragedy, real roman and history weaving everyday, I suffer, suffer, leading the life I do" (Faust 1990, p. 1205). The contributions and courage of Confederate women have been memorialized since 1904 in the form of a statue at the state capital in Jackson, Mississippi (Faust 1990).

But, perhaps the two most famous women of the time to grace the American landscape were Molly Pitcher, who never received attribution until some 70 years following the Battle of Monmouth in 1778 (DePauw 1998; Holm 1992), and Harriet Tubman, a slave, born Araminta Ross (Allen 2006; DePauw 1998). Although the identity of the now-famous Molly Pitcher is still unidentified, she is believed to have been the wife of John Hays who after witnessing the mutilation of men in the Seventh Pennsylvania Regiment, including her husband, is said to have taken up arms to defend the fort until she was replaced by an artillery man in the regiment (Holm 1992). Some also believe that Molly Pitcher is actually Mary Ludwig Hayes McCauley who had achieved such exploits or perhaps Margaret Corbin who had done so two years earlier at the Battle of Fort Washington. Today, as DePauw (1998) retorts, Molly Pitcher, whatever her identity, is worthy of more than being consigned to a rest stop off the New Jersey Turnpike that was dedicated to her memory. But unfortunately for a woman who assumed such functions, it is not surprising that she has not been given the fitting recognition as concurred by Holm (1992). To Holm, regardless of her identity, Molly Pitcher is not a fictional character. She is the paragon of women who served in the Continental Army, and more importantly, she stands as a symbol of America's independence.

Almost 100 years later and during the Civil War, another woman distinguished herself sheroically and has been dubbed by Sarah Bradford in 1869/1961 as "The Moses of Her People" (as cited by DePauw 1998). Harriet Tubman escaped the arduous life of slavery and the brutal beatings of her slave master to assist similarly situated slaves to freedom. While there have been multiple literary works about this giant in American ourstory, Allen (2006) resurrected Tubman's life, where among her many exploits, she served as a spy for the Union Army. Once she fled to freedom, Harriet Tubman used the now-famous Underground Railroad in helping others to freedom. In her later years, Tubman twice petitioned to the U.S. government for compensation for wartime service (Hall 1994). Her second attempt though resulted in the receipt of a $20 per month stipend for the rest of her life. According to Hall (1994, p. 166), "Harriet Tubman was an extraordinary human being, and possibly the most underrated and underappreciated person of either sex or any race, from the Civil War period." Most recently, it was apt of President Barack Obama, the country's first African American president, to designate a 480-acre property located in Dorchester County, Maryland, as Tubman's birthplace, and under the management of the National Park Service built a monument to coincide and commemorate the 100th anniversary of her death on March 10, 2013 (Fritze 2013).

The literature is filled with women's experiences in WWI for the British, German, and Russian women who served as both unofficial combatants as spies and the like and noncombatants as nurses who, despite their role, were nevertheless on the front lines of the war (DePauw 1998; Goldstein 2003). But for the purpose of this book, I will continue to delve into the discussion of war in terms of the American experience from WWs I and II to the more recent campaigns of Operations Enduring Freedom, Iraqi Freedom, and New Dawn. In 1901, Congress authorized the establishment of the Nurse Corps as an auxiliary arm of the Army (Holm 1992). However, at the time, nurses were devoid of military rank, pay, or benefits. The Navy followed suit in 1908. So, when WWI broke out, the Secretary of the Navy Josephus Daniels ascertained that there were no restrictions that a yeoman could not be a woman. During WWI, approximately 13,000 women were mobilized by the U.S. Navy (Goldstein 2003). Most worked as clerks with full induction into the military in both rank and status. The Army hired women to work primarily as nurses. Then Director Anita Phipps drafted a plan that would integrate 170,000 women into the Army, but not as an auxiliary for wartime (Goldstein 2003). But, as a War Department official replied, such a plan would "tend to avert the pressure to admit women to actual membership in the Army" (Treadwell 1954, pp. 18 and 88). By the war's end, approximately 34,000 women had been mobilized for the Army, the Navy Nurse Corps, the Navy, the Marine Corps, and the Coast Guard (Holm 1992). But, accordingly, WWI had brought about the impression that women were only to be involved in the war effort in such capacities as clerks, telephone operators, and nurses; essentially in support roles only.

In 1941, Congresswoman Edith Nourse Rogers (R-MA) advised Chief of Staff General George Marshall that she intended to draft a bill for establishing a Women's Army Corps (WAC; Monahan and Neidel-Greenlee 2010). Nourse Rogers grew impressed with the fact that British women had gained full status as military veterans but that their American counterparts had not yet achieved that status in any of the military services. Moreover, in her role, she was more than familiar with the discrimination that American women had encountered during WWI but without the protection of the military especially if they were injured, killed, or became prisoners of war (POWs). As a consolation, the bill was passed, not in its entirety as Nourse Rogers intended, but as the Women's Army Auxiliary Corps (WAAC) in 1942 (Holm 1992; Monahan and Neidel-Greenlee 2010) and without the full complement of benefits as veterans afforded to men in the military. Oveta Culp Hobby was tapped as its first director at the rank of Major, the highest ranking woman in the WAAC (Goldstein 2003; Monahan and Neidel-Greenlee 2010). She later rose to the rank of Colonel, the highest rank a woman could attain in the military at that time (Monahan and Neidel-Greenlee 2010).

Following the attack on Pearl Harbor in 1941, the WAAC became the WAC, a part of the Army (Holm 1992). Shortly thereafter, legislation was passed to establish the Women Accepted for Volunteer Emergency Services (WAVES). The military then turned to the expertise of primarily academic women for counsel on creating programs for women. Barnard College Dean, Virginia Gildersleeve, became the first Chair of what then became the Defense Advisory Council on Women in the Services (DACOWITS) (Holm 1992; Monahan and Neidel-Greenlee 2010). This appointment was timely as the recruitment of both the enlisted and commissioned corps was at their peak along with the establishment of specialty schools for enlisted women (Holm 1992). As Goldstein (2003) remarked, much was to be learned during this period about the performance of women in the military. For instance, it was observed that women were as dedicated to the performance of their duties as men. Yet, health problems given the feminization of certain occupations resulted in different rates of injuries. Consequently, women WACs experienced far less hospitalization downtime than men, although surprisingly injuries and accidents that were not combat related were similar for both sexes. Women were more likely to sustain accidents that were unrelated to their jobs and that were to be attributed to their wearing of poorly fitting military shoes while men incurred more vehicular accidents. Women also experienced undue fatigue that brought about the prevalence of overweight given the nature of their sedentary jobs and a disconnection to any relationship with the war effort (Treadwell 1954). Questions about the Army's food also became an issue as were bouts of menstruation, although of little consequence, the condition was aggravated by the Army's requirement that women be hospitalized for two days for those experiencing cramps while those who served as pilots in the Army Air Force were grounded. But the rule was unenforceable (Goldstein 2003). And, should a woman become pregnant, she was immediately discharged from military service (Goldstein 2003; Treadwell 1954) to fend for herself without the assistance of the American military.

As for discipline, challenges varied from location to location that surfaced because men had difficulty in dealing with women overall (Goldstein 2003). It was the problem of disciplining women, which Goldstein (2003) suspects that might have reinforced the need to keep the sexes separate and render women as noncombatants. Plus, as the Army's 1946 field manual stated "the necessity for discipline is never fully comprehended by the soldier until he has undergone the experience of battle" (Goldstein 2003, p. 89; Treadwell 1954, p. 676), an experience for which women were not sanctioned. Despite these challenges, the discipline and morale among the WACs remained quite high. Yet, women's response to the hierarchy was different, for in spite of the reputation as collaborative, according to WAC Director Culp Hobby, "women need to remain as individuals" (Goldstein 2003, p. 90; Treadwell 1954, p. 675). And, contrary to the military's *esprit de corps* culture, the women tended to function separately and as individuals (Goldstein 2003). Yet, unlike the male to male relationship, the WACs loathed the idea of separating commissioned from enlisted women, especially in light of the fact that some of the women officers had emanated from the enlisted corps. For the women, leadership was synonymous with being fair, unselfish, and caring for one's troops. Blind ambition was an unattractive trait in their eyes. The WACs were also known as better communicators than their male peers. For example, they were particularly adept at deciphering Morse codes for long periods of time. The Women's Air Service Pilots (WASPs) ferried planes and served as test pilots, the Navy's WAVES served in various capacities including air traffic control, naval air navigation, and communications. The Marine Corps reserve lost 18 women in WWII while in total, approximately 200 to 300 women died, although but a few were as a result of enemy fire.

Though judged by today's standards, mentioning the following challenge may seem simplistic, if not a waste of valuable space and time, but the experience spoke of an evolving military, perhaps at the time out of necessity yet was nevertheless prevalent enough that it could not be ignored. The uniforms designed for the WACs became an issue (Holm 1992). While WAC Director Culp Hobby was consulted in terms of its construction and procurement, the Army proceeded with the undertaking despite its lack of expertise in either the design or purchase of women's clothing. Again, though Director Culp Hobby was consulted, when convenient, her input was only in an advisory capacity. Even as the head of the WAC. She had no power of veto in such final decision making. Besides, the uniforms had a masculine appearance and the most ill-advised manufacturers of men's clothing secured the contracts. The result was that women's uniforms were designed, developed, procured, and manufactured, including the type of material selected, all by men for the purpose of military women's wear. And because of this debacle, the low quarter shoes, also designed for men's wear, and for which women were also to be attired, gave way to a frumpy and masculine appearance of women in uniform. This discomfort was coupled with the fact that the female recruits received incomplete sets of uniforms. But, this was only the Army's experience. Contrast this "bureaucratic nightmare" (p. 40), as Holm (1992) framed it, to that of the Navy for the WAVES uniforms. Mildred McAfee, or "Captain Mac" (Holm 1992, p. 37) as she was endearingly called, was described as a colorful character whose flair for articulation from the lowest to the highest ranks in the Navy, and known for her straight talking and no-nonsense approach, was indeed consulted in almost, if not every, phase of the process, but one. Thereafter at McAfee's insistence, the Navy would not allow the WAVES to wear gold stripes. This infuriated McAfee to say the least. Nonetheless, following WWII, the Navy unwillingly capitulated to this *fait accompli*.

At the height of WWII in 1943, women's participation rate grew in the military to 150,000, although short of the initial aspiration of recruiting 1.5 million women (Goldstein 2003; Holm 1992; Soderbergh 1992); approximately 90,000 in the WAVES; 25,000 in the Marine Corps and the Coast Guard's SPAR (Semper Paratus, Always Ready) (U.S. Coast Guard 2013); and 75,000 commissioned officers who were nurses (Goldstein 2003; Soderbergh 1992). But the recruitment rolls in the military, and particularly for the Army, fell woefully short of its goal of 1.5 million because the Army was rocked by a scandal that began in 1943, some referring to the period as a slander campaign, all for the purpose of dissuading women from joining the military (DePauw 1998; Goldstein 2003; Holm 1992). Though the rate of many of these myths and rumors about women in the military have declined with the passing of time and through the increase of and exposure to women in the military, overall, the more contemporary interviews in this book of former women in the military, despite the passage of time, for one reason or another, reveal that many of these same myths and rumors about military women still persist. This slander campaign during WWII was rumored to be the work of Nazi sympathizers (DePauw 1998; Goldstein 2003; Holm 1992; Monahan and Neidel-Greenlee 2010). No doubt though and especially for Director Culp Hobby who was dedicated to building a credible force of women in the Army and put to the test that women were just as skilled as their male counterparts, the scandal could not have been more untimely. And, the problem with a scandal of this magnitude at the time was that, given the fledgling force of military women, women and the military were perceived as related whereas even before the scandal, women in the military were already viewed with suspicion (Holm 1992).

DePauw (1998) partially attributes this attitude, even by men, of wearing the military uniform, with a sign of disrespect as unlike our European allies, wearing the military uniform was the attire that was to be adorned by aristocrats, the elite, or royalty. But this tradition of a call to arms has been different in the United States. So, by having large numbers of women in the military in uniform during WWII, it was not unexpected that people would have thought the worst about them. Outraged, Director Culp Hobby sought an immediate investigation, even prompting the Federal Bureau of Investigation (FBI) to get involved (DePauw 1998; Holm 1992; Monahan and Neidel-Greenlee 2010). The rumors were salacious in nature. They ranged from that military women were serving as prostitutes to becoming pregnant (DePauw 1998) and had low morals (Goldstein 2003; Monahan and Neidel-Greenlee 2010). This only served as fodder for dirty jokes and gossip that were circulated in the military and to the media (Holm 1992; Monahan and Neidel-Greenlee 2010) and broke out in the column of the *Capital Staff* headings as "Contraceptives and Prophylactic Equipment will be furnished to the WAAC according to a super-secret agreement reached by high ranking officers of the War Department and the WAAC Chieftain, Mrs. William Pettus Hobby. It was a victory for the New Deal Ladies … Mrs. Roosevelt wants all the young ladies to have the same overseas rights as their brothers and fathers" (Treadwell 1954, p. 203).

To compound matters, it was discovered that an organized group of prostitutes were sporting military women's uniforms making it difficult to distinguish a legitimate woman in the military from a prostitute in uniform (DePauw 1998). Even nurses who were customarily viewed as nurturing did not go unscathed by the scandal as they, the nurses, according to a so-called scholarly study by Hershfeld, carried bed pans around as one way of connecting sexually with the male soldiers (DePauw 1998). Even First Lady Eleanor Roosevelt became involved by denouncing the scandal as the work of Nazi propaganda (DePauw 1998; Holm 1992). No doubt, as a result, and despite laudable attempts, female recruitment into the military declined precipitously (Goldstein 2003; Holm 1992; Monahan and Neidel-Greenlee 2010). And to Marines Corps Lieutenant General Thomas Holcomb's credit, who like First Lady Roosevelt, was moved enough to direct his commanding officers by reminding them of their responsibility for the conduct of their male marines toward female marines (Holm 1992). Yet, interestingly, for those women who were already in the military, given the high moral standing that in many ways was required for female recruits, on average, women in the military were more educated, possessed a higher level of intellect, were older, and their selection process in terms of personal character and backgrounds were more stringent than required for male recruits (Holm 1992). In effect, it was the quality of the female recruits that made the military's enlistment recruitment successful and in turn successful for the services overall. According to Goldstein (2003), while demobilization following WWII resulted in a decline in military women, the growing pains reaped valuable lessons learned that continue to remain as a yardstick of performance for integrating women into the American military.

The Korean conflict remains an anomaly to this day in the sense that it is a war that was not declared, nor has it been formally concluded (DePauw 1998). Yet, because of the military's challenge in recruiting its goal of employing a force strength equal to 2% of women in the military, the Korean conflict, albeit unexpectedly, was fortuitous in providing a narrow window of opportunity to set the stage for the increase of women in the military. Faced with this now-growing recruitment charge given the conflict afoot, and with some prodding by Senator Margaret Chase Smith and upon recommendation of the then Assistant Secretary of Defense for Manpower, Anna Rosenberg, Secretary of Defense General George Marshall, who commissioned DACOWITS, was now called to advise the Secretary on how to achieve this goal (DePauw 1998; Holm 1992). The Committee was comprised of prominent women in society, some of whom were former directors of the various women corps of the military, academicians, business women, and women from other disciplines, all influential in their own right. It was charged with promoting the need to recruit women to the public, allay parents' fears about their daughters' welfare in the military, educate women about career opportunities in the military, and improve the stature of women in the military, especially in the eyes of the American public (DePauw 1998; Holm 1992). The goal was to recruit 72,000 women within one year into line positions over the traditional non-line positions such as health (DePauw 1998). However, not only did the plan fail abysmally, the Army experienced a net loss of women, although both the Navy and the Marine Corps experienced moderate gains. This so worried the Secretary of Defense that he immediately drafted a proposal for selective service for women as per the legislation that imposed a peacetime draft of men only (DePauw 1998; Holm 1992).

But as asserted by Holm (1992), the recruiting plan failed for a number of reasons. First, Americans had become war weary and were anxious for their troops to return home. While WWII had ignited the fervor of patriotism, this was not the case for the Korean conflict. Moreover, the military had not heeded the lessons learned from WWII. There was the assumption that because 300,000 women were galvanized for the war effort, recruitment for one-third the size of the required force of women would be easily attained for the Korean conflict. Second, a call to arms for women in the military revived the public's attitudes about the moral turpitude of women who joined the military, not to mention those who were suspected of exhibiting masculine characteristics. Third, unlike WWII that accompanied specific objectives, those established for the country's entry into the Korean conflict were questionable at best, and raised concerns. The military's low salaries, coupled with its low standard of living, were unattractive and did nothing to quell concerns about pursuing a viable career. To exacerbate the situation, both the military and civilian employers were recruiting from the same pool of candidates that was only worsened by a shrinking labor pool of qualified workers along with a decline in the birthrate of available women because of the Great Depression. Finally, enlistment criteria for women in the military were far more stringent than those for men. However, not only was no action taken on the Secretary of Defense's proposal to impose the conscription of women into the military, but the Korean conflict ended almost as immediately as it began (DePauw 1998; Holm 1992). And, the afflictions of recruiting women into the military only worsened.

Although women, unlike men, were not subjected to a peacetime draft, their numbers in the military remained small relative to the targeted goal of 2% of the military's workforce (DePauw 1998; Holm 1992). Further, more rumors only circulated to reinforce the anemic recruitment levels of women such as in 1959 when it was believed that Congress was planning to enact legislation to eliminate women altogether from even serving in the military during peacetime (Holm 1992). Then in 1963, the Department of Defense (DoD) was dealt a blow, this time supported by data from the then U.S. General Accounting Office (now U.S. General Accountability Office; GAO), that the attrition rate for enlisted women was as high as 70%–80% and this was before the conclusion of their first term of enlistment. This in turn resulted in the replacement rate of 50% of women lost or about in excess of twice the replacement rate for men enlistees, although it was found that male draftees had still higher rates of attrition. Yet, to Holm (1992), the hypocrisy lied in the fact that those at the helm, or males who were the most alarmed about these losses, were also the least fitting to change the policies that brought about such losses. And, accordingly, the incomplete data analysis by the GAO only rendered the situation far much worse than it actually was. The agency concluded that premature discharges of women for such conditions as pregnancy, marriage, and what the military dubbed "unsuitability" (Holm 1992, p. 163) was costing DoD about $12 million annually. The GAO recommended that the Department decrease the attrition or replace such positions via the Federal Civil Service which Holm (1992) said would have resulted in a shortsighted and unsustainably costly move. For as Holm argued, in light of the exceedingly higher dependent rates of enlisted men than their female counterparts, which did not even factor into the overall cost of funding civil servant replacements in terms of salaries, medical benefits, and the like, would have proven to be cost prohibitive for the military. In the end, the military came to the defense of its women's programs. And, while it acknowledged the need to reduce premature attrition among women, the military was committed to the retention of such programs.

The buildup to yet another undeclared war, this time the Vietnam conflict, also produced no discernible dent in recruiting women into the military. In fact, every one of the military's women's programs experienced a decline in its force, even as the military turned to men to fill requirements for what Holm (1992) referred to as "the quicksand in Southeast Asia" (p. 178). By this time, there were no more than 30,000 women in line positions in the armed forces combined. The military looked increasingly to men instead of women to serve its needs through selective service. But of the military women who served during this era, most did so in the traditional role as nurses (DePauw 1998). But many nurses witnessed more death than many of the soldiers did as combatants (Smith 1992; Van Devanter and Morgan 1983; Walker 1985; Walsh 1982). As a result, nine nurses in the Army died in Vietnam. Few women served in line positions but found the experience to be equally debilitating (DePauw 1998). They lacked the equipment, training, and clothing to be effective in the field. More disturbing, and especially during a major conflict, was the military's campaign to downplay in its recruitment of women the possibility of exposure to combat. This was also a time that a similar effort was underway to expand the women's movement even though for some reason women in the military were never factored into this equation by feminists in the civilian sector (Holm 1992). Holm took issue with this perhaps unintentional slight by feminists who were so concerned with the fight for equal pay and the like that they barely took notice of a similar fight for their sisters in arms. Even more regrettable was the fact that the women service directors did not question and more pointedly were not troubled by these insensitivities. They rationalized that women should not compromise themselves with men as "it behooves every woman to remember she is not going to be asked to put her life at stake as the men are" (Chandler 1967). Holm (1992) saw this unofficial dictum, which was in many ways being reinforced by the military women in leadership positions, as tantamount to upholding a double standard at best, and given this reason, the women's programs functioned as akin to auxiliary programs than as women in the military. In addition, women in the military following WWII and the Korean conflict, despite the enlightenment of the civil rights movement in concert with the women's movement, suffered a retrenchment in progress. Where women were once selected for such functions as driving trucks and repairing engines, to name a few, these occupations were now deemed to be unsuitable and unladylike. Many previously opened occupations were being closed to women. The Pentagon, it appeared, began preparing finishing schools for women and what little gains had been made for women in the military had eroded and became what Holm (1992) amounted to a "token force" (p. 185).

Yet change was stirring, not because of the women's movement per se but because of a confluence of events that collided to create an unanticipated opportunity for military women. The Vietnam conflict was now spiraling out of control and the resultant casualties that it produced, and so much so, that despite the draft which was due to expire in mid-1967, men no longer aspired to military service while many others avoided this compulsory obligation by seeking safe haven in other countries (DePauw 1998; Holm 1992). Even so, involvement in Vietnam was becoming unpopular with the American public and the forces of feminism, along with a civilian labor force that was increasingly expanding women's roles as a result, appeared to conspire against the military to bring about change within the institution (Holm 1992). President Lyndon Johnson, upon the recommendation of the National Advisory Commission on Selective Service, invoked national security as the pretext to continue the draft of another 100,000 men for the war effort and in doing so mandated the recruitment of an additional 6,500 women, the first such increase of women post the Korean conflict. Holm (1992) cynically referred to similar reticence to employ the services of women in the military as preferring "dogs, ducks or monkeys" (p. 187) instead of women, if it was possible. But between 1965 and 1967, the troop requirement mounted to half million and so did the casualties. A one year rotation to Vietnam was established. However, women, except nurses, and especially those in line occupations, were excluded from deployment to the region. But, inexplicably, while women in line positions were excluded from this assignment or that would bring them into a situation where they would either witness and/or experience combat, military nurses, women who worked in the Red Cross, and even female journalists and other civilian women, were allowed and accommodated in the region. Even more ludicrous was that many of the jobs that were traditionally held by women such as typists and secretarial support were now being held in the theater of operations, meaning in war, by men.

A comment by one female WAC lieutenant summed up the misguided and shortsighted policy:

> What kind of delicate creatures do the brass think we are? There's a war going on in Vietnam but you have to be a civilian to get assigned there. Women are fighting in the jungles with the Viet Cong. Yet, we aren't allowed to dirty our dainty hands. (Haas 1991, pp. 16 and 17)

And, despite the one-year rotation policy, male enlistees were incentivized into completing multiple tours through the lure of generous bonuses in the form of hostile fire pay (Holm 1992). But, military women, again those in the line occupations, were further marginalized because completing a tour in Vietnam became the pretext on one's record for future critical assignments (follow on assignments) and/or accelerated promotions. But, as the war accelerated, excluding commissioned and enlisted women from the theater of operations grew increasingly unrealistic, not only given the shortage of men with certain requisite skills but because of the commensurate increase in paperwork associated with the war's activity. Then Colonel Jeanne Holm, Women in the Air Force (WAF) director, shot a letter to the Personnel Center in 1967 stating the following:

> WAF airmen continually ask me why they are not allowed to "pull their share of the burden" in Southeast Asia when men who have families must go involuntarily, and some may now be threatened with second tours. These women know that nurses, civil service employees, WACs, and Red Cross women are serving in Southeast Asia and they can find no logical reason why enlisted women in the Air Force should be considered unacceptable by their own service. While lack of adequate housing may have been a good excuse initially, it becomes less and less acceptable as time goes on. (Holm 1992, p. 222)

She faced the real prospect that in the midst of a war, Air Force women and specifically enlisted women were being denied deployment to the Southeast Asia (SEA) theater because of hollow reasons provided such as lack of accommodations when other women, including nurses and civil service employees, were already in Vietnam. More troubling though was the fact that men with families were being sent involuntarily to the theater while skilled and able-bodied Air Force women were being forced to standby stateside, if at all, even though they were eager and willing to serve.

By far, most of the uniformed women who served in Vietnam were nurses, especially from the Army (DePauw 1998; Holm 1992). Yet, no amount of experience or training could have prepared them for the unprecedented death toll and injuries that they encountered. In 1967, Army Chief Surgeon Major General Byron Ludwig Stegner extolled the virtues of the valiant and collective work of the nurses: "The injuries they handled are unprecedented, ... because this war is fought largely with small arms—booby traps, punji sticks, clay more mines, high velocity bullets. Nearly all inflict multiple wounds of the most vicious mutilating kind" (Drake 1967, p. 75). Nurses were different from those on the line in the sense that they knew that given their expertise, they would witness war for which their training prepared them (Holm 1992). And, like male soldiers, they were as adept at selecting camp sites, pitching tents, and reading maps and compasses. Similarly, they were as proficient in the fundamentals of disaster preparedness, using field equipment and sanitation. But it was the Tet Offensive, like no other event, that not only proved the competence of military women and their ability to perform under fire but in its aftermath, it also proved as overwhelming for the American psyche in that the war, at least for the Americans, could not be won militarily. No one was immune from the attack that the Viet Cong launched which caught the American military by surprise. In other words, the Tet Offensive so changed the character of the war that it exposed all of the American military to combat that finally forced President Johnson to concede, although not altogether, in exchange for a ceasefire. And, though the fighting continued, the event was pivotal in helping to wind down the Vietnam conflict. In all, 7,000 military women had served with a record of 58,000 American military casualties, and with even more civilian women getting to the front lines of combat than military women were allowed (Solaro 2006).

The end of the Vietnam conflict marked a record integration of women into the military along with the advent of the all-volunteer military in 1973 (Goldstein 2003). For one reason, the men were no longer present to fill the void in recruiting levels (Solaro 2006), especially in a post-Vietnam environment. Once again, this call to action, though during peacetime, mimicked the trajectory of past wars, although unlike during peacetime, this turn to women became a necessity in a now-all-volunteer military. Previous levels that were unattainable in recruiting women into the military at 2% were surpassed during the 1972 through 1980 period from 8% to 14% of the military force in 1999 (Goldstein 2003) prior to 2001, or Operation Enduring Freedom, and 2003, Operation Iraqi Freedom. Current force levels of women as a percentage of the total military force lies at 14.8% (Population Representation in the Military Services 2012), although this figure varies among different sources. These data exclude the U.S. Coast Guard (now part of the U.S. Department of Homeland Security) whose personnel are only activated under the auspices of the U.S. Navy in a national emergency, crises, or war.

Subsequent major and minor military campaigns show women's increased participation in the military, more importantly beyond the role of health professionals especially nurses and increasingly in line positions that blurred the distinction of what and what did not constitute combat and the military's rhetoric that women by law are not to be engaged in direct ground combat. A brief skirmish during the Reagan administration under the guise of rescuing U.S. students who were attending medical school on the island of Grenada ensued in 1983 (Wright 1984). According to Zunes (2003), nothing could have been further from the truth. On the dawn of what Zunes refers to as the "Vietnam syndrome," or that which makes the American public question the reasons for becoming involved in another sovereign country without just cause, it was rumored that the administration used the students as a pretext for the invasion (Zunes 2003) dubbed Operation Urgent Fury (Holm 1992; Zunes 2003). One hundred and seventy female soldiers were deployed and served in a number of capacities from platoon leaders of the military police (MP), to helicopter pilots, crew chiefs, maintenance, intelligence specialists, and for transportation to detonate unexploded ordinances (Wright 1984). And, although not well publicized, both Air Force and Army women came under fire (DePauw 1998). Captain Linda Bray's command of troops in returning fire upon being fired upon during Operation Just Cause in 1989 welcomed both praise and condemnation (DePauw 1998; Goldstein 2003; Holm 1992; Monahan and Neidel-Greenlee 2010). However, the campaign also reignited an issue that the military would safely sidestep for another two decades until doing so was no longer feasible.

In reality, during the fall of the same year, and following Bray and her troops' triumph over the Panamanian Defense Force (PDF), DACOWITS seized the opportunity to use the case about Linda Bray's leadership in battle to introduce and elevate the argument that more occupations, including combat, should be opened to women (Monahan and Neidel-Greenlee 2010) at least for a pilot period of four years. Congresswoman Patricia Schroeder (D-CO) also grabbed onto the opportunity to use the DACOWITS recommendation together with a *Newsweek* poll that revealed 79% of Americans supported women's role in combat to introduce legislation in an attempt to repeal the combat exclusion policy (Francke 1997). This was Congresswoman Schroeder's second but failed attempt at such legislation. The Army wanted no part of it and instead of showering its own Captain Bray with accolades, it vilified her to the point of discredit that resulted in Bray's disillusionment and premature separation from the Army (DePauw 1998; Francke 1997; Harris 2009; Titunik 2000). The question of a woman's place (Harris 2009) would again resurface for debate during Operation Desert Storm. When Saddam Hussein assembled his forces and subsequently crossed into Kuwait, the action not only troubled the American government but such provocation signaled instability in the region and emboldened Hussein's army to become the largest and most powerful as well to pose a threat to one of America's allies, Saudi Arabia (Holm 1992). By then the composition of the American military was 11% and 13% female in the active and reserve components, respectively (Holm 1992). But more important than the question of amassing American forces in a desert 7000 miles from the United States was the reemergence of the question of the roles that women in the military would play in the campaign.

As Holm (1992) correctly identified, there was little recognition, if any, that the issue had been repeatedly revisited even though women in the military had always performed brilliantly in previous military campaigns. So, it would appear that the discussion, as was demonstrated in the past, was in essence, and once again, moot. But, for one reason or another, women were once again perceived as the "Achilles heel" (Holm 1992, p. 439) to military readiness, a ploy for large-scale exclusion or imposed segregation. Yet, when all was said and done, over 40,000 women were deployed to Saudi Arabia and distinguished themselves during Operation Desert Storm (Francke 1997; Holm 1992; Monahan and Neidel-Greenlee 2010). Of the 375 U.S. casualties, 13 were women (Enloe 1993; Francke 1997). While a far cry from the 90 women who were taken as POWs during WWII, two were taken as POWs during Operation Desert Storm (Holm 1992). But yet again, what the mobilization of women for a major campaign taught the military was that military women proved to be a reliable contingent, not to be taken for granted, time after time (Holm 1992). Women's involvement in every phase of the war had no limits as their capabilities in every aspect of the operations abound. Senator John Warner (R-VA) was taken aback by the level of military women's involvement in the war (Holm 1992). The extent of this involvement was such that it first exposed the American public to women's roles in the military but more importantly to the inconsistencies regarding combat and where women could and could not be assigned.

In Operation Allied Force, women constituted 10% of all the U.S. forces in Bosnia. Goldstein (2003) described the largely peacekeeping mission, especially the relationship between military men and military women as "easygoing and untroubled" (p. 99).

However, given the protective gear issued to all troops, women and men were rendered indistinguishable. Take one infantry officer who after one week came to realize, to his surprise, that the military police (MP) who were assigned to his protection detail comprised all women. As a matter of practice and in the same vein, one of the direct contradictions in light of the combat exclusion policy, the Army routinely assigned women to the front lines during peacekeeping missions and more so than the assignment of men in the infantry and armored units to the same posts (Moskos 1998; Priest 1997a, 1997b, 1997c). Accordingly, when practical, the Army found ways of making things work by deliberately assigning women to off limit posts. Yet, despite the relatively good relations between female and male troops, the female troops found it necessary to assume a male-like posture through their overt display of behaviors such as smoking cigars, using profane language, and engaging in other thrill-seeking behaviors like firing their guns. One woman colonel, who commanded an MP battalion, defended these actions by stating that it is important for a female soldier to adopt a warrior spirit: "If a woman thinks like a warrior, believes she is a warrior, then she'll do what it takes. Most women don't think they have it in them, but once you let that spirit loose you find that aggressiveness" (Priest 1997a).

If all previous military campaigns have collectively failed in proving women's worth in war or at least convince the skeptics that without women no war can be won, then surely their stellar performance during Operations Enduring Freedom and Iraqi Freedom must have, for the initial phase of troop withdrawal from Iraq and a similar withdrawal from Afghanistan have been a tipping point. But, as stated at the outset of this book's introduction, although I speculate that it was a confluence of factors that collectively served as a catalyst for the repeal of the combat exclusion policy, perhaps it was these later wars, particularly Operation Iraqi Freedom, that blurred the lines of demarcation more than ever of the conditions on the ground and in the theater of operations of what defines direct ground combat. As a consequence, even if assigned, providing that you keep within the heavily fortified green zone, in this case in Iraq, did not necessarily render those within its confines any less vulnerable than those who were actively exposed in the field. As you will see, even those women whose occupations as medics signaled them as noncombatants, like nurses, the nature of their occupation and training inevitably placed them into direct combat. Therefore, calling into question what distinguishes the front line from those in the rear of combat. While the number of women in the military who have participated in both wars in terms of hard numbers has not yet been ascertained, what is known is that women constituted 11.4% of the force that participated in Operations Enduring Freedom and Iraqi Freedom (SWAN 2011b). And, in accordance with a study conducted by the Pew Research Center, and based on the population report for the military services in FY 2010, 15% of women and 35% of men, respectively, self-identified as having served in combat, despite the existing combat exclusion policy on women in the military (Patten and Parker 2011). These findings, according to the report, contrast with those of the pre-1990s where women were found to have been exposed to combat at a rate of

7% compared to the post-1990s findings of 24% of female veterans' exposure to combat. Considering the military population report for FY 2010, these data are in keeping with the overall commensurate and significant increases of women in both the enlisted and commissioned corps.

Monahan and Neidel-Greenlee (2010) see America's most recent wars, that is, Operations Enduring Freedom and Iraqi Freedom, as like no other as unprecedented in both military and American ourstory. While the missteps during the early years of especially Operation Iraqi Freedom signaled overly ambitious predictions on the part of the civilian administration coupled with its failure to heed the counsel of its military leadership (Sanchez and Phillips 2008), the wars served, if not for anything else, to finally put to rest the question of women's capability in the military, and more directly, woman's capability and role in combat. As have always been the case in previous wars or major campaigns, women served in positions as noncombatants in combat even in non-line support positions as nurses, medics, and the like. Operations Enduring Freedom and Iraqi Freedom were no exception, but like the Vietnam conflict, the latter, especially in Iraq, was tantamount to guerilla warfare. Also, perhaps unlike the Vietnam conflict, women were caught in the crossfire, for as Solaro (2006) and others (i.e., Corum 1996; Holm 1992; Monahan and Neidel-Greenlee 2010) have pointed out, the enemy makes no distinction in gender during times of war.

As of early 2013, of the 4475 total number of U.S. military casualties sustained during Operations Iraqi Freedom and New Dawn (post-Operation Iraqi Freedom), 110 were women (Fischer 2013). Likewise, of the total 2122 U.S. military casualties during Operation Enduring Freedom, 42 were women. Combined, and while low compared to the overall death rate for military men, as a reflection of their total participation, 152 women have paid the ultimate sacrifice (Fischer 2013), with 3 being taken as POWs (WIMSA 2011, for Operation Iraqi Freedom only). The schematic representations of women's participation in the American military are given in the following. Table A1.1 (see Appendix 1 in Chapter 1) shows the increasing participation rates of women in military campaigns since the Civil War along with the number of women declared as POWs. Table A1.2 is a breakdown by military branch of women's composition as a percentage of the total military force. Table A1.3 represents the numbers of women who have paid the ultimate sacrifice, including those wounded in action, during each major military campaign beginning with the Civil War through present. Table A1.4 displays the occupations in which women in the active duty component of the enlisted corps are distributed. Table A1.5 reflects similar data for enlisted women within the reserve components of the military (Reserve and National Guard). Table A1.6 has similar data for women within the commissioned corps on active duty while Table A1.7 shows the same data where women officers are distributed within the various occupations according to military branch and component. Note, however, that these data reflect information for FY 2011, or prior to the repeal of the combat exclusion policy. While there might have been minor movement afoot in terms of moving women into positions and assignments designated as combat and combat related, the data here might not have changed, if any, since they were collected for the FY 2011 report.

The dearth of recorded information about women's participation in the military reflects the very important yet often unrecognized roles throughout the American experience during war that women have actively played. And, where women in one way or another have assisted men on and off the battlefield, as reported, for the most part, these have been primarily in support roles. As is evident, the writings are scant about women's involvement during the war of 1812, for instance, as is information from subsequent and major campaigns such as the Mexican-American War of 1846 (Bellafaire 2010). What we do know, however, has been garnered from information of those women who wrote letters to their loved ones at home and about their escapades in either accompanying their significant others, as nurses, or many who participated by cross dressing or serving as spies. What we also do know, for example, is that it was the experience of the Spanish-American War of 1898 that resulted in the Army's and Navy's establishment of a permanent corps but which did not occur until 1901 and 1907, respectively. Records do show, however, that at least 1500 women participated in this major conflict (Bellafaire n.d.).

World War I

Navy Secretary Josephus Daniels employed a little known legal loophole to begin recruiting women into the Navy and Marine Corps Reserve (Bellafaire 2010; WIMSA n.d.). Known as yoemanettes, the women commanded the same compensation, including benefits as the enlisted men, and served in such jobs as clerical support, draftspersons, translators, and other positions as required. The intent behind recruiting women was to release the men for more dangerous assignments overseas. Women, however, did serve overseas as telephone operators, although ironically unlike their yoemanette and Marine peers, they were denied both the status and benefits as veterans until 1978. But, as will be repeatedly shown throughout the journey in this book, women's uneven and as some regard begrudging yet tokenized call for participation in the military, Congress subsequently amended the Naval Reserve Act at the end of WWI to further deny women's participation in the military, making such participation eligible to only male members of the citizenry (Holm 1992).

World War II

Accordingly, WWII is considered to be the most documented war (Bellafaire 2010). Further, its 50th anniversary resulted in a wealth of memoirs and other documents, especially surrounding the experiences of nurses. Although a record number of women, including civilian women, at 400,000 (Bellafaire n.d.), were galvanized for the war effort, 150,000 women were recruited for the military (Bellafaire 2010). A total of 90 women were taken as POWs (Bellafaire n.d.).

The Korean Conflict

Known as the "Forgotten War" (Bellafaire 2010, p. 2), approximately 50,000 women were recruited into the military, with 1,000 women deployed to the theater of operations (Bellafaire n.d.). This marked the period when the Women Armed Services Integration Act was enacted in 1948 along with the establishment of the DACOWITS in 1951 by Executive Order 10240 (Bellafaire 2010).

The Vietnam Conflict

Approximately 11,000 women served in Vietnam during the conflict, 90% of whom were nurses (Vietnam Women's Memorial Foundation n.d.). But, while nurses in Vietnam were heralded by the American public, little has been documented about the many servicewomen who served in Europe and at military installations around the United States (Bellafaire 2010). Yet, this period marked one of consciousness: while military women were largely ignored, the women's movement took center stage in the United States. At this time, then law professor Ruth Bader Ginsburg of Columbia University, successfully argued in front of the U.S. Supreme Court that a military woman's right to have her male-dependent husband secure the same benefits as a military man for his dependent wife was constitutional (Bellafaire 2010). Therefore, the denial of such benefits in the military was illegal. It is also of interest that the sole litigant, who was in the Air Force at the time, is one of the 17 women being featured in this book. Also in this book is the main litigant who later successfully challenged the Navy for disallowing women aboard ships.

Operations Urgent Fury and Just Cause

One hundred and seventy women were deployed for Operation Urgent Fury in Grenada in 1983, while 770 women were deployed during Operation Just Cause in Panama in 1989 (Bellafaire n.d.). It was during the second campaign when Linda Bray, then a Captain in the Army, was hailed as the first woman to lead troops into battle (Holm 1992; Mazur 1998; Monahan and Neidel-Greenlee 2010), yet was vilified for having done so (Harris 2009; Titunik 2000). According to Holm (1992), this was perhaps the first snapshot that the American public had received that women in the military's roles were much more involved than was ever acknowledged by the military. In fact, Holm

(1992) quoted Charles Moskos who said at the time that women's involvement in combat operations in Panama resulted in "a shot heard around the world, or at least in the Pentagon" (p. 435).

Operations Desert Shield/Storm

The operations in the Persian Gulf, known as Operations Desert Shield/Storm, witnessed the largest number of women or over 41,000 deployed for any military operation since WWII (Holm 1992). Women's collective performance was unparalleled, although the conclusion of the war effort for women came to be reputed more for the challenges of deploying mothers and adjustment challenges for children of dual military families than it was for women's performance. The war was instead dubbed by the press as "Mommy War" (Holm 1992, p. 441). Two women were taken as POWs (Bellafaire n.d.).

Operation Enduring Freedom

While we do know that military women, like military men, were deployed to Afghanistan during Operation Enduring Freedom, there are no statistics to provide the specific number of American military women who participated. Yet, according to a summary, as per Burrelli (2012), DoD reported that as of February 2012, more than 20,000 female soldiers have served in Operations Enduring Freedom and Iraqi Freedom. What we also do know is that in 2009, the Marine Corps began training female engagement teams (FETs) to assume the task of "calming, interacting and building relationships with Afghan women," and their jobs also entailed engaging in hostile fire given their frequent assignments in "hot zones" (SWAN 2011a). Additionally, the Marine Corps assigned 40 of such teams to Helmand Province in early 2010. However, to circumvent the requirement of the combat exclusion policy, that is, to keep women out of ground combat situations thus preventing them from serving in positions against the law as combatants, women were attached to combat units, not assigned. According to SWAN (2011a), this was "a bureaucratic sidestep" to allow the military access "to servicewomen's labor in combat situations without having to acknowledge them as combatants" (p. 4).

Operation Iraqi Freedom

Of the over 1.6 million troops who served during Operations Enduring Freedom and Iraqi Freedom (U.S. Army OneSource n.d.), it is estimated that over 11% of them were women (Iraq and Afghanistan Veterans of America [IAVA] n.d.), although estimates vary to data as high as that one out of every seven military personnel deployed in these wars were women (Curphey 2003). It was during Operation Iraqi Freedom in 2003 that the Army began employing all-female teams, together known as Lioness, to accompany Marine Corps combat units into Ramadi, Iraq (SWAN n.d.). By utilizing female soldiers in these teams, the primary purpose was to mitigate the cultural challenges associated with conducting raids, checkpoints, or of places where Iraqi women felt threatened by the presence of male soldiers. Team Lioness were primarily utilized for the search of explosives and weapons by the Iraqi insurgency. Their presence also functioned as a "calming effect" (SWAN p. 3) for the women and children. Moreover, like their male counterparts, the all-female teams of soldiers were themselves combatants who confronted and operated within the same hostile and insurgency infested environment. And, without the use of these all-female teams, the mission could not have been accomplished. Three women were taken as POWs during Operation Iraqi Freedom (Bellafaire n.d.).

Operation New Dawn

Effective September 1, 2010, U.S. military operations in Iraq transitioned to that of a reduced and more support role under the banner of Operation New Dawn to advise and assist. However, data as to the number of troops that remain, including those who are women, have not been ascertained and are scant but what has been gleaned is that of the 295 recorded who have been wounded in action to date, 12 are women (Defense Manpower Data Center [DMDC] 2013).

Chapter 4

Marginalized, Yet Accountable: The Irrationality of the Combat Exclusion Policy

As modern leaders and heads of states, like men, women have consistently demonstrated their political prowess during wartime. Women like Indira Gandhi, Golda Meir, and Margaret Thatcher ably led their countries through wars (Goldstein 2003). Others like Benazir Bhutto and Corazon Aquino visibly grappled with restraining their respective militaries. Aquino outlived seven assassination attempts and during the 1990s, TanSu Ciller of Turkey led a callous war to crush Kurdish rebels while President Chandrika Bandaranaike Kumaratunga of Sri Lanka waged war against the Tamil separatists following her failed peace initiatives. Nicaragua's Violeta Chamorro achieved peace despite the warring factions tangled in a ruthless civil war. Female heads of states in such countries as Norway and Iceland have come to power during times of war and peace (Carras 1995; Fraser 1989; Harris 1995; Richardson and Howes 1993). And, it was during these times that these heads of states shrewdly employed both feminine and masculine styles of leadership (Goldstein 2003). For example, Corazon Aquino of the Philippines was known for her diplomatic acumen that she skillfully used during a 1986 visit to the United States. Yet, such skills, where she capitalized on her femininity, proved to be liabilities following each coup attempt in her own country where she was forced to resort to military rhetoric to cede control of the military and government that were masculine in both tone and content. Nevertheless, when addressing the population, Aquino shifted to more feminine phrases of Tagalog (Boudreau 1995). According to Goldstein (2003), women political leaders like their male counterparts were equally adept at leading their countries during times of war and peace by calling upon skill sets as the situations dictated. Women, like men, are no more peaceful, no less prone to exercising violence or nonviolent means to resolve conflicts, and/or no less staunch about maintaining sovereignty or the principle of territorial integrity. Thus to understand the combat exclusion policy is to understand that when the legislation was enacted to accept women into the military, it was inherently written to legally subordinate them to the command of the will of men. The Women's Integration Act of 1948 was framed as follows:

1. Women can constitute no more than 2 percent of the total force.
2. The number of women officers can total no more than 10 percent of the 2 percent.
3. Promotion of women officers is capped above pay grade 0–3 (Captain/Lieutenant). Pay grade 0–5 (Lieutenant Colonel/Commander) is the highest permanent rank women can obtain. Women serving as directors of WACs, WAVES, WAFs, and Women Marines are temporarily promoted to pay grade 0–6 (Colonel/Captain).
4. Women are barred from serving aboard navy vessels (except hospital ships and certain transports) and from duty in combat aircraft engaged in combat missions.
5. Women are denied spousal benefits for their husbands unless they depend on their wives for over 50 percent of their support.
6. By policy, women are precluded from having command authority over men.
7. The coast guard is not included in this legislation, but a few SPARS remain in the Women's Coast Guard Reserve (Women's Research and Education Institute [WREI] 2005, pp. 4 and 5).

And, accordingly, women's talents only become a necessity when there is an impending threat to national security or in a national emergency (Monahan and Neidel-Greenlee 2010). Regrettably though, neither women's acceptance into the military nor their painstaking gains in the institution, despite their remarkable performance each time, ever came from the realization of either the military leadership or Congress that this was just the fair and right thing to do in light of the outright and codified discrimination against them (Monahan and Neidel-Green 2010). But, the irrationality and misguided justification behind the combat exclusion policy can be best explained through this awkward but illuminating exchange between former Senator William Cohen (R-ME) and former Air Force Chief of Staff, General Merrill McPeak, following the conclusion of Operation Desert Storm.

Cohen: Suppose you had a woman pilot ... of superior intelligence, great physical conditioning in every way she was superior to a male counterpart vying for a combat position. Would ... [you personally] because you would not want to see the risk to her life increased ... pick the male over the female under these circumstances?

McPeak: That is correct.

Cohen: So in other words you would have a militarily less effective situation because of a personal view.

McPeak: Well, I admit it doesn't make much sense, but that's the way I feel about it. (In Goldstein 2003, p. 101; Holm 1992, p. 484; from Testimony June 18, 1991)

Yet, in the same vein, General McPeak admitted that the policy was openly discriminatory to military women and candidly acknowledged that when it comes to G forces (gravitational forces), women pilots have demonstrated that they are clearly superior to men (Goldstein 2003; Holm 1992). He cowardly sought refuge though to rationalize his position by stating that while it was not his desire to expose women to such risks, the Air Force would not prevent qualified women from flying fighter aircraft (Goldstein 2003; Holm 1992).

Former Marine Corps Commandant General Robert Barrow presented an emotional exaggeration that

> exposure to danger is not combat. Being shot at, even being killed, is not combat. Combat is finding ... closing with ... and killing or capturing the enemy. It's KILLING. And it's done in an environment that is often as difficult as you can possibly imagine. Extremes of climate. Brutality. Death. Dying. It's ... uncivilized! And, WOMEN CAN'T DO IT! Nor should they even be thought of as doing it. The requirements of strength and endurance render [them] UNFIT to do it. And I may be old-fashioned, but I think the very nature of women disqualifies them from doing it. Women give life. Sustain life. Nurture life. They don't take it. (Holm 1992, p. 483)

In fact, he added that to have women in combat units would "destroy the Marines Corps ... something no enemy has been able to do in 200 years" (Holm 1992, p. 483). The Chief of Naval Operations (CNO) was less dramatic, but like General McPeak, cowered into offering his sympathy to women who are exceptional aviators yet are disqualified from combat because of the long-standing policy. And, while tripping himself, the CNO gave cause for doubt as to women's aspirations for such roles when he added that even women themselves have unanimity on the issue. According to Holm (1992), the fallacy of these arguments, at least, for the Air Force, is that since the 1980s, women have been assigned to geographically remote locations around the country to intercept; that is, to strike down enemy targets using intercontinental ballistic missiles

(ICBMs) with nuclear warheads (Holm 1992; Mazur 1998). And, during the Gulf War, the Army assigned women to both target and launch Patriot missiles by distinguishing what constitutes defensive versus offensive combat (Holm 1992). But the McPeak testimony so incensed Air Force women that they felt betrayed particularly since he inserted his personal feelings to influence his judgment about the combat exclusion policy. The Army and the Marine Corps have been the most resistant of the services to women in combat (Goldstein 2003). And, the Army's interpretation of the policy in the form of an assignment system dubbed Direct Combat Probability Coding (DCPC) based on the probability of being engaged in situations of low to high combat to determine the types of assignments for women drew a terse response from Brigadier General Evelyn "Pat" Foote to the then Army Chief of Staff General Carl Vuono as follows as to the irrationality of the Army's DCPC system:

> I know of no more dysfunctional military policy in effect today than the much-despised and unquestionably inoperable [DCPC] system which places gender-based restrictions on the assignments of highly trained Army women ... [N]o amount of factual, authenticated data from the field attesting to its unworkability has dented the iron wall of resistance dictating its perpetuation by those who lead the Army. (Holm 1992, p. 406)

For this reason, the Army continued to utilize the system fearing that its discontinuation would invite more questions than allay them even though this practice was designed to limit the number of women in combat (Holm 1992). But in 1994, the Army was forced to open 20,000 positions that were previously closed to women, a decision that legally moved women ever closer to the front lines of combat (Goldstein 2003).

To Holm (1992), the premise for the combat exclusion policy was so absurd that she likened it to *Through the Looking Glass*' Humpty Dumpty who was reprimanded by Alice for speaking in circles by invoking the same words to denote different definitions. Specifically, Holm was referring to the inconsistency in the application of the policy by each of the military services. The crux of the matter was that what constituted combat differed with each branch of the military. In turn, this divergence within and among the military services created the illusion, at least from the public's perception and as interpreted by agents of the media, that women were barred from all situations defined as combat. It was not until 1989, during Operation Urgent Fury in Panama when Captain Linda Bray was branded as the first female to lead troops into combat, that the truth about women's roles in combat came to light (DePauw 1998; Francke 1997; Holm 1992; Monahan and Neidel-Greenlee 2010). And, it was not until Operation Desert Storm that many long-held myths about the degree to which women participated in the military was finally demystified (Holm 1992), although it still took another 21 years for the law to eventually converge with reality.

Yet, for all intents and purposes, the notion of combat exclusion only pertained to the Navy and Air Force involving combat missions on ships and aircraft (Holm 1992). At least the idea of women engaged in direct ground combat was not the expressed intent of Congress in the original Act as it was written. With clear yardsticks as to what comprised combat exclusion, the military branches concocted their own interpretations of the policy. Per se, many positions that could have been deemed noncombatant increasingly became categorized as combatant, thus barring them to women (Holm 1992). Since the sanctioned approval of women in the military services under the Truman administration, though recognized but tepidly as one of substance, has always been subject to debate (Harrell et al. 2002), but for much of this time, the civilian and military leadership's indecisions about women's role in combat have essentially conspired to keep them out of combat (Sheppard 2007). As well, the goal was to retain an all-male domain with career benefits (Francke 1997). And, arguably, in today's asymmetric warfare environment, adhering to an archaic law whose function was consistently out of step with the realities on the ground was no longer viable. Attempts to craft the application of the law in terms of women's competency to perform in combat during the Carter and Reagan administrations were itself inconsistent as when pressed for clarity, the military's leadership sought refuge in stating that such changes must be derived from the public's will through Congress and not the military (Holm 1992). Yet, the testimony of Martine Ferber, Senior Associate Director of the National Security and International Affairs Division, in November 1987 before the Subcommittee on Military Personnel and Compensation of the House Armed Services Committee signified the conundrum in reconciling the policy across the services while simultaneously admitting that then the 40-year-old policy that has evolved overtime is no longer in keeping with the reality of an increasingly different battlefield. In addition, was the recognition that a reexamination of the policy was warranted in light of the changing roles of women in the civilian workplace. Foremost though were the changing conceptions of what defined combat (U.S. General Accountability Office [GAO], November 19, 1987), for even then the lines of the battlefield were blurring.

For the Army, despite its motto "Be All That You Can Be," the meaning had actually devolved into "Be All We'll Let You Be" (Holm 1992, p. 400). Hence, the Army was arbitrary in applying its definition of combat exclusion in ways that deliberately opened up previously closed positions to women yet stringently imposed new criteria for enlisted occupations, caps on female accessions, and dubious policies regarding assignments, all for the purpose of controlling women's access to these jobs. To the issue of competence, the Army justified the aforementioned as ways of ensuring that women were qualified in the required skill sets for such positions (Holm 1992). For these reasons, multiple studies of Army women were conducted, many of them beyond their targeted dates of completion. Many women in the Army labeled these delay tactics as a ploy for obstructing their advancement. Then the highest ranking woman in the Army in 1987, Major General Mary Clarke, who had just retired, wrote an open letter to women in the Army but which was designed for its leadership as follows: "The duty performance of the average soldier is a solid, quality performance—too good ever to return to an all-male force with only a few token women" (Holm 1992, p. 402). This warning was also in response to the Army's decision to rescind the practice of coeducational training for which the General, as the Commander of Fort McClellan, Alabama, is to be credited. But even the Army's own studies on unit performance, namely, MAXWAC and REFWAC, yielded positive results citing that women performed as well as men on tasks and that, if any, there was no statistical significance in adverse effects. More recent Army studies showed that mixed-gender units were superior in performance than single-gender units (U.S. Army 2002).

The results of a subsequent study, dubbed Women in the Army Study or WITA, during the 1980s threatened to close military occupational specialties (MOS) that were either remotely or totally unrelated to combat such as plumbers and electricians (Holm 1992). The study came with strident criticisms from Defense Advisory Committee on Women in the Services (DACOWITS), especially the new DCPC system that was purportedly designated to control the number of women assigned to positions that were categorized as low to high probability in combat. While then Army Secretary John Marsh, Jr., publicly denounced parts of the study, particularly with regard to its restrictions of positions under DCPC, in reaction, the Army planned for an increase of 70,000 enlisted women for qualified women but was quick to point out that more validation of the study's data would be needed. The morale of Army women plummeted in light of these events as it was again believed that the comments were simply a proxy for conducting more studies and consequently another pretext for delaying the opening of positions to women. Disgusted, DACOWITS Chair, Dr. Mary Huey, wrote a letter to then Secretary of Defense Caspar Weinberger under the Reagan administration as being suspect of the Army's intentions, chiefly the DCPC system and the multiple studies that had only served to reevaluate women's positive performance. Fundamentally, it appeared that DACOWITS was asking the Army to what end did these studies seek to find something? Or, more pointedly, the studies appeared to be solutions in a perpetual search of problems.

While the Navy was less contentious in its approach to the combat exclusion policy and begrudgingly agreed to expand women's roles on ships, still, there was growing angst among its leadership about the boundary of what they hoped was only a fledgling expansion (Holm 1992). Harkening back to the days of Congressman Carl Vinson (R-GA), the influential chair of the House Naval Affairs Committee was not in the cards when he threatened to derail any legislation that would call for the inclusion of women on ships, barring Navy families of commanders and nurses, to keep women out of what he considered to be the heart of the Navy, that is sea duty, by saying "Just fix it so they cannot go to sea at all!" (Gordon and Ludvigson 1991, p. 264). And, although as the interpreted Navy policy stated that women were to be barred from ships and/or aircraft engaged in combat missions, the fact of the matter was that women were already at sea, not only on oilers, ammunitions, and supply ships but were serving as pilots on the USS *Lexington* (Francke 1997). Unfortunately, the Navy chose to go the way of the Army despite the Secretary of the Navy's plan for an additional 600 ships (Holm 1992). But to many, the Navy seemed more hell bent on preserving its seafaring tradition for its men folk than adhering to the law, which by the 1980s had evolved into one where women could be assigned and rotated for temporary duty on noncombat ships that were not expected to be deployed for combat missions. However, the degree to which women were assigned to ship duty was capped and opened to manipulation by the Navy. Again, this was during the 1980s. As late as 2002 in a study conducted by RAND and sponsored by the Department of Defense (DoD), Harrell et al. (2002) found that certain occupations that on record were open to women were in effect closed to women because the particular jobs were coded for certain skill levels that were closed to women. While this finding was not limited to the Navy, the nature and date of the finding given the earlier suspicious manipulation is stark. It is equally important to note from this same study that the labor intensive or physical nature of the work was an unreliable predictor of women's propensity to be attracted to certain occupations. In fact, the opposite was true. Women were no more likely than men to be deterred from occupations that called for harsh or austere working conditions (Harrell et al. 2002). But, this was nothing new.

As early as 1981, as a collective and per the results of a DoD Background Review, commanders were singing the praises of Navy women who not only performed in an exemplary manner but by all indications had exceeded expectations, and so much so, that commanders overwhelmingly preferred the work ethic of women who were found to be more detail oriented and more dogged in researching problems than their male peers (Holm 1992). They demonstrated that they were willing and better able to endure the austere working conditions (Holm 1992). However, Navy women were undermined in the face of stellar performance when once again the proverbial lightening rod issue about readiness reared its ugly head when retiring CNO Admiral Watkins questioned the Navy's reason for recruiting more women when he called into question its adverse impact on readiness as purportedly serving in more desirable billets than men (Bush 1986). Though CNO Watkins was generally considered congenial to Navy women given his often positive comments about them within the commissioned and enlisted corps, his outgoing comments as their chief spokesperson was tantamount to a betrayal as noted in this letter to the Editor of the *Navy Times* on August 4, 1986:

> I was outraged at the comments apparently made by the CNO during his "outgoing interview" concerning women in the Navy. It seems to me that energies of this nature would be better directed toward legislation to allow us to serve on combat units and within the ranks that are now "men only" rather than continue to limit when and where we can serve our country, then put us down for those very limitations. (Letter to the Editor, 1986)

Another, second-class builder in the Seabees, Katherine Goodwin, framed her outrage more personally.

> I bust my butt for the Navy and I work very hard for the respect of the men I work with. I have worked very hard for the position which I hold today. I am damn proud of my job and my country and, put in the position, I would do my best or die for this country. Just one thing I refuse to do, and that is to be the scapegoat for any one of our Navy policies … it [the CNO's comments] makes me feel as though all my work and pride have been in vain. (Letter to the Editor, 1986)

The collective outcry forced the Navy's hand. This time, under the guise that it was increasing its enlisted force of women by opening another 1000 positions, along with two prepositioning ship squadrons while surreptitiously closing other squadrons where, for instance, six ships classified under combat support force (CSF) would become "other combatant" (p. 410) as another tactic to limit women's movement into combat classified positions (Holm 1992). To add salt to an already festering wound, the newly appointed CNO, Admiral Frost, announced a moratorium on the total end strength of enlisted women in the Navy blaming Congress for its failure to increase its overall end strength. In a subsequent interview with the *Navy Times*, retired Admiral Fran McKee blamed the new plan as simply "another reflection of the very fragile nature of any long-range planning concerning the utilization of women in the Navy. For years we have witnessed the cyclical use of women as a valve to adjust the Navy's manpower picture."

While decisions such as these are not directed at affecting morale, they do indeed have a most unsettling effect on Navy women regarding their professional future and true value to the Navy in accomplishing its mission (Purcell 1987). And, David Fraser, a Naval Affairs writer, questioned that in reality, whether Navy women were being used as scapegoats because how can the 10% of its force of women have such an adverse impact on the rotation scheduling of its remaining 90% of its workforce who are men. While the uproar moved Secretary of Defense Weinberger to scrap such plans, the relief was short-lived only to be replaced by Navy Secretary James Webb, Jr., who was well reputed for his negative views about the integration of women into the Navy beyond traditional support roles (Holm 1992). In his quest to become the next Secretary of the Navy, the grilling at his confirmation hearing was enough to sensitize him to the plight of women in the Navy and Marine Corps. However, once confirmed, Webb ordered that promotion selection be based on "demonstrated outstanding performance in demanding assignments" (Holm 1992, p. 412). The fallout from these statements only served to reinforce what an already demoralized contingency of Navy women felt about its leadership. And, a review of Navy and Marine Corps installations by DACOWITS revealed the magnitude of the fallout. Chairwoman Dr. Jacqueline Davis was candid in her assessment about her findings to Weinberger and Webb. Yet, what appeared to have moved Webb to take action was DACOWITS' findings that were reported by the national media.

A study of over 2500 Navy personnel at 10 installations ensued to culminate into the Navy study's Group Report on Progress of Women in the Navy (Holm 1992). What resulted was to bring clarity to the definition of combat exclusion and the increase of assignments at sea for women, the creation of a special assistant to the Chief of the Navy Personnel for Women Policy for a female incumbent. Another follow on study only further illuminated the gravity of problems for Navy women including the perception by Navy men of their failure to equally contribute to the mission, not to mention the stalling of many careers given the combat exclusion policy (Holm 1992). Under a review of all ships and aircraft directed by Secretary Webb, the Navy forecasted almost the doubling in the total force of women into the Navy to move from 13% in 1991 to 25% in 1996. Despite these unprecedented moves, it was still evident that while Navy women's opportunities were visibly expanding, its leadership had no intentions nor any desire to repeal the combat exclusion policy.

For the Marine Corps, the smallest, the most combat heavy, and the branch with the lowest number of women as part of its force as well as the least integrated in terms of assimilating women into its occupations, according to Holm (1992), it was still determined to remain "A Few Good Men" (p. 414), for it represented "the last bastion of the classic fighting man" (p. 414). Yet, the service could not immunize itself from the sea change of the times, so to speak. With an anemic force that was 4% female, the Marine Corps drew its interpretation and conversely implementation of the combat exclusion policy from both the Navy and the Army. To its credit, the Marine Corps commissioned a study of first its enlisted women, then three years after that of its female officers in an effort to determine the requirement for its overall female force. The Marine Corps concluded that women would serve in all occupations except infantry, artillery, tank, and assault amphibian and pilot/naval flight officer. In effect, all occupations that were designated as combat were off limits to women, although the number of enlisted and commissioned positions for women significantly increased. Subsequently, it became a requirement for women to receive weapons training with the expectation that they could technically encounter situations deemed as combat. Women's qualifying capability on the shooting range exceeded all expectations at 98% (Jones 1986). But the DACOWITS' report describing rampant sexual harassment, abuse, and discrimination at installations in the Pacific Rim doused any cause for revelry. A task force finding at the order of Secretary Webb to be convened by the Marine Corps Commandant Alfred Gray produced disturbing results that the aforementioned were pervasive among male Marines toward their female counterparts. This was found to have been borne of negative attitudes at every level of the command. And although the Commandant himself reacted appropriately by directing that all women be treated respectfully as they are all Marines, his actions spoke otherwise. For example, he vetoed recommendations from his senior officers that would allow women to serve in previously closed assignments such as security forces, embassy guard units, pilots, and to engage in offensive combat training though he did allow women's participation in defensive basic warrior (Moore 1988). But then Secretary of Defense Carlucci rejected this decision to the public consternation of the Marine Corps Commandant by posting the first three women as embassy guards in France, Germany, and Switzerland respectively (Holm 1992). For the most part though, the Marine Corps held to its original goal for the accession of women by not exceeding the number of noncombatants to positions to align with that of the general civilian population. And, where there was a shortage to meet force requirements, the Marine Corps simply backfilled these positions with men thus controlling the number of women who were recruited. So, whereas the remaining military branches were significantly expanding their female force, the Marine Corps' use of women grew from 2% to only 5%.

Unlike its sister services (the irony that this term is invoked when referring to the familial kinship between the branches of the military), the Air Force did not employ a system that required separate criteria for women and men (Holm 1992). In fact, the Air Force was in an enviable position that called upon the highest caliber from all of its recruits, thereby holding fast to the number of women that it recruited and without having to ever substitute men for women in any position given across the board application of the standard. And, again, unlike its sister services, in light of their respective missions, the Air Force was impacted by the combat exclusion policy the least as women were only barred from serving on aircraft involved in combat missions. This did not mean, however, that the Air Force was any more receptive to recruiting women than the other services as, like its sister services, it found ways of excluding women from jobs that were remotely related to either aircraft and combat missions, even occupations that were expressly defined as noncombat in nature by invoking that these jobs may have a "high probability" of encountering "direct combat or exposure to hostile fire or capture" (Holm 1992, p. 419). The policy even applied to nonflying squadrons. Yet, in spite of these exclusions, because the Air Force's occupations largely mirrored those found in organizations within the civilian sector, it enjoyed another advantage in its ability to recruit women. But to deliberately control the number of enlisted women recruited, the Air Force developed an intricate mathematical model to internally manipulate its objectives and caps that estimated the likelihood of women to enlist in the Air Force. Despite this convoluted approach, the plan was found acceptable to the Office of the Secretary of Defense (OSD), but this was short-lived.

Congress later imposed new incremental goals for the recruitment of women in the Air Force, from 19% in 1987 to 22% in 1988, and in 1989 under the National Defense Authorization Act (NDAA), the Air Force was then disallowed from setting any restrictions for accessing women other than those established under combat exclusion (Holm 1992). Congress' intent was that neither baselines nor ceilings be created by allowing both women and men to compete for such positions. Consequently, the revised combat exclusion policy which later became the risk rule resulted in lifting the ban on 2700 positions to women, but not without DACOWITS' intervention in questioning compliance. By then, a whopping 97% of the Air Force's occupations, at least in principle but not in practice and with 14% of its workforce, comprised women (Holm 1992).

The Coast Guard, then a peacetime arm of the U.S. Department of Transportation (WREI 2005), was receptive to women's integration into all occupations and never imposed a combat exclusion type policy (Holm 1992). Further, the Coast Guard was not a part of the original legislation or the Women's Armed Services Integration Act of 1948 though at the time during wartime, the institution could be subsumed under the Navy (Francke 1997). The Coast Guard was unequivocal in its support to repeal such laws (Francke 1997) and since 1978 had decided that there would be "absolutely no arbitrary restrictions based solely upon sex" (Holm 1992, p. 421). According to the then Commandant Admiral James Gracey in 1982, "My view on the performance of women in the Coast Guard is that they are Class A! They are great! They have performed up to all my expectations and beyond most people's expectations" (Holm 1992, p. 421). But in contrast to the Navy, the Coast Guard's assignment policy provided especially its female officers unprecedented opportunities at sea, including being in command of ships. However, during wartime, when the Coast Guard is subordinated to the Navy, it is subject to its laws resulting in the removal of women from certain positions in light of the combat exclusion policy (Francke 1997). This subsequently remained a bone of contention between the Coast Guard and the Navy regarding the assignment of its female personnel (Holm 1992). While there were challenges on ships in meeting privacy requirements for enlisted women on mixed crew ships, the Coast Guard vowed that it would do whatever was necessary to meet such accommodations.

Ironically, at the time, a study of the Coast Guard directed by Commandant Paul Yost revealed that, given the demographic trends on women and minorities within the general civilian population, and specifically in comparison to the military branches of DoD, it was woefully underutilizing women in its active duty component at only 7.8% (Holm 1992). The report resulted in a 20% increase in the number of women accessed to active duty in the future. As well, the report addressed the entrenched differences between the Coast Guard and the Navy in the event of wartime mobilization. The Coast Guard's concern in light of its policy and practice about women's integration into all occupations is whether or not this transfer to the Navy would result in the restriction of its female workforce aboard its vessels. Doing so, the Coast Guard's leadership believed, would severely compromise operational readiness. Fortunately for the Coast Guard, the Navy Judge Advocate General (JAG) erred on its side ruling that under any national emergency the Navy's laws would not usurp those of the Coast Guard's regarding the assignment of its female workforce (Holm 1992). The aforesaid 1990 study echoed these sentiments by reaffirming the integral role of women in the Coast Guard whose removal, according to Commandant Admiral Yost, would "have deleterious effect on the operational and military readiness of their vessels" (Holm 1992, p. 423). Admiral William Kime, Yost's successor, concurred with and promised to implement the recommendations of the study by expanding the degree to which the Coast Guard recruits and utilizes women. More radical in its policies was the approval of no more than two-year sabbaticals for both women and men, enlisted and commissioned, for the purpose of caring for newborn children (Holm 1992). This policy was specifically devised as a strategy for improving the retention levels of critically trained personnel.

Like the Navy's holy grail in restricting the command of ships to women, the flying community was similarly fervent in its culture, bound and determined to prevent women from fighter jets believed to be the sole domain of men. What was interesting though was that the U.S. military was pathetically behind its North Atlantic Treaty Organization (NATO) counterparts in its treatment of women in the military, specifically in its assignment of women to combat cockpits (Francke 1997) even as the U.S. Air Force was already involved in training women from NATO countries on combat/fighter aircraft as early as the 1980s (Holm 1992). Giving up these prized assignments, however, was only a matter of time, albeit at a snail's pace, but it came at great expense to the military following the loss of skilled women pilots who prematurely separated from the military because of the legally imposed glass ceiling on their careers. Yet, the comments below of one pilot, a Canadian, perhaps best demonstrated the fight to the death, in a manner of speaking, even in the face of an embarrassing loss, as to why leaders in the aviation community, including its proponents within the U.S. military, were steadfast in not yielding a morsel of their perceived territory to women in the American military.

Captain Jane Foster was one of the first two female fighter pilots in the world (Holm 1992). Following a simulation where she not only dispelled any associated myths about women lacking the right stuff to be fighter pilots, but in flying a CF-18 Hornet, she destroyed the AV-8B Harrier of a U.S. Marine with a missile (Bird 1989). One observer stated that, having lost to a woman, the Marine was so angry he hurled his helmet across the hangar. According to one flight safety officer, Captain Pierre Ruelli, stationed at the Canadian Forces Base Cold Lake, "We like to think [flying fighters] is a man's job, but it's not" (Bird 1989; Holm 1992, p. 429E). And, "it's more a matter of women entering the ranks. Fighter pilot has been a male territory up until now," said one Norwegian pilot who flies F-18 jets on exchange with the Canadian forces. This, it is believed, is the same macho attitude that resonates among aviators within the U.S. military, hence, the slow pace at which women have been assigned to such opportunities and the resistance to repealing the combat exclusion policy (Holm 1992). A 1988 report by the GAO was replete with the manipulative steps to which the Air Force went to restrict such positions to women and that was even restrictive in practice than the law allowed. Air Force leadership was of the mindset, despite women's repeated performance, that women could not endure the stress of real combat situations. And, the few women who were finally accepted to this exclusive community were subjected to demands not made of men.

Take Captain Troy Devine, a 1985 Air Force Academy graduate who had received her silver wings and by all indications was destined for an illustrious career as a fighter pilot, if only she had been a man (Holm 1992). So, she settled for an assignment with the Ninth Strategic Reconnaissance Wing at Beale Air Force Base (AFB) in California, was not only forced to sign a waiver that for at least one year she promised not to become pregnant, but was further humiliated by consenting to pregnancy tests every two weeks. In effect, the Air Force's arbitrary interpretation and corresponding practice in its implementation of barring women from combat aircraft assignments were actually more restrictive than even the Navy's (Holm 1992). And essentially, the Navy's implementation of the combat exclusion policy was more in keeping with the law than that of the Air Force because the Navy based such restrictions on the mission, not the type of aircraft. While on par, this practice did not necessarily yield more opportunities for Navy women in light of the law's dual restriction of women on combat ships, its practice nonetheless afforded experience to Navy women not enjoyed by women in the Air Force. For instance, as early as 1975, Navy women like then Lieutenant (Junior Grade [JG]) Rosemary Conatser (Mariner) was the first military woman to become qualified to fly a high-performance jet aircraft (Holm 1992). In 1990, she was also the first woman to take command of a Navy tactical electronic warfare squadron. Likewise, in 1985, Navy women were already flying an array of combat aircraft that were off limits to Air Force women. Still, because carriers represented the center of gravity for the Navy, although women took off and landed on them, they were never assigned to squadrons onboard these vessels except the USS *Lexington* (Holm 1992). This twin exclusion for Navy women, that is, from combat aircraft and ships, produced a negligible effect in the cadre of women pilots and navigators totaling only 1.8% and 1.2% for each occupation.

The Army differed markedly from its sister services given its interpretation and application of the combat exclusion policy. By employing its DCPC system, this allowed the Army free reign in determining what constituted high to low probability assignments to legally exclude its female workforce from what it deemed to be combat-related missions such as flying the Apache Attack helicopters yet flying the Black Hawk and Chinook helicopters in support of combat soldiers (Holm 1992). As with the other services, despite the conveniently deployed jargon, all intended to restrict women from any assignments that were even remotely considered to be combat related and in the face of women supporting combat support missions, such as the Army and Operation Just Cause in Panama where women functioned flawlessly under hostile fire while transporting troops or supplies into enemy territory. And women's uniformed performance during Operation Desert Storm all but settled the performance issue even though they were still barred from flying Apache helicopters. But as Holm (1992) correctly highlighted, the so-called noncombatant helicopters ferrying troops and supplies in and out of the battlefield were as much a target as the designated combat helicopters. The Marine Corps was left intact by providing convincing justification that, unlike its sister services, all of its flying functions were combat and therefore automatically excluded women. Even following the recommendations of an internal task force in 1988, the Commandant ruled against his senior officers without any repercussions from the civilian leadership.

A testimony to Congress in early 1990 by Lieutenant General Thomas Hickey, Chief of the Air Force Personnel to the Armed Services Committee, who stopped short of recommending the repeal of the combat exclusion policy, gave some indication as to the possible mindset, at least of the Air Force, toward the integration of women, when he talked about the performance of women in the Air Force that

> They can fly fighters, they pull Gs, they can do all those things. They are physically [and] emotionally capable … the issue is if you want us to put them there, just change the law and the Air Force will do that. (Holm 1992, p. 432)

But it was not the repeal of the combat exclusion policy that Congress was after but simply an exercise to find a way of clarifying the law while reconciling the differences in the interpretation and implementation of the separate policies between the services. DoD's response to seek clarification of the combat exclusion policy was to craft what subsequently came to be known as the risk rule (Holm 1992; Solaro 2006). The risk rule was owing to Secretary of Defense Weinberger's establishment of a Task Force on Women in the Military to address such issues as career, morale, utilization, and quality of life for military women and based upon the recommendation of DACOWITS following a trip to the western Pacific. Among DACOWITS' recommendations was to adopt a clear standard on what positions constituted combat that were closed to women. The premise was to restrict the degree of interpretation by each service resulting in the widest breadth in providing assignments and opportunities for women. This attempt at clarification was also designed to abolish any inconsistencies in assignments among the services, especially in similar positions across the services. While the risk rule stated that "risks of exposure to direct combat, hostile fire, or capture are proper criteria for closing noncombat positions or units for women, provided that … such risks are equal to or greater than that experienced by associated combat units in the same theater of operations" (Harrell et al. 2002, p. 2; Holm 1992, p. 433). Unfortunately, even the risk rule was a poor compromise devised to protect women from what Holm (1992) terms a profession that is inherently risky as "misplaced chivalry" (p. 433). Similarly, Solaro (2006) and Francke (1997) question this moral logic, even though at the time women were already assigned to intercept enemy targets by launching ICBMs with nuclear warheads while being barred from using conventional weapons (Holm 1992). This was the absurdity of it all, said Holm (1992). By then, the Canadian Forces had integrated women into all occupations, including those categorized as combat, with the exception of submarines (Francke 1997).

Operation Desert Storm was a display of the largest number of women to be mobilized since WWII (Holm 1992; Monahan and Neidel-Greenlee 2010; Solaro 2006). Nonetheless, 40 years later, Congress again had chosen to frame the issue of women's suitability for combat by revisiting already debated concerns, among them morale and unit cohesion, which ironically the military had used some 40 years earlier to provide as a rationale for excluding African Americans from integration into the military (Holm 1992). To Monahan and Neidel-Greenlee (2010), the performance of women during Operation Desert Storm was once again all but forgotten during peacetime even though it proved more than ever before that the war could not have been won without women (Francke 1997; Monahan and Neidel-Greenlee 2010; Solaro 2006). However, the period from 1992 through 1994 began experiencing somewhat of a sea change (Harrell et al. 2002). The 1992 NDAA repealed the original 1948 Women's Armed Services Integration Act that barred women from combat yet appointed a commission to study the matter further while providing the Secretary of Defense the authority to set aside the remaining exclusion in the law for tests to be conducted of women who were assigned to combat positions (Holm 1992).

The President's Commission on the Assignment of Women in the Armed Services hearings soon devolved into one about values. Accordingly, given the values issue, it was never about women, but about how men would feel about women being captured as prisoners of war (POWs) as occurred during Operation Desert Storm (Francke 1997). The hearings appeared to be more about social policy than what were the best decisions for the military (Monahan and Neidel-Greenlee 2010). The debate became hostile (Francke 1997). Reportedly, one white male Commissioner even quoted the scriptures using the Bible and proclaimed that he was a Christian in his fight against women in combat. Retired Air Force General Robert Herres, head of the Commission and formerly the Vice Commander of the Joint Chiefs of Staff, was impassioned in declaring that there were no overriding arguments to allow the ban on women flying combat aircraft to stand (Monahan and Neidel-Greenlee 2010). Unfortunately, the conservative wing of the Commission prevailed. The vote for lifting the ban on women serving on Navy vessels and to reinstate the same against women flying combat aircraft descended into using, of all arguments, the problem of menstruation (Francke 1997). The Commission went as far as calling for the reinstatement of the risk rule.

Fortunately, President Clinton disregarded the Commission's recommendations, adopted the diversity strategies in accordance with the Defense Equal Opportunity Management Institute (DEOMI), and abolished the risk rule by directing the Secretary of Defense Les Aspin to order that combat flying positions be opened to women (Francke 1997; Monahan and Neidel-Greenlee 2010; Solaro 2006). In 1994, the Navy lifted its ban on combat ships to women and under pressure from Army Secretary Togo West, the Army opened 32,000 positions to women, although those occupations that engaged in direct ground combat like infantry, field artillery, and armor remained closed to women (Francke 1997;

Monahan and Neidel-Greenlee 2010). With combat aviation and combat vessels, excluding submarines, opened to women, the Secretary of Defense not only ordered full rescission of the risk rule but that women could now be assigned to units but not units "below the brigade command level whose primary mission is to engage in direct ground combat" defined as

> engaging an enemy on the ground with individual or crew served weapons, while being exposed to hostile fire and to a high probability of direct physical contact with the hostile force's personnel. Direct ground combat takes place well forward on the battlefield while locating and closing with the enemy to defeat them by fire, maneuver, or shock effect. (Secretary of Defense, Les Aspin 1994, as cited by Harrell et al. 2002, pp. 3 and 4)

It is unfortunate though that otherwise intelligent men, and such female co-conspirators like Elaine Donnelly, head of the Center for Military Readiness (CMR), would not only denounce DACOWITS and its work but laud the capture of Private First Class (PFC) Jessica Lynch during the initial phases of Operation Iraqi Freedom as evidence that women do not belong in the military (CMR 2002). As Harris (2009a) points out, Donnelly and others decry the exemplary work of women in the military by choosing to portray them in battle as "damsels in distress" (p. 1), preferring not to call attention to such sheroes as PFC Lori Piestewa in the same platoon as PFC Lynch, who died during the same period. For this purpose, those who oppose women's full integration into the military, stoop to such low levels to conquer, and fly in the face of the overwhelming evidence, by turning to and grasping at conjecture, at best, of women's so-called incompatibility with the military. One such instance that gained unnecessary exposure was the unfortunate incident that resulted in the death of Navy Lieutenant Kara Hultgreen, the first female combat pilot to meet such demise (Francke 1997). Lieutenant Hultgreen was about to land her F-14A aircraft onto the USS *Abraham Lincoln* when she crashed into the Pacific Ocean after losing an engine. Ironically, Hultgreen was one of 10 pilots to lose their lives flying the same aircraft during training exercises since 1992. Yet, it was only upon her death that questions emerged concerning Navy "political correctness" and the compromise of pilot standards (Francke 1997, p. 236). The anonymous accusers alleged that women were being accelerated through pilot training and as a consequence women flight skills were deemed inadequate.

Hultgreen's mother, an attorney, fired back by immediately releasing her daughter's flight records which showed that of the seven combat pilots in her class, Hultgreen ranked third with an overall score of 3.10 out of 4 but above the average score of 2.99 for the class (*Nightline* 1995). The Navy's exhaustive investigation, which included a reenactment of the last 10 seconds of Hultgreen's landing, but in a flight simulator, also resulted in a crash. Critics nonetheless chose to cherry pick the evidence that pointed to the inordinate cost of the investigation. And, to add more salt to an already infested wound, of the Navy pilots who lost their lives during simulator training exercises in the same combat aircraft, only Hultgreen received the distinction of being laid to rest at Arlington National Cemetery, a ceremony that was attended by top Navy brass, including the Secretary of the Navy (Pexton 1995). Even worse though was when it was leaked that Hultgreen's accident could have been attributed to pilot error as much as a malfunctioned engine (Francke 1997). It was as if this situation was destined to defame not only the deceased pilot but more importantly what she represented—a woman who was not only in the military but she had the audacity to pursue a vocation that was perceived as the sole prerogative of the white male as a pilot and flying in a combat aircraft to boot. But following Hultgreen's accident, the opponents chose not to underscore that another pilot had also died while attempting to land on the USS *Abraham Lincoln* along with the loss of four combat aircraft (Garrison 1995b). The slander campaign expanded to include flight records of fellow pilot Lieutenant Carey Dunair Lohrenz aboard the USS *Abraham Lincoln*, all for the purpose of discrediting women as pilots (Francke 1997) and reinforcing Donnelly's CMR to highlight the alleged substandard qualifications of women (Barnes 1995; Chavez 1995).

In turn, the Donnelly report only served to add more fuel to an already roaring fire that resulted in the new Wing Commander for the USS *Abraham Lincoln* ordering evaluation hearings for four of seven female pilots that questioned their qualifications (Francke 1997). The fallout from this witch hunt was stark. Two of the women voluntarily left Navy aviation, another was placed on probation with the forewarning that the next mistake would be her last, while the fourth resigned her commission (Barnes 1995). But the height of the hypocrisy only became evident after the only male combat pilot who had crashed his F-14A aircraft into the ocean yet was returned to flight status (Garrison 1996). In a cruel twist of faith, poetic justice or even perhaps more pointedly one of vindication, this same male pilot died while performing daredevil stunts in Nashville, Tennessee, nine months later.

The scandal only widened to overshadow the successful maiden voyage of the USS *Dwight Eisenhower* to the Mediterranean, the Arabian Gulf, and the Adriatic Sea where it was asserted that of its 415 women aboard, 39 became pregnant (Garrison 1995a). Said Francke (1997), the academies steeped in "white male cultures" (p. 259) were no less immune from these salacious incidents. In the case of the Army's U.S. Military Academy at West Point, in 1995, 15 female cadets were groped and paraded in front of an assembly of 200 football players (Campbell 1995). In an attempt to downplay the significance of this event, the academy's findings were that the likelihood of reporting misconduct had increased among both male and female cadets. However, what the findings deliberately failed to mention was that the three male cadets who reported the incident were all African Americans. Yet, as one feisty female veteran declared, "The men can try and knock me down, but they haven't managed to stop me yet. That in itself keeps me going"

(Francke 1997, p. 259). This last statement is illustrative of the 17 former military women who are profiled in this book, for, despite the level of opposition that they encountered during their military careers, quite coincidentally it is this very same level of opposition that fueled their resolve to never succumb to the enormous pressure at hand.

Holm (1992) pointed to the number of myths that have been held about women by men as to their roles in society that have only served to conspire against women in their continuing quest for recognition and equality in the military and arguably in society at large. Specifically surrounding the issue of combat, Holm refers to the phenomenon as the "humpty dumpty factor" (p. 398). The issue has been deliberately framed in such terms as a cloak in order to bar women from certain jobs, occupations, units, ships, aircraft, and missions under the semblance of combat or combat related. And to add to the confusion, the varying contradictions in how the military branches chose to interpret the policy was a sure fire way to ensure that women never succeeded in filling these roles. Further, as part of this larger conspiracy, many positions, occupations, units, ships, aircraft, and missions that were technically noncombat were changed to block women from them (Holm 1992). This conception was based on the myth that the original 1948 Women Armed Services Integration Act barred women from all positions of combat when nothing was further from the truth and it was only through media coverage of Operation Just Cause in Panama in 1989 when the extent of women's roles in the military was finally revealed to the American public for the first time. But, by design, what made the argument against this nonexistent policy even more convoluted was the lack of standardization in its interpretation across the services. So, Holm's (1992) Humpty Dumpty factor then, as portrayed at the outset of this chapter, as to the ludicrous nature of the combat exclusion policy in the frustrating and nonsensical exchange between Humpty Dumpty and Alice in *Through the Looking Glass* is emblematic of the discourse by decision makers. Thus, Alice's retort in how can one use the same words to mean so many different things following Humpty Dumpty's proclamation that his use of words is just what he chooses those words to mean speaks of this frustration for the women who live it and for those lawmakers and civilian and military leaders who honestly attempt to change the policy's arbitrariness for the combat exclusion policy is only a problem for those who experience it (McElrath 1992).

These myths as espoused, according to Holm (1992) and others (i.e., DePauw 1998; Eltshain 1987; Fenner 2001; Francke 1997; Goldstein 2003; Herbert 1998; Monahan and Neidel-Greenlee 2010), and as articulated by still others are perceived as truths (i.e., Maninger 2008; Mitchell 1997; van Creveld 2000, 2002) that have become the drivers of the case against women in the military and specifically against women in combat. The first myth about women in the military is that they should be protected from being exposed to combat (Holm 1992). The reality as it stands is that the enemy does not discriminate in combat, for them a target is a target. Nonetheless, what is illogical about this myth is that women as nurses, reportedly as early as WWI, have been on the brink of the front lines of war and where no other U.S. military women could legally venture, although female civilian journalists were routinely at the tip of the spear (DePauw 1998; Eltshain 1987; Goldstein 2003; Holm 1992; Monahan and Neidel-Greenlee 2010). And, while vicious in description as well as intent, American women have been known to carry out the murder of Native Americans and the lynching of African Americans (DePauw 1975, 1998). American women's roles in combat even harkens back to the days of the Revolution when they battled for the militia in the countryside, the most famous of whom is Molly Pitcher, who not only nursed wounded troops but following the death of her husband on the battlefield, took up arms by firing his cannon (DePauw 1998). Likewise, during the Civil War, women disguised mostly as men, fought on both sides (DePauw 1998). The large-scale injuries and deaths that military nurses encountered are legendary (Holm 1992). Their training prepared and suited them well for war. The indiscriminate lines of demarcation of what defines combat is then perhaps the most profound modern-day example where even the female military medics, as per the personal interviews in this book of pioneering, prominent, and/or elite former military women, were forced to pick up arms. In addition, the use of female engagement teams by the Marine Corps during Operation Enduring Freedom (DACOWITS 2009) alongside the embedding of teams of women by the Army was known collectively as Lioness during Operation Iraqi Freedom (Alvarez 2009; Lioness Report 2012; McLagan and Sommers 2010). One such veteran is portrayed in this book. So, in essence, this myth is essentially a myth but is still being depicted as truth.

The second myth about women in the military is that they are an unreliable contingent for deployment (Holm 1992). It is obvious that nothing could be further from the truth. During every major military campaign, including those during the early days before the founding of America as a republic, women have always found ways to serve at their own peril and when sanctioned for service from WWI through Operations Enduring Freedom, Iraqi Freedom, and New Dawn. Women have consistently heeded the call to arms and their repeated and increasing en masse mobilization by the military and valiant performance during each campaign underscores their recognition as an invaluable resource. But this continually speaks to the "cultural amnesia" (Segal 1995, p. 761) that takes effect following demobilization from each military campaign and smacks of Solaro's (2006) metaphor of the use of women by the military to that of a mistress only to be taken for granted and repeatedly used as a matter of convenience. Pregnancy has been used as one of the many wedge issues that allegedly render women nondeployable even though studies by Harrell and Miller (1997) and others (i.e., Harrell et al. 2002) show that pregnancy has not been an issue that adversely impacts the mission. Further, being ever mindful of their perception as a weak link in the chain of military readiness, women go to extreme lengths to time their pregnancies so as never to detract from their units' missions (Harrell and Miller 1997; Harris 2009b).

Solaro (2006) explains that pregnancies in the military fall into three categories—Congratulations!, Oops!, and Get me out of here! Congratulations comprise planned pregnancies for women in the military. These normally occur during non-deployable assignments such as attendance at schools and the like. Oops! pregnancies are those that are unplanned, are unexpected, and tend to disproportionately occur among junior enlisted women. One enlisted soldier, upon learning that she was pregnant, to her commander's chagrin, wanted so much to return to her unit in Iraq that after she was evacuated to the continental United States (CONUS), she received an abortion. Yet, Get me out of here! sometimes illustrates the few military women who do employ pregnancy as a tactic to avoid overseas deployment and/or multiple and frequent deployments. Regrettably, these are rare incidents that still call unnecessary attention to and thus the resonance of this myth. The reality then stands that this straw issue for opponents has never been one that was credible enough to be advanced, despite the repeated attempts to do so. This is not to say, however, that myth or not, the issue has not gained traction. Another myth that is obviously refutable is that women do not have what it takes to perform under pressure in combat (Holm 1992). Women's collective performance during every single major military campaign has only served to disprove this still widely held myth. And, because combat is perceived as the sole province of men (Harrell et al. 2002; Hosek et al. 2001; Jeffreys 2007; Maninger 2008; Petronio 2012; Simons 2000), this myth has achieved footing. Even with the recent repeal of the combat exclusion policy which in itself represents the cumulative record that this is not the case, it may never dissuade those who are hell bent on proving otherwise. But more importantly, women's official entrance into combat as now a matter of law is the last feature that will no longer distinguish what men do versus what women do. At least in theory, until the repeal of the policy is implemented as a matter of practice, women and men for the first time will be on equal footing and unlike the past where men assumed the competitive edge given the combat advantage, and where women were routinely relegated to second-tier assignments, especially for promotions, women's records too will legally reflect this distinction.

The next myth reinforces the belief of women as the fairer, the more delicate, and the weaker of the sexes, all to imply that they are ill equipped for the strain of combat. This suggests that because American women enjoy a certain high standard of living at home—as do men—they would be unable to adapt to the rugged terrain within a combat zone (Holm 1992). There is a partial truth to this myth though in terms of the country's standard of living. However, at no time when called to duty were women in the military unable to or incapable of translating these so-called creature comforts (Holm 1992, p. 462) to those of a combat zone. Nurses, given their training during the Vietnam conflict were notorious for their knowledge about the basics of field sanitation and capably pitched tents, camped out at various sites, read maps and compasses, used field equipment, planned for disaster preparedness through exercises, road marching, and practicing likely chances that would be encountered in the field. The aforementioned declaration by the then Army Chief Surgeon Major General Steger about the nurses' performance in an insurgency style war was indicative of the horrors that they witnessed and endured. And, as described by Holm (1992), women quickly adapted to the crude elements of war zones by living like "grunts" (p. 462). As a matter of fact, during Operation Desert Storm, women were at a greater disadvantage than their male comrades in many ways, among them lacking personal hygiene supplies even though there was an abundance of shaving cream for men. Many women dealt with incidents of sexual harassment in an environment in which they constantly had to prove themselves.

Unaccustomed to the cultural mores of women in the Persian Gulf, women's freedom was severely curtailed which in many cases hindered their ability to accomplish their jobs, not to mention some of the racial discrimination that was experienced by African American women (Monahan and Neidel-Greenlee 2010). The harshness and hostility of the environment, especially during Operation Iraqi Freedom, that unnecessarily imperiled military women as noncombatants, even as they performed combat duties for which in many instances they lacked both the training and equipment for protection, exposed military women to dangers not experienced by military men. For example, in the case of the Army, women were officially not assigned to units engaged in direct ground combat below the brigade level (Solaro 2006). Yet, when placed in units below the brigade level, women were inaccurately considered attached to them. This confusion in designations and assignments that was frequently at odds with the realities on the ground gave way to women carrying out assignments in lieu of their male counterparts for which they were left unprotected. This was a routine scenario as described by some of the interviewees in this book who are Army veterans and who were involved in many fire-fights during the early phase of Operation Iraqi Freedom. Needless to say, they found themselves patrolling areas alone yet often did not receive the credit for such valor as technically they should not have been placed in these assignments. Additionally, these women trained many of the men who were in turn promoted because of this training but they themselves did not receive similar recognition. One of the interviewees in this book graphically detailed the lengths to which she went to overturn a decision to place a less qualified male subordinate into the theater of operations, even though she was far more qualified than this male soldier. And, in the end, she never received credit for this designation. In fact, she only suffered the repercussions as a result. Ostensibly "in the military, if you are not assigned to a unit, you are an 'orphan'" (Solaro 2006, p. 70).

The fifth myth, like the others that have been rebutted time and time again, yet persists, is that the presence of women will destroy unit cohesion and correspondingly male bonding (Holm 1992). Rosen et al. (1999) define unit cohesion as a comradeship or type of interpersonal bonding that is essential among military members in a unit. It is believed that it is the key ingredient to meeting a unit's mission. Not only does the integration of women in the military not detract from a unit's cohesion, morale, and readiness (Harrell and Miller 1997; Harrell et al. 2002;

Rosen et al. 1996, 1999), but the Army's own research has shown that performance is noticeably increased in mixed-gender units (U.S. Army 1996, 2002). Training was also integral to increased performance in mixed-gender units (U.S. Army 1996, 2002). What these studies uniformly illustrate is that what is most important to unit cohesion and thus bonding among unit members is leadership. The presence of women was secondary and functioned in the same manner as would separation according to rank or occupation (Harrell and Miller 1997). It was found that under fire, men and women coalesced into effective teams during Operation Desert Storm (Holm 1992). Captain Cynthia Mosley, who was the commander of an Army combat support company that came under fire said, "When the action starts every soldier does what they are trained to do. Nobody cares whether you're male or female. It's just: can you do the job?" (Holm 1992, p. 463). And, West Point graduate Captain Carol Barkalow, who was attached to the 24th Infantry Division at the time, believes that unit bonding grows out of respect and shared hardships.

The sixth myth, as described by Holm (1992), constitutes what Harris (2009a) calls the two prevailing views about women in the military. One view, as those on the right believe, is that women's disruptive nature in an otherwise cohesive unit of men only serves to lead men astray (Harris 2009a). Yet, the other view, or as advocated by those on the left, attempts to dispel the myth that the military is the last stronghold of masculinity where women are subordinated to second-class citizenship or even worse as sex fiends (Harris 2009a). Rosen et al. (2003) found that in units where only males were present, there was a direct relationship with this concentration and hypermasculinity or the notion of a true sense of machismo or manhood. But, at the individual level, this was not the case. There was a negative relationship between hypermasculinity and unit cohesion and readiness. Even more revealing, and again at the individual level, was that men also rated their units low in cohesion and readiness. Yet, at the group level, those groups that were rated high in hypermasculinity were considered to be high in unit cohesion, even while many of the same individual members scoffed at the hypermasculinity activities in which their groups engaged. Solaro (2006) views this dilemma that male unit members face is that even though they dislike such activities, for survival at the individual level, the men simply "go along to get along" (p. 311). She deduces that what is unfortunate in any scenario of male bonding is that it is "the scumbags" in the units who assume the enviable position of setting the tone (Solaro 2006, p. 311). As well, at the individual level, unit members are forced to succumb to partaking in these Neanderthal activities in order not to appear "unmanly" (p. 311). So, when women are integrated into these otherwise hypermasculine units, it becomes less attractive to be hypermasculine. And, in these less hypermasculine units, members coalesce at subgroup levels according to shared backgrounds either because they are married, are college educated, or are of the same ilk in some way, these groups form relationships at the subordinate levels that become positive for the unit overall (Solaro 2006). Rosen and Martin (1998) show though that when women soldiers feel rebuffed by fellow male soldiers, they experienced chronic levels of stress.

Similarly, male soldiers who work with these female soldiers appear to empathize with their female cohorts by experiencing the same levels of psychological stressors such as intimacy deficits, loneliness, and depression. To Solaro (2006), this maybe the case but such suffering is not painful enough in male soldiers to motivate them to align themselves with the female soldiers as their consciences and loyalties are torn.

But there is actually a third view about women as offered by one of the pilot interviewees in this book. When women in the military are not classified as "whores," the other default is that they must be "lesbians" if they fail to cooperate to engage in sexual relations with male unit members (Firestone and Harris 2008). According to Herbert (1998), the military ensures that there is the separation of the sexes to avoid any sexual relationships and thus adultery or fraternization. The same mechanism was used to avoid any sexual relationships by preventing the recruitment of either lesbians or gay men into the military. The belief was that while preventing sexual relationships among heterosexuals, it must also go without saying that such liaisons between homosexual men and women must be prevented as well. Further, the military successfully advanced the argument that such privileges should be denied to homosexuals that are not offered to heterosexuals. Solaro (2006) offers a poignant example to elucidate the fallacy of this myth.

In 2003, *Time* magazine graced the American soldier as its Person of the Year. Army soldiers Romesh Ratnesar and Michael Weisskopf were the Tomb Raiders from the Third Field Artillery Regiment, First Armored Division, while Army Specialist Billie Grimes, a woman, was attached to the Tomb Raiders from another unit. While embedded, Weisskopf's hand was blown off when a grenade was hurled into his Humvee by an Iraqi assailant. Without hesitation, Specialist Grimes rushed from her Humvee to treat the wounded soldier. Solaro (2006) recounts that given this myth, nowhere did Grimes's presence bring about disaster. Moreover, according to the folklore, Grimes should have been raped or the men should have fought it out to see who would be the luckier of the two to eventually engage in sex with her. And, given the nature of her job, that is, in combat, Grimes should have been incapable of carrying out her duties under such circumstances since she should not have been either physically or emotionally strong enough to endure this undue pressure. Nevertheless, in the heat of it all, the men were not supposed to have exercised sound judgment by leaving their post to protect her. No such incident took place. Solaro (2006) points out that while it was commendable that Grimes, along with the men, were recognized for bravery, the media largely missed a window of opportunity to highlight the significance of the event. In effect, no one noticed that Grimes is a female. Especially during Operation Desert Storm (and the same sentiments most likely applied during Operations Enduring Freedom and Iraqi Freedom), there was the notion that enemy soldiers, particularly Arabs, would never yield as prisoners to a woman (Holm 1992). But what really occurred debunked this myth.

The Iraqi soldiers surrendered willingly, in this case during Operation Desert Storm, and did not appear to discriminate between the soldiers, just as long as they were American. In one testy exchange when an Iraqi soldier insulted a female military police officer by calling her a "bitch," she simply roared back "Prisoner!" (Eskind 1991, p. M2). This response more than settled the score in terms of who was in charge of whom. Sergeant Connie Ross Spinks, who subsequently received the Purple Heart for wounds sustained when a suicide bomber rammed into her vehicle, was with the Army Reserve assigned to the 426th Civil Affairs Battalion (Scott 2006), when she was deployed during Operation Iraqi Freedom, she was surprised to find the Iraqis to be respectable of her as a woman and African American given what she had learned about how Iraqi men disrespected their women. But, pleasantly she found her experience to be contrary. More importantly, she said that as a U.S. soldier, she found the Iraqi men with whom she worked and interacted to be respectful. This is not to say, however, that there were no such problems. Prior to her arrival in Iraq, a female soldier on guard duty was raped resulting in the institution of a battle buddy system to prevent such further attacks (Monahan and Neidel-Greenlee 2010). The premise of this myth is that women and men cannot work together because sex inherently occurs as a consequence of their interaction (Holm 1992) and in so doing may compromise the mission and by extension military readiness. For while fraternization occurred in mixed-gender units during Operation Desert Storm, there was little evidence that these relationships adversely impacted the mission (Holm 1992). A survey of personnel in those units who served in Operation Desert Storm also confirmed these findings (Francke 1997; Moskos 1993). While the survey yielded findings of sexual relationships within and among members in these units, there was little to no discernible impact on morale or readiness. Another survey, however, proved these results inconclusive. Mixed-gender unit personnel engaged in sexual relations that were found to negatively impact unit morale (Moskos 1993). Studies on the Nicaraguan Sandinista guerrilla army, for instance, show that women and men worked so well together that soldiers who were wounded and taken to the hospital would deliberately slip back into their units to fight with comrades (Randal 1981; Randal and Yanz 1995).

A final myth held about women in the military is that the American public has neither the tolerance nor the will to stand for women being taken as POWs or returning home in body bags (Holm 1992). Female or male, the American psyche is reputed to have little tolerance for both, and more so as it applies to women. But the public's memory is short (Fenner 2001). This is an appeal to the most basic and instinctive of arguments where women are perceived as victims. In particular and most emotional of all is the thought of seeing military women being returned from combat in body bags. Supposedly, the argument goes that military men would be so overcome by this sight that they would compromise military readiness and therefore the mission. A similar argument is advanced for female POWs. Yet, the evidence provided is to the contrary. During WWII, the enemy was known to send women into combat to infiltrate the enemy (Fenner 2001). Throughout the period of the Tet Offensive in Vietnam, women were forced to fend for themselves as male soldiers sought cover (Breuer 1997; Fenner 2001; Saywell 1985). It is then ironic that women's experiences during Operation Desert Storm and most certainly during Operations Enduring Freedom and Iraqi Freedom have still not debunked this myth even though during previous wars there was no such public outcry. Actually, the American public reacted no more terribly about the reality of women POWs and casualties (Fenner 2001; Francke 1997; Holm 1992; Monahan and Neidel-Greenlee 2010; Solaro 2006).

An interesting finding during the Air Force's survival, escape, resistance, and evasion (SERE) training contrary to what was hypothesized that male aviators would instinctively turn to the rescue of female aviators shot down over enemy territory was not borne out (Fenner 2001; Francke 1997). The training revealed what military women already knew was that if military male POWs surrendered because their female comrades were beaten, the female comrades would be further brutalized. And, most illuminating was that the men in the training were no more likely to retaliate when the enemy was a predator on their female comrades than they were when males were ill-treated. It is believed that this hysteria is to be attributed to the U.S. Congress, the U.S. military, the U.S. media, and historians (appropriate use of this term given the lopsided chronicle of events) combined (Monahan and Neidel-Greenlee 2010). Its constant repetition along with a record of misinformation in books has caused this myth to not only persist but to spiral out of control. Notwithstanding the myths as proposed by Holm (1992), other myths about women in the military abound, hence, the rationale for excluding them from combat. Many such arguments were employed to keep African Americans from being integrated into the American military holding that the military was not an institution for social experiments (Fenner 2001). Women's integration into the military has been similarly plagued as a social experiment or for the purpose of the feminist agenda (Fenner 2001; Francke 1997; Holm 1992; Solaro 2006).

Another myth is that the military brings women in by lowering its standards (Fenner 2001). Even the women recruits during WWII were found to be more educated than their male counterparts partly because the military's recruiting criteria for women were far more stringent than for men (Holm 1992). A 1977 DoD study entitled Women and the Military indicated that 90% of female recruits between 1971 and 1976 possessed a high school diploma compared to 63% of the male recruits (Francke 1997). Women recruits were found to score an average of 10 points higher than male recruits on entrance examinations. The retention rate for women was also higher and seemed to have correlated with having a higher level of education than men in the military (Francke 1997). Seventy percent of the women who entered the military in 1973 were still in the military in 1976 compared to 64% of men who entered the military during the same period. Women in the 1979 and 1980 cohorts scored higher on the Air Force Officer Qualifying Test (AFOQT) for entrance to the Air Force Officer Training School (Fenner 2001). As a result, the military accessed the most intelligent women into its ranks. And, because there was a cap on women's recruitment in the military, moving from 2.5% (until 1967) to approximately 20% today, the military has never had to access women who scored in the lowest intelligence category (Category IV) (Fenner 2001). In 1978, a DoD report admitted that its female recruits were far brighter than its male recruits (Francke 1997). It stated that "the trade-off in today's recruiting market is between a high quality female and a low quality male. The average woman available to be recruited is smaller, weighs less and is physically weaker than the vast majority of male recruits. She is also much brighter, better educated, scores much higher on the aptitude tests and is much less likely to become a disciplinary problem" (see Francke 1997, p. 16).

The Army has traditionally moved to access men from the lowest intelligence category when it was in jeopardy of meeting its recruiting goals yet failed to access more intelligent women (Holm 1992). In fact, the Army instituted a little known practice of bringing onboard within its enlisted ranks approximately 5%–10% of its recruits without a high school diploma (Harris 2003). This is known as the "dumbing down effect" but following the September 11, 2001, attacks, to meet its recruiting goals, the Army began to progressively lower its recruiting standards (Inkeep and Bowman 2008; Kaplan 2008). These decisions no doubt resulted in many regrettable and some criminal incidences that occurred during Operation Iraqi Freedom. One of the most gruesome involved Army PFC Steven Green whose troubled childhood at home and school, including three arrests, should have immediately set off multiple alarm bells had even adequate attention been given to the caliber of person who was being recruited into the military (Monahan and Neidel-Greenlee 2010). Moreover, given Green's questionable background, a war zone like that of Iraq became the ultimate venue for his mischiefs. To spare the reader of the details of this heinous crime that was committed, I will only say that Green coopted with three other soldiers—Sergeant Paul Cortez, Specialist James Barker, and PFC Jesse Spielman—while two others, Sergeant Anthony Yribe and PFC Bryan Howard, served as the lookouts. After identifying and staking out a house for the purpose of carrying out this crime, Green and his cohorts not only repeatedly raped a 14-year-old Iraqi girl but they killed the girl, her sister, and parents, doused the house in kerosene, and set the house on fire with the deceased bodies inside, all with the intent of concealing the evidence. The soldiers disposed of any clothing or weapons that would have implicated them in the crime (Monahan and Neidel-Greenlee 2010). It was only a crisis of conscience by one member of the same unit, PFC Justin Watts, who knew of the incident and who after mentioning it to his counselor, did this crime come to light. But by that time, PFC Green had already been honorably discharged from the Army in 2006 but with a diagnosis for combat stress of a personality disorder (Finer and Partlow 2006). While not absolving the soldiers for committing this atrocity, Monahan and Neidel-Greenlee (2010) hold the military and specifically DoD and the Army, as a failure in leadership in that "It is that military hierarchy that sets the tone for all military situations and environments" (p. 404). Thus, as long as leadership continues to turn a blind eye and by doing so directly and/or indirectly condones these acts, these and similar behaviors as those committed by PFC Green and his cohorts are likely to continue and to the detriment of the military, its reputation, and perhaps even to national security by providing the enemy just cause for retaliation.

Another myth about women in the military that has been needlessly perpetuated is regarding the issue of parenthood and where the media functioned as the primary conduit for this propaganda. Apparently, not only were "Mommies going to war" (Fenner 2001; Francke 1997; Holm 1992) but the military was becoming a repository for unmarried mothers (Fenner 2001). Admittedly, Operation Desert Storm revealed for the first time some of the family and parental challenges never before experienced as the consequence of a major military deployment (Fenner 2001; Francke 1997; Holm 1992). Yet, in many ways, it was the military that fostered this culture and environment (Francke 1997). Longer deployments required more technically trained personnel. This phenomenon inevitably corresponded with military personnel's child-producing years. Unlike the conscription years of the Vietnam era that required two-year enlistments, the all-volunteer military called for two-year, four-year, and six-year enlistments. As a result, the average age of the military force increased to reflect this stability. By Operation Desert Storm, the average age of recruits was 26.7 years as opposed to those conscripted during the Vietnam conflict at an average of 19 years (Francke 1997). In addition, more than half of the enlisted corps were married. But as far as the military was concerned, having an overwhelmingly married workforce was to its advantage. This situation lent itself to a more stable workforce prone to less disciplinary problems and drug and alcohol abuse.

Also, a stable and married workforce increased the likelihood of re-enlistments (Francke 1997). This state of affairs promoted the establishment of family-oriented programs that in turn cultivated this culture. Such benefits as housing, medical, dental, and the like for families during the post–Vietnam conflict became attractive for young families. Single parents were drawn to these benefits as well. Ironically, single fathers were particularly attracted to these benefits and during Operation Desert Storm, perhaps attributable to their proportion of the total military force, single parents were disproportionately men (Francke 1997). Nevertheless, but inexplicably so, it was the single mothers, not the single fathers, who appeared to prove the more challenging for the military. The Navy established a policy that forbade new recruits from retaining custody for their children. Violators were "discharged for fraudulent enlistment" (Francke 1997, p. 140). But, reportedly, a 1992 survey of the Navy uncovered that in all such enlistments, the children were residing with their parents (Thomas and Thomas 1992). Single female parents became the pariahs for every so-called indiscretion committed in the military, from pregnancy to lost time on the job given the perception by Navy detailers that these women would be more burdensome than productive when they deployed. In doing so though, the detailers spent an inordinate amount of time locating positions for the dual military couple while ostracizing the single mothers (Thomas and Thomas 1992). As a result, single mothers were to be avoided at all costs. Even when highly trained, these women were instead consigned to performing menial tasks (Francke 1997). As one single military mother noted, "This guy in my unit takes time off to take his kid to the doctor and everyone says 'Oh, isn't he wonderful?' I take my kid to the doctor and my supervisor marks it down as time lost off the job" (Francke 1997, p. 140).

Whereas single fathers were more likely to have multiple children resulting in higher costs to the military, it was the single mothers who bore the blame (Francke 1997). Neither the Navy nor Army chiefs and commanders wanted them in their units. This prejudice against single mothers resulted in an unintended consequence for them as well. According to one Army Reserve commander, "They're not just weekend soldiers. They need the money and they really want to be there and make it work" (Francke 1997, p. 141). But, as stated, Operation Desert Storm exposed the extent to which this war, at least as perceived by the media, was about mothers going to war. This was not the problem for single mothers but one of personnel management (Holm 1992). It represented a distortion of the truth to the American public while giving way to the implication that single mothers were incapable of managing their family and military careers simultaneously. Ironically, the problem was never attributed to single fathers. More poignantly, it simply suggested that women in the military with children were unable to have a family while pursuing their careers. Holm (1992) categorically refuted that this was simply not the case. As she saw it, having children, and by extension a family, was an outgrowth of the all-volunteer force. But columnists like Fred Reed saw it differently. He asserted that the military had become a home "for unwed mothers" (Reed 1999). At the time, the Pentagon reported that of the 67,000 single parents, two-thirds of them were men (Holm 1992). Still, Reed (1999) alleged that most of the single parents in the military were women. But while the number of dual military parents deployed during Operation Desert Storm was unprecedented and heightened for the first time the exigency and therefore the need for more family support programs, the recruitment impact on deployment was unsubstantiated (Francke 1997). Essentially, of the 23,000 single parents and 5,700 couples with children who were deployed during that period, less than 5% were not deployed for reasons not having to do with the family (Sagawa and Duff Campbell 1992).

For all the pomp and circumstance over the years surrounding the combat exclusion policy and the rationale provided for women's continuing exclusion from combat, although the wheels of progress have been painstakingly slow, the irrefutable evidence and an ourstory of exemplary performance have erred on the side of military women all along. Watchdog groups like DACOWITS have consistently held DoD and the military's feet to the fire. In its most recent report of 2012, the Committee cited that one of its overriding concern as the military draws down its forces from Operations Enduring Freedom and Iraqi Freedom (now Operation New Dawn) is the retention of "highly qualified" women (Executive Summary). This was prompted as a result of the Military Leadership Diversity Commission's (MLDC) finding in 2011 that unlike men, and especially in light of the drawdown posture, military women were more likely to voluntarily separate and not make a career of the military. Consequently, DACOWITS (2012) made the following recommendations. First, the military must continue to develop strategies that ensure the retention of "highly qualified men and women." Even more important was that, in the process, the military should not lose sight of retaining both diversity and talent: the hallmarks of a strong force. Second, the military must remove the combat exclusion policy that bars women from combat and any corresponding rules that restrict such assignments to women. As well, all career fields, schools, training, and assignments that were previously closed to women should be opened. To accompany this removal, the military should develop "gender-neutral physical standards" as one of many modalities to integrate women into formerly closed combat positions. Finally, because military readiness and thus performance are at issue, women as a group should not be excluded from combat assignments. Such assignments should be based on individual performance and in accordance with the requirements of each position.

The MLDC (2011) was commissioned by Congress as a product of the NDAA of 2009 to examine military policies with regard to the promotion and advancement of certain groups in the military, namely, women and racial and/or ethnic minorities. With specific regard to women, the MLDC concluded that women are underrepresented in senior leadership in the military. And according to the Commission, this still stark disparity in leadership when compared to the demographic composition of the force who are led at present and for the foreseeable future, the military must take immediate steps to mitigate the problem before it becomes more acute. Because the findings that result in this persistent gap includes that women and racial and/or ethnic minority officer accessions are low, women and racial and/or ethnic minorities are underrepresented in the career fields that would increase their likely advancement to the general officer ranks. The rates for these groups are also low at the mid-career level in both the commissioned and enlisted corps along with equally low promotion rates. In light of these data, the MLDC was moved to conclude that the DoD and the military must repeal the combat exclusion policy as one of many strategies for creating equity among military personnel by removing the barriers and inconsistencies that prevent women from certain assignments. Selection for assignments should be based on qualifications, not gender. The recommendations by DACOWITS (2012); the MLDC (2011); the legal challenges afoot, including those that brought about the repeal of the Don't Ask, Don't Tell, and Don't Pursue policy; and even the ensuing and rampant sexual assault in the military have all independently and together provided the crucial weight to finally topple the last archaic remnant of a gone bar era; that is, the combat exclusion policy, which has far outlived its initial purpose.

Chapter 5

The Enemy Within: Sex Crimes and the Evils of Asymmetry

To address the plight of women in the military with regard to the combat exclusion policy cannot be accomplished in a vacuum without delving into the sexually related challenges that have reached epidemic proportions in the military. As perceived by those whose writings have indelibly reflected their animus toward women in the military, such as the likes of Mitchell (1989, 1997) and van Creveld (2000, 2001), to name a few, and even ourstorian Charles Moskos (if he were alive today, he most certainly would have taken issue with this denotation), the military represents the last bastion, the sacred grove, or haven, if you will, in which white men can be communal and without the seeming interference of women, unless they are to be served by them, of course. And, if these men are to relinquish this exclusivity in the boys' club, it will not be without a fight, for to put it bluntly, the military has long treated its women more like a married man does his mistress (Solaro 2006). The mistress remains somewhat of a secret. But, even if acknowledged, unlike his wife, the mistress has no rights unless legally compelled and enforced by the courts. This scenario depicts the frequent and conveniently deployed collective amnesia by the military and its civilian leaders, for that matter, following a major call to arms about the performance of women in the military. The mistress, who is being used here as a proxy for women in the military, is only employed at will or when situations call for her talents. Otherwise, once the imminent danger has passed, there is no more need for her services until the next call to arms or another emergency.

And, during peacetime, particularly should the married man divorce, the mistress presents her arguments once again for now that he is single and therefore free to marry her, she is yet again told that he, the lover, will reexamine the issue when he already knows full well that his mistress is justly overdue her recognition and publicly so as his partner. But, when the mistress again mounts even more compelling evidence of her performance, as another delay tactic, the now single man resorts to conducting a study of the matter or that he will further ruminate about it. Goldin (2006) describes how these jobs, in this case, those reserved as combat, have become gendered through pollution theory. I will use the same argument to explain the attitudes that were advanced once upon a time against African Americans to thwart their integration into the military that have been similarly unleashed against women in the military. For women, pollution theory encompasses the asymmetry that must be maintained between men and women in the workplace. Goldin effectively employs the occupation of firefighters and how it is statistically determined to exclude women when they attempt to enter the profession. Men perceive women's entrance into their domain as a threat to the prestige of the profession and will do all that they can to keep women out, thus retaining the profession as all-male, exclusive, and prestigious.

In many ways, the sexual assault epidemic of especially women in the military speaks persuasively and is symbolic of the reasons why they have been so treated, particularly with regard to combat. For 2012, the Pentagon's annual report on sexual assault shows an alarming rise in such cases, up 6% from fiscal year (FY) 2011 to 3,374 or from 19,000 previously to 26,000 during FY 2012 (Department of Defense [DoD] Sexual Assault and Prevention Response Office [SAPRO], FY 2012). It is important to note that these data represent only the reported cases. These rates of occurrence have so outraged lawmakers in Congress that there is an unprecedented level of unanimity in the call for an overhaul of the Uniform Code of Military Justice (UCMJ) system that gives commanders wide discretion in the manner in which such cases are adjudicated, including the need for prosecution (Cassata 2013). One only needs to watch the documentary film *The Invisible War* (2012) or listen to National Public Radio's (NPR's) recent coverage about the struggles of the survivors of sexual assault in the military (Lawrence and Penaloza 2013a) to begin to fathom and scratch the surface about the severe price that women must pay for being in the military. More reprehensible is that the enemy no longer only resides on the battlefield. The tragedy is that the enemy also resides within the ranks of the military and with and against whom women in the military are simultaneously forced to fight.

According to retired Air Force Brigadier General Wilma Vaught in *The Invisible War*, who is also one of the 17 women portrayed in this book, "When does this end?" She added that a female soldier stood a greater chance of being raped by a fellow soldier than being killed by the enemy. Still more alarming is the degree to which such cases, if any, are prosecuted. And, even more appalling is that even when these cases are justifiably reported by victims, the culture of the military is such that commanders either turn a blind eye or in effect slaps the perpetrator on the wrist for committing these crimes (Lawrence and Penaloza 2013b; Montagne and Lawrence 2013). As have been recently demonstrated, where such crimes have been rarely and successfully prosecuted, many commanders choose to ignore their own legal counsel by overturning the convictions.

The rate of sexual assault and related crimes committed by those in the senior ranks and/or the level of indifference is so entrenched that the women who become victims constructively discharge given the overwhelming hostility, they short-circuit their careers by leaving the military. According to Senator Kirsten Gillibrand (D-NY), who is also a member of the Senate Armed Services Committee, "There's a shift in the debate, that we need real reform and accountability. The recent cases have demonstrated just how severe the problem is" (Whitlock 2013d). Representative Howard "Buck" McKeon (R-CA), Chairman of the House Armed Services Committee (HASC), echoed his disgust with the situation and that essentially his confidence in the military to control these crimes has been "deeply shaken" (Whitlock 2013e). But more than the severity of prevalence of sex crimes in the military, what makes lawmakers in Congress so troubled is that many of these acts are being committed by the guardians of redress for the victims of these crimes. In one instance, a senior field grade officer, Air Force Lieutenant Colonel Jeffrey Krusinski, who oversees the Air Force's sexual assault and prevention program at the Pentagon, was charged and arrested with sexual battery after groping a civilian woman in an Arlington, Virginia, parking lot while intoxicated (Editorial Board, *The Washington Post* 2012). In another incident, a soldier at Fort Hood, Texas, who is the equal opportunity adviser and Sexual Harassment/Assault Response and Prevention Coordinator, is being investigated for sexual assault and specifically for "pandering, abusive sexual conduct, assault and maltreatment of subordinates" (Skinkman 2013). The soldier's name has been withheld pending an investigation.

Air Force Chief of Staff General Mark Welsh's testimony at a recent Senate hearing about the prevalence of sexual assault, appeared to reveal more about the senior leadership's attitude about the malady than it did to allay Senators' concerns about the military's efforts to control the prevalence of sexual assault as well as to provide a system of redress for victims. In effect, General Welsh indicted the "Lookup" culture among young people as the primary cause for such problems (Clift 2013). Additionally, the nomination of Lieutenant General Susan Helms as Vice Commander of the Air Force Space Command was delayed in the Senate amid concerns about using the UCMJ that gives commanders broad authority to overturn military jury convictions and alter sentences for perpetrators (Editorial Board, *The Washington Post* 2012). While these are only few of many such incidents, altogether, it appears that a system that was designed to punish perpetrators and protect victims has only managed to protect the perpetrators by revictimizing the victims. A study of 558 female veterans who served in the military between the Vietnam era but before Operations Enduring Freedom and Iraqi Freedom unmasked the devastating and long-term psychological, physical, and health effects of sexual assault from rape, physical assault, and dual victimization identified as both rape and physical assault while in the military (Sadler et al. 2000). On average, the women in the study entered the military at age 18 and separated with 11.5 years of service. Described as a "sequence of violence" (Sadler et al. 2000, p. 477), the authors point to the implications for military women as a public health concern. Almost half (48%) of the sample experienced violence while in the military, which included rape (30%) or dual victimization (16%). Those who were either raped or physically assaulted continued to experience significant low quality of life in terms of their health, including limited physical and emotional health. Those who were dually victimized experienced the poorest health status, including severe physical and emotional limitations in health as well as problems in attempts to attain financial and educational stability, and recurring problems with work and social interests. At least 5% of those who were raped had been gang raped. Over half (58%) had been raped at least twice while those who had been physically assaulted had been assaulted at least twice. The authors of the study note the need to conduct routine health assessment ourstories for evidence of sexual violence.

Solaro (2006) views sexual assault as "corrosive" (p. 317) in mixed-gender units in that there are men who not only prey on women but there are men in these units, for the sake of brotherhood, who refuse to part with the perpetrators failing to see that the many who are injured are their sisters-in-arms. But what is more insidious is the military's reluctance to punish the perpetrators and protect the victims. In 2003, a survey by the Veterans Administration (VA) showed that women who had become vulnerable to sexual harassment stood a four times more likely chance of being raped than women who had never had such experiences (Solaro 2006). Yet, in mixed-gender units where sexual harassment did not occur, there was no such risk to women. It is not surprising then that units located overseas, that is, in Republic of Korea, where there is human trafficking and sexual violence, experienced higher rates of sexual violence than those units that are based within the United States. After all, units are only a subset of the larger civilian culture. However, as Solaro (2006) sees it, the problems of rape are not taken seriously in the military, even when men in the units know that that these individuals are predators yet fail to confront them about their misdeeds. Solaro blames that sexual assault is not limited to the military but is a problem for society at large in its failure to pursue perpetrators and hold them accountable. It is also paradoxical that while it is the victim who is brave enough to report the incident, she is the one who suffers from her actions since others knowingly conspire to protect the predator by covering up the incident. This, says Solaro (2006), is most damaging to unit cohesion.

During the Total Force Subcommittee of the HASC in June 2004, known as Sexual Assault Prevention and Response in the Armed Forces, former Assistant Secretary of the Air Force for Manpower and Reserve Affairs, Michael Dominguez, testified by citing Dr. David Lisak, a renowned expert on rape, that "sexual violence on that scale can only exist in a culture that facilitates it" (Solaro 2006, p. 320). Essentially, he said, that the country has provided an environment where such behavior against women is allowed to thrive. Yet, John McHugh (R-NY), Chairman of this committee, having chided the then Undersecretary of Defense for Personnel and Readiness that despite the 18 studies about sexual assault in the military during the past 15 years, the military had done little, if anything, in the way of instituting programs for the purpose of prosecution, prevention, and response. Again, this was almost 10 years before the recent reported rates of sexual assault in the military had reached such pandemic levels (Solaro 2006). Further, McHugh continued that while he was considerate of Chu, "we are at a crisis point here. I happen to believe we are at a juncture ... I think we are in real danger of losing the faith and trust of the female contingent in the United States military" (Solaro 2006, p. 320). Representative Vic Snyder (D-AK) was more pointed in his criticism of the military after advising both Chu and William Nava, the Assistant Secretary of the Navy for Manpower and Reserve Affairs of the findings of a 2003 survey that military women, at the rate of 4%, had either experienced sexual assault or abuse (Solaro 2006). Therefore, these rates were not an anomaly as Navas was suggesting, said Representative Snyder,

> If you took a four-year career and add that up, at the end of the career, it would be a significant number. So, you can fool yourself a little by coming up with an over-twelve-month number when those are additive. I mean, the same four percent in 2003 is very likely not going to be the same four percent in 2004 or 2005 or 2006 (Solaro 2006, p. 321).

At the hearing, another administration official, but this time, the only female, Frances Murphy, Undersecretary for Health Policy Coordination for the Veterans Health Administration in the Department of Veterans Affairs, said in her testimony that for military sexual trauma/assault (MST), or veterans who experienced sexual assault while in the military, only about 20% of the women and 1% of the men reported to the VA as ever having had this experience (Solaro 2006). Besides, it was unlikely that any of these assaults were ever reported to a law enforcement agency. What should have given the military cause for pause, however, but apparently did not, was when Murphy testified as to the low number of veterans who failed to register a response about MST following the administration of a VA survey to approximately one million veterans from the Vietnam era forward to determine the rate at which MST occurred in the military. Approximately 3,000 women and 34,000 men declined to respond to that question. According to Murphy, "They did not say no. They just would not answer. And I think that this is very telling" (Solaro 2006, p. 322).

The fallout from sexual misconduct began to rear its ugly head as more women have been integrated into the military. According to a 1997 Air Force report, through 1988, no adultery charges had been brought against any Air Force women but that 16 had been brought against Air Force men (Murnane 2007). But by 1996, that number had increased to 67 cases of adultery with one including both men and women. Murnane (2007) believes that it is the increasing integration of women in the military that introduced sexuality as a challenge for the military. More importantly, though, it is the glaring manner in how the military has responded to the challenge, given similar violations of a sexual nature by both men and women in the military. The April 1980 publication by *Playboy* magazine of seven scantily clothed uniformed women from all branches of the military, including the Coast Guard, created a furor of reactions, but there was a uniformed response by each branch of the military that the women should be involuntarily separated (Stiehm 1989). Yet, the military men who also posed nude for the same magazine were not similarly punished. Only one male Marine officer was given a letter of reprimand but was not discharged. The more recent case of a female service member, Air Force training instructor, Staff Sergeant Michelle Manhart, led to an investigation and her actual discharge for posing nude in *Playboy* magazine (Murnane 2007). Against this decision reinforced the nature of the response by the military when its female and male service members commit such acts of indiscretion.

In 1986, Lieutenant Colonel David Shober, then a manager at the Officers' Club at Wright-Patterson Air Force Base (AFB), Ohio, was charged with engaging in sexual intercourse with a subordinate and taking nude photographs of her (*United States v. Shober* 1986). The U.S. Court of Military Appeals upheld the decision of the Air Force Court of Military Review holding that

> not every deviation from high standard of conduct expected of an officer constitutes conduct unbecoming an officer. The nude photographs were taken with the consent of the subject and were given to her upon her request. There is no indication that while the appellant had the photographs he used them for an illicit purpose ... Under the language of this allegation, any officer who has an interest in photography had best limit the subject matter to still-life, landscapes and fully-clothed models. (Murnane 2007, p. 1080)

However, while Lieutenant Colonel Shober was not involuntarily discharged from the military, he was found guilty of both offenses but the sentence was modified to be less severe in the form of a letter of reprimand plus the forfeiture of $1500 per month for a period of one year along with the forfeiture of all pay and allowances and returned to active duty. Then the Fifth Air Force Chief of Staff stationed at Yakota Air Base, Japan, in December 1989, and after repeated warnings by superiors to cease and desist in his adulterous affairs with subordinate enlisted members, Colonel Cisler, a decorated fighter pilot from the Vietnam era, was charged with twice violating the orders of his superior officer and for adultery with a female enlisted service member who was an air traffic controller (*United States v. Cisler* 1991). He was sentenced to two years in prison with the forfeiture of $2,000 per month of his pay for the same period of incarceration plus a fine of $10,000. The subsequent prosecution of an Air Force Captain (Hebert) while on deployment during Operations Desert Shield/Storm underscored the tacit environment of adultery and public display of such acts and without retribution on the part of its participants. Hebert was charged with engaging in sexual behavior with two enlisted women and in the presence of one of his lover's roommates (*United States v. Hebert* 1993). Hebert, on appeal, mounted in his defense that this type of behavior was the norm during such deployments. Further, he was imprisoned for three years for this activity while his female conspirators only received letters of reprimand. But, it was the Tailhook Convention scandal that took center stage and brought the problem of these illicit sexual activities and the degradation of military women to light.

The Tailhook Association was a privately held organization comprising active duty, reserve, and retired members of the Navy and Marine Corps aviators (Murnane 2007). During this particular convention in Las Vegas that was attended by the Secretary of the Navy, the Chief of Naval Operations (CNO), including 29 admirals from active duty, two Marine Corps generals, three admirals from the Navy Reserve, other retired flag officers, and defense contractors (Murnane 2007), a reported sea of drunken aviators engaged in a three-day activity of subjecting fellow female aviators to a gauntlet whenever they were forced to walk through the corridors to their respective rooms in the hotel (Kempster 1993). Approximately 200 aviators descended into this activity where the corridors wreaked of alcohol, urine, and vomit and groped at the breasts, buttocks, and legs of approximately 83 fellow female officers, many of whom forcibly lost their clothing in the process. According to DoD's Inspector General (IG), this type of behavior was not the typical fraternity style behavior but depicted those of public indecency and assault (Kempster 1993). Many such acts included streaking through the corridors of the hotel, mooning others by exposing their buttocks, "ballwalking" where officers exposed their testicles, butt biting, belly or navel shots where both men and women drank alcohol from each other's navels, and the shaving of pubic hair in which some women participated. Adding to this backdrop was the number of strippers and prostitutes present to peddle their wares in an environment filled with pornographic videos and liquor. Yet, what was most deplorable, according to the DoD IG report was

> that similar behavior had occurred at previous conventions. The emerging pattern of some of the activities such as the gauntlet, began to assume the aura of a tradition. There is even some evidence to suggest that Tailhook '91 [1991] was tame in comparison to earlier conventions... In fact, many of the younger officers who attended the Tailhook '91 convention felt the excesses that occurred were condoned by the Navy (Kempster 1993).

Despite the despicable nature of the raucous event that brought ill repute to the Navy and Marine Corps and ultimately to the military and perhaps which more so served as a warning for both potential female and male recruits, even the damning indictment by the DoD IG report did not move the Navy to punish any of the offenders (Murnane 2007). A Naval Criminal Investigative Service (NCIS) official, Thomas Powers, was in disbelief that officers sworn to protect and defend the country's Constitution would uniformly lie under oath to ensure that those who engaged in these criminal acts were not implicated (Vistica 1995). Powers said that "It's as if they take an oath to the Navy and not to the nation." In 1993 (*United States v. McCreary* 1995) and again in 2012 (Whitlock 2012), Air Force instructors found themselves mired in sexual assault scandals. In 1993, an Air Force instructor was charged with five violations, namely, sodomy, indecent assault, issuing a threat, dereliction of duty, and disregarding a regulation that involved his conduct with female trainees assigned to his unit (*United States v. McCreary* 1995). In rendering its decision about the instructor's behavior, the Air Force Court of Criminal Appeals stated that the Sergeant's position was unique as he had power over the trainees where such acts and specifically sodomy would be deemed as forcible in nature. The Sergeant received a dishonorable discharge and reduction in rank from E-4 to E-1.

More recently, approximately 12 Air Force instructors at Lackland AFB in Texas are being investigated for assault, harassment, and engaging in sexual behavior with female recruits (Whitlock 2012). The Air Force Commander of the Air Education and Training Command (AETC), General Edward Rice, cited aggressive efforts on the Command's part to get to the bottom of the problem. Evidently, it is suspected that such activities may be more widespread within the Command and may involve multiple units. Approximately 25% of instructors in the 331st Training Squadron were either already charged with or are under investigation for sexual assault. One such trainer was charged with rape and sexually assaulting approximately 10 recruits. In 1996, the Army was rocked by a sexual misconduct scandal of its own, resulting in the conviction of Sergeant Major Gene McKinney who was charged with harassing at least six women for sex (Whitlock 2012). Then McKinney, with 29 years of service, was the Army's highest ranking enlisted member. Ironically, while McKinney was charged with multiple acts of sexual impropriety, including adultery and threats, it was the tape recording of the pressure for sex by one of the women where she had only requested information about career development that helped to bring about his conviction. McKinney was reduced in rank to E-8 and saved face by being allowed to retire.

An email generated by an Air Force cadet in 2003 about the level of sexual assault within the Air Force Academy's chain of command resulted in an investigation of the institution over a 10-year period given at least 57 sexual assault allegations brought by cadets (Murnane 2007). Reportedly, the Board of Visitors had known about the problems yet failed to investigate these allegations (Murnane 2007). The commander of the 12th Air Force, Lieutenant General Thomas Griffith, was relieved of duty after 28 years of service for an affair with a civilian woman (Murnane 2007). He was reduced to the rank of Major General and allowed to retire honorably. Air Force Lieutenant Colonel Shelly "Scotty" Rogers, commander of the 90th (F-15) Fighter Squadron, who was selected for promotion to the rank of Colonel, suffered a $2789 forfeiture of his pay for four months and was reprimanded for this indiscretion.

The Navy was particularly sensitized by the Tailhook Convention scandal. In the wake of unearthing evidence of sexual misconduct by three of its senior officers who had been advanced for consideration to flag rank, the Navy removed all three Captains from such consideration and prosecuted them separately commensurate with the offense committed (Schutt 1995). Captain Everett Green, the Navy's top officer for equal opportunity, was subsequently court-martialed for the sexual harassment of two female aides (Schutt 1995). The second officer, Captain Mark Rogers, was assigned to the White House but who upon investigation was found to have repeatedly used vulgar and debasing language at work even though his coworkers complained about it (Schutt 1995). The third Naval officer, Captain Thomas Flanagan, who was the commander of a submarine unit, was accused of pursuing a relationship with a subordinate officer, a female lieutenant.

Charges of sexual assault, including rape, was brought by female enlistees at two of the Army's training facilities: Aberdeen Proving Ground in Maryland and Fort Lee in Virginia (Murnane 2007). Staff Sergeant Delmar Simpson and other instructors from Aberdeen Proving Ground were convicted of such crimes while Staff Sergeant Jeffrey Ayers, Sr., was convicted of similar offenses (*United States v. Simpson* 2003). Other convictions were made at Fort Leonard Wood in Mississippi. Staff Sergeant Andrea Reeves, an Air Force training instructor, was convicted in 2001 of maintaining sexual relations with four trainees (*United States v. Reeves* 2005). As egregious was that she violated five counts of a regulation by advising one of the trainees to secure an attorney, but not to cooperate with the investigation. Reeves was demoted from E-5 to E-1, dishonorably discharged, sentenced to incarceration for six years which was reduced to three years, and forfeited all pay and allowances. Lieutenant Kelly Flynn, an Air Force Academy graduate and the first woman pilot to qualify to fly the B-52 bomber, was charged with engaging in an adulterous affair with a married man, lying, and insubordination by failure to obey the orders of her commander. According to Murnane (2007), this incident ignited a debate, at least in the public, that women and men are held to different standards when it comes to sexual misconduct in the military. Though such charges in the past were subject to court-martial, Congress recommended that Lieutenant Flynn be administratively discharged from the military which Sheila Widnall, the first female Secretary of the Air Force, endorsed allowing Flynn to evade court-martial (Murnane 2007). In 1997, both the Navy and Army relieved general officers from duty due to sexual misconduct. Rear Admiral R.M. Mitchell, Jr., of the Navy Supply Systems Command in Mechanicsburg, Pennsylvania, was relieved of duty for making unwelcomed sexual advances to a military subordinate (Kim 1997; Priest and Spinner 1997), and Brigadier General Stephen Xenakis of the Army's Medical Operations in the Southeastern region of the United States was relieved of duty given allegations that he committed adultery with the civilian nurse who was taking care of his ill wife (Priest and Spinner 1997).

In 1997, another female and graduate of the Air Force Academy, Lieutenant Christa Davis, was found guilty of engaging in adultery with one of her instructors, a married Air Force officer (Murnane 2007). Because of the heightened scrutiny and publicity surrounding the Flynn case, however, Davis's sentence was reduced to nonjudicial punishment where she was fined $2000, a letter of reprimand, forced to reimburse the cost of her Air Force Academy tuition, and discharged from the

Air Force (Murnane 2007). The Army's Aberdeen Proving Ground became the subject of another high-profile investigation for sexual misconduct, this time at the highest level of the command. Major General Longhouser, who was the commander of Aberdeen Proving Ground, was allowed to retire with a demotion in rank to Brigadier General, following a tip from an anonymous call to a hotline that was established after female trainees lodged complaints of rape by their drill sergeants (Murnane 2007). The general was accused of having an affair before 1992. Also, in 1997, General Joseph Ralston, Vice Chief of Staff in the Office of the Joint Chiefs of Staff, was accused of committing adultery some 13 years before his appointment to the post (Becker and Hennenberger 1999). In spite of this revelation, General Ralston was allowed to not only remain in the military but was assigned as the Supreme Commander of the NATO forces in Europe. He withdrew his name as a candidate for the Chairman, Joint Chiefs of Staff in 1997 but was quick to point out that the country perceived that he was similarly situated as the Lieutenant Flynn case in that there was suspicion of a double standard since he, a man, was not involuntarily discharged from the military. Even many in the military criticized the decision not to relieve General Ralston of his duty as well as to discharge him because only two years earlier, General Ralston, who was Lieutenant General Griffith's superior, forced Lieutenant General Griffith to retire for committing adultery with a civilian (Shenon 1997).

Ironically, prior to General Ralston's appointment as the NATO Supreme Commander, Major General David Hale, a NATO Commander in the Army, was convicted of having affairs with the spouses of four of his subordinates (Murnane 2007). The General's sentence included forfeiture of $12,000 of his retirement pay for a period of one year and a fine of $10,000. But, this marked a reduced sentence that had previously included serving an 11-year prison term (Cruz 1999). Other courts-martial include the conviction of an Air Force pilot for fraternization, conspiracy, and obstruction of justice (Murnane 2007) and the discharge and conviction of 15 days in prison of Captain Joseph Bell, a tanker pilot, for an adulterous relationship with a junior enlisted female (Howard 1999). In 2005, Major General Thomas Fiscus, another Air Force Academy graduate and then the Air Force's Judge Advocate General (JAG), was reduced to the rank of Colonel and retired for conduct unbecoming an officer, fraternization, obstruction of justice, and involvement in inappropriate relationships with three women which included other JAG officers, enlisted service members, and civilian personnel (Murnane 2007). This move was unprecedented marking the first time that the JAG had been charged with such misconduct, including sexual misconduct spanning a 10-year period (Ricks 2004). To be fair, though, the level of sexual misconduct, especially against active duty women, has become so rampant that listing other such cases would be daunting, although one of the most famous and recent cases, not in the form of a legal challenge, involved General David Petraeus, a highly decorated Army veteran and then Director of the Central Intelligence Agency (CIA), who resigned in late 2012 after admitting to an adulterous affair with his biographer Paula Broadwell, who was also married and with children (Shear 2012). But since his fall from grace, General Petraeus, now a private citizen, has apologized for this fatal lapse in judgment (McDonough 2013).

According to the 2012 Workplace and Gender Relations Survey of Active Duty Members who experienced some level of unwanted or unwelcomed sexual conduct, three overriding reasons prevented them from not reporting these incidents (DoD SAPRO Report, FY 2012). Of the respondents, 70% did not want anyone to know, 66% said that they did not feel comfortable making such claims while 51% were suspicious that their claims would remain confidential. Of the few active duty men who stated that they had such experiences, 22% were of the belief that making such disclosures would result in retaliation against them, 17% said that no one would find their claims as credible, and 16% believed that reporting would prove detrimental to their careers. Thus, DoD acknowledges that underreporting of sexual misconduct remains a problem in providing victims with the necessary assistance while holding offenders accountable. Other unsettling findings by DoD revealed that active duty women are at an increased risk of experiencing intimate partner violence and sexual violence when they deploy than active duty women with lower deployment levels. And, in the wake of the unparalleled attention and commensurate increase in reported sexual misconduct, "sexual assault remains a persistent problem in the military" (DoD SAPRO Report, FY 2012, p. 16). Further, while "current efforts to improve the Department's investigative and prosecutorial capabilities are important, … another acknowledgment is that they are not enough to solve the problem" (pp. 16 and 17). The active duty women who were most recently surveyed signaled their lack of confidence in the UCMJ system to prosecute offenders, despite the rhetoric from the military's leadership. At least 50% of the active duty personnel sampled believed that even when sexual assault is reported, nothing would be done about it, whereas 43% of the personnel vicariously learned from the reporting of these negative experiences by others not to report it given the backlash (DoD SAPRO Report, FY 2012).

The DoD also acknowledges the challenges in upholding the confidentiality of reported information by the victims of sexual assault (DoD SAPRO Report, FY 2012). Even more sinister is that many such violations are committed by first responders. Still, to Goldstein (2013), the issue is not that the most recent DoD report showed an increase in sexual assault for the past three years consecutively or that the FY 2012 report showed that, of the women who reported these offenses, "62 percent suffered retaliation for speaking up." In fact, it is not that those charged as the guardians of the victims of sexual assault were themselves implicated for committing sexual assault. What Goldstein (2013) finds most incriminating is that in spite of the prevalence of sexual assault for the past two decades, the military has allowed these crimes to persist.

Three independently filed lawsuits have emphasized a military culture mired in its tacit acceptance of sexual misconduct. In *Cicoca v. Rumsfeld et al.* (2013), the litigants Kori Cioca and 27 other current and former service members filed a lawsuit in federal court against the then Secretary Donald Rumsfeld in December 2011 (Goldstein 2013). The case was dismissed, citing similar cases that ruled that the civilian courts should not become involved in military discipline (Kime 2011). However, U.S. District Court Judge Liam O'Grady, found the allegations of sexual assault against the military to be "troubling." The second lawsuit, *Marquet and Kendzior v. Gates et al.* (2012), was filed on behalf of two military academy cadets, who both alleged that they were raped by fellow classmates at the U.S. Military Academy at West Point and the U.S. Naval Academy at Annapolis (Katz 2012).

The final lawsuit, *Klay and Hellmer v. Panetta et al.* (2013), was filed on behalf of eight women (one active duty enlisted Marine and seven others who served in the Navy and Marine Corps) (Tucker 2012). The lawsuit alleges rape and attempted sexual assault and accused the military of having a "High Tolerance for Sexual Predators in Its Ranks" (Tucker 2012). In at least two of the aforementioned lawsuits against DoD (*Klay and Hellmer*), the military was alleged to have retaliated against the victims for reporting the crimes with Klay attempting suicide. In an even more condemning assessment of the military's wave of sexual assault, Nancy Parrish (2012), President of Protect Our Defenders, went as far as saying that "The Pentagon Is Camouflaging the Truth about Rape in the Military" (Parrish 2012). Parrish asserted that, despite the Pentagon's efforts to spin the data, given the optimistic report that the level of reporting of sexual assaults has increased and correspondingly the number of courts-martial, she said, was designed to "confuse" and "misinform" as to the actual facts when in effect what has actually occurred is that the number of charges have declined and consequently so have the number of courts-martial and convictions. But as Murnane (2007) proclaims, even when charges of sexual misconduct are upheld, the level of un-evenhandedness or double standard that is not only applied across the board for men and women but certain leaders dismiss similarly situated men while successfully mounting an affirmative defense for their own actions.

Case in point. General Ralston forced his subordinate, Lieutenant General Griffith, to retire even as he committed the same indiscretion (Murnane 2007). Moreover, almost uniformly high-profile cases involving women were junior in rank and who were discharged from the military. Almost always, the men who committed such crimes were senior in rank but whose cases were disposed of as non-judicial punishment. It then begs the question, says Murnane (2007), how the military can explain to its public that the UCMJ is being fairly and impartially applied. Murnane fails to see, for instance, how a female posing partially nude for a magazine is a dischargeable offense yet a senior field grade officer who engaged in a sexual relationship with a subordinate employee, then took photographs of her in the nude, escaped discharge from the military because the relationship between the two, despite the power difference, was consensual and he returned the photographs that he took of her. What is also inexplicable is that men at a military convention who subjected their fellow women officers to lewd behaviors, including groping and the like, suffered no adverse actions. The DoD IG, Admiral George

Davis, believed that it was tantamount to going on a witch hunt to locate the culprits (Solaro 2006). After all, the Navy had condoned this behavior in the past. And, the Commander of NCIS, Rear Admiral Duval Williams, Jr., concurred with Admiral Davis by saying that in essence that "men simply did not want women in the military" (Solaro 2006, p. 173). Barbara Pope, the then Assistant Secretary of the Navy for Manpower and Reserve Affairs, was so incensed that she got into a vociferous argument with him whereby he, Davis, referred to women naval aviators as "topless dancers, go-go dancers or prostitutes" (Solaro 2006, p. 173). As part of the investigation, Davis chose not to question any of the Admirals about Tailhook and why they had tolerated such activity. Instead, he ensured that he maintained close oversight of the investigation to control its outcome as one could only but speculate (Solaro 2006). When discussing one of the aviator's behaviors with a female NCIS agent and her language, Davis's ignorance and narrow-mindedness became even more apparent when he stated that "Any woman that would use the F-word on a regular basis would welcome this type of activity" (Solaro 2006, p. 173).

This is not to say, however, that once the incidents surrounding Tailhook came to light, especially via the media, that failure to take action, particularly by flag officers, did not end some otherwise promising careers. Lieutenant Paula Coughlin, Rear Admiral Jack Snyder's aide, who was featured on CBS' *60 Minutes*, described her ordeal. For example, Rear Admiral Synder failed to consider her complaints credible that she was groped (Solaro 2006). He was relieved of duty. Rear Admiral Wilson, whose attitude was such that he believed if a woman used expletives to describe how she was being mistreated, then that implied that she actually condoned such treatment, was retired. Admiral Frank Kelso, CNO, involuntarily retired. Vice Admiral Richard Dunleavy, former Chief of Naval Aviation, and Rear Admiral Riley Mixen, Director of the Air Warfare Division in the CNO's office, were reprimanded (Zimmerman 1995). Allegedly, the NCIS investigators were obstructed at every turn in the process, although no one was imprisoned, and in exchange for immunity, a Lieutenant Gregory Geiss implicated his colleagues (Solaro 2006). Of the 140 officers who were being investigated for participation, over 50% of the files were removed. Forty-three officers received nonjudicial punishment in the forms of fines, letters of reprimand, and letters of counseling. Six officers were court-martialed but the charges that were made against the only officer who was tried were dropped. And, claiming ignorance, the conscience of another officer, Robert Stumpf, Commander of the Navy's Blue Angels at the time of Tailhook, came back to haunt him following his promotion to Captain. His promotion was delayed because some senators voiced their concerns about his behavior at the 1991 convention.

But Rear Admiral Davis's need to control the outcome of the investigation of the activities during the Tailhook convention together with the nouns that he used to describe his own female naval and Marine aviators is not that particularly far removed from how women are viewed by many in the military. It is a culture borne of norms and rules (Hunter 2007). And, one medium employed to indoctrinate the newly recruited to those norms is via boot camp at a time when recruits are the most developmentally vulnerable (Harris 2009). This is an intense acculturation process that is designed, at least for those within the enlisted corps, to "break them down, so we can build them up our way" according to a Marine Colonel (Briggs 1997). Fundamentally, the military sheds any recruit of her or his civilian culture and requires that recruit assume a new identity, that is, the military culture. Hence, the issue of new clothing and the cutting of the hair and "send his possessions home, and tell him he doesn't know a damn thing, that he's the sorriest thing you've ever seen, but with my help" ... continued the Colonel, "... you're going to be worthwhile again" (Vistica 1995, p. 151). Yet, with that culture and indoctrination comes the use of degrading language, all for the purpose of instilling the warrior spirit in each recruit. However, this process of degradation comes at the expense of another segment and still a minority of the military's population—women. As part of the socialization process, certain effeminate terms are routinely hurled as insults to motivate the recruit, such as "girlie" (Snyder 2003, p. 192). Drill instructors regularly invoke such phrases as "You wuss, you baby, you goddam female" (Francke 1997, p. 155) to instill this warrior spirit. To Harris (2009), for any recruit, female or male, to write home about such taunts of humiliation through the use of slurs about women, who as per the most recent census, constitutes 50.9% of the country's general civilian population (U.S. Census 2010), would be disheartening to any parent and the American public. This practice would seem more than anything to breed hostility among men against women, render women as inferior to men in the military, and acculturate women to believe and act in kind as inferior beings to their male peers. It should then come as no revelation that women as a group in the military are treated with such blatant disregard given the open level of animus toward them which has permeated the American culture in such slights as "You run like a girl."

Hunter (2007) describes military slangs as laced with raunchy sexual smears throughout, all intended to objectify one's target. For instance, the start of each academic year at the U.S. Military Academy at West Point is officially designated as "reorganization week," yet the term is more endearingly referred to as "re-orgy" (Hunter 2007, p. 17). And, in the mess hall, following the completion of cutting and serving desserts in an immaculate manner, it is customary for the dessert corporal to shout "Sir, the dessert has been raped and I did it!" (Janda 2002, pp. 88 and 92). Likewise, certain cadence calls are infused with both sex and violence (Hunter 2007). In essence, sexual assault has never been about sex (Hunter 2007). The act has been about violence meant to inflict pain, terror, and dishonor. Such words as "faggot" and "cunt" may be used to vilify a particular target for abuse (Hunter 2007, p. 20). Cadets at the U.S. Military Academy do not perceive their female peers as normal women like mothers, sisters, and girlfriends who are worthy of respect. To address fellow cadets through the use of such language is to deliberately dishonor them. Rape not only becomes an instrument of war but should the victor hold fast to the same untoward views about the enemy following the war, the sexual assault of those citizens will likely occur (Hunter 2007). When speaking about the rape that was committed during the Vietnam conflict, squad leader John Smail said "That's an everyday affair. You can nail about everybody on that—at least once. The guys are human, man" (Hersh 1970, p. 185). But "It would be comforting to believe that sexual assaults occur during the heat of battle when emotions run high, but Americans commit 66 percent more sexual assault when serving as an occupational army than as a combat force" (Brownmiller 1975).

Copelon (1994) explains that sexual assault and thus rape allows troops to ventilate emotions. It is ultimately an act of power. Copeland goes on to expound that during the Vietnam conflict, after the members of the 11th Brigade had gang raped and killed a woman, they would leave the brigade's patch in between the victim's legs. This symbolic act following this brutal crime acknowledges the level of loyalty to each member of the brigade and to each other. And, undeniably, sexual assault, and specifically rape, is most prone to occur during war (Hunter 2007). Another factor that makes especially rape most likely during war in the military is the social class in the form of rank that the military attaches to its members (Hunter 2007). This "social distancing makes it more likely that sexual assault will occur" (Hunter 2007, p. 21). Moral distancing, or the belief that one is religiously superior to other groups, hence warrants acts of sexual abuse against women and the reference of homosexuals as "ungodly" (Hunter 2007, p.21). The confluence of culture and social and moral distancing may itself emerge as a potential rationale for justifying sexual abuse (Hunter 2007).

What came to be known as Rape of the Nanking, Japanese soldiers committed wholesale acts of rape against women, 65% of whom were raped at least once, and many of whom were gang raped, and where the women were left to die of the injuries that they sustained (Brownmiller 1975; Hunter 2007). Men were also castrated and anally raped (Chang 1997). When asked why they devolved into performing such vicious acts against the Chinese, the Japanese soldiers said that they considered the people to be inferior to them (cultural difference) (Hunter 2007). Only Chinese civilians with resources had the means to flee the city leaving the poor to fend for themselves (social distance). And, the Japanese soldiers felt the moral authority (moral distance) on behalf of the Emperor to scourge the earth of the enemy through violence, so they "could do no wrong" (Hunter 2007, p. 22). According to Hunter (2007) though, frequently military personnel who have and have not served in combat are able to psychologically compartmentalize how to treat certain comrades even when they feel animus toward certain groups. So, to disrespect women in some regard while still regarding other women as one of the guys who are entitled to respect or holding the belief that homosexuality is wrong yet accept others of the same sexual orientation as "Sure he's gay, but he's not like regular faggots, he's all right" (Hunter 2007, p. 22) is counterintuitive.

Hunter (2007) invoked the Stanley Milgram experiments and the profound ways in which the teachers, who became participants as a result of a newspaper advertisement and who had nothing to gain from the experiments, were essentially used as pawns to administer shock to learners who had not complied with verbal instructions from the teachers. And, yet, what is surprising is that these teachers willingly complied to administer the shocks when they were instructed to do so by a perceived authority figure, the researcher. Hunter views the Milgram experiments as parallel to the military's culture in that someone is more responsive to authority to inflict pain to others despite the desperate pleas of victims when these shocks were administered. Lieutenant Colonel Grossman summed it up well by saying that "if this kind of obedience could be obtained without a lab coat and a clipboard by an authority figure who had been known for only a few minutes, how much more would the trappings of military authority and months of bonding accomplish?" (Grossman 1995, p. 143). This same logic was employed to explain the behaviors of Army soldiers at Abu Ghraib prison during Operation Iraqi Freedom. Sergeant Javal Davis alleged that he was told by intelligence officers to "rough" up prisoners or "to loosen them up" for interrogation (Hunter 2007, p. 25). Davis admitted to Army investigators that morally he was concerned about some of the things that he was asked to perform by Army intelligence, yet he rationalized that "Yes, I could have said no to anything. But that would have been disobeying an order. So either you can get in trouble for not doing what you're told or get in trouble for doing what you're told" (Hunter 2007, p. 25). Sergeant Davis was charged with dereliction of duty in failing to protect detainees from abuse, mistreatment of those detainees, making false statements, assault, and conspiracy to mistreat detainees.

What became the Abu Ghraib prison scandal culminated from four separate reports from Amnesty International about the abuse of detainees—in July 2003, the 800th Military Police Brigade, commanded by Brigadier General Janis Karpinski, of the overcrowded 7000 detainees that was purportedly understaffed by 90 poorly trained military personnel; two reports issued by the Red Cross in October and November 2003, respectively, citing abuses at Abu Ghraib; the CIA IG's investigation of the suspicious death of two Iraqi prisoners at Abu Ghraib; and the Army's Central Command's own investigation of prisoner abuse that began in January 2004 (Monahan and Neidel-Greenlee 2010). Major General Antonio Taguba became the point man for the investigation, but who later found himself and his report about the Abu Ghraib abuses, as subjects of another investigation. While it was a compact disk (CD) to the Army Criminal Investigation Division (CID) of the photographs about the military women who were involved in the abuse that later prompted instructions for General Taguba's investigation, it was the content of the CD that was most startling. The photographs highlighted a parody of sexual enslavement of the prison detainees by military personnel in the forms of coercing the prisoners to expose themselves to the prison staff; naked male prisoners were being mocked by female military personnel as they looked at their genitals; prisoners were forced to perform lewd acts on one another; military personnel were seen attacking the detainees by hitting and/or pulling them with a lead that was part of collars or choke chains affixed around their necks; detainees wore hoods with wires to dispense electric shock; male detainees were being threatened with military police dogs; while others were forced to don women's undergarments on their heads (Monahan and Neidel-Greenlee 2010). In all, there were approximately 100 photographs and a videotape that documented the abuses at Abu Ghraib prison.

However, General Taguba became suspicious. He was convinced that given the military hierarchical culture of top–down command, no military personnel, especially those within the enlisted corps, would have voluntarily carried out such deviant acts unless ordered to do so by officers, contractors, and government officials (Monahan and Neidel-Greenlee 2010). General Taguba believed what military veterans know the world over—enlisted personnel do not take the initiative to start new programs, let alone to run a cell block into X-rated reality television programs where offenders take snapshots and videos of their unlawful and immoral actions (Monahan and Neidel-Greenlee 2010) but that these enlisted personnel had been deceived by superiors to break national and international laws (Monahan and Neidel-Greenlee 2010). General Taguba was also of the belief that military personnel at Abu Ghraib prison were manipulated by intelligence personnel to do their bidding in preparing detainees for interrogation (Monahan and Neidel-Greenlee 2010). Following the submission of his report and amid an investigation about himself, no doubt due to the report that he submitted, but more importantly, because the report went public, General Taguba had plans on returning to an assignment with the Third Army (Monahan and Neidel-Greenlee 2010). He was reportedly placed at the Pentagon instead, according to a retired four-star General who confided in Taguba that the purpose of this assignment was to monitor his actions.

According to Hunter (2007), military personnel suffer from what he calls a double bind when it comes to following orders that they might find to be objectionable. On one hand, if they obey an order from a superior that is later deemed as illegal, they are held accountable and must suffer the consequences. But, on the other hand, disobeying the orders of a superior, if later found to be justified, may be grounds for court-martial or insubordination. The issues and fallout of these issues stemming from Abu Ghraib are only a few of many such examples. The gruesome rampage and murder of the Iraqi girl and her parents and siblings by the Army's Private First Class (PFC) Steven Green and his cohorts, together with the findings of General Taguba's investigation, are all evidence, according to Monahan and Neidel-Greenlee (2010), and were the most lamentable signs of the lapse in military leadership. Not unlike the raucous acts of sexual misconduct by aviators at the Tailhook Convention, such behaviors could not have been carried out without the tacit approval or at least knowledge of military leadership, for after all, it is those in the military hierarchy who create the tenor and environment that condone these transgressions (Monahan and Neidel-Greenlee 2010). By the same token, though, Lieutenant General Ricardo Sanchez described the battlefield during Operations Enduring Freedom and Iraqi Freedom in Afghanistan, Iraq, and Kuwait as environments of "360-degree combat zone" infused with such inordinate levels of stress as to perpetuate the sexual assault of female soldiers by their male peers (Sanchez and Phillips 2008). But repeated deployments to these regions only heightened an already stressed force borne of posttraumatic stress disorder (PTSD). As one Army officer, Orlinda Marquez, who served during the 1980s, said, both the level and indifference about the sexual assault of female soldiers by those within its own ranks was not news (Bowser 2004).

In the Public Broadcasting System (PBS) program *The Newshour* entitled "Rape in the Ranks," Ms. Marquez illustrated a story about one female soldier who reported sexual assault. The soldier was vilified and left to her own devices given the command's response. The command said "Your peers begin to turn against you. Your command turns its back on you. This business that we take care of [our] 'own,' once you're the victim, you're no longer 'their own' that they take care of. They persecute the victim while they protect the offender." (Bowser 2004). This story by Orlinda Marquez and others share a common but despicable theme about the military—the victims of sexual assault are overwhelmingly women and whom male soldiers view less as peers but as a means of sexual gratification (Monahan and Neidel-Greenlee 2010). More deplorable is that such acts are carried out against the woman's will through violence and rape. Now, place these same soldiers—women and men—in a hostile environment where conditions of war create to echo what Lieutenant General Sanchez calls a 360-degree combat zone. The female soldiers in this environment were not only fighting the known enemy coupled with the associated risks and other adversities for which they were not protected because of the combat exclusion policy, but were also forced to contend with sexual assault with the enemy within their own ranks—their comrades in arms who are men. Monahan and Neidel-Greenlee (2010) describe this confluence of events as a "no rule zone" (p. 406) where a male soldier was privy to take whatever was necessary to ensure that he remained in pristine condition for combat. And, by inference, female soldiers became the vehicle for this end.

What is even more insidious is that the military did not have a policy on sexual assault until 2005 despite calls for its development as early as 1992 (McHugh 2004). The women then in Congress were urging the military to adopt policies that not only would punish the perpetrators of sexual assault but would provide a means of redress for the victims. At the time, Representative Carolyn Maloney (D-NY) invoked the 18 studies that had been conducted during the past 16 years about the prevalence of sexual assault in the military yet the rate of sexual assault against women in the military has been unrelenting (McHugh 2004). Given this level of apathy on the part of the military, the rate of sexual harassment has increased exponentially and the plight of military women continue to be compromised even as many women were forced to contrive strategies to their own peril, all for the purpose of protecting themselves from the enemy within, their fellow soldiers. And, as the number of sexual assaults in the military has increased, so did the rates of suicides associated with sexual assault, notably rape (Monahan and Neidel-Greenlee 2010). For instance, in 2004, 17,000 cases of sexual assaults were reported by military women (Monahan and Neidel-Greenlee 2010).

Of this total, 329 men were charged with sexual assault. Monahan and Neidel-Greenlee (2010) pronounced this as a tepid attempt by DoD in the place of numbers of sexual assault, rape, and sexual harassment, cases against military women by military men to quell the rate at which such incidents occurred. Moreover, in the wake of Operations Enduring Freedom and Iraqi Freedom, along with troops in Kuwait, sexual assault was becoming "commonplace" (Monahan and Neidel-Greenlee 2010, p. 406). And, the rates had grown to such untenable levels that DoD was forced to act. In response, DoD issued the Task Force Report on Care for Victims of Sexual Assault Overview Briefing in May 2004. The report issued the following:

Findings (Broadly Characterized)

- DoD policies and standards need to focus on sexual assault.
- Services' stovepipe policies need to be integrated for effective prevention and response.
- Commanders need guidance, resources, and emphasis on prevention and response.
- Victim response capabilities need more resources and uniform guidance.
- Efforts to hold offenders accountable need to be made more transparent.

Recommendations

- Establish a single point of accountability for addressing sexual assault matters.
- Discuss leadership responsibilities at May Combatant Commanders Conference.
- Fill gaps in sexual assault information through DoD-wide communication outlets.
- Convene a summit to develop strategic courses of action on critical, unresolved issues.
- Develop DoD policies for prevention, reporting, response, and accountability.
- Establish an Armed Forces Sexual Assault Advisory Council.
- Provide manpower and fiscal resources to implement required policies and standards.
- Develop an integrated strategy for sexual assault data collection.
- Establish program evaluation, quality improvement, and oversight mechanisms (Task Force Report on Care for Victims of Sexual Assault, Overview Briefing, May 13, 2004, as cited by Monahan and Neidel-Greenlee 2010, pp. 406 and 407).

But, as Monahan and Neidel-Greenlee (2010) bemoaned, even in light of the Task Force report's findings and recommendations, the lackluster response of DoD was characteristic of its response about providing body armor to troops in Iraq.

Nevertheless, four years later, or in 2008, nothing had been done to take action on the task force's recommendations in light of its findings (Monahan and Neidel-Greenlee 2010). In many ways, as to make a mockery of the situation not unlike previous attempts to deny women of their equality in the military by invoking the combat exclusion policy as well as the countless numbers of studies as a delay tactic of their recognition and thus for full inclusion in all career fields in the military, DoD appointed this time a civilian task force of 15 to address the epidemic of sexual assault in the military. It was discovered that apparently neither the military nor its civilian leadership were serious about addressing the blight of sexual assault against women in the military. In effect, both factions had conspired that by not doing anything, the problem would miraculously disappear. A cover-up was disclosed to just do nothing, notwithstanding the subpoena from the U.S. House of Representatives' Subcommittee on National Security and Foreign Affairs to combat the problem of sexual assault. The principal Deputy Undersecretary of Defense, Michael Dominguez, directed Dr. Kaye Whitley, Chief of SAPRO, to not to comply to the order nor to discuss the reasons that after the findings and recommendations of the 2004 task force that not even its first meeting had yet been held. But, as former military officers, Monahan and Neidel-Greenlee (2010) know all too well that the culture of the military is so ingrained that if the military's goal was to hold its commanding officers accountable and to rid its ranks of the scourge of sexual assault, it would have readily and quickly done so through courts-martial. Books like *Generally Speaking* (Lieutenant General Claudia Kennedy) and *Women in the Military: An Unfinished Revolution* (Major General Jeanne Holm) as well as various interviews and conversations by Monahan and Neidel-Greenlee (2010) with Chaplain Major Priscilla Mondt, Colonel Carolyn Carroll, and Captain John Miller and other data serve as evidence (Monahan and Neidel-Greenlee 2010). But, this was not the case.

The prevalence of reported cases of sexual assault in the military skyrocketed to 2371 (Pupovac 2005). But perhaps as a strategy to affect the reported data and correspondingly to decrease the actual number of sexual assaults, again, on those incidents that were reported, DoD moved the parameters of reporting these data from calendar year to fiscal year in 2005. The 2006 reported incidents of sexual assault showed a 24% spike over the previous year and an astonishing 73% over the reported ones in 2004. And, of the 2668 cases of sexual assault that were reported in 2007, 60% of them were the result of rape. As early as 2004, Murdoch et al. (2004) in discerning the prevalence of sexual assault among combat and noncombat veterans both in-service and post-service and who were seeking disability benefits for PTSD from the VA, of the 3337 veterans sampled, 69% of the women were classified as combat veterans and 86.6% of noncombat veterans experienced sexual assault.

The researchers found these numbers to be higher than the cases reported for sexual assault within the general civilian population.

To obviate the likelihood of falling prey to rape, especially in the combat zones of Afghanistan, Iraq, and Kuwait, many female soldiers unwittingly took matters into their own hands by employing tactics to protect themselves, some dying in the process. As part of the battle dress uniform (BDU), soldiers wore protective armor in the often 115-degree temperatures (Monahan and Neidel-Greenlee 2010). However, because female soldiers faced sexual assault, rape, and worse yet, murder, many withheld drinking fluids after 3:00 p.m. each day to avoid going to the latrines in the evenings (Cohn 2006). In January 2006, in a testimony to the Commission of Inquiry for Crimes against Humanity, the deaths of at least three female soldiers were attributed to dehydration (Cohn 2006). Worse yet, Colonel Jania Karpinski implicated the Army as covering up the individual causes of death. According to the testimony

> Under orders from [Lieutenant General Ricardo S] Sanchez, he [Major General Walter Wojdakowski, Sanchez's top deputy in Iraq], directed that the cause be no longer listed on the death certificates or other documents that were likely to be seen by the media and the public. For all intents and purposes, women were needlessly dying because the U.S. Army did nothing substantive to lower the risks of sexual assault and rape. Here, we have three deaths of military women, and still there have been no orders to prevent future crimes in these categories were taken. This was just one more crime compounded by a cover-up in an environment of hostility and misogyny. (Cohn 2006)

In one of the many interviews conducted by Monahan and Neidel-Greenlee (2010), Captain John Miller, a retired Navy pilot, said, "If the military wanted to fix the problem, it would already be fixed. It's leadership … leadership can change it [sexual assault] … It's all about what a CO will put up with, and what he will not tolerate … As you know, a CO has a tremendous amount of discretion" (Monahan and Neidel-Greenlee 2010, pp. 409 and 410). The following cases then provide blatant examples of a conspiracy by the U.S. Army to conceal evidence, mislead as to the truth about the evidence, and/or lie to obfuscate evidence leading to the death of three female soldiers who, it was later found, were all raped (Monahan and Neidel-Greenlee 2010).

In the first case in July 2005, the deceased body of PFC LaVena Johnson was found in Bagdad, Iraq (Monahan and Neidel-Greenlee 2010). The death was labeled a suicide after purportedly the soldier's body showed signs of self-inflicted wounds from an M-16 rifle (Wright 2008). From the outset, once PFC Johnson's body was returned to her parents Dr. John and Mrs. Linda Johnson, they became suspicious as to the actual cause of death of their daughter. After examining his daughter's body, Dr. Johnson became even more convinced that her wounds were inconsistent with the Army's proclamation that she had committed suicide. Besides, the frequent conversations that the Johnsons had with their daughter during her time in Iraq, there was no indication of depression much less to the point of committing suicide. As a matter of fact, by all indications, PFC Johnson was happy and well-adjusted. Her commanding officer, Captain David Woods, supported her alleged state of mind while she was stationed in Iraq as "in good health, both physically and emotionally" (Monahan and Neidel-Greenlee 2010, p. 410). Stonewalling by the U.S. Army to provide information led the Johnsons to request information via the Freedom of Information Act as to the actual cause of their daughter's death. It is worth noting that it took two and a half years for the Army to finally relent by providing the requested materials to the Johnsons but not without the assistance and prodding of the Congressional office.

The evidence uncovered that contrary to the Army's findings and disposition, PFC Johnson did not die of wounds sustained from self-inflicted injuries. PFC Johnson was raped and then murdered (Monahan and Neidel-Greenlee 2010). The M16 found across her body, the bruising on her face and body, and uniform white gloves that were glued to her hands were all attempts by the assailants to cover up the crime (Wright 2008). The photographs showed that it appeared that following the attack, the M16 was used to strike a blow to her face and given the dirt found on her back, her body was dragged from one location to another suggesting that she was taken from another contractor's tent into the contractor's tent where her body was finally found. PFC Johnson's body had bruises, teeth marks, burns, and scratches. More diabolical was that a corrosive fluid had been poured over her genitals, again, to conceal the evidence that she had been raped (Wright 2008). Yet, when found, PFC Johnson was fully clothed. Her body was dragged to the tent and then set on fire. PFC Johnson's death was labeled a "homicide" which, and without additional explanation, was changed to "non-combat wound—self-inflicted suicide" (Wright 2008). And, in spite of repeated calls for the Army to reopen and reinvestigate the case, it refused on condition that it rendered its original disposition of the case as "complete and fully thorough" (Wright 2008).

In the second case, PFC Tina Priest of the Fifth Support Battalion, First Brigade Combat Team within the Fourth Infantry Division, at Fort Hood, Texas, was raped and then murdered by a fellow soldier in February 2006 at Camp Taji, Iraq (Monahan and Neidel-Greenlee 2010). Again, like PFC Johnson's death, not only was an M16 rifle found on her body but her death was also ruled self-inflicted and therefore a suicide. Mrs. Priest, PFC Priest's mother, challenged the Army's findings, for as she stated, that even following the rape, in speaking with her daughter, she was nowhere suicidal. And, even after the sperm from PFC Priest's body implicated a fellow soldier as the rapist, these charges were dropped (Wright 2008). Instead, the soldier received what amounted to a slap on the wrist for insubordination in that he disobeyed an order, forfeiture of $714 for two months, was confined to his military installation for a period of 30 days, and given an additional duty for 45 days. In the third case, PFC Amy Duerksen, also out of Fort Hood,

Texas, was assigned to the Fourth Combat Support Battalion, First Brigade, Fourth Infantry Division (Jones 2006; Wright 2008). PFC Duerksen's death, like the previous two cases, was also ruled a suicide by the Army. And, oddly enough, PFC Duerksen's death only occurred one week following that of PFC Priest's. However, PFC Duerksen's diary chronicled that she had been raped in training when she consumed a drink that contained a date rape drug. Although the individual that PFC Duerksen mentioned in her diary as the rapist was arrested following her death, and despite evidence to the contrary that she could not have committed suicide, once again, the Army refused to investigate the case for the possibility of her death being the result of a homicide (Jones 2006).

But, as warped and devious as the aforesaid acts are, understanding what motivated them is key in identifying the military mind in terms of consent. This act of consent said Archard (1998) comes down to those involved, providing their permission to do something that also takes into consideration the rational interests of others who are not substantially harmed. But giving consent suggests that in doing so one must have the capacity to be informed about what is involved, what are the risks, and must possess all faculties to make an informed decision. As well, capacity may be compounded, for instance, if one is intoxicated. Consent may be given before one becomes intoxicated. However, this may not be the case when the situation involves sex. Hunter (2007) states that there are some individuals who might be more susceptible to sexual assault. For example, those who have been the victims of sexual abuse as adults were more likely to have experienced sexual abuse as children more so than those who have never had such experiences as children. Under such conditions, the trauma may cause the child to become passive or "frozen" (Hunter 2007, p. 26). Unfortunately, as an adult, the response is similar when faced with unwanted sexual advances or assault. Therefore, when consent is coerced where the victim is threatened with violence, this does not constitute valid consent. Threats can be both explicit and implicit in nature. And because men have been socialized to believe that unless a woman is expressly vocal in not giving consent, her silence then means that she is giving consent.

To Hunter (2007), in light of these conditions, then the mere silence of a dead person could be equally rationalized as giving consent (MacKinnon 1982). Consequently, women's socialization, and especially those who have been victims of sexual abuse, tends to comply with this behavior even in the face of sexual assault (Pateman 1988). It is hence safe to assume that if consent for sex by a woman has not been expressly given, then consent for sex has not been given for "the harm to a woman of unconsented sex is much graver than that of the loss to a man who refuses from proceeding to have sex with consent" (Archard 1998, p. 36). Besides, for a woman, "Fear invalidates the consent" (Archard 1998, p. 51). But, given the nature of the military, there is always the expectation that there will be losses—personnel will be maimed, injured, or killed as a consequence of the mission (Hunter 2007). So, collateral damage as victims of sexual assault or those who have been killed is perhaps just part of the course.

The U.S. Supreme Court has repeatedly held that the purpose of the military is such that there must be a subordination of the individual self for the good of the organization (*Orloff v. Willoughby* 1953). This ruling was essentially upheld at the lower federal district court in the case of *Cicoca v. Rumsfeld et al.* (2013) as similar cases of sexual assault have been filed yet were dismissed for not being within the purview of the civilian courts even though in *Cicoca v. Rumsfeld et al.*, the presiding judge found the allegations of sexual assault against the military by the 28 litigants disturbing (Goldstein 2013). However, the litigants had no other recourse but to turn to the civilian courts for redress since DoD and by extension the military had uniformly refused to address the widespread problems in its ranks.

But, what amounts to another form of victimization is that the civilian courts refuse to rule in the matter by choosing to dismiss the lawsuits outright when it is the civilian leadership to which the military must look for its charge. And, paradoxically, the civilian courts have never shied away in the past from inserting themselves when necessary by adjudicating on military matters. It is this very attitude that Hunter (2007) says contributes to the proliferation of sexual assault in the military. By refusing to confront the issue head on and worse yet, suppress it, this ensures that such reports, especially to civilian bodies, will keep the military's unblemished reputation intact. Hunter views the military's treatment of sexual assault as akin to not airing the institution's dirty laundry to particularly outsiders like civilians that the military believes will simply not understand. More insidious though are attempts by the military to keep the family secret even as the victims are forced to absorb the personal, professional, and emotional costs, all for the purpose of continuing to extol the virtues of the institution while a segment of its population suffers. Hunter (2007) again invokes another frequently used ploy to silence the victims of sexual abuse, this time against victims of incest as in "If you tell anyone about what happened, Daddy will go to jail and then everyone in the family will suffer, and it will be your fault" (p. 29). By duping the victim into feeling both guilty and responsible for preserving this well-kept secret, the victim is revictimized to her peril as a way of protecting the perpetrator, an adult, who knowingly committed the crime.

In a sense, the military's apathy toward sexual assault wreaks of the recognition that like war, fairly or unfairly, women become collateral damage. And, in a manner of speaking, this is analogous to viewing women as simply the spoils of war. Army psychologist Lawrence LeShan puts this fatalistic mentality into perspective by delineating a series of steps that move a nation to the brink of war (LeShan 2002). The enemy is first identified after which it is established that the enemy is evil. Given this determination, the sheer presence of the enemy becomes intolerable. So, by eliminating the enemy through a preemptive strike, much will be gained and the world will be a better place. To not concur with these self-evident truths, as the perpetrator sees it, is the sign of a traitor who must then support the enemy. In essence, there is no middle ground. You are either with us or against us. Thus, placed within the context of sexual assault in the military, because the individual must subordinate oneself for the good of the institution, sexual assault then becomes one of the many factors that constitute "the price of doing the business of war" (Hunter 2007, p. 29).

After all, for military men, prostitution and consequently the vilification of women through sexual assault become a reward of sorts for being in the military. Actually, 84% of military men admitted that they had at least one sexual encounter with a prostitute while in the military (Moon 1997). What is counterintuitive though is that the military has always considered prostitution as one of the conduits through which to satisfy the welfare of its men. But sadly, the military has reconciled the implications of prostitution as important to both combat readiness and foreign policy, not as an issue of either moral importance or one that overwhelmingly affects women (Hunter 2007). Some host nations like Republic of Korea, for example, go as far as to publicly exalt the benefits of prostitution to the U.S. military and in turn the economic benefits to the country to the tune of 25% of its gross national product (GNP) (Moon 1997). This unspeakable truth has not only been acknowledged by Republic of Korea's government and its Minister of Education but that the Korean International Tourism Association actively aided and abetted the growth of the industry on behalf of U.S. military service men by training their women to serve as prostitutes.

What is even more appalling though is the accompanying mentality that sex is a man's inherent prerogative and regularly at best (Hunter 2007). But the life of the profession of arms is such that military men, for the most part, are away from their significant others such as wives and girlfriends and for extended periods of time. As such, it is therefore necessary to fulfill this physiological need via prostitution. However, as Meredith Lehr, a military spouse, can attest and has declared, this duty of providing sex to military men is not limited to prostitutes. This function is expected of wives as well. "Model military wives" must remain faithful to their husbands knowing full well that their husbands have been engaging in sexual activity outside of marriage (Lehr 1993, p. 89). This hypermasculine view of men holds that depriving men of a regular dose of sex will increase the likelihood of their involvement in sexual assault (Hunter 2007). This myth concomitantly holds that it will also be important for host nations to then provide the U.S. military with prostitutes to prevent them from harming the more upstanding women of the same populations in the forms of sexual assault and the like. We are reminded to some degree of the cavalier attitude of the U.S. military toward the indiscretions of their own when such crimes are committed.

In 1995, three U.S. military men were convicted of raping a 12-year-old Japanese girl in Okinawa, Japan, in a rental car (Enloe 1996). Admiral Richard Macke, then the Chief of the Pacific Command, quipped that "I think it was absolutely stupid, as I've said several times. For the price they paid to rent a car, they could have had a girl prostitute" (Enloe 1996, p. 15). And, in March 2013, two U.S. Navy service men received 10-year and nine-year sentences, respectively, for raping a Japanese woman in an Okinawa parking lot in late 2012 (Watkatsuki and Shaughnessy 2013).

Sometimes the U.S. military would couch its own defense innocently for not curbing the solicitation of prostitutes by U.S. military men by claiming the desire not to interfere in host nations' internal affairs because such problems existed before the arrival of U.S. military personnel (Hunter 2007). Further, the United States was not in a position to force American values on those of its host countries.

Yet, as Hunter (2007) muses, the U.S. military has intervened on behalf of its own personnel when doing so threatened its own interests. For example, during the 1960s through 1970s, businesses overseas catered to U.S. military men. The business of prostitution, however, limited itself to catering either to a black male or white male clientele. But, this was also during the period of civil rights in the United States and black men stationed in Korea became intolerant of the racist system. Consequently, like their brethren in the United States, black men in the military began demanding equal access to Korean businesses and when these demands were unmet, the U.S. military, specifically the Commanding General of the Second Infantry Division, moved to ban U.S. personnel from patronizing certain parts of the town (Hunter 2007). The ban worked, forcing businesses to capitulate to the U.S. military's demands for business access to both black and white male military personnel. And during Operation Desert Storm, the U.S. military banned U.S. military men from soliciting the services of prostitutes in host nations like Saudi Arabia, vowing that to do so could have an adverse impact on its mission (Butler 2000).

The aforementioned then represents only a few of the multiple examples where the will of the U.S. military was imposed and successfully enforced. But to take this one step further, the U.S. military grew suspicious that sexual relations of its male personnel with English-speaking prostitutes could potentially compromise secret military information by those prostitutes who may well be functioning as spies for their respective countries (Hunter 2007). This became problematic as some U.S. military personnel began legitimizing many prostitutes by marrying them. Moreover, many of these women were foreign born. The U.S. military sought to address this perceived problem by issuing regulations, dubbed "Problems to Be Considered," one of which included "prostitutes," or those who "have engaged in or profited from prostitution" (Hunter 2007, p. 69). Moon (1997) said that many military towns or businesses that develop beyond the outskirts of military installations within the United States and overseas comprise tattoo shops, bars, and massage shops, all for the purpose of providing comfort for U.S. military men. Overseas, these conveniently geographically located towns help military personnel forgo having to learn about host countries by going beyond the conveniences of the towns to such a degree that military personnel are under the misnomer that such countries are "populated solely with poor, thieving people, groveling for U.S. soldiers, and lacking in national culture and pride" (Moon 1997, p. 118). And, incidentally and principally so in the Pacific Rim, as late as 1997, the U.S. Army published its attempts to stem the tide of the use of even child prostitutes by U.S. military personnel (Hunter 2007) citing threats to the national interests of the United States, protection of the soldiers, as well as welfare of the children themselves (Hunter 2007). Unfortunately, many of these child prostitutes were the offspring of prostitutes who became pregnant and were abandoned by American military men. The Philippines is just one of the many examples where a reported 30,000 children have ties to U.S. military men (Enloe 1989). Approximately one-third of these children who are homeless roam the streets as prostitutes, beggars, and thieves. And, there have also been an innumerable number of abortions that have been performed on many pregnant prostitutes. But even more despicable is the warped mentality that is associated with prostitution that "Man should be trained as a warrior and woman as recreation for the warrior" (Seifert 1994, p. 64). Suffice it to say, where men only interact with women as prostitutes, it then becomes the foundation for sexual assault (Hunter 2007). And, where men secure sex from those who are socioeconomically disadvantaged, they learn to do so with impunity for they are immune from punishment. Likewise, when military men perceive military women as merely "sex machines" or for the sole purpose of self-gratification, they are prone to hold military women in the same regard. No doubt, this attitude displayed through behavior sets them up for the sexual assault of military women.

So what are the conditions that render organizations like the military ripe for sexual assault? Says O'Hare and O'Donohoe (1998), there must be a confluence of circumstances that facilitate its occurrence. The perpetrator is induced in some way to become involved in sexual assault and the perpetrator is then overcome by any internal reticence in his unit to follow through with such acts. Finally, the perpetrator follows through and receives little to no commensurate resistance as the act is being carried out against the victim. Nevertheless, and more importantly, the extent to which sexual assault occurs is contingent upon the degree to which it is perceived that the organization's leadership will condone its behavior. Units where commanders do not take such issues lightly and are proactive in ensuring that unit personnel clearly understand such policies and where any violation is vigorously enforced are likely to never experience any type of sexual assault given the culture of intolerance in the command (Hunter 2007). In this case, the occurrence of sexual assault is widely perceived as a problem for the unit. Conversely, units where sexual assault is tacitly tolerated, where the "Get over it. Learn to deal with it" or where the issue only becomes a concern between two people as in "You two learn to get along," sexual assault is more likely to occur (Pryor 1995). Also, those who have the audacity to report such incidents either as victims or witnesses are perceived as troublemakers for the commander and its leadership (Hunter 2007). Here, ineffective leaders are at the helm. To no surprise, an earlier DoD study showed that units where the command was perceived as either neutral or apathetic to sexual assault, sexual assault was more likely to occur (Pryor 1995). These units were also characterized by the lack of procedures for redress against sexual assault, the work environment was determined to be unprofessional, and the existence of sexist attitudes permeated. Worst yet, in the face of sexual assault, when victims seek out leaders for assistance, they not only turn a blind eye to the problem by failing to act, but tacitly encourage or even participate in the abuse (Hunter 2007). Victims of sexual assault in these units then learn that to report any occurrence invites punishment.

More recently, three sexual assault cases have come to the attention of Congress that have so outraged lawmakers that they questioned the decisions of commanders to grant the accused clemency contrary to military prosecution or legal counsel without ever having attended the trials, and in the latter case, one senator has indefinitely blocked the promotion and appointment of the second commander (Whitlock 2013a). The first case drew the consternation of Congress after the Air Force's Lieutenant General Craig Franklin, Commander of the Third Air Force in Europe, overturned the conviction of fighter pilot, Lieutenant Colonel James Wilkerson, for sexual assault (Whitlock 2013a). Particularly female lawmakers probed the legitimacy of the commander's decision and the dismissal of the pilot's conviction of sexual assault without explanation. Accordingly, the commander concluded that there was "insufficient evidence to prove guilt beyond a reasonable doubt" and that he "could not in good conscience, sustain the conviction" (Whitlock 2013f). To Senator Claire McCaskill (D-MO), who is also a member of the Senate Armed Services Committee and herself a former prosecutor, "It looks like somebody taking care of one of their guys."

In the second and more recent case, the appointment and promotion of an Air Force rising star, ironically a woman, and the first in 1993 to travel into space as one of the crew members on the space shuttle Endeavour, to become Vice Commander of the Air Force Space Command, is being blocked and placed on indefinite hold (Whitlock 2013f). Lieutenant General Susan Helms dismissed the conviction of an unnamed Air Force captain who was found guilty of sexual assault and, as in the first case, against the recommendation of her legal adviser. More deplorable was that the fact that the commander cited her decision based on the grounds of finding the accused to be more credible than the victim. Again, Senator McCaskill (D-MO) was out front on this case by stating that, notwithstanding the commander's 30-year military career, "With her action, Lieutenant General Helms sent a damaging message to survivors of sexual assault" that "They can take the difficult and painful step of reporting the crime, they can endure the agony involved in being subjected to intense questioning often aimed at putting the blame on them, and they can experience a momentary sense of justice in knowing that they were believed when their attacker is convicted and sentenced, only to have that justice ripped away with the stroke of a pen" (Whitlock 2013a).

This fatal decision by Lieutenant General Helms is most likely to be a career-ending one. The most recent case against three football players in the U.S. Naval Academy serves as yet another reminder of the widespread sexual assault in the military and the urgent need for action, if not by the military, but by Congress to spur the military into action. On Wednesday, June 19, 2013, three football players were charged with raping a female midshipperson and lying about it (Shin 2013). But the charges only came to light after the victim secured an attorney because although the incident was reported to the NCIS about what sparked the incident over an year ago in April 2012, Susan Burke, the victim's attorney, accused the Navy of dragging its feet. In fact, the victim was reportedly told by one of the perpetrators not to cooperate with NCIS. One of the perpetrators was also prevented from graduating and hence obtaining his commission, pending a decision by the Naval Academy Superintendent on whether to proceed with an Article 32 hearing given the findings of NCIS.

While some of these high-profile incidents of sexual assault in the military have derailed some promising careers in the past, namely, the Navy's Tailhook and the Army's Aberdeen Proving Ground and those of the Abu Ghraib prison during Operation Iraqi Freedom, to name a few, with the reported epidemic levels of sexual assault in the military and the multiple civilian litigation afoot against civilian leaders by former military personnel for their failure to either intervene on their behalf or for creating a culture where sexual assault is condoned, federal lawmakers, specifically Congress, are no longer willing to tolerate such outlandish indiscretions, even to the point of calling for the overhaul of the long-standing UCMJ. Interestingly enough, in previous years, in response to the problem of sexual assault in the military, Congress considered returning to the days when the military employed separate training programs for women and men (Shenon 1997). However, in 1997, in a convincing testimony to the Senate, Vice Admiral Patricia Tracey, then the Navy's education and training chief, weighed in by stating that "Men and women who suspect they have been trained to different standards cannot have confidence in one another to boldly go into harm's way" (Shenon 1997). And, given the most recent cases that, for all intents and purposes, have resulted in ruined careers, and otherwise distinguished reputations disgraced, put on the line or being forced to walk the gauntlet, so to speak, the military, perhaps for the first time, is not only being forced to acknowledge the often-invoked term of "cancer" within its ranks, but the preponderant need to take action in light of lawmakers' uniformed disgust.

This disgust recently resulted in the passing of competing legislations in the House of Representatives to attack the problem (Lardner and Cassata 2013). The first legislation was approved to circumvent the power of military commanders to grant clemency for assault and rape cases and at least, the mandatory discharge of anyone in the military who has been convicted of any form of sexual assault. Seemingly though, this represents a compromised version of the original proposed bill. Military commanders confessed of not being judicious in addressing the problem of sexual assault yet convinced lawmakers that putting the discretion in the hands of military prosecutors over military commanders would be a mistake. But while Representative Jackie Speier (D-CA) was pleased with proactive steps to intervene on behalf of the victims of sexual assault in the military, she believed that given the objection of the military, the aforementioned legislation did not go far enough to protect victims of sexual assault (Lardner and Cassata 2013). Therefore, Representative Speier introduced independent legislation that would also be independent of the military to create a SAPRO of military and civilian experts. And, after refusing to become serious enough about the matter, much less to take action that is far overdue for the victims of sexual assault, past and present, owing to the credible threat by Congress to not only take the discretion of the system for redress of sexual assault out of commanders' hands but to overhaul the UCMJ for prosecuting such cases, the military has decided to finally relinquish by giving the epidemic in its culture the needed attention. But, perhaps not before receiving the most profound of messages yet.

The most incriminating warning shot to the military about its dereliction of duty to protect especially its female workforce was fired by Senator Susan Collins (R-ME) who told the American public that they should beware of allowing their daughters to enlist in the military (McDonald 2013). And, in a dramatic move by the consummate veteran and perhaps one of the staunchest supporters of the military in Congress, Senator John McCain (R-AZ) joined his colleagues in condemning sexual assault in the military (Briggs 2013). But even more significant was his public statement that he would not encourage women to join the military until the institution has resolved its sexual assault crisis. This served as yet another wake-up call to the military, that Congress was simply fed up and has become intolerant of its inactions as well as that its ability to carry out its mission and a primary constituent upon whom it has always relied to accomplish that mission was being jeopardized. For example, following the arrest and conviction of sexual battery of Lieutenant Colonel Jeffrey Krusinski, the former head of the Air Force's SAPRO, the Air Force appointed Major General Margaret Woodward to shake things up in an effort to restore order and confidence to the broken system (Burns 2013).

Anu Bhagwati, Executive Director and cofounder of the Service Women's Action Network (SWAN), spoke of her own travails with sexual assault as a Captain in the U.S. Marine Corps (Bhagwati 2013). She recalls having to listen to "rape jokes" that were the order of the day, about the degradation of women in the forms of such adjectives like "weak" or "lazy," and that women do not belong in the Marines along with the common reference to pornography that are commonplace and within proximity of many U.S.-based and overseas military installations. Bhagwati described the Marine Corps' Parris Island Marine Corps Recruiting Depot as one infused with a culture of predators ready to pounce upon innocent trainees and particularly against junior personnel. Besides, at other Marine Corps installations, the attitudes and corresponding behaviors about sexual assault were not of condemnation but one of condoning such behaviors, including the associated violence by senior commissioned and noncommissioned officers. Bhagwati confessed that it was tantamount to career suicide to report these incidents. However, she became so fed up after reporting to her commander that such violations were being committed against her troops by the executive officer that she sought redress outside of her command by lodging an equal opportunity complaint against the officer. And, even though the executive officer was charged with sexual misconduct, Bhagwati's (2013) command simply ignored the findings and went as far as to promote the perpetrator in a cruel irony, "to command the company filled with women whom he had harassed." Bhagwati said that she sought to make the problems known to the civilian media, to no avail. Not only was she ostracized for her courage to stand up against sexual assault for her subordinates, but she was dealt a decidedly lethal blow to her own career as a result. And, as is the norm when women complain to their chain of command about sexual assault, Bhagwati was labeled as being too "sensitive" or that she "took things too personally." But, as Bhagwati put it, those with career aspirations to rise within the ranks of the military are forced to become complicit in the quagmire by remaining silent. Doing so, of course, only serves to exacerbate the problem by elevating the perpetrator while destroying the lives of victims in the process.

But, like the overdue but fortuitous repeal of the combat exclusion policy, it would have been remiss, if not unconscionable, to not cover the issue of sexual assault that overwhelmingly plagues women in the military and is as much a problem of asymmetry given the existence of the combat exclusion policy as it is about the cultural perception of women as a group. To not cover this topic as part of this book would have proven as a disservice to the women whose lives have been so valiantly portrayed as a representative sample of women in the military. And, while regrettable, the prevalence of sexual assault in the military constitutes part of the very fabric that justified the combat exclusion policy and its adverse effects on women. This second-class status couched in a legal form of asymmetry has no doubt contributed to the ongoing marginalization of women in the military and in turn the culture of sexual assault. Lest we forget, though, it is important to mention that sexually related behavior, including sexual harassment, sexual assault, and its worst manifestation as rape, particularly in male-dominated organizations like the military, is ultimately a tool of control to maintain hegemony and power over women. Connell (1987) provides a theory of hegemonic masculinity as one way of explaining the rationale for the occurrence of such behaviors like sexual harassment in the workplace. It is argued that sexual harassment is one medium through which men, as a privileged sect, exemplify normative behavior and in so doing helps us to understand the roles of sexual harassment, gender, and power. Equally true is that men who are perceived as effeminate by other men become as vulnerable to sexual harassment (DeSousa and Solberg 2004; Waldo et al. 1998) as are women who are perceived to challenge gender-appropriate roles. Nonconformity with perceived gender-appropriate roles then results in sexual harassment (West and Zimmer 1987). The same premise can be employed to explain sexual assault against women in the military for failure to comply or pursue what is understood by men as gender-appropriate roles. Moreover, even when women rise to positions of power, positional power and the accompanying authority for these positions in no way guarantees that the women will not themselves become targets of sexual harassment (Rospenda et al. 1998).

Lieutenant General Claudia Kennedy, then the highest ranking woman in the Army, comes to mind when she accused a subordinate male officer, Major General Larry Smith, of sexually harassing her in 1996 (Marquis 2000). Perhaps borne of embarrassment and validated findings by the Army's IG, Lieutenant General Michael Ackerman, led the Army to issue a letter of reprimand to the accused who ultimately saved face by seeking early retirement. While the incident had taken place nearly four years earlier when both were of equal rank, Lieutenant General Kennedy said that she was moved to press charges when Major General Smith was subsequently selected to become the Army's deputy IG, a position for which he would have responsibility to investigate such personnel misconduct as sexual harassment. The vulnerable-victim model hypothesizes that marginalized groups such as women and minorities are more susceptible to harassment in the workplace while the power-threat model proposes that women who are perceived to threaten male dominance become even more frequent objects of sexual harassment (Chamberlain et al. 2008). A longitudinal study by McLaughlin et al. (2012) not only supports this research but holds that women supervisors are more likely than not to be sexually harassed in the workplace. As well, given women's disproportionate target for sexual harassment because of gender, their organizational rank becomes inconsequential. And, when organizational rank or status is perceived as illegitimately earned, due perhaps to the notion that the woman only attained a certain position that is at least partly attributed to her gender, then her male peers and supervisors are more likely to engage in "equalizer" tactics where harassment is more about control and power, and less about sexual desire (Berdahl 2007a, 2007b; Schulz 2003).

The wealth of literature on sexual harassment in the civilian workplace need only be a reminder of its prevalence even as the participation of women increases and they are infused throughout the different levels of hierarchy in the workplace. It will also be interesting to observe how these dynamics will play out as more women are integrated into formerly closed combat and combat-related fields in the military within a post–combat exclusion policy environment. What is equally important to know though is that the various manifestations of sexual harassment and by extension other sexually related abuses such as sexual assault and rape markedly diverge along gender lines. For example, sexual harassment results in a psychological blow to women's self-esteem (Gruber and Bjorn 1982), PTSD (Dansky and Kilpatrick 1997), lower job satisfaction (Culbertson et al. 1992; Schneider et al. 1997), decreased job performance (Magley et al. 1999), and other health-related maladies (Fitzgerald et al. 1999). Harris (2009) asserts that the incidence of sexual harassment and other sexually related behaviors then call into question gender integration and the role of women in the military. The military has acknowledged this challenge as a largely unsettled issue (DoD 2005) and while sexual harassment is an affliction in society at large, it has always been particularly menacing for the military.

From their research, Magley et al. (1999) surmised that because the primary offenders of sexual harassment are men who can be victims of sexual harassment themselves, the construct of sexual harassment and by implication the experience of women and men to sexual harassment may be different. Yet, men who are sexually harassed do experience such adverse effects as women, albeit less frequently. But, because of the frequency of sexual harassment, for instance, for women, the adverse effects are magnified and these effects become more acute for them as a group. As the authors note, given these effects, and since women unlike men become targets of such behaviors by men simply because of gender, although not exclusively, measuring such effects are both problematic and complex because women, not men, are overwhelmingly the target of these behaviors. For example, when men are sexually harassed, it is because they are perceived to exude feminine traits that are atypical of men (Magley et al. 1999). This is known as enforcement of the heterosexual gender role. To complicate this conundrum, Magley et al. address whether or not men have the same reactions as women when they view pornography, as one possibility, or witness crude jokes or view unflattering materials that objectify women, as another. And, while the authors admit that such materials may indeed offend some men, men are usually neither the target nor are such materials distributed at their expense. Further, given the fact that, unlike women, can men experience such acts or even experience hostile work environment? The authors speculate that men may psychologically construct such behaviors differently from women as a coping mechanism. The U.S. Supreme Court's ruling in *Oncale v. Sundowner Offshore Systems* (1998) has settled this question.

Joseph Oncale worked as a roustabout on a crew that was located on an oil rig in the Gulf of Mexico (Gutman 2005; Pynes 2009). After repeated complaints to his supervisors about the sexual assault that he endured in the forms of even the threat of having a bar of soap forced into his anus by fellow employees, two of whom were supervisors, Oncale constructively discharged from the company for fear of rape. He insisted that his record reflected that he left because "I felt that if I didn't leave my job, that I would be raped or forced to have sex" (*Oncale v. Sundowner* 1998, p. 71). The question at play in this case was whether or not prohibited sex discrimination under Title VII of the Civil Rights Act (CRA) of 1964 also covers same-sex discrimination. The answer is yes. According to Justice Antonin Scalia, there is no foundation for excluding same-sex harassment under Title VII of the CRA (Gutman 2005). Further, same-sex harassment was not the primary driver when Congress passed the original legislation. Therefore, Title VII must be extended to same-sex harassment. Justice Scalia said:

> The real social impact of workplace behavior often depends on a constellation of surrounding circumstances, expectations, and relationships which are not fully captured by a simple recitation of the words used or the physical acts performed. Common sense, and an appropriate sensitivity to social conduct, will enable courts and juries to distinguish between simple teasing or roughhousing among members of the same sex and conduct which a reasonable person ... would find hostile or abusive. (Gutman 2005, p. 69)

Several other precedent-setting cases by the U.S. Supreme Court, including *Meritor Savings Bank, FSB v. Vinson* (1998), *Harris v. Forklift Systems* (1993), and *Johnson v. Transportation Agency, Santa Clara County* (1987), were cited and formed the basis for the Court's ruling. In a unanimous decision, the High Court held that, although Title VII does not explicitly bar against verbal and physical harassment in the workplace, it does prohibit discrimination on the basis of sex (Gutman 2005). Regardless of the victim's gender, if the discrimination is actionable, then it places the victim at a disadvantage. The ruling of the case is unprecedented because it provided guidance on same-sex harassment and was the first of its kind to be elevated to the High Court. However, particularly in same-sex harassment situations, the context of the situations must first be considered before such decisions can be rendered (Pynes 2009). As such, to resolve the issue on whether or not men can experience sexual harassment and specifically under hostile work environment, given the context of the situation, men, like women, can indeed experience hostile work environment based upon sex.

Pryor and Fitzgerald (2003) also offer sexual harassment in the workplace and by implication sexual assault as a form of bullying but that women view such unwelcomed behaviors as vastly different from men despite citing earlier studies by the U.S. Merit Systems Board Protection (USMSBP) (1981, 1987, 1994) and Gutek (1985), respectively, that contradict this evidence. But, methodological differences make it difficult to compare the findings of these studies (Pryor and Fitzgerald 2003). Pryor and Fitzgerald list multiple antecedents or risk factors that increase the likelihood for sexual harassment in the workplace. First, the job gender context is an important determinant (Fitzgerald et al. 1999); second, the female to male ratio or the degree to which both genders have the opportunity to interact or make contact (Gruber 1998; Gutek et al. 1990). This may be parallel to Kanter's (1977) tokenism contending that it is important for women to achieve at least a 15% critical mass in any occupation within an organization to avert undue attention to themselves in being perceived as tokens. Nevertheless, Kanter warns that achieving a critical mass by women in any organization in no way guarantees that they will not be perceived as tokens given contrast and hyper-visibility, two byproducts of tokenism. And, even as the size of women increases, women may still become vulnerable to such labels thereby reinforcing their stereotype as tokens.

A third factor, according to Pryor and Fitzgerald (2003), that increases the propensity for sexual harassment in the workplace occurs when there is a minority of women in male-dominated organizations (Kernoff-Mansfield et al. 1991). Fourth, where women are likely pioneers in predominantly male organizations such as the military, sexual harassment is also likely to occur (Niebuhr 1997), similar to Dansby and Landis's (1998) findings about minority female officers who suffered the triple effects and the associated burdens of being pioneers in the military as are female officers who are routinely underevaluated in performance by male superiors strictly owing to their small representation in the military (Pazy and Oron 2001). A female with a male supervisor also increases the likelihood of sexual harassment (USMSPB 1994). This substantiates the finding that women are at least three times more likely than men to experience sexual harassment and typically by a male supervisor. And, women in the military who are sexually harassed are more likely to be younger than age 25 and single with little to no experience with sexual assault. Other risk factors for the occurrence of sexual harassment includes the absence of effective leadership accompanied by an indifference by that organization's leadership that serves to undermine organizational efforts to stave off sexual harassment (Gruber 1998; Pryor and Fitzgerald 2003). The military considers such behavior as punishable under the UCMJ. But, to report this behavior, especially against one's own, would be unthinkable given the military's communal environment. For the significance of unit cohesion in the military and the subordination of self for the good of the unit trump, the individual's need to report on a fellow unit member (Rosen et al. 1996).

Another factor is that women and men define sexual harassment differently in terms of what constitutes hostile, intimidating, or offensive behavior, for example (Katz et al. 1996). Moreover, only those who perceived a situation as sexually harassing are likely to report it (Malovich and Stake 1990) because sexual harassment is perceived differently by women and men (Uggen and Blackstone 2004). In light of the military's culture and organizational norms, what frequently determines the fitness of a member's survival in a particular organization is the extent to which these norms, which may come in the forms of lewd jokes and/or the obscene gestures about women, are accepted. Doing so then distinguishes unit and other organizational outsiders (Miller 1997). Because the military culture can be hostile "toward" and "about" women, men may also experience social pressure to engage in such behaviors not only to reinforce the organizational norms but as a strategy for organizational survival in that they, as unit members, must remain in good stead with their peers (Firestone and Harris 2008). The paradox though is that unit cohesion actually functions to "include" men, while on the other hand "exclude" women (Firestone and Harris 2008; Harrell and Miller 1997; Rosen et al. 1996). Women, too, employ a strategy for organizational survival that may confound the already complex mix by engaging in behaviors that help them to become "one of the group" at the expense of vilifying women in general (Firestone and Harris 2008, p. 9). Many women who do so escape the label as lesbians but in the process they compromise themselves by subordinating their own values and becoming involved in consensual sexual liaisons with their male peers. And, while in the short term these women gain protection from being sexually harassed, in the long term they may acquire a reputation as prostitutes or sluts, for lack of a better word. Yet, women who refuse to engage in such brinkmanship may also pay a price. They risk being labeled as lesbians (Firestone and Harris 2008). Either way, military women are caught in an untenable and no-win situation wherein they become devalued for they, not the men, are forced to contrive techniques to mitigate these perceived situations against sexual assault.

However, these perceived schisms in organizational justice and inherent contradictions function as yardsticks for an organization's actual tolerance for maladaptive behavior like sexual harassment (Adams-Roy and Barling 1998; Dekker and Barling 1998). Therefore, men are more likely to engage in such maladaptive behaviors when, despite the existence of policies against sexual harassment coupled with forms of redress, the organization's leadership is perceived as undermining any formal structures by informally condoning these behaviors. For example, the rate of reporting sexual assault by women in the military is commensurate with the extent to which men believed that their leadership tolerated these behaviors (Pryor 1995). Besides, a unit in the military that is perceived as overlooking the incidence of sexual assault shows this indifference that in turn contributes to the rate of sexual assault (Williams et al. 1999). Pryor and Fitzgerald (2003) concluded that in organizations where there have been repeated and consistent incidences of sexual harassment, it is safe to deduce that this behavior proliferates in an environment of tolerance. However, Pryor and Fitzgerald attempt to clarify that while not all men are sexual harassers, those men who do almost always thrive in organizational environments of tolerance. This finding is corroborated in similar findings by Dekker and Barling (1998).

Using data from the 2002 Armed Forces Sexual Harassment Survey, Firestone and Harris (2008) found that a pervasive climate of sexual harassment in the military negatively impacts not only women's propensity to reenlist on active duty but that of men as well. An earlier study by Segal et al. (1998) supports this finding. Moreover, the "norm" as Segal et al. (1998, pp. 4 and 5) found in terms of this climate of masculinity may increase women's fears that their career opportunities will be limited because of gender. The study concluded that sexual-related behaviors, including sexual harassment, contributed to this perception. With the recent announcement of the repeal of the combat exclusion policy together with the expected infusion of more women into formerly closed career fields, positions, and units that are categorized as combat or combat related, it will be interesting to observe whether or not the level of sexual assault against women will increase beyond the current epidemic levels as an open form of backlash against the increasing presence of women in these career fields, positions, and units.

There are innumerable cases on sexual assault in the civilian sector, specifically sexual harassment, that can be instructive for the UCMJ and hence the military in heeding the lessons learned from civilian case law, particularly with regard to the impact of such sexually related offenses on women as a group. More importantly, this case law is germane because women, like men, represent a subset of the general civilian population and from which the military recruits. But women, unlike men, have a heightened sense of awareness when it comes to sexual abuse (Sochting et al. 2004). And much of the research that has been conducted on college campuses speaks of this vulnerability (Day 1994; Norris et al. 1996; Sochting et al. 2004). Yet, paradoxically, even in an impaired state such as after consuming alcohol, some women feel overly optimistic about their ability to overcome their aggressors (Norris et al. 1996). This is relevant because women in the military often know who their attackers are and given their military training may feel overly confident of their ability to overcome their attackers.

Three cases in particular illustrate the attendant fallout of the effects of sexual abuse on women in the civilian workplace. The first precedent-setting case is *Meritor Savings Bank, FSB v. Vinson* (1986) which established the parameters and legal definition of what constitutes sexual harassment and, more pointedly, a hostile work environment, which, by all indications, describes the environment and culture toward women in the military. Michelle Vinson was employed by Meritor Savings Bank (then Capital City Federal Savings and Loan Association) for four years, beginning as a bank teller trainee in 1974 until her dismissal in 1978 for allegedly misusing sick leave time. During her tenure with the bank, while Vinson achieved multiple promotions, she stated that she was subjected to repeated and unwelcomed sexual advances by the branch manager and vice president of the bank, Sidney Taylor. Ms. Vinson testified that Taylor's sexually harassing behaviors included but were not limited to inviting her to dinner, recurrent offers for sexual relations which resulted in sexual intercourse approximately 40 to 50 times, raping her on numerous occasions, exposing himself to her, following her into the women's bathroom, and molesting her in the presence of other bank employees. Upon termination, Vinson responded with litigation under Title VII of the CRA of 1964 citing sex discrimination on the grounds that she was sexually harassed because of her gender. The bank mounted an affirmative defense that not only did it have a policy against sexual harassment in place but that Ms. Vinson neither reported the incidents nor took advantage of its complaint system of redress against such claims. When asked why she failed to do so, Vinson replied that not only did she fear losing her job, but she was even more fearful because such complaints had to be directly reported to her supervisor, Sidney Taylor. While the lower courts at the district and appellate levels struggled with defining the voluntariness of the complied behaviors by Vinson in acquiescing to Taylor's advancements, upon appeal to the U.S. Supreme Court, the High Court ruled unanimously that Title VII of the CRA prohibits *quid pro quo* sexual harassment where such harassing behaviors are perpetrated in exchange for some employment-related protection such as the situation that would have led to the loss of employment even if the victim failed to comply with the perpetrator's demands. The Court found Vinson's testimony credible enough to constitute sexual harassment under the condition of a hostile work environment. More importantly, the Court found that such advances were unwelcomed. And, while the Court did not find that employers were automatically liable for the behaviors of their supervisors, in the same vein, the Court was quick to note that the absence of notice to employees does not necessarily insulate employers from liability for violation of the policy.

In *Ellison v. Brady* (1991), the second landmark case, the definition of what a "reasonable person" would find sexually harassing was clarified. Kerry Ellison, the litigant, was a revenue agent with the Internal Revenue Service (IRS) within the Department of the Treasury, based at its office in San Mateo, California.

During orientation in 1984, she met her colleague, Sterling Gray, who began engaging in a series of what might be considered as stalking behavior toward her. Ellison's initial encounter with Gray came with an unscheduled stop to Gray's home under the guise that he had forgotten his son's lunch after Gray asked Ellison to lunch. Following this encounter, Ellison noticed that Gray began to loiter around her office cubicle and pestered her with questions. Gray subsequently asked Ellison out for a drink but she declined. Gray began to increase his communiqués with Ellison, for instance, in writing via a telephone message slip on which he expressed his feelings for her. It was at this point that Ellison began to become alarmed by these unwanted advances from Gray and shared the information with another woman, her immediate supervisor, who immediately recognized the pattern of communication as one of sexual harassment. However, Ellison requested to her supervisor that she not intervene on her behalf. Instead, Ellison asked a male colleague in the office to convey to Gray that she was not interested in him.

Ellison subsequently left for training in Missouri and while there, she received a card and a type single-spaced three-page letter from Gray expressing more of the same about his feelings for her but the contents of which Ellison put as "twenty times, a hundred times weirder" than Gray's previous communiqués (*Ellison v. Brady* 1991). Ellison again shared the information with her supervisor, Bonnie Miller, by forwarding a copy of the information to her. Miller, in turn, shared the information with her immediate supervisor, Joe Benton. Gray was immediately counseled by Miller and was told that he was entitled to union representation but that he should leave Ellison alone. Gray subsequently transferred to the San Francisco office but after prevailing in a complaint to the union pertaining to the reason for his transfer, he transferred back to the San Mateo office. Hearing this, Ellison became frantic. She received a letter from IRS management of its intent to resolve the matter by way of a six-month separation. Still, despite the warning from management, Ellison received another letter from Gray. Ellison entered into a formal complaint charging sexual harassment against Gray and requested a transfer to the San Francisco office when Gray was scheduled to return to San Mateo. However, the Department of the Treasury dismissed Ellison's complaint issuing that a pattern of sexual harassment by Gray had not been established. As a consequence, Ellison filed suit in federal court charging sexual harassment where the court held that she had not established a *prima facie* case showing a pattern of sexual harassment and awarded summary judgment to the Department of the Treasury.

Ellison sought resolution upon appeal to the U.S. Court of Appeals where she prevailed on the following (*Ellison v. Brady* 1991). First, the court reversed the lower court's decision and found on Ellison's behalf that she had indeed established a *prima facie* case showing a pattern of sexual harassment by the accused. Second, there was no indication by the employer as to whether or not the accused was punished for his behavior. Third, it was inappropriate for the employer to have allowed Gray to transfer back to the San Mateo office where his presence could continue to create a "sexually hostile environment." Given the above, transferring

Ellison to San Francisco as a result of Gray's return to San Mateo would in essence result in adverse effects for the victim (Ellison). Fourth, the Department of the Treasury failed to establish that it took remedial steps to avoid liability of Title VII of the CRA of 1964. Finally, and most pivotal to the court's ruling and thus its significance is that a sexually hostile work environment should be defined from the perspective of a reasonable woman. The court rejected the notion of a reasonable person perspective erring on the side of the reasonable woman because doing so would likely "ignore the experiences of women" by inserting the perspective of a male instead (Reinders 1992). The court in its wisdom astutely cited that though men do experience sexual assault, albeit rarely, women are the disproportionate victims of these crimes and therefore their perspectives on the matter will be radically different from men. Using *Meritor Savings Bank, FSB* (1986), the court stated that while the case had resolved the matter of the definition of hostile work environment under sexual harassment, Gray's behavior was off putting enough to constitute, and no pun intended, a gray area that was somewhere between "forcible rape" and "the mere utterance of an epithet." Further, the court opined that these conditions were "sufficiently severe and pervasive to alter the conditions of Ellison's employment and create an abusive working environment." Moreover, according to the court,

> We realize that there is a broad range of viewpoints among women as a group, but we believe that many women share common concerns which men do not necessarily share. For example, because women are disproportionately victims of rape and sexual assault, women have a stronger incentive to be concerned with sexual behavior. Women who are victims of mild forms of sexual harassment may understandably worry whether a harasser's conduct is merely a prelude to violent sexual assault. Men, who are rarely victims of sexual assault, may view sexual conduct in a vacuum without a full appreciation of the social setting or the underlying threat of violence that a woman may perceive. (Forell and Matthews 2001, p. 141)

Therefore,

> By acknowledging and not trivializing the effects of sexual harassment on reasonable women, courts can work towards ensuring that neither men nor women will have to "run a gauntlet of sexual abuse in return for the privilege of being allowed to work and make a living." (Forell and Matthews 2001, p. 141)

What is remarkable about the aforesaid holding in the *Ellison v. Brady* (1991) case is the stunning revelation of openness and sensitivities displayed by what is surmised to have been a largely male-dominated court. In fact, the court inferred that Gray envisioned his behavior as analogous to a "modern day Cyrano de Bergerac, wooing his lady through unrequited letters" (Pinkston 1993, p. 375). But the court's ruling and hence jurisprudence supported what had already been validated empirically about women's and men's views about sexual harassment. Gutek (1985) showed that women and men diverge in their sensitivities about sexual harassment. For one study, she presented what are deemed affirmative comments of a sexual nature in the forms of compliments, social invitations, or illustrations of admiration. While 27% of the women found the comments to be odious, only 11% of the men reacted similarly. And, when shown what were defined as undesirable comments of a sexual nature such as profanity, jargon, labels, or sexual propositions, 63% of the women found them to be offensive while 48% of the men did so. In a second study by Gutek (1985), less than 17% of the women found certain invitations from a coworker to be flattering, whereas a whopping 67% of the men found the same invitations as flattering.

Finally, in the third example of civilian case law that can prove instructive for the military in its handling of sexual assault, the term "vicarious liability" of an employer, and therefore liability for the behaviors of its supervisors, is introduced. The case *Faragher v. City of Boca Raton* (1998) considered the creation of a sexually hostile work environment even when the employer, the City of Boca Raton, should have known about these behaviors because such behaviors were so pervasive in the workplace, and therefore the City could potentially become liable for its failure to prevent these behaviors. The plaintiff, Beth Ann Faragher, was a part-time lifeguard for the City's Marine Safety Section of the Parks and Recreation Department while she attended college from 1985 through 1990. Faragher constructively discharged her employment from the City because her immediate supervisors, Bill Terry, David Silverman, and Robert Gordon, had created a sexually hostile work environment replete with unwelcomed sexual advances that included touching, making lewd remarks, and discussing women in vulgar terms. Faragher entered the charge citing a violation of Title VII of the CRA (1964). Faragher alleged that she was also threatened when Silverman told her to "date me or clean the toilets for a year!" and Terry frequently chided that he could never promote a woman to the rank of lieutenant. These supervisors were bold in both their gestures and behaviors in how they treated the female lifeguards. For example, according to Faragher, Terry repeatedly touched female employees without invitation, would put his arms around Faragher often touching her buttocks, make a sexual simulation motion to one of the female lifeguards, and derided Faragher in public about her figure. During an interview with a female candidate, Faragher witnessed when Terry directly remarked that female lifeguards had intercourse with male lifeguards and the candidate would agree to do so if she was hired. Faragher also remembered being grabbed by Terry who remarked that had it not been for her physically unsightly shape, he would have had sex with her.

Faragher admitted to complaining to Gordon but did not consider doing so through the formal complaint system (*Faragher v. City of Boca Raton* 1998). Further, although other female lifeguards confided in Gordon about their experiences regarding the inappropriate and unruly behavior of his colleagues, he neither reported them nor believed that it was his place to do so. Besides, as he was alleged to have stated, "the City just [doesn't] care." Prior to Faragher entering into constructive discharge, a fellow female lifeguard finally complained to the City's Personnel Director via a letter citing inappropriate behavior by Terry and Silverman. A subsequent investigation by the City substantiated the complaint and resulted in the City's reprimand by way of a suspension without pay and forfeiture of the supervisors' annual leave time. In a 7–2 decision, with Justice David Souter rendering the majority decision, the Court held that an employer could be found vicariously liable for the behaviors of its supervisors. Likewise, the only way that an employer could be absolved of these charges is for said employer to satisfy two conditions. First, demonstrate that it exercised reasonable steps to prevent such behaviors and promptly correct the behaviors and, two, demonstrate that victimized employees failed to take advantage of the system for redress available to them. Additionally, merely having a policy against sexual harassment will not suffice (Pynes 2009). Employers must actively educate their employees about the policy, advise employees about the system for redress, and take immediate steps to resolve complaints.

Of note is that many victims of sexual assault in the military use the term "survivor" to describe their ability to live with the ordeal and for which they are more likely to be blamed for inflicting upon themselves (Solaro 2006). Suffice it to say, women find themselves having to explain what it is that they did wrong to elicit the perpetrator's behavior. It is they, not the perpetrators, who are blamed for the criminal behavior while the actual criminals go unscathed. The survivor's life is thus subjected to a microscopic examination. Dr. David Lisak, a national expert on rape and who has been consulted by the military, primarily the Air Force, shared some enlightening insights about understanding the psyche of a rapist (Solaro 2006). The unarmed rapist, Dr. Lisak said, knows his victim and has no compunction about his repeated violations of the victim (Lisak 2002). The rapist's weapon of choice is psychological in that he effectively employs power, control, emotional manipulation, and when necessary, will resort to physical violence, to achieve his goal. But what is astounding about Dr. Lisak's counsel is that the perpetrator's desire is to leave no traces of his transgressions. Alcohol is almost always used as a tool to render the woman vulnerable to attack but is also used by the perpetrator as a cover-up. Solaro (2006) calls this myth "We both had too much to drink" (p. 326) excuse that functions for the perpetrator's purpose and is all part of the grand scheme to overpower the victim once she is in a compromised state, both mentally and physically. Yet, this very ploy is what makes reporting such crimes in the military so difficult. As Solaro (2006) attests, the use of alcohol is very much a part of military culture.

In an interview with Solaro (2006), Dr. Lisak likened rapists or anyone who commits sexual assault to that of a child molester, for the perpetrator, in a sense, becomes the expert at identifying their prey and thus the most vulnerable among them. The perpetrator's activities are premeditated given the time invested in planning the assault. More stunning is that rapists do not consider their actions as one of rape and because they do not perceive their actions as wrong, they experience no remorse. In his more than 20 years of research, said Dr. Lisak, he conceded that no rapist, serial or single offender, has ever been remorseful. In addition, as far as the investigation goes following the rape, the scheming rapist relies upon the investigators' misunderstanding that the incident was all due to miscommunication between the rapist and the victim:

> Rapists say, it was all a misunderstanding, we were both drunk, and investigators are so prone to believing this that they don't investigate the guy's background; if there are one, two, three incidents, is it really a misunderstanding? From listening to predators think and talk over many, many years, I am struck—by their proclivity for controlling, taking advantage of, and dominating people," Dr. Lisak continued (Solaro 2006, p. 327).

What is even more dubious is that investigators captured the perpetrator's outright confessions yet did nothing to prosecute them (Solaro 2006). In at least three cases that were cited in this HASC report in 2004, the forensic evidence was indisputable. Yet, investigators chose to err on the side of the perpetrator (Solaro 2006).

The testimony of an Army sergeant who was raped in Afghanistan and who reported it sums up the apathy toward the victims of sexual assault in the military especially when such incidents are reported. "Some male soldiers accused me of being at fault for the rape to include making false allegations" (Solaro 2006). Solaro recalls her interview with Colonel Jim Kurtz, an Army veteran who stated how ignorant he and the Army were in terms of understanding the cultural aspects of working with women. He said that

> stuff that the Army leadership thought would be a big deal, like sharing sleeping spaces and latrines, isn't for this new generation. It's almost as if the Army leadership attributed to their subordinates all the evil stuff going through their own minds. One thing that really must have intimidated women was the "jodies" [running chants—then often profane—that troops sing]. But it was my generation that did that, that taught the troops those jodies, and we sang them running through housing areas. I look back and I'm appalled. I'm appalled at what I thought was funny then, that now is so clearly boorish behavior. The only time I remember talking to people about sexual harassment was during race relations training. No one ever talked to us about how to work with women, about how not to offend them, about how to lead units with women in them; and for my generation, it would have helped. (Solaro 2006, p. 329)

Colonel Kurtz was clearly remorseful about how he and his generation of men in the military had treated women. As he put it, unlike the present generation of men, his generation was less likely to know women as peers or even as friends.

Solaro (2006), however, offers a less timed, and indeed more direct, approach to resolving the sexual assault malady in the military. No sensitivity training, she says. Enough is enough! Solaro (2006) subscribes to some small initiatives like that of the Marine Corps where outwardly manly men, for lack of a better term, confront the perpetrators with the likes of "You disrespect or mistreat our sisters or betray their trust, you are not our brother" (Solaro 2006, p. 330). This approach will make more of an impact on the "would-be thugs" than any sensitivity training can (Solaro 2006, p. 330). Solaro also firmly endorses Congresswoman Louise Slaughter's (D-NY) call for an office of the Victim Advocate to be established by DoD. This office should be given the authority and the corresponding clout not only to follow upon sexual assault cases but to be vested with the power to prosecute those leaders who are accessories to these crimes. As Solaro (2006) sees it, one strategy in dealing with sexual assault and more cynically than any sensitivity training can hope to accomplish is simply by punishing the perpetrators and in her words "collaborators" who exacerbate the situation for victims. She envisions when the rates of punishment for sexual assault decreases and where doing so would facilitate the rate at which such crimes are reported. A third prong of this strategy should include the collection of data on the perpetrators to be shared with law enforcement agencies, including those within the civilian sector, since perpetrators are likely to be repeat offenders. Solaro (2006) concludes by invoking the national expert Dr. Lisak's sage advice about the problem of sexual assault when he stated that "Our whole society has trouble dealing with this issue. The only solution is long-term cultural change" (p. 331) while others like Sochting et al. (2004) recommend self-defense training for women.

As Harris (2009) notes, rightly or wrongly, these indignities to women in the form of sexual assault are more than likely to force women to conclude that their presence in the military is unwanted. This, Harris states, becomes a profound measure of the military's ability to recruit and retain women as a group. And, while attrition occurs within all segments of the military's population, the most disconcerting trend occurs among white females at 43% according to an unpublished study by Charles Moskos (Park 1999). Similarly, white females are the least likely of any group in the military to complete their first term of enlistment. The attrition rates for Army enlisted personnel reflect a parallel trend for white females who entered the military in 2000 and after 36 months of service (Moskos via e-mail, January 7, 2005). The retention rates for white female officers also follow similar trends as they are the least likely to remain in the military between promotion cycles and, as a result, are slightly less likely to be promoted (Hosek et al. 2001). But these smaller promotion rates for white female officers do not necessarily explain their attrition rates. Consequently, this domino effect results in much shorter retention cycles for white female officers. Why then should the military be concerned about these disturbing attrition rates for especially white women? Because white females represent the largest group of women from which the military recruits. And, while all groups of women are important to the military, the white female, more so than others, is the most supportive of gender equality in the military (Wilcox 1992). It then becomes counterproductive for the military to alienate its most staunch supporter of gender equality (Harris 2009). This becomes even more urgent now that the combat exclusion policy, at least in theory, has been repealed.

But despite this support, aside from the clear and present danger of sexual assault, unlike minority women, the research shows that, in effect, white women do not benefit in the civilian sector from having military service (Cooney et al. 2003). As well, post-military earnings for white women indicate that they are actually penalized for such service (Mehay and Hirsch 1996; Segal and Segal 2004). In other words, as Harris (2009) concluded that because white women do not necessarily consider the military a viable career option, if the military is perceived as a hostile work environment for women given the current epidemic levels of sexual assault, women as a group will not aspire to military service. Parents will discourage this endeavor for even their sons (Harris 2009). The military could lose the public's support and in turn much needed funding, which together may serve to widen the already gaping civilian–military chasm despite the more recently earned accolades from service during Operations Enduring Freedom and Iraqi Freedom for as more evidence comes to light about sexual assault, the military's performance becomes less stellar and woefully wanting. But as Harris (2009) predicts, this fall from grace may not be limited to military women. This phenomenon may reverberate throughout as not only spouses, female and male, will discourage their respective partners from pursuing the military as a career, but even civilian women, in a symbolic support of military women, may no longer aspire to either service in the military and/or the DoD as an employer of choice. Fundamentally, this domino effect along with the long-term effects of sexual assault for the military in the recruitment and retention of women and even men could be far reaching. And, while the recent appointment of a fast and rising prominent general female officer, in this case to head the Air Force's SAPRO, will finally highlight the overdue gravity that is being given to the malady, as Ann Bhagwati (2013) of SWAN insightfully forewarned, for any person, female or male, to thrive in the U.S. military culture, acquiescence to the norm will become the order of the day. In other words, if those at the helm of each service's SAPRO offices are to succeed in their respective careers, will they be willing to "draw a line in the sand" by making unpopular decisions that will be politically disadvantageous to their careers? Or, as is widely held, will these new leaders be more likely to go the way of protecting their own careers at the expense of the mounting rates of victims, and by this negligence, protect the predators of sexual assault in the process?

The U.S. General Accountability Office (GAO) issued reports on the prevention of sexual assault in the military for 2011, 2012, and 2013, all of which found that DoD's response to protect the victims of sexual assault are both uniformly and abysmally lacking (January 2013, GAO-13-182; September 2011, GAO-11-809). Amid the backdrop of opposition by the SAPRO chiefs given concerns that the results of their annual climate surveys not be made available to higher authority under the condition that they be held accountable for the results and that such assessments should not be part of their performance appraisals, DACOWITS (2012), to its credit, issued bold recommendations on what the military must do to rid the blight of sexual assault within its ranks. First, the Committee recommended that the Secretary of Defense assign the responsibility of sexual assault prevention and response in DoD to an individual with the level and authority for the oversight and assessment for the implementation of these initiatives in the military. DACOWITS's concern stems from the lack of accountability by commanders and civilian leaders to "personally read, understand, and implement the Lines of Effort, the initiatives do not assign responsibility for their implementation, nor has there been any supplemental DoD directive or other guidance to do so. Without such responsibility, there is no way of ensuring accountability for and consistency of the implementation of the initiatives" (DACOWITS 2012, pp. iii, 12).

Second, that the command climate surveys include gauges of sexual harassment and sexual assault to each commander as well as to the next level of authority within their chain of command (DACOWITS 2012). The Committee is concerned that, while DoD requires the administration of climate surveys within 120 days of assuming command and annually thereafter, it is vague as to whether or not the command should include any measures for sexual harassment and assault. Having this information, said the Committee, will provide early warning signs of problems within the command. Further, although they should be, these climate surveys and assessments are not shared with supervisors above the individual's commander. Finally, and the most forthright of its recommendations, the Committee stated that the overall assessment of the climate surveys on sexual harassment and sexual assault should be incorporated as part of each commander's performance appraisal. The DACOWITS (2012) recommendations are meaningful and profound in that they are clearly designed to pressure DoD, and more importantly, hold it accountable for the outcomes of implementation. However, as is commonly the case, until they are forced to do so, will DoD and in turn the military balk in heeding these recommendations? It is difficult to say given the military's record of self-denial and is obstinate in its failure to recognize its own shortcomings and the need for change, especially where issues surrounding women in the military are concerned and particularly when recommendations by the likes of DACOWITS are offered.

Eugene Fidell, the cofounder of the National Institute of Military Justice and a Yale University professor of military justice, and himself a former military defense attorney, is adamant about overhauling the UCMJ, a threat that many lawmakers in Congress hope to make good on (Harkins 2013). Fidell is fervent that commanders should no longer possess the wide discretion that they currently enjoy under the system. In addition, to Fidell, the UCMJ harkens back to the days of Britain's King George III and is antiquated. In his opinion, Congress, and specifically the Armed Services Committees in both the Senate and the House, must interact with the military by becoming more familiar with its justice system. Fidell said that owing to the current levels of sexual assault, Congress cannot be passive. He describes the UMCJ as command-centric and says that the system is past due a respectable demise. Although unsuccessful, Fidell testified in 2009 before Congress in an effort to urge lawmakers to repeal the Feres Doctrine of the UCMJ by allowing military personnel the right to sue should they become victims of medical malpractice. And, as the system relates to the current malaise of sexual assault in the military, Fidell notes that, especially given the decision concerning Lieutenant James Wilkerson who was convicted of sexual assault but where the conviction was overturned by Lieutenant General Craig Franklin, "It's rare that we have the stars aligned in quite this way and people's attention focused on the otherwise obscure field." But, as Fidell aptly points out, the stars may indeed be aligned this time around for change in light of this sexual assault scandal, for altogether, the military's apathy toward its victims has reached the ultimate tipping point of intolerance. It is hopeful then that lawmakers will no longer be under the illusion that the military can be entrusted to take care of its own (as is often its mantra), who are women and overwhelmingly the victims of sexual assault. This means that the American public can no longer idly stand by while its daughters are treated as collateral damage, the consequences of war or of being in the military, for that matter.

In a rare move, the Army Air Force Exchange Services (AAFES) recently took the unusual step of removing magazines that display sexually explicit contents from the shelves of its 3100 facilities around the world (Lunney 2013). While the watchdog group Morality in Media does not consider such outlets as *Playboy* and *Penthouse* in that category, the Military Honor and Decency Act of 1996 of Title 10, Section 2495b of the U.S. Code, bars the sale of sexually explicit materials on any DoD properties. But, according to Morality in Media, while such materials do not in themselves cause sexual assault, they may be contributing to the problem. It is hoped, however, that the other branches of the military will follow suit. But, although Media in Morality welcomes this decision by AAFES, it questions what it calls hypocrisy by the Navy to remove some magazines with salacious material but not others.

Nevertheless, by all indications, the military has betrayed the trust and confidence of its civilian public from whom its female workforce is drawn. And, unfortunately, as is often the case, when the military fails to act, this inaction indicts the whole institution. Since the military is unwilling to act on behalf of its own, in this case, for women in the military, who are maimed and scarred both physically and mentally and, in some cases, have needlessly paid the ultimate price as the casualties of sexual assault, then civilian leadership is obligated to intervene, for after all, the military must submit to civilian leadership. Failure to act become matters of not only the morale and welfare of its most precious resource, that is its workforce, but the clear and present danger of sexual assault is one of such compelling government interest for it threatens national security and military readiness. Thenceforth, the urgency lies with the civilian courts and/or Congress to intervene now to force a change in the military's culture by ridding the institution of the bane of sexual assault and working tirelessly to restore the public's trust and to hopefully regain its once flawless reputation.

WOMEN IN WAR
Living Legends: Sisters-in-Arms under Combat Exclusion

II

This section paints a powerful portrait of 17 women whose lives have been chronicled as profiles in courage and what represents the basis of this book on pioneering, prominent, and/or elite former military women. These warriors are by no means ordinary for together they capture a tapestry of extraordinary accomplishments yet what they all humbly reflect upon as just doing their jobs while they did so under the oppressive yolk of the combat exclusion policy. But, for the reader though, of importance is the fact that what constitutes a pioneering, prominent, and/or elite former military woman is not limited to any singular criterion. Collectively, these criteria embody a broad array of triumphs that fall within the purview of women who have assumed precedent-setting roles under the combat exclusion policy as a result of their unique achievements in still what are considered nontraditional occupations, critical assignments, and/or promotions held. The women profiled here stand as a rich panoply of boldness, dogged determination, grit, strong-willed, obstinate, relentless, unyielding with a steely resolve, persevering against innumerable and impenetrable odds, and with a penchant for challenging the boundaries that were established to confine them to ill-conceived notions of what womanly behaviors are supposed to be.

Not surprisingly, the oldest interviewees, now at ages 95 and 94, held markedly divergent beliefs from their much younger sisters-in-arms about the role of women in the military even as they themselves shattered barriers that created a new trajectory for their successors. Many of the women bucked the system not to be deliberately defiant but to simply question the sense of unfairness or what they deemed to be right and wrong and in the process unknowingly paved the path for what military women and men, for that matter, take for granted today as the norm. Some of the women did so all the while knowing the high personal and professional costs that they would pay in going up against Goliath. Others were facilitated either by a person or situation that fortuitously presented itself. For example, two of the women who attained general officer rank—one, the first African American in the Air Force to be promoted to the rank of Major General, the other, the first woman, also in the Air Force, to reach such heights within the comptroller occupation—attributed their successes to the direct intervention of Colonel Jeanne Holm, then the Director of Women in the Air Force. Ironically, Colonel Jeanne Holm went onto not only achieve the rank of Major General but was the first woman in the military to do so. Still, others devised innovative methods of navigating the structural barriers that were erected and inherently unfair by legally circumventing the system and/or working at least twice or thrice harder than their male counterparts while hoping that when all was said and done, despite the prejudices, fairness would inevitably prevail.

But what is still more remarkable is that even within the midst of fighting a blatantly unjust system, these women at no time blamed the military per se as an institution for the cause of these inequities or their uncalled for struggles, although they questioned the nonsensical rationale for their exclusion. In fact, they generally laud the military and were more likely to place the blame on the individuals whom they viewed as the symbols and proselytizers of injustice within the system. In short, the women profiled here are simply amazing and their indomitable spirit continues to reside in the hearts and minds of their present-day sisters-in-arms and will no doubt do so perpetually in future generations of military women and to whom all women inside and outside of the military are forever indebted for collectively they are truly an inspiration for overcoming adversity. Finally, as a fellow veteran and the author of this research and book, I am indeed honored that the women portrayed here have selected me as the instrument through which to convey their stories about life in the military.

The 17 women interviewed are profiled according to the following four categories that form the four chapters: Taking Command: The Generals; Commanding the Air: The Aviators; Commanding the Sea: The Mariners; and Commanding the Land: The Soldiers.

Please note that all interviews were conducted in accordance with the same information mentioned in the text of each chapter in this section for the respective interviewees.

Chapter 6

Taking Command: The Generals

Major General Marcelite J. Harris, U.S. Air Force, Retired

First African American Woman to Attain the Rank of Major General in the U.S. Military
First African American Woman Major General in the U.S. Air Force
First Female Aircraft Maintenance Officer in the U.S. Air Force
First Female Vice Commander of a Major Military Aircraft Maintenance Depot
One of the First Two Female Commanders of the U.S. Air Force Academy
First Female Director of Maintenance for the U.S. Air Force

This accomplished military officer has achieved an unprecedented number of firsts throughout her illustrious career in the Air Force. Not only was she the first African American woman to achieve distinguished heights by gaining the rank of Major General in the U.S. Air Force and the first African American woman to attain the grade of Major General in the U.S. military, she was also the first woman to serve as an aircraft maintenance officer in the U.S. Air Force; the first of two women commanders at the U.S. Air Force Academy; the first woman to be the Vice Commander of a major military aircraft maintenance depot; the first woman to be the U.S. Air Force's Director of Training; and the first woman Director of Maintenance in the U.S. Air Force. With such a record of achievements, Major General Harris has set the bar high for breaking the glass ceiling for women in the military. But to those who know her and her family, it comes as no surprise that she has amassed this record. Major General Harris comes from a family with a rich legacy of firsts.

She was born at the Houston Negro Hospital (now Riverside Hospital) in Houston, Texas, which was the first fully equipped hospital for African Americans in Texas. This hospital was designed by her grandfather, an architect, Wendell Phillip Terrell, one of the first African American graduates from the Massachusetts Institute of Technology, and his father, her great grandfather, Isaiah Milligan Terrell, who secured the funding for this fully equipped hospital. Also, from her maternal side came the first African American mayor in the United States. This former slave, Pierre Caliste Landry, became the mayor of Donaldsville, Louisiana, in 1869. Major General Harris attended Spelman College where she received her undergraduate degrees in speech and drama, and from the University of Maryland's University College she got a degree in business management.

Major General Harris was the first female in her family to enter military service, which she considered a conduit to gain work experience at a time when securing employment was particularly difficult for blacks. Her final year at Spelman College was spent as part of a drama troupe that traveled Europe and performed at various United Service Organizations (USOs) in Army installations. It was this experience that provided the rationale for the Major General to not only join the military but to travel while doing so. And, at age 22, after completing an additional semester of law school, she decided to join the Air Force. Her father joined the Navy during WWII but after only three years of service became ill from a virus that he contracted and so was medically unable to serve in the war. Coincidentally, her brother had previously joined the Air Force but soon succumbed to a sickle cell anemia attack that short circuited his completion of basic training. The culmination of these events, together with the fact that blue was her favorite color, provided the impetus for securing her commission through the Air Force's Officer Training School (OTS). After a year and a half at Travis Air Force Base (AFB) in California, the Major General was assigned to Bitburg Air Base located in the Eifel Mountains of Germany. Starting out as an administrative officer in a missile squadron in Germany, the Major General soon ended up taking one small step that led her on her journey to greatness. Faced with the fact that the military decided to eliminate the MACE missile, she was given a new career field—aircraft maintenance.

It was Colonel Thompson, then in charge of maintenance, supply, and distribution, who approached her about becoming an aircraft maintenance officer. She subsequently assumed the position as a maintenance analyst. As such, she was responsible for discerning the cause for a myriad of maintenance problems on the F-4D aircraft. It was her being asked to conduct a study on the reasons for the failures of the boundary layer control on the F-4 together with her unfamiliarity with the technical jargon and her inability to intelligently converse in the language of the Air Force Specialty Code (AFSC) that moved Major General Harris to apply for the aircraft maintenance officer course. She was initially denied admission to the course, citing as a reason that her administrative career field was too critical a field to lose her skill sets. Determined and not fully satisfied with the reason provided, the Major General reapplied and for a second time was denied admission, the reason cited this time being that she had applied too late to be considered. Still undeterred by these unsubstantiated excuses even after being turned down twice, Major General Harris applied for a third time. But this time she sent a copy of her application with a letter to the then Colonel Jeanne Holm, the Director of Women in the Air Force (WAF). Incidentally, Colonel Holm was later advanced to become the first female two-star General in the military and specifically in the Air Force. Miraculously and within six weeks, and by then a Captain, Major General Harris received a class date for entry to the aircraft maintenance officer course. This notification of acceptance was accompanied by a letter from the Military Personnel Center.

The contents of the letter stated that this was the only way in which women could secure admission to the aircraft maintenance officer course. In essence, women would need tenure in the Air Force in order to cross train into the aircraft maintenance career field. Major General Harris now regrets not retaining that letter, for, as she pointed out, its verbiage served to demonstrate how openly discriminatory they were at the time against women in the military who desired to enter nontraditional career fields. Ironically, although the only woman and amazingly the only African American to be attending the aircraft maintenance officer course, and at the rank of Captain, Major General Harris was also the highest ranking student in her class. For this reason, she served as the class leader.

Major General Harris went onto her first supervisory assignment in aircraft maintenance that included supervising a little more than 40 men at Korat Royal Thai Air Base in Thailand during the Vietnam era conflict. Subsequent assignments included being commander of a field maintenance squadron (engines, electrical, hydraulics, and corrosion control) and commander of an avionics squadron (radios, radar, electronics of aircraft). During her dual assignment in Kansas, she was again first the commander of a field maintenance squadron, then for a second time was the commander of an avionics squadron.

While serving as a squadron commander of cadets at the Air Force Academy, she met her husband, who was also an Air Force pilot. Other more high level assignments included being the Vice Commander for the Oklahoma City Air Logistics Center where she was responsible for 27,000 personnel at Tinker AFB, Oklahoma. Prior to retirement, Major General Harris was the Air Force's first woman Director of Maintenance responsible for the governance and adherence to policies and doctrines for more than 120,000 personnel, with a budget of $260 billion that included the entire fleet of aircraft in the Air Force. Major General Harris believes that it is important for women in the military to know that in addition to her professional achievements, she also served as a wife and mother. More importantly though, as a wife and mother, and despite the pressure that accompanied her military positions, at no time did she feel the necessity to relinquish her responsibilities for those of a wife and mother. When asked, and in light of the times, how she successfully and simultaneously managed a career and family, she advised that as it turned out, even though her husband was the consummate traditional man, he became "the wind beneath my (her) wings." Throughout her career, when she was unexpectedly called away on temporary duty assignments (TDY), he remained supportive by caring for their children and home. She was also fortunate in the sense that she had a supportive extended family, including her mother, on whom she could call for support. The Major General acknowledges that in her case, it really took a community of caregivers to raise a child and it was frequently her community that came to the rescue in her moments of need. She remembers taking her then 13-month-old daughter on her assignment to Okinawa, Japan. Approximately three months after arrival, she was suddenly called to report to Hawaii. It was her friends who immediately stepped in to function as surrogate parents, thus making such spur-of-the-moment trips possible. Friends, such as these, provided the Major General the opportunity to travel without having to needlessly worry about leaving her daughter behind.

Along with many assignments within the continental United States (CONUS), Major General Harris has also been stationed overseas. It was in Germany, her first overseas assignment, where Colonel Thompson encouraged her to become an aircraft maintenance officer. Following her graduation from the aircraft maintenance course, he was instrumental in getting her assigned to Thailand during the Vietnam conflict. While in Thailand, the Colonel also had to thwart subsequent attempts to place her in an administrative position despite her qualifications in aircraft maintenance. She received a Bronze Star for her role in the Vietnam era conflict. Eighty percent of the fighter aircraft that flew into Vietnam were flown from fighter aircraft bases in Thailand. And, it was in Okinawa, Japan, where Major General Harris became the first woman Director of Maintenance for the Pacific Air Force (PACAF) Logistics Support Center. In this capacity, she was responsible for repairing the engines of all aircraft that flew into the Pacific theater (the Philippines, Korea, Japan) and for the repair of avionics equipment. Throughout her career, the Major General was responsible for the F-4 fighter jets, KC-135 refueling aircraft, and C-130 cargo aircraft (flown as the airborne command and control and the hurricane hunters) and the E-3 airborne command and control aircraft. But the paradox was that even as a noncombatant, the Major General commanded squadrons that maintained combat aircraft; however, personally she was never placed in harm's way.

Yet, while performing these precedent-setting roles, Major General Harris neither perceived herself as breaking barriers nor as serving as an exemplar for those who would follow. She simply viewed herself as an ordinary woman who had a job to do and without complaining about it despite the multiple obstacles that she confronted in the process. The Major General saw as her overriding concern that there were people who depended upon her to ensure that the airplanes flew and were mission ready. She also enjoyed the responsibility as a wife and mother, for at the end of each day when she returned home, she was greeted by her family with such questions as "What's for dinner?" It never dawned on any of them that she was a person with enormous responsibilities. In essence, Major General Harris never considered herself as being special nor did she recognize the survival strategies she employed when faced with discrimination. She applied these strategies without realizing at the time that she was being discriminated against. It is only in retrospect that she now fully grasps the intensity of the racism and sexism that she encountered. Major General Harris was medically retired after more than 31 years of military service as the highest ranking female in the Air Force and the highest ranking African American woman in the military. Prior to retirement, as aforementioned, she obtained a second undergraduate degree in business management from the University of Maryland's University College.

It is interesting to note that Major General Harris wanted to become a spy before joining the military. But after becoming an aircraft maintenance officer, in her own words, the field just "popped off my radar." And, prior to her assignment as an administrative officer, she had even requested an assignment to the intelligence field. Major General Harris was always of an adventurous spirit and said that if all career fields were open to women at the time of her commission to the military, she probably would have selected one that increased the likelihood of her being placed in harm's way.

The Major General explained her definition of citizenship as being akin to how she raised her two children. That is, to exercise their rights and freedom but not to do so in a manner that would either conflict or deprive others of their rights or freedom. Further, without the American public, the notion of citizenship cannot be upheld. She deeply values the importance of being an American citizen. While stationed overseas at the time of Martin Luther King, Jr.'s, assassination, her landlord asked, "Why do you want to return to the United States?" Major General Harris replied that, regardless of what happened, "The United States is still my home." There, she believed, she had the opportunity to be whatever and whomever she aspired to be despite the many hurdles that she would have to overcome in the pursuit of that goal.

While the Major General admits that there were multiple occasions while on active duty that gave her cause for pause, she regards her overall experience in the military as very positive. She believes that her military service only represents one part of fulfilling that role as a citizen. The Major General was quick to distinguish between how the military, as a group of fair-minded individuals, treated her as a citizen versus how some individuals within the military have treated her. She declared, "It is this military that promoted me to the rank of a two-star General." Besides, being barred from certain career fields in the military by no means meant that she was not treated as a full citizen. She said, invoking another one of her husband's sayings, "The service is not what defines me as a person, rather it is I who must make that definition."

While still on active duty, Major General Harris became the first African American woman to serve on the Board of Directors of the United Services Automobile Association (USAA). USAA is a company that was not only started by military officers but perhaps today continues to serve as the largest insurer of military personnel and their dependents. By extension, her husband became the first male spouse of one of the Directors on the Board of USAA. Major General Harris concedes that it was at this moment that she and her husband realized how far they had come, now that they were hobnobbing with the likes of both the Chairman and Vice Chairman of the Board of USAA and were being chauffeured in limousines. Her husband jokingly described his first ride in a stretch limousine as a vehicle longer than the first house he had lived in.

Despite being the traditional male, the Major General's late husband, Maurice A. Harris, was her most staunch supporter. He gave up his own career in support of and for the advancement of hers. She remembers when her husband asked her to marry him. He said that she was a rising star but that he, as a pilot, was "on the downhill side of a mediocre career." Therefore, it was important to concentrate on her career alone. Major General Harris speaks of her husband with admiration and fondness when she describes him as the quintessential spouse who was secure enough in his masculinity to allow her to grow, although there were times that he simply wanted her to be a wife. For these reasons, the Major General admits that she has lived "a charmed life."

When asked about the combat exclusion policy, Major General Harris offered a sobering yet enlightened view. She said that she has never understood why the country has always seemed to value women as more special than men. Upon further reflection, she ascribed this schema perhaps to childbirth as the sole domain of women. To the Major General Harris, placing men in harm's way is just as critical as placing women in harm's way. She believes that placing women in direct ground combat or in theaters of operations where conflict occurs will not deter the country from being able to launch future wars if the need occurs. Regardless, she feels that women, like men, can perform the jobs of admirable combatants. She is also of the opinion that by opening certain career fields to women, which were previously closed to them, the services can create and/or adhere to the established standards for those career fields. The Major General said that these career fields would be better defined and refined for both men and women. For example, the military did not have weight-lifting standards for aircraft maintenance, for example, the ability to lift 40 pounds. When women were admitted into the career field, such a standard was established, among others. So, she believes that only by creating standards for the career field and placing women with the best abilities as combatants will the military fight much smarter. Yet, notwithstanding the existence of the combat exclusion policy and discrimination during her own career, Major General Harris does not believe that the policy has impacted her career decisions. But, she is emphatic that the combat exclusion policy should be repealed. As she sees it, repealing the combat exclusion policy would enable the military to fine-tune its selection criteria for the recruitment and retention of women as well as men. In doing so, it would also facilitate the military's selection process for getting the very cream of the crop, thereby vetting those who really want to serve in the military, and in matching the individual to their chosen career field. Thus, the services' ability to accomplish a job well in all areas is enhanced with personnel ready, willing, and able.

According to the Major General Harris, the repeal of the combat exclusion policy will, over time, have a positive impact on the ways in which military men relate to military women. She is taken aback by the level of disrespect and the number of sexual harassment cases that women presently endure in the services. In fact, she does not recall this degree of disrespect during her tenure of military service and cites a study that she conducted while stationed at the Pentagon. The study measured the degree of change in the attitudes of men after they have been exposed to women performing jobs in career fields previously closed to women. By revisiting the same sample of men two years after the baseline was established, the study revealed that men's exposure to the performance of women significantly and positively altered their attitudes about women's capabilities. Because the Major General is against discrimination of any kind, she sees the repeal of the combat exclusion policy as yielding positive outcomes for the services. Here, she believes that the military can take the lead and function as the model of equality for women, including those within the civilian sector.

Regrettably, Major General Harris does not describe her experience in securing employment within the civilian sector post retirement as particularly positive. She has discovered that while the path for whites and especially white male general officers following retirement is one that includes lucrative offers as chief executive officers, to name a few, the same cannot be said about African American general officers who are forced, despite their military status, to launch their own businesses in an effort to create opportunities for themselves. She said that in some respects, the private sector may experience a challenge in seeing how what she, as a general officer, has done that can translate to their own organizations. For this reason, Major General Harris believes that government organizations are more receptive to her leadership expertise. She concluded her interview by saying that the United States must move into the twenty-first century as there is no room for prejudice and discrimination if the country is to maintain its leadership role in the world. (In-person and telephone interviews on August 28, 2012 and August 31, 2012)

Brigadier General Wilma L. Vaught, U.S. Air Force, Retired

President, Women in Military Service for America (WIMSA) Memorial Foundation
First Woman to Deploy with an Air Force Bomber Unit
First Female to Attain the Rank of Brigadier General from the Comptroller Occupation

At 5'2" and with a commanding voice and bearing that resonate like one much taller in stature, this no-holds-barred-speaking retired Air Force general officer delivers a potent punch that is worthy of her rank, despite her size. As president of the Women in Military Service for America (WIMSA, Women's Memorial) Memorial Foundation, which built the first and only memorial of its kind in the United States that celebrates and commemorates the "ourstory" (history) and contributions of women in the military services, Brigadier General Wilma Vaught is herself a larger-than-life symbol of this monumental effort. And, perhaps no one else could have been more resolute in her conviction to assume the mantle and lead the charge toward realizing this vision of what might have seemed an improbability at the time. But, even beyond this achievement, Brigadier General Vaught boasts multiple firsts of her own as the first woman to deploy with a bomber wing in the Air Force as well as the first female in the Air Force to attain the rank of general officer within the comptroller AFSC.

Born in Pontiac, Michigan, to a father who worked in the Pontiac division of General Motors and raised in a small rural community in Illinois known as Scotland, Brigadier General Vaught represented the first female in her family to enter the military. In 1952, when she graduated from college with an undergraduate degree in commerce and business administration, the only role models for women in the workplace were that of secretaries, teachers, and nurses. And, if not employed, women were simply married.

But for Brigadier General Vaught, she was not interested in pursuing any of these endeavors. Given her five years of experience with the Dupont Company, then a male-dominated workplace, she did not see any opportunities that would strategically position her for management, a role to which she aspired. However, after receiving a recruiting letter from a woman Army major describing a program in which she could be directly commissioned by the Army as a second lieutenant and, more importantly, where she could manage others, Brigadier General Vaught chose to be commissioned in the Air Force instead. The decision to go with the Air Force followed conversations with neighbors who had served in the Army and the Air Force but who advised that, for women, serving in the Air Force would offer more opportunities. Further, at the time, 85% of the careers in the Army were combat related and closed to women while many more in the Air Force supported the flying mission and were open to women. Additionally, the likelihood of overseas assignments was greater in the Air Force, whereas those in the Army were basically limited to Germany and Korea.

At age 27, in 1957, Brigadier General Vaught was initially commissioned with an eyesight waiver in the Reserve Component of the Air Force. Within three months of her commission, she was called to active duty. In 1959, the Surgeon General of the Air Force instituted new eyesight standards that called for all nonrated officers to meet the same eyesight standards as pilots (rated officers)—20/70, correctable to 20/20. In addition, this new standard adversely impacted many nonrated Air Force officers with eyesight problems even though such problems did not affect their job performance and even if their eyes were correctable to 20/20 vision. This newly established eyesight requirement nearly resulted in Brigadier General Vaught's discharge from the Air Force. At the time, Brigadier General Vaught had successfully applied for a Regular commission, was selected, sworn in, taken her physical, applied for an eyesight waiver, and was sent overseas. Nearly a year later, she learned that the Surgeon General's office had denied the waiver and she would be reverted to Reserve status. Unbeknown to her, the delay in notification caused her to miss a critical window to submit her application for Indefinite Reserve status. To make matters worse, this change came at a time when the military was drawing down its forces and was looking for ways for people to leave military service. All of this together saw her facing discharge within 90 days. Provoked, she decided to challenge the discharge decision. With a date of separation, Brigadier General Vaught sought the assistance of her senator, Paul Douglas (D-Illinois), to successfully fight the discharge as well as to be given Indefinite Reserve status. The Board for Correction of Military Records approved her request. It was not until 1967 that her status changed, when she was advised, again, that she had been selected for a Regular commission.

During her eminent military career as a line officer, Brigadier General Vaught served in a number of roles. She served as the commander of a 250-person WAF squadron as an additional duty; headed a data automation office and a management analysis office; and worked as a budget officer, comptroller, and finally as the commander of the U.S. Military Entrance Processing Command with responsibility for some 3300 personnel. The command headquarters relocated to Great Lakes Naval Training Center from Fort Sheridan, Illinois, shortly after Brigadier General Vaught took command. In addition to multiple assignments within the CONUS and a four-year tour in Spain, she was deployed to Guam on a TDY with a bomb wing. The deployment made her the first woman to have ever been deployed with a bomb wing on an operational combat mission. She worked directly for the Wing Commander as a management analyst in support of the B-52 missions over Vietnam. While her deployment was unique given the combat exclusion policies of the day, Brigadier General Vaught assumed that the commander had obtained the necessary permission for her to deploy. With the deployment to Guam, she became one of the first female line officers at the time to serve in direct support of the Vietnam conflict. And, while as a noncombatant, Brigadier General Vaught did not personally experience combat, she was, nevertheless, assigned to a unit with a combat mission.

Upon return to CONUS, she obtained her master's degree in business administration. Other notable assignments for Brigadier General Vaught included a one-year tour to Vietnam during the Vietnam conflict followed by assignments at CONUS installations. She became the first female Air Force officer to graduate from the Industrial College of the Armed Forces after which time she was assigned for the next four and a half years to the Office of the Comptroller at the Pentagon. Brigadier General Vaught was then assigned to Andrews AFB as the Director of Budget for Air Force Systems Command. There, she was subsequently promoted to the rank of Brigadier General. Brigadier General Vaught also served as the Air Force representative to the Defense Advisory Committee on Women in the Services (DACOWITS). Following her assignment at Andrews AFB, she was assigned as the commander of the U.S. Military Entrance Processing Command. During this time, she also chaired the NATO Committee on Women in the NATO Armed Forces. In 1985, after 28 years of military service, Brigadier General Vaught retired from the Air Force.

Incidentally, given her AFSC as a management analyst, her role often placed her in unique positions where she had first-hand knowledge and/or dealings with the mission wherever she was stationed. Brigadier General Vaught recalled that she had hoped to go to Vietnam because she felt that as a career officer, it was important for her to be a part of it. Her selection for assignment to Vietnam, she believes, can be attributed to the then Colonel Jeanne Holm, the Director of WAF. It was Colonel Holm who, a few years earlier, had challenged the discharge requirement for non-rated officers with eyesight problems. As it happened, Brigadier General Vaught had written a response to Colonel Holm's letter of congratulations upon her selection for a Regular commission after competing with her peers. Brigadier General Vaught replied by thanking the Colonel, but in the same vein questioned the identity of her peers since this was about the fourth time that she had competed and was selected. This not only got Colonel Holm's attention, it resulted in her effort to change the Air Force physical standard policy. It also seemed to have brought Brigadier General Vaught to the Colonel's attention, which may have influenced some of her future assignments. As an aside, then retired Major General Holm later served as a judge in selecting the design of the Women's Memorial.

While the Air Force has earned the reputation as the most-female-friendly branch of the military, Brigadier General Vaught said that she entered the Air Force at a time when women scarcely represented seven-tenths of 1% of the Air Force. Yet, she always viewed this minority status as an advantage of sorts in the sense that wherever she was stationed, the women were few and well known. And, it was this minority status that often distinguished her and for which she may have received more visibility than she deserved since she was competing "in a sea of men." Moreover, as aforementioned, being a management analyst provided her with unique opportunities not necessarily afforded to other AFSCs. For instance, she had the opportunity to review the performance of missiles, pilots, and aircraft that most women, at the time, were not in a position to do. Yet, Brigadier General Vaught noted that the selection of her AFSC was not of her doing but the Air Force's. In fact, although she had indicated that neither the comptroller's office nor management analysis was what she desired, it was exactly what the Air Force had in mind for her and in which she was subsequently placed. She was actually interested in pursuing the field of aircraft maintenance and even took various related correspondence courses. And, her interest in maintenance was reinforced when she scored well on the tests. She knew, however, that even though she did well in the courses, the field was not open to women at the time. Brigadier General Vaught also recalled that her ambition throughout her formative years from grade school to high school was to become a medical doctor. Determined to pursue her dream, she enrolled in college as a pre-med major. But after a college course in chemistry, she quickly concluded that medicine was not to be her career field and so changed her major to business administration instead.

When it comes to the subject of citizenship, Brigadier General Vaught believes that a person's role can range from serving a small part in one's community to playing a larger role in national service, as well as helping others succeed. She realizes how fortunate she is to be an American citizen, especially having been assigned overseas and witnessing how others live. She lamented, however, that many Americans do not value this citizenship to the degree she thinks they should. According to Brigadier General Vaught, being a good and active citizen is a lifelong role. She also acknowledged that despite the deficiencies in the military, particularly with regard to women, the institution has treated her well as a citizen. Nevertheless, she dubs some of the military's shortcomings with respect to women as merely "the height of silliness." She pointed to such examples as a servicewoman who married a military man with children. In accordance with policy at the time, the servicewoman would have been involuntarily separated from the service because she now had dependent children in her household. However, slowly but surely, over time, these outdated policies have changed. When asked if being barred from certain career fields in the military made her feel less than a citizen, Brigadier General Vaught was more diplomatic. She simply replied that all career fields should be opened to military women if the woman is capable, trained, and qualified. Likewise, commanders should be given the latitude to place the best qualified person, female or male, in the roles for which they are most suited without constant reference to a law that limits what should and should not be done based on gender.

Brigadier General Vaught described her overall experience with the military as favorable, despite some moments she could have done without. Yet, she indicated there were experiences as a result of her military career that were beyond belief— she has shaken the hands of and/or engaged in conversations with the likes of every U.S. President from Ford to Obama; as well as First Ladies such as Rosalyn Carter, Hillary Clinton, and Michele Obama; along with the Secretaries of State, Defense, Veterans Affairs, and U.S. Supreme Court justices who came to know her. She has had lunch with the actress, Loretta Swit, star of the television series *MASH*; and counts actress Connie Stevens as a personal friend. Despite all this, she still continues to be amazed that someone of her humble background has had such opportunities. According to Brigadier General Vaught, had it not been for her career in the military, particularly given her general officer rank, she would not have been able to marshal the forces crucial to securing the funding to erect the memorial honoring America's military women. In light of these accomplishments and, again, given the Air Force's reputation as the most-female-friendly of the military branches, when asked if she had chosen one of the other military branches would her experience have been different, Brigadier General Vaught quipped that given her outspoken personality, the other services might not have tolerated her.

Brigadier General Vaught believes that women's overall treatment in the military has translated into the improved treatment of women within the civilian sector as well. One such example includes the U.S. Supreme Court ruling after an Air Force female officer successfully sued the Secretary of Defense over denying benefits for her male dependent simply because she was a woman. The High Court concluded that these benefits should apply to everyone without regard to gender— military and civilian alike. A second example cited by Brigadier General Vaught of how improvements for military women have translated to women in the civilian sector, is the integration of African Americans in the military. She added that an examination of many of the strides that have been made within the civilian sector would reveal roots in the military.

While Brigadier General Vaught believes that the combat exclusion policy should be repealed, she never saw the policy as impacting the decisions she made during her military career. Her only recall of how the policy might have remotely impacted her career was during her assignment in Vietnam when she was restricted from going out into the countryside.

Brigadier General Vaught was uncertain as to whether or not repealing of the combat exclusion policy would have any discernible effects on either the recruitment or retention rates of women. She observed that the military has experienced difficulty in retaining women especially for promotion to higher ranks. For example, at the field grade through senior officer ranks, and after 20 years of military service, when they are eligible for retirement, many women begin to reexamine their priorities and the demands of military service. As a consequence, it has been challenging for the military to retain these competitive women for promotion to higher ranks. As Brigadier General Vaught indicated, in some cases, these women are simply tired of being in the military. Other times, it is the desire to have time to be with their children.

There is a perception by some that, because of the combat exclusion polices, women do not bear an equal burden of war, therefore marginalizing women's contributions and creating resentment. Brigadier General Vaught believes that repealing the combat exclusion policy, as has been done, will change this, and at some level, the way that military men relate to military women.

To the question of whether or not there might be a backlash against women in the military with the repeal of the combat exclusion policy, Brigadier General Vaught replied that for some men, there will be acceptance. For others, however, nothing will ever change the minds of some men about women in the military. Essentially, she said, it will depend upon the situation, as it is usually the first cohorts of women who are placed in any nontraditional career field who take the brunt and burden for those who follow. Some men will view the introduction of women as intrusive, forcing them to change their behaviors; for example, use of foul language. So, assimilating women into certain occupations, according to Brigadier General Vaught, will not be easy. And, she went on to say that backlash may occur against all women in a particular field if a woman fails to perform to standard. Key to success then will be the extent to which the leadership at every level of the organization supports the introduction and integration of women into the combat fields. Otherwise, in the absence of leadership, "chaos may rule." Leader support is crucial to both individual performance and the overall effectiveness of the organization. Without leadership's support, there will be no appreciable change.

Brigadier General Vaught spoke to the recent integration of women in submarines, and believes that the Navy's decision was borne out by the fact that a decline in the number of young men seeking the requisite technical degrees caused the service to look more favorably toward accepting women into the field. With the increasing number of women acquiring the types of technical degrees the submarine community needs, it was a logical and prudent decision for the Navy. With nearly three years into the decision, the integration of women into the submarine career field, by all accounts, has been seamless.

Following retirement, for a few months, Brigadier General Vaught did some consulting work that, admittedly, she said she did not particularly enjoy. She was also involved with work on the Star Wars program at the Pentagon. Beginning in 1987, she increasingly began devoting her time to the Women's Memorial Foundation and has continued doing so ever since. She continues to credit her military service and her general officer status, without which, her successful launching of the Women's Memorial Foundation and subsequent Women in Military Service for America (WIMSA) Memorial Foundation with its 33,000 sq. ft. education center would not have been possible. (In-person interview on August 23, 2012)

Chapter 7
Commanding the Air: The Aviators

Mrs. Anna Flynn Monkiewicz, Women Airforce Service Pilots (WASP)

Recipient of the Congressional Gold Medal—more than 60 years after her Military Service One of the Original "Fly Girls" for the U.S. Military Who Started It All

At 93 years young at the time of this interview and with an airplane propeller mounted in her living room as a mark of her remarkable past, Mrs. Anna Flynn Monkiewicz is the symbol of genuine humility about the unprecedented role that she played as one of the original cohort of "Fly Girls" who served as pilots for the U.S. military and for which she was finally recognized in 2010, more than 60 years later, with the Congressional Gold Medal, the highest award to be conferred on civilians by Congress. Little did she know then, but Mrs. Monkiewicz and her cohort of fellow females started it all by being the first women to fly for the Women Airforce Service Pilots (WASP), beginning in 1943. Later, following in the footsteps of her uncles who both served in WWI and like her brother in WWII, she joined the military owing to an early fascination, at age 8, with Charles Lindbergh's maiden flight in 1927. This fascination with the idea of flight never left Mrs. Monkiewicz's mind though at the time there were no females in the career field to serve as role models. Nevertheless, at age 24, she persevered in pursuing that dream and joined the civil service as a pilot attached to the U.S. Air Force. Although at the time the notion of launching female civilian pilots as a component of the Air Force was a temporary endeavor, depending on the assignment and/or station, Mrs. Monkiewicz and her female cohorts did so in military uniform while on active duty. Mrs. Monkiewicz admitted that this kind of service in the military made her status, as well as that of her fellow female pilots, ambiguous, for even though they were considered civilians, they were attached to the military in the Ferrying Division of the then Air Transport Command. Women then utilized the credentials of their civilian pilots' license to fly for the military.

Prior to working for the military then under the guise of the civil service, Mrs. Monkiewicz worked for and obtained her pilot's license through Piper Aircraft, where she learned to fly at a greatly reduced rate, thanks to the owner, Mr. Piper, who believed that all of his employees, both women and men, should know how to fly. But to do so, it was necessary to secure a pilot's license. Ironically, even then, being female with the desire to become a pilot never struck Mrs. Monkiewicz as an obstacle, for according to her, flying was what she wanted to do and so she went about securing the necessary skill sets to do just that. While at Piper Aircraft, she worked in a manufacturing plant making riveting ailerons and like her female coworkers was able to take time off from the job for flying lessons at the nearby airport. These women were also recruited by the military as pilots. Mrs. Monkiewicz's parents, and particularly her father, at first objected to their daughter joining the War Department but soon came to accept it as this is what she wanted to pursue.

While in the military Mrs. Monkiewicz was stationed at Sweetwater, Texas, for cadet training for six months and upon graduation was assigned to Romulus Army Air Base in Michigan. She served during the initial phase leading up to America's entry into WWII for 20 months from mid-1942 to December 20, 1944. While she was assigned to the continental United States (CONUS), she never experienced combat; however, she left the program (i.e., the WASP) only because it was prematurely disbanded even though the then Director of the Women in the Air

Force (WAF), Jacqueline Cochran, wanted the WAF to be militarized. And, it was the cadre of female pilots from the Ferry Command at Long Beach, California, and Wilmington, Delaware, at New Castle Army Air Base who even volunteered to do so for the military as long as the need existed for no more than an annual cost of $1. But, according to Mrs. Monkiewicz, such a request was ill-timed despite having to disband some 1100 women pilots. Further, militarizing the women pilots would have required having to establish a separate military branch. And, as stated, even if the WASP became militarized, doing so would come at the expense of subsuming the WASP, and thus the WAF under the command of the Women's Army Corps (WAC). And, even when offered, Cochran declined having to work under Oveta Culp-Hobby, then the WAC Director. While Cochran's intentions for the WASP were clear, it appeared that her primary concern was the potential loss of the WASP's identity. Additionally, Cochran was afraid that her pilots would lose their status and possibly be reverted to working in other occupations such as clerks and typists. So, according to Mrs. Monkiewicz, "We (the WASP) had the dubious distinction of being the first unit to be disbanded before the war was even over." She believed that this was the outcome of Cochran's trying too hard and she believed that politicking might have played a role in these decisions since Cochran was married to a rich and influential man who was a personal friend of President Roosevelt. It was believed that she, Cochran, thought that she could benefit from such connections with the President.

When asked if she had a choice of careers would she still have chosen to become a pilot, Mrs. Monkiewicz answered in the affirmative, although she conceded that she would have served in combat only if sent and would not have volunteered. As an American citizen, Mrs. Monkiewicz sees herself in the roles of both giver and receiver and considers herself awfully fortunate to have had that luck of the draw. Mrs. Monkiewicz continued by saying that not only is she proud to be an American but that the role of citizenship begins at the cradle and ends at the grave. She said that the military has treated her as an equal citizen, although a female pilot's treatment was contingent upon where she was geographically stationed within the United States. For instance, at some military installations, female pilots were treated as and received the accompanying status of officers while at other locations they were considered as enlisted personnel. This arbitrary status though dictated, for example, where they dined, in the officers' club or the enlisted club. In other words, the female pilots' status was at the whim of the military installation to which they were assigned. But, interestingly enough, Mrs. Monkiewicz did not mind being assigned as an enlisted as she found the food at the enlisted club to be more favorable than the often stiff atmosphere of the officers' club. Her overall experience in the military was enjoyable as she believed that she was contributing to the greater good. And, it was only following her military service, that as a collective, did the female pilots come to realize, as she put it, that they were the luckiest people in the world to have had the opportunity to fly for their country. Also, at the time, no one realized that as women they were playing a pioneering role as well. Further, had they not disbanded the WASP, Mrs. Monkiewicz said that she probably would have remained in the military even if the WASP had not been militarized, and would probably have also made a career of it. During her military career, Mrs. Monkiewicz flew various aircrafts such as the P51, P47, P39, P63, and P40 and accrued approximately 700 flying hours.

Following separation from the military, Mrs. Monkiewicz went onto secure her instructor pilot's license and completed charter work, until she got married and began having children. She flew private charter flights from California to Mexico as one of many such routes. Although her husband preferred that she did not work, the economics of the day forced her to do so, albeit on a part-time basis and in such employment as working on a chicken farm, a liquor store, and as a legal and medical secretary. At the time of her separation from the military, women as civilians were then barred from positions such as airline pilots, though some of her cohorts later went on to break barriers as civilians in that field. Mrs. Monkiewicz, however, never aspired to this kind of endeavor as she thought that doing so was akin to flying a truck.

While the existence of the combat exclusion policy was unfamiliar to Mrs. Monkiewicz as the policy was not instituted until following her military service, she does not believe that women belong in combat. When asked to provide a reason for as a female she broke the barrier for women not only to serve in the military but also to serve as pilots, Mrs. Monkiewicz still believes that a woman's primary role is in the home; that of having children and raising a family and therefore women "shouldn't go help to kill them off." She acknowledged that the modern woman thinks differently and should be given every opportunity to pursue whatever field she aspires. Further, she said that no woman should be denied from doing so because of the existence of the combat exclusion policy. Yet, despite her personal beliefs about women's roles, Mrs. Monkiewicz said that the combat exclusion policy should be repealed as she thinks it would positively impact women's recruitment, promotion, and retention rates in the military. Yet, in the same vein, she also believes that when women and men are placed together, one should expect nothing but trouble, for as she remarked, it is just the nature of things that such indiscretions as sexual harassment could occur. And, even though she thinks that repealing the combat exclusion policy would in turn prove advantageous to civilian women as well, Mrs. Monkiewicz said that women should proceed carefully with these advancements because they may generate animosity from men. She confessed though that her way of thinking is perhaps generational in nature as she would not want to see a man donned in an apron, for instance.

For some time, Mrs. Monkiewicz did not disclose to prospective civilian employers about her pioneering role and military service. It took until 1978 when a group of fellow female pilots were designated veterans yet could never claim the status for benefits. And, even when they were finally given the designation, the funding for such benefits was depleted although, like Mrs. Monkiewicz, one could secure low interest loans for home improvement. Mrs. Monkiewicz retired from state government in 1985 and then served as a reserve police officer in her community for about 10 years. For several years after her retirement, the cadre of original woman pilots from WWII would convene every two years. However, in light of the dwindling numbers caused by the passing away of the veterans, these gatherings have not been as frequent. Mrs. Monkiewicz has also become a celebrity of sorts, given frequent speaking engagement requests and a 1990 visit to Denmark where she spoke at an airshow. (In-person interview on July 11, 2012)

Colonel Pamela Rodriguez, Army National Guard, Retired

First Female Aviator, Kansas Army National Guard
First Female Commander, Kansas Army National Guard
First Female Battalion Commander, Arizona Army National Guard
First and Only Female Commander of the Army National Guard's Western Army Aviation Training Site
Second Woman to Fly the Skycrane Helicopter in the U.S. Army

Everything about this senior military officer indicates that she is very much a lady. Yet, her hard-charging demeanor and sometimes candid use of what she refers to as "salty language" for which she makes no apology says that this is a woman who must be taken seriously and is not to be messed with. Colonel Pam Rodriguez has earned all of her military honors by studying in the school of hard knocks and outperforming her competition in a career that is still considered today by many to be a boys club. As the first female aviator in the Kansas Army National Guard (KSARNG), the first female Company Commander and Commander at any echelon of the KSARNG, the first female Battalion Commander of the Arizona Army National Guard (AZARNG), the first and only female Commander of the Army National Guard's (ARNG) Western Army Aviation Training Site (WAATS), and only the second woman in the entire U.S. Army to fly the Skycrane helicopter, Colonel Rodriguez is every bit the overachiever she had to be when the perception for women aviators was that they lacked the right stuff to be pilots. She is the second female in her family to join the military; her father is a veteran of

WWII. Colonel Rodriguez had not considered the military as a career until her sister joined the KSARNG and convinced her to follow suit. And, ironically, it was not until sometime later in her mid-career that she discovered that her father was the subject of a famous WWII unit.

Unbeknown to her and while writing a paper about it two years prior, Colonel Rodriguez discovered that her father was part of the 37th Tank Battalion, and Lieutenant Colonel (LTC) Abrams after whom the tank was named, during the Ardennes campaign of the Battle of the Bulge. Colonel Rodriguez described her father's unit as the "tip of the spear," a term that she frequently invoked during the course of this interview. LTC Abrams devised a tactic which was modified and adopted by the Army during the 1980s called the Air-land Battle Doctrine. At the time when Colonel Rodriguez was writing her paper, she had no knowledge that this was her father's unit. Coincidentally, it was only following the release of the movie *Saving Private Ryan* that when her husband probed her father in an effort to ascertain to what unit he belonged during this period did she learn of this fact. Her father served as the company clerk but never shared this information with his family. Even after probing him for information about his experiences during WWII, he was simply unwilling to talk about it, like many of that era. So, while for Colonel Rodriguez this discovery about her father was fascinating, it was nevertheless regrettable for had she had prior knowledge, she suspected that she would have written a more enlightening paper from her father's perspective on the role that he played during the war. According to Colonel Rodriguez, following the war, her father simply pursued his successful life as an electrical engineer and never looked back.

Colonel Rodriguez described her joining the KSARNG as a fluke because at the time, the KSARNG had an enlistment bonus that enticed her. She was also fortunate in being assigned to an aviation unit and was later recruited to become a pilot. Prior to military service, Colonel Rodriguez described herself as "adrift." She was considered a bright child in school but was not challenged and who over time experienced boredom. Following high school, she moved to Ft. Lauderdale, Florida, and for approximately four years, lived the life of Shangri-La but soon realized that, especially upon her return home to Topeka, Kansas, her high school cohorts had already graduated from college while she seemed to be going nowhere. So, the challenge of joining the military also appealed to the adventurous side of her personality. Colonel Rodriguez was 24 years old when she joined the enlisted corps. She was the first female in an aviation unit of 250 men and functioned as the administrative support, given her secretarial skills as a civilian. However, according to the Colonel, "they didn't know what to do with me." During the first year of her assignment, even as a member of the unit, she was disallowed from accompanying the rest of the unit in the field because, as they explained, someone had to remain in the unit should the men's wives call. But, little did Colonel Rodriguez know that she was actually following the path of another woman who was only attached but not assigned to the unit yet who failed abysmally because she lacked the army field experience, unlike the then Private First Class (PFC) Rodriguez. PFC Rodriguez was approached by the Unit Commander and told that they would give her a chance and for several years she remained the only female in the aviation unit.

A good natured but blunt comment by one of the men in the unit at the time more or less summed up the attitude of the unit members: "You know what, before you got here, I used to be able to get up in the morning, go outside my tent and just take a piss. And, now I can't do that." To Colonel Rodriguez, as the only female in the unit, and especially during field exercise, they would often forget about her, as unlike the men who shared a tent, she was in her own tent. And, it was only following meetings that the unit realized that they had forgotten about her and/or failed to include her in the given activities. Throughout this ordeal, Colonel Rodriguez learned to cope with these convenient lapses by developing a sense of humor and never complaining, as her goal was to gain acceptance of the unit members through assimilation. She believed that to do otherwise, that is, by complaining, would have been shortsighted on her part and considered it the best compliment that she received from a unit member when he remarked that sometimes he would forget that she is a woman.

Sometime in 1980, one of the pilots in the unit approached her about becoming a pilot as the National Guard was instituting a new initiative in the Reserve Officer Training Corps (ROTC) program through the University of Kansas that would enable enrollees to bypass the first two years of training in light of their completion of basic training in the enlisted corps. Colonel Rodriguez secured her undergraduate degree through the program, earning her commission as an officer in the KSARNG. She remembered going through the program with a male classmate from a neighboring university who proclaimed that he wanted to become an officer because officers "don't do anything." The irony is that the male classmate failed the program and never received his commission. So, for Colonel Rodriguez, her experience told her that "an exceptional woman was only accepted as much as a mediocre man" and a mediocre woman would never have made it through the program. While this level of mediocrity was troubling to Colonel Rodriguez, she learned to accept it. Similarly, as then the only female in the unit, she found little to no acceptance by the wives of the male unit members. But, realizing the dynamics of her existence at the time as the only female in multiple media (i.e., in the unit, in an aviation unit, and as a pilot), especially given the aviation environment, and her use of colorful language as a helicopter pilot, this lady-like yet candid aviator summed it all up that to remain in the military, she would have been perceived as either a "lesbian" or a "whore," for those were the only two boxes in which women were placed at the time.

Colonel Rodriguez's no-nonsense approach in getting things done identified her as a leader as early as during her days in basic training when she prematurely replaced her predecessor due to poor leadership. Subsequently, she progressed from the supervision of a platoon to commanding a battalion. One of her last assignments in the AZARNG was as the Commander of the ARNG's WAATS where she was not only selected to lead the training of flight and crew members in their transition from the Cobra helicopters to Apache helicopters, but she was also honored by having an 80,000 sq. ft. hangar on a bronze plaque named after her. While Colonel Rodriguez has never served overseas, she has participated in the preparation of deploying troops forward during Operations Desert Shield, Desert Storm, Iraqi Freedom, and Enduring Freedom. Particularly during Operations Desert Shield/Storm, despite her goal to deploy to Saudi Arabia, the leadership believed that her skills could be more invaluable at the stateside headquarters, in deploying the required troops for the war effort. However, Colonel Rodriguez was keenly aware that even though as a woman and pilot, she had served in combat heavy attack units, given the restriction on where as a woman she could and could not be assigned, for professional mobility, it was important for her to move to the operations side for battalion level command experience. She subsequently transferred to a combat support unit as its operations officer, although this was to a non-aviation unit, to gain operations experience. Though Colonel Rodriguez could have delayed for another two years, after 27 years of military service and bouts of a form of degenerative arthritis, she retired from the AZARNG. Plus, she opted to join her husband, himself a veteran, who was retiring for a second time, now from his civilian employer. At the time of her retirement, Colonel Rodriguez had completed a graduate degree from the U.S. Army War College.

Colonel Rodriguez explained that for most of her career, the ARNG seemed to be burdened with aircraft and equipment that the active duty U.S. Army counterpart no longer wanted. So much so that the following saying was coined by her "Give us your tired, give us your poor. Give us your airplanes you don't want anymore." During her career, Colonel Rodriguez flew the utility helicopter (UH) 1 or Huey as it is more often called, the Skycrane, and the BlackHawk helicopters. She credits her selection as an aviator to being in the right place at the right time and has enjoyed being a pilot so much that she could not believe that she was being paid to do what she loved. Yet, given the culture of combat attack aviation units at the time, it was almost intolerable to remain, yet she did for as she put it she "was too stupid to know that she [I] was to go away." She heeded the advice of one of her male counterparts who counseled her to put blinders on and not to pay any attention to the circus around her. She described herself as taking a lot of spears mid-career and thereafter, particularly following the retirement of many of her mentors and supporters.

Unfortunately, following retirement, Colonel Rodriguez regrets that she no longer flies because "they beat the love of it" out of her. She described the aviation units as sometimes hostile environments and believes that because of her gender, while in her view many male peers basically achieved what they did by just running once around the block, she was forced to run twice and thrice around the block to achieve the same in light of this bias. Colonel Rodriguez disclosed that after 27 years of military service, tolerating these stressors had finally taken its toll on her.

While in retrospect she would have still selected her lifelong occupation in the military as an aviator, she had fantasized earlier in her career about being in the Special Forces. She was intrigued with both the uniqueness and elitism of the discipline and felt that if all careers were opened to women in the military at the time of her commission, she would definitely have selected an occupation that increased her likelihood of being in combat.

Upon reflection, Colonel Rodriguez sees citizenship as where one obeys society's laws, gives back to society, and does whatever one can do to make the world a better place. She said that patriotism and the like often come to mind around the notion of being an American citizen and by being in the ARNG, she believes that she has fulfilled her role as a citizen, thus the frequent invocation of the term "citizen-soldier" when referring to either reservists or someone in the National Guard because they live and work in the communities in which they serve. And, despite being barred from certain occupations in the military and even amidst the outright sexism that she experienced, Colonel Rodriguez still believes that the military has treated her as a full citizen and still looks back fondly upon her military career. But, fortunately, for Colonel Rodriguez, her sacrifices have paid off handsomely. She now receives two forms of retirement, one as a federal employee as a former full-time technician in the ARNG, the other as a military officer given her work with the ARNG and following retirement, her work with the state of Arizona. Interestingly enough, the latter type of employment constitutes a third but nominal type of retirement. Thus, this formerly adrift starter has over time more than compensated for lost time.

Colonel Rodriguez described the combat exclusion policy as an idea whose time has long expired. She said that given women's most recent roles in Operations Enduring and Iraqi Freedom, and given the asymmetrical nature of war, there is no more defined front line. As such, the policy has now become irrelevant because the lines of demarcation are now blurred. The existence of this policy had forced Colonel Rodriguez during her mid-career to seek opportunities in a combat support unit because she was forbidden to remain in a combat attack aviation unit below the grade of Brigade Command if she was to consider herself for promotions. She opined, however, that should the combat exclusion policy be repealed, as with any change, those who were denied in light of its existence all know too well that failure in a post-combat exclusion policy environment is not an option. Colonel Rodriguez remembers, while a Captain, attending an advanced course where she was the only woman as well as the only reservist or National Guard person in her assigned group and that none of the men spoke to her. After one month of this experience, and when they began speaking to her, she learned that it was not her per se as a woman or that she was not liked but that the bite on active duty of any perceived fraternization or sexism with a female was so severe that such action was like committing career suicide. But, Colonel Rodriguez believes that the same ends can be achieved if the consequences of noncompliance in a post-combat exclusion policy environment were of similar bite or as punitive in forcing compliance.

Furthermore, how military men will begin relating to military women will change, although there will be growing pains in that adjustment as well.

Colonel Rodriguez believes that repealing the combat exclusion policy will definitely improve the performance and thus the overall effectiveness of the military as this action will result in a stronger and healthier force now that women will no longer be excluded from combat, not because many lack the capability but because it was the law that restricted them from doing so. In addition, repealing the policy would facilitate on par advances of women within the civilian sector, although such advances are already being witnessed by women in such occupations as firefighters and police officers. In conclusion, despite residence in a remote area, Colonel Rodriguez attributed her civilian employment to her military experience. And, her civilian experience has been positive as she has never called attention to her military rank and deliberately does not disclose information about her military service. (In-person interview on September 8, 2012)

Dr. Rita F. Sumner, U.S. Air Force

One of the First Cohorts of Women Navigators in the U.S. Air Force

Born and raised in Clearwater, Florida, Dr. Rita Sumner is the first female in her family to enter the U.S. military. After earning an undergraduate degree in biology and while working with the Pinellas County Health Department in Florida, Dr. Sumner's entrance into the military was significantly influenced by a coworker in the Environmental Health section who had retired from the Air Force as a C-130 navigator. As luck would have it, this close relationship and her inquisitiveness in probing her colleague about his military career led to her inquiry and subsequent commission through Officer Training School (OTS) to the Air Force on active duty as a navigator. In 1980, Dr. Sumner became one of the first females in the military, and specifically in the U.S. Air Force, to attend navigator training at the Mather Air Force Base (AFB), California. Her first assignment after earning her "navigator wings" was to Castle AFB, California, for training in her assigned aircraft, the KC-135 air refueling tanker. She was selected to upgrade to instructor navigator, during which time she supervised and trained newly assigned squadron navigators. As far as she can recollect, she was one of the few women in the third cohort of 20 navigators to be trained. She is aware that there were previous cohorts prior to her arrival at Dyess AFB, and does remember that there were two women ahead of her while she was stationed at Mather AFB. There was also another woman whom she did not know when she arrived at Dyess AFB, Texas, who was in one of the classes ahead of her. What Dr. Sumner can ascertain, however, is that she was the only woman in her cohort. Thus, Dr. Sumner was one of the first females in the Air Force to complete navigator training. At the time of her permanent change of station (PCS) to Dyess AFB, she served in the 917th Air Refueling Squadron (now inactive), a flying squadron which was part of the 96th Bomb Wing, then under the Strategic Air Command (SAC). The KC-135 aircraft and B-52 bombers (later replaced by B-1 bombers) were collocated at Dyess AFB.

Though at the time when she served, as well as at the time of this interview, all females in the military were still designated as noncombatants, Dr. Sumner was in a combat support squadron with the mission to offload fuel to B-52 bombers and other combat aircraft during times of conflict. Her career took her to such temporary duty (TDY) deployment overseas in England and Guam (U.S. territory) and though she has never experienced direct ground combat, she and her crew completed refueling missions in the air and where ground skirmishes occurred, such as in Saudi Arabia and during classified operations out of Alaska. After almost six years in the Air Force, Dr. Sumner voluntarily separated to continue her academic education. Ironically, Dr. Sumner's choice to pursue a career in the military was to do so as a pilot and while she was successful in passing both the pilot and navigator examinations, the physical examination revealed that her vision required correction to achieve the required 20/20 criterion. As a result, she defaulted to her second military career choice as a navigator. According to Dr. Sumner, during her service as a navigator, the vision requirement for pilot selection changed, and had she entered the Air Force at a later time, she would have been selected for pilot training.

Dr. Sumner admits that her love for the military and even her concept of citizenship have both evolved over time as her formative years were spent during the height of the Vietnam conflict. It was not until she spoke with former military personnel, particularly her coworker who had retired from the Air Force, that her attitude about the military began to change. While Dr. Sumner believes that her career in the military represented one of citizenship, she has never perceived her role as a citizen as having a finite date of completion attached to it. As she puts it, particularly in education, she views her responsibility as one affecting policy through increased civic engagement in her community. In essence, as with the military, so too has her concept of citizenship evolved over time and she thinks that the military has treated her as a full citizen even though she concedes that it is only in understanding how organizations evolve in terms of the acceptance of certain groups like women, that one, in this case herself, can come to terms with being barred from certain career fields in the military. Yet, at no time while she was on active duty did Dr. Sumner feel that she was treated by the institution as less than as a citizen. She views her role in the military, especially when serving underground in bunkers during alerts as then the only female occupying the same physical space with the male KC-135 and B-52 crews for one week rotations. For example, during these assignments and as the only female in the crew, Dr. Sumner was assigned a male chaperone to stand guard for her to even take a shower. Dr. Sumner believes though that for her survival, she simply had to "roll with the punches" by adapting to the situation at hand, as over time, things did improve for her. Further, the female navigators who followed derived the benefit of having female bathrooms among other improvements. Overall, Dr. Sumner speaks very positively about her experience in the military. However, she is uncertain as to whether being in the military has helped or hindered her treatment within the civilian sector following military service.

Without a doubt though, Dr. Sumner believes that the combat exclusion policy that barred women in the military from pursuing certain occupations should be repealed. She cites an event while on active duty in the military when her base hosted and invited the civilian public to view the display of the squadron's fleet of aircraft. Donned in her flight suit, Dr. Sumner was participating in a static display of aircraft open to the public and was standing next to one of the airplanes when a little girl enthusiastically approached her proclaiming that she wants to become a B-52 pilot. Dr. Sumner hopes for the day when such aspirations of all little girls will become a reality. She sees that repealing the combat exclusion policy would be positive for women because to her knowledge military personnel who have witnessed direct ground combat are more likely than not to be selected for prime assignments and thus are more frequently tapped for promotions. Currently, given the combat exclusion policy, such plum assignments are reserved for men only. And, should the policy be repealed, how receptive military men will be to these changes and in turn how they relate to military women will be contingent upon how the military's leadership and the ensuing culture is prepared to accept women.

As a subset of the general civilian population, Dr. Sumner predicts that by integrating women into all career fields in the military, the military should experience an increase in its performance and effectiveness. This equal footing for women that would be in keeping with the rest of the country will facilitate the foundation toward equality for women in the military. Again, to Dr. Sumner, key will be the institution leadership's preparation for this change in culture. Conversely, repealing the combat exclusion policy to engender the equality of women in the military would facilitate similar advances for women in the civilian sector. Further, doing so would offer former military women opportunities within the defense industry as a whole. Other than claiming the advantage of receiving additional points as a veteran, Dr. Sumner does not believe that her veteran's status, particularly as a female, has affected her selection for positions in civilian employment and she always proudly declares to prospective civilian employers about her military service. In fact, Dr. Sumner believes that she has been advantaged because of her military service, although to her knowledge she is unaware as to whether or not her status as a female veteran has facilitated or hindered her employment compensation.

Dr. Sumner is currently an assistant professor in the Mark O. Hatfield School of Government, Division of Public Administration, at Portland State University, Oregon. (In-person interview at her place of employment on June 12, 2012)

Chief Warrant Officer 5, Trish Thompson, U.S. Army, Retired

First Cohort of 15 Women Warrant Officers to Complete Flight School in the U.S. Army First Female Chief Warrant Officer 5 Aviator in the Colorado Army National Guard

The command of the air became an overriding passion when this senior warrant officer learned to fly her father's Cessna Cardinal 177 aircraft. For her, flying was like riding a motorcycle without a helmet as it gave her an immense sense of freedom, unconstrained by boundaries, and she found it to be an exciting endeavor. But, to a great degree, Chief Warrant Officer (CWO) 5 Trish Thompson's early life was like the open road and in many respects could be compared with the lyrics of the Christopher Cross' song "Ride like the Wind" but without the associated imminent doom. Born in Delhi, Louisiana, but raised all over the world as a military brat, CWO5 Thompson became a citizen of the world, so to speak.

For instance, her kindergarten years were spent in Japan and middle school years in France with the remaining years of her formal education in different parts of the United States. While on active duty in the U.S. Army and subsequently in the Colorado Army National Guard (COANG), CWO5 Thompson became the first cohort of 15 women warrant officers in the Army to complete flight school and catapulted in rank to CWO 5, one of the only two such ranked position vacancies in the state of Colorado and within the COANG. While CWO5 Thompson was not the first member of her family to join the military, her father served during the Korean and Vietnam conflicts and three of her brothers served in each of the respective military services, she was the first female to do so.

Before joining the military, CWO5 Thompson was already married with a child but at the time had not yet found her passion in life. What she did know, however, was that she loved flying, having been taught by her father, who later encouraged her to pursue a career in the military as a pilot. CWO5 was successful in passing all of the required tests, and in 1980 was in the first cohort of 15 female warrant officers in the Army to complete flight training. She was initially enlisted in the Army at the rank of E-3 and immediately upon assignment to flight school was promoted to E-5. It was upon completion of flight school that she was commissioned as a warrant officer. She remained on active duty in the Army for six years before transferring to the COANG as an active guard reservist (AGR) until she retired. While on active duty CWO5 Thompson was deployed multiple times overseas, and she feared that as a single parent she would be separated from her daughter for long periods of deployment. Consequently, and because her request for short overseas assignments was declined, she transferred from active duty to the National Guard where she also served as an aviator. CWO5 Thompson flew such aircraft as the UH-1, also known as the Huey; observation helicopters (OH) 58 and 06; and the UH-60 BlackHawk helicopter. One of CWO5 Thompson's assignments during her career included commanding a 64-person launch and recovery maintenance company in the COANG. Throughout her career, she has served within the CONUS and overseas to such places as Honduras, Guyana, and Germany with deployments during Operations Desert Shield/Storm and Enduring and Iraqi Freedom in aviation or combat support units. CWO5 Thompson retired after 26 years of military service with an undergraduate degree in aviation technology. Upon retirement and after spending 18 months traveling, CWO5 Thompson became bored and easily secured civilian employment as a subject matter expert in aviation for the Department of the Army. Further, given her military service and as a woman business owner who is also disabled, these factors provided her with some advantages as a small business in working with the federal government.

While technically, and particularly as a female and noncombatant, CWO5 Thompson has not served in a combat zone, she was identified as a combatant while serving in Honduras and El Salvador during the time of Daniel Ortega, the Sandinista National Liberation Front and the Central Intelligence Agency

(CIA)-backed Contras. The Contras were taking form and place along the border with Honduras. CWO5 Thompson's responsibility included patrolling and conducting missions for which she received a combat patch. According to CWO5 Thompson, this 1985 assignment most certainly placed her in direct ground combat. She also recalled returning on a flight from Germany when the male pilots on the C-141 aircraft asked her to join them as they had never seen a female military pilot before. CWO5 Thompson was so captivated with the size of the aircraft that she wanted to see what the pilots did to navigate across the ocean, since she flew only helicopters. She discovered that the gadgetry in the C-141 aircraft console, while larger, was similar to that of many of the helicopters she had flown. In those days, as CWO5 Thompson pointed out, there was no GPS to guide pilots on how to get from points A to B. She found this skill to be intriguing for it was necessary to be able to visualize from the map the chart of one's destination using navigational aids by way of beacons that flashed signals that were read by one's aircraft to discern one's way and thus the direction.

CWO5 Thompson was always cognizant of the fact that as a woman, she had to outperform her male peers to be seen as an equal. And, in doing so, she could never let them see her sweat. She was also uniquely aware of the precedent-setting role that she played as an aviator at the time and felt that it was imperative that she and the other women serve as exemplars for those women who would follow. CWO5 Thompson was fortunate in that she was commissioned in the Army when the career field of aviation was just being opened to women. Yet, even though she was able to pursue aviation, she believes that if all career fields were opened to women at the time of her commission, she confessed that she would have loved to have been a fighter pilot.

For CWO5 Thompson, citizenship means that every person in the United States should serve their country in some way, and doing so she believes could instill pride in those who serve in helping the citizenry as a whole. She reflected upon her own life as a child overseas and how this experience helped her in understanding that other cultures are different and that there is never just one way of exemplifying one's culture, despite the differences. CWO5 Thompson said that she is very proud to be an American and the wonderful things, including humanitarian work, that the U.S. military engages in all over the world. But even after 26 years of military service, she does not believe that her role as a citizen has been completed as it is important to help those who cannot help themselves. CWO5 Thompson paused though as she pondered on whether or not the military has treated her as a full citizen. She responded that inherently the military does not treat its members, female or male, as full citizens given its own laws that result in restrictions of what one can and cannot do. As such, she recognizes that the military constitutes a very different world from that of its civilian counterpart. However, she acknowledged that by being barred from certain fields, the military has not treated women on an equal footing with men and therefore as full citizens. To CWO5 Thompson, this practice simply conveys that women are not good enough to perform in certain milieus as men. Worse yet, by having the combat exclusion policy that only applies to military women, it says that military women, not military men, cannot measure up to men. She believes that these decisions in turn have a cumulative and adverse effect on military women's careers for, unlike men, they are excluded from meeting given career targets toward the achievement of their own career goals. Hence, military women are thereby forced to circumvent this injustice by working to gain an advantage. For example, to achieve the highest level as a warrant officer, such as CWO5, CWO5 Thompson learned to do things differently to achieve the same promotion pursuits as her male peers. She learned quickly, when deterred by gender bias, to engage in educating herself, to pursue every military occupational specialty (MOS) producing course available and to go above and beyond the call of duty to render herself more competitive. For her, this was the key to success.

But, as fate would have it, six months before her retirement, she was on an authorized training mission with two fellow pilots who had recently returned from Operation Iraqi Freedom and wanted to demonstrate to her their technique for landing in the sand which they compared to landing in the snow. At approximately 10,000 feet up in the Colorado mountains and donned in night vision goggles with CWO5 Thompson in the rear seat of the helicopter, the pilots thought that they had landed firmly on the ground but had not. The helicopter drifted into the trees and, in effect, destroyed the aircraft. While injured, fortunately, there were no fatalities. As for the combat exclusion policy, CWO5 Thompson did not mince words. She said that the policy is simply "ridiculous!" She said that the military knows, and has known for a while now, despite the policy and accompanying rhetoric to the public, that women have been in combat roles and therefore in direct harm's way. Yet, she believes that when the military is caught doing something and that which is not in keeping with the conditions of the policy, the military in turn seems to get angry at women, not itself. To CWO5 Thompson, women again must pay the price and are deliberately held back from attaining their career goals. The backlash against women also comes in the form of resentment by men because they, the women, are excluded from certain occupations. Correspondingly, women are seen as a liability, as Commanders must strategically think about where they are placed regardless of skill sets, given the combat exclusion policy.

These restrictions are then considered where Commanders are unnecessarily forced to place any pilot in key positions that should be filled by the best pilots. As a result, female pilots' ratings are not be as highly ranked as male pilots because Commanders cannot place female pilots where they are needed to utilize their best skills. CWO5 Thompson believes that this uneven application and employment in deploying personnel in pursuit of the mission eventually hurts unit cohesiveness. Similarly, when her unit was deployed to Iraq, no female pilot was selected for that tour of duty even though the women wanted to go. And, according to CWO5 Thompson, because she is a woman, she was constantly perceived as a liability, but has had to learn to strategically craft alternative ways to level the playing field in order to increase her competitiveness for ratings, assignments, and promotional considerations. In response, during her career, she has consistently endeavored to be the best and the most proficient in her career field. But, as she said, unfortunately, even if the combat exclusion policy is repealed, it will take some time to change the behaviors of men as there will be growing pains for its adjustment to positively impact the recruitment, promotion, and retention rates of women. The policy's repeal over time though would positively result in how military men eventually relate to military women. CWO5 Thompson maintained that the combat exclusion policy gives military men an unfair advantage over military women. And, by repealing the policy, the level of resentment by military men against military women would decrease. In fact, in her experience, this resentment is generational in that older military men become more resentful of military women for not having to serve in combat as they are required to do. Furthermore, CWO5 Thompson believes that these changes will result in increasing the performance and effectiveness of the military. She believes too that the repeal of the combat exclusion policy will give an equal footing to women everywhere to be treated as equals, including in the civilian sector. Further, these advancements and given their experiences in military service, would encourage women to demand more by pushing the envelope for equal treatment. Thus, this regular exposure of military men to military women as partners in combat will have similar effects on women working in the civilian sector.

When CWO5 Thompson retired from the military, and following her 18-month hiatus, she stated that while she was seeking employment within the civilian sector, it was actually civilian employment that found her, ironically, while playing golf, of all things. She confirmed that it was essentially her military service that facilitated both her ability to secure civilian employment and the compensation that she garnered but, to her knowledge, her gender was never a consideration given her expertise in aviation. Yet, while her overall experience in the military was a positive one, she believes that the Veterans Administration (VA), at least in her experience and that of others of whom she is aware, has a long way to go in its treatment of women veterans. CWO5 Thompson recoils from ever having to visit the VA because she finds such trips to be burdensome and slow, so she utilizes the services of Tri-Care instead. She said that as a female veteran, she neither feels welcomed nor comfortable when she has visited the VA because the notion of women who have been in the military and claiming benefits for being disabled is unexpected. CWO5 Thompson was candid when she stated that the women behind the counter who service the veterans, but who themselves are not veterans, are especially rude. In some ways, said CWO5 Thompson, there is no sense of compassion in these women to other women and, more importantly, no such compassion is ever displayed when they learn that the women who are there to be serviced are veterans. To CWO5 Thompson's chagrin, the treatment of male veterans has been far better than that bestowed on female veterans. (In-person interview on September 7, 2012)

Master Sergeant Judith Hatch, Air National Guard (ANG), Retired

First Woman to Successfully Challenge the National Guard Bureau's Policy against Enlisting Single Females with Dependents in the National Guard or Branch of the U.S. Military Reserve
Inductee, the State of Arizona Veterans Hall of Fame

This senior noncommissioned officer is the type of person who calls a situation as she sees it because she has a penchant for getting to the bottom of the matter and unmasking the truth. A self-described daredevil who is unabashed and unapologetic about her beliefs as well as in her defense of others, especially the vulnerable, or when she perceives that someone is being sidelined, Master Sergeant (MSG) Judith Hatch is a force to be reckoned with. Today, MSG Hatch's unwavering commitment to helping veterans of the U.S. military is unquestioned and the plethora of activities in various military organizations is a reflection of her passion. As perhaps the first woman to have successfully challenged the National Guard Bureau and by extension the Reserve component of the military's policy, in barring the enlistment of single-parent females with dependent children into the military, she is also an inductee into the State of Arizona's Veterans Hall of Fame, a coveted title reserved for the rare few. MSG Hatch's life is a compelling journey of what it means to stand up to overcome injustice. And, while her understanding of her family's military ourstory (history) is less clear except that she had an uncle who was an ace pilot during WWII, what MSG Hatch is keenly aware of is that she is the first female in her family to have ever served in the military.

Born in Evergreen Park, a suburb of Chicago, and raised in Chicago, Illinois, MSG Hatch had always envisioned a life much more exciting and worthy of realizing her dreams than working in a bank vault filing canceled checks. And, at age 18, she believed that such work was befitting of an elderly woman with nothing else to do than a young woman with so much of life still ahead of her. Contact with an Air Force recruiter resulted in a remarkably high score on the battery of tests and entrance to active duty in February 1961. While on active duty, MSG Hatch married and became pregnant with her first child. Unfortunately for her at the time, women who were in the military and became pregnant could not continue to serve in the military. Consequently, MSG Hatch was involuntarily separated from the Air Force in July 1962. In April 1972, following a divorce from her husband, MSG Hatch again longed for the association with the military, and this time she decided to join the Illinois Air National Guard (ILANG) as an AGR. But, entrance to the ILANG was a challenge in and of itself, although she subsequently transferred to the Arizona Air National Guard (AZANG).

As a young divorcee with one child at the time, MSG Hatch was seeking a second income to augment her salary as an employee at Montgomery Wards' department store in Chicago, Illinois. Joining the Air National Guard not only provided the means for an additional income but subsequently became the primary source of income. The series of events that brought her to the ILANG began following a conversation with a coworker whom she found out was a Colonel in the Air Force Reserve, but who recommended that she join the Air National Guard "as they have more fun." Unaware as to the meaning of this remark, MSG Hatch completed the necessary documents to join the ILANG. However, as she was completing the paperwork, the recruiter noticed that she was the parent and primary guardian for her son and advised that she could not join the Air National Guard for this reason unless she was willing to sign over the custody of her child to a guardian. MSG Hatch explained to the recruiter that her son was in boarding school and therefore the issue of custody was moot. She related this difficulty to her coworker, the Reserve Colonel, who advised her that he would bring in an article from the Air Force Reserve magazine that addressed the very issue. Armed with the magazine in hand, MSG Hatch returned to the ILANG and showed the article to the person in charge of the personnel office. She noticed that, upon scanning the article, the Colonel began grinning from ear to ear and contacted the National Guard Bureau office in Washington, DC, to not only bring the article to its attention but the basis for the article which the Colonel read to his counterpart in Washington, DC, was that "refusing women in the Guard and Reserve programs on the basis of dependency" was discrimination because at the time men were enlisted into these programs even if they had custody as single parents.

A few days later, the National Guard Bureau advised the ILANG that it could not receive a waiver to bring MSG Hatch on board but instructed the ILANG to go ahead and enlist her to just wait and see what would happen. MSG Hatch was enlisted into the ILANG without incident, thus making her the first known female to successfully challenge the National Guard and Reserve's existing policy that barred all single women with dependent children from entering these components of the military. As a result, and specifically within the ILANG, single female parents were subsequently enlisted. It is also speculated that because of MSG Hatch's challenge, as the first woman to challenge this policy, she may have also impacted the status of other single women with dependent children to not just enter the National Guard and Reserve but join active duty as well.

While most of MSG Hatch's assignments were within the CONUS, she did get the opportunity for an abbreviated tour to Norway. She recalled her desire for deployment to Saudi Arabia during Operations Desert Shield/Storm, but as the primary coordinator for the squadron's family support program, her request was denied. Ironically, while she was on active duty in the Air Force, and because her posting was in personnel administration, MSG Hatch became privy to information that revealed that contrary to the United States' repeated denials to the public of its role at the time in Vietnam, she was responsible for processing the orders for the personnel who were being deployed to that country. However, for several years, she was barred from speaking about what she knew and until the U.S. government made such information known. A little known fact, according to MSG Hatch, to conceal such information, the personnel orders for deployment were only marked "classified," yet the deployment destination was conspicuously absent from such documents. But at the time of processing these orders, MSG Hatch said that she neither had a clue of what was really going on nor knew the critical role that she was playing in the lead up to the Vietnam era conflict. So, for all intents and purposes, MSG Hatch served during the initial phase of the Vietnam era conflict. During Operations Desert Shield/Storm, she served in combat support squadrons and in an air refueling wing for the Air National Guard. And, after almost 30 years of military service, 22 years of which constituted active service with the Air National Guard, MSG Hatch retired with approximately two years of college and skill set qualifications in two Air Force Specialty Codes (AFSCs), namely, personnel administration and administration.

According to MSG Hatch, she played no role whatsoever in the selection of her career field in the military. While in basic training, she was assigned to her first duty station at Travis AFB in California and was told to report for on-the-job-training (OJT) as an administrative assistant. Moreover, women were restricted to primarily three career fields at the time: personnel, administration, and medical. MSG Hatch wanted a career that involved flying and though positions as flight attendants periodically became available, when she applied for such opportunities, she was advised that the field was mysteriously closed. And, left to her own devices, she would not have selected either of the two career fields that she eventually pursued in the military. In fact, if all career fields were opened to women at the time of her enlistment in the military, MSG Hatch said that she would have liked to have pursued a career as an aircraft mechanic, as her score on the battery of tests for the military indicated an acumen for electrical engineering. Further, if all career fields were open to women at the time of her induction into the military, particularly those that would have increased the likelihood of her direct involvement in combat, given her risk-taking nature, MSG Hatch said that she would have selected one of them. At one time she said that she considered herself a tomboy and felt that the positions in combat would have been the kind of excitement that she would have sought and relished.

MSG Hatch described citizenship as having the freedom and rights to choose, the right to defend ourselves, and to even protect the rights of others from undue interference from the government. She believes that the type of system that we have in the United States is superior to any other system in the world. MSG Hatch was very passionate as she delineated her notion of citizenship. And, as an American citizen, to MSG Hatch, it means belonging to the greatest country in the world. While she believes that she has served her country through military service, it is her belief that her role as a citizen will continue in the service of fellow veterans until the day she dies. Nonetheless, MSG Hatch does not believe that the military has always treated her as a citizen, although she was quick to point out that one learns in the military that there are just certain things that are not to be questioned. Ironically, and despite her experience, MSG Hatch does not believe that in being barred from certain career fields in the military she is less than a citizen, for, as she explained, it was the culture at the time, and through her own struggles, she has created a pathway for other women to follow. She continued that the fact that women are proving themselves in many of the positions formerly closed to them, primarily in the Navy, such as those in submarines, as fighter pilots in the remaining services, and women on the front lines in combat, is a clear indication of this progress. When asked about her overall experience while she was in the military, MSG Hatch described her experience as analogous to having a large family of members with whom you may have served and then later encountering them at various veterans' events. She explained that being in the military was like meeting a lost cousin or having a friend on whom you can always depend. She considered this experience in the military to have fostered a special bond between her and her fellow veterans, where each person is always present to assist the other.

On reminiscing about her time in the military, MSG Hatch provided an example during her tenure in the Air National Guard when a particularly petite female was assigned to the engine shop to work on the very large jet engines. Accordingly, it was eventually acknowledged by those in the squadron that there were certain functions that this female member would not have been able to carry out. Consequently, there was immediate resentment from the male members in the unit until they discovered that there were actually certain things that she could not do yet there were also many things that she could do but which they could not. For example, given the size of this female member's hands, unlike her male counterparts, she could reach into the jet engines and make repairs without having to disassemble the engines to do so, a skill that the males did not have and which necessitated them having to take the engines apart to make such repairs. The male members in the unit soon realized that their female peer did not detract from but simply complemented the functions of the engine shop and over time came to accept her.

MSG Hatch believes that the combat exclusion policy is slowly eroding in light of the increasing changes in the military to break down the barriers for women, for, she explicated, women are already out there proving themselves. She sees that many of these rules are being changed as women are increasingly being placed on the front lines and recalled a situation in 1975/1976 that dealt with her squadron's self-defense teams that at the time comprised only men. Not one to idly sit back as the passive recipient of what she views as an injustice, MSG Hatch went to her commander and questioned the rationale of using all male-only teams when in reality these teams could also be confronted by obnoxious women. She said that given the country's culture, men are taught not to hit women. But, as she pointed out to her commander, in light of this psyche, how will the self-defense teams then deal with female protesters who threaten them? MSG Hatch said that she was able to convince her commander to thereafter utilize the skills of female unit members as part of these self-defense teams to counteract some of the cultural nuances that male members will be unnecessarily forced to negotiate when in the line of fire. Further, as MSG Hatch explained, the split second that a male team member would have hesitated to combat the attacks of a female rioter could possibly cost him his life. Whereas, when a female self-defense team member confronts a female rioter, they will be less likely to hesitate to take action. In convincing the Commander, MSG Hatch astutely invoked the Israeli Defense Force's employment of female service members on the frontline as it does its male members. She made the compelling argument that war attacks will not just be against men but against the entire community. After much consideration, the Commander revisited the issue and thereafter began including women as part of these self-defense teams.

While MSG Hatch agreed that the combat exclusion policy has not adversely impacted her career decisions, she was always hopeful that things would change to increase women's role in the military. Likewise, she sees no purpose for the existence of the policy. Additionally, to honor the integrity of the system and thus equality for all, MSG Hatch finds that it will be imperative that the criteria for combat be on par for men and women. More importantly, if women can hold their own, as she stated, then they should not be excluded from battle. Doing so, she believes, will raise the bar for all involved in the pursuit of meeting the mission. She hopes that, should the combat exclusion policy be repealed, the often token gestures of recruiting and promoting some women, as one of many examples, will cease, for such gestures add no value to the military if these women are promoted for purely symbolic reasons but are not the best qualified in their career fields. MSG Hatch believes that although some women will be attracted to the military, to secure a college education, as one reason, entrance to the institution gives young women, and men for that matter, a conduit to help them to mature and accept responsibility without having to worry needlessly about the consequences of their actions when they make foolish mistakes, like squandering their paychecks, for they will always have "a roof over their heads, clothes on their backs and food in their stomachs." In effect, because they are in the military, these men and women will never be in need of anything and because the military is the only institution "that begins to train its recruits at the outset for leadership."

Her many years of military experience, MSG Hatch said, convinced her that the military can only benefit from repealing the combat exclusion policy. While she admitted that getting over the male ego resentment will be challenging initially, it can be done. Repealing the policy will also help to dispel some of the long-held beliefs and stereotypes about not only why women join the military but about women in general. MSG Hatch talked about the active roles that the wives of the Minutemen played during the American Revolution war effort. Therefore, repealing the combat exclusion policy can only result in improving the overall performance and effectiveness of the military, and women in the civilian sector will also be likely advantaged as a result of the removal of barriers to women in the military.

Finally, MSG Hatch noted that following military service there were very few positions for which she applied within the civilian sector and did not secure employment. She most assuredly attributes this success to her military service, given the reputation of the military as an institution and the work ethic of its members in getting the job done. MSG Hatch went as far as to say that the work of the military, and by extension its members, surpasses that of many organizations and members within the civilian sector. And, now as a private citizen, she believes that, it is her military service that has enabled her to function as an exemplar for women within the civilian sector. (In-person interview on September 8, 2012)

Sharron Frontiero Cohen, U.S. Air Force

First Person to Successfully Sue the Department of Defense for Its Unequal Treatment of Women Service Members in Pay and Dependent Benefits

It was a matter of economics, pure and simple, that led the then "pissed off" second lieutenant and now self-described feminist to challenge a system that was unequal in its culture and endemic in its application of how men and women in the military were compensated, including the benefits that were ascribed to their respective dependents. While at the time many might have viewed it as an act of feminism, the then Second Lieutenant Sharron Frontiero Cohen saw this as an inequality that punished her as a woman and in turn her husband as a dependent. She felt that this wrong had to be righted. Yet, at the time even after talking to the crotchety old sergeant in payroll who attempted to convince her otherwise, citing that she was lucky as a woman that the military even gave her the opportunity to serve, she continued to perceive the discrepancy as simply a payroll error. Justifiably though, her anger culminated in the lawsuit, *Frontiero v. Richardson* (1973), the first ever challenge against the then Secretary of Defense Elliott Richardson, that advanced to the U.S. Supreme Court in record time and resulted in its 8:1 ruling that sex discrimination was as offensive in nature as discrimination based on race or national origin. Further, as the ruling noted, all classifications based on sex were "inherently suspect." The majority, with the lone dissenter Justice William Rehnquist, opined that "Traditionally sex discrimination was rationalized by an attitude of romantic paternalism which, in practical effect, put women, not on a pedestal, but in a cage."

Sharron Frontiero Cohen, then Sharron Perry, was born in Greenfield, Massachusetts, but raised throughout the eastern part of the state that eventually brought her to graduate from the high school in Gloucester, Massachusetts. While she would not consider military service as a family tradition, four of her uncles on her father's side of the family served during WWII and so did two of her mother's brothers following WWII. However, she was the only female, and continues to be the only female in her family, who has ever served in the military. Frontiero Cohen then joined the military, specifically the Air Force, because she needed the money to finance her college education, and during her final year at the University of Connecticut, she secured a commission through the Air Force Institute of Technology (AFIT) as a physical therapist. She served on active duty for four years rising to the rank of Captain after which time she separated from the military to assume the traditional role of a housewife. During her career in the 1970s and the Vietnam era conflict, Frontiero Cohen was never deployed overseas and was stationed for most of her military service within the CONUS at Maxwell AFB in Alabama. She said that she chose physical therapy as her career field because of her grandmother who was a rehabilitation nurse and whom she considered to be the most powerful person in her family. Likewise, even if all career fields were opened to women in the military at the time of her commission, Frontiero Cohen stated that she would have still chosen to pursue physical therapy and not any other career field, particularly one that would have placed her in the line of combat.

Yet, the series of events that brought Frontiero Cohen to file the lawsuit are important to recount as no less than an act of courage. She considered that it was a confluence of three factors that ultimately led to its successful ruling. First, she attributed what she called "the spark" or her anger that provided the impetus for taking action. She discovered that the male second lieutenants were receiving a housing allowance that amounted to an additional $120 per month. Their wives also received medical and dental care, courtesy of the U.S. military. However, in contrast, her husband was not entitled to such benefits. She was, in essence, being penalized for being a woman and the payments for such benefits came at her and her husband's expense. So, she began making inquiries at the personnel and payroll offices as she continued to naively presume at the time that it was just an error. But, following her memorable encounter with the payroll sergeant, she became so enraged that she felt that it was incumbent upon her to do something about it. So she did. In fact, as she recalled that the, "Up yours" attitude was the figuratively, lady-like and polite way that she would have liked to have ended the encounter with him. She believed that by receiving less pay for the same rank or work performed inherently reduced her to that of a second class status and thus one of disrespect.

The original lawsuit filed in the federal district court as *Frontiero v. Laird* (1970) by the Southern Law Poverty Center, advised her that this was no clerical error but one that was a matter of law. Melvin Laird was then the Secretary of Defense. This, or the discovery that the inequity in pay was a matter of law, not a clerical error, represented the second factor to which Frontiero Cohen attributed her lawsuit's success and which she described as "the opportunity." However, the three-judge panel upheld the statute for the purpose of administrative efficiency. The panel stated that in light of the fact that given the ratio of married enlisted men and commissioned male officers in comparison to then the only 6000 married women in the military, accordingly as the panel concluded, "women were not being denied a benefit … Men were being given a windfall." But, it was upon appeal that the case was joined by the American Civil Liberties Union (ACLU) with a young upstart, then as head of its Women's Rights section, Ruth Bader Ginsburg. Frontiero Cohen said that her case's brief consisted of 200 pages while that of the government was only 8 pages. And when questioned, the young attorneys at the time who were working on the case on behalf of the government confessed to reporters that, at least for this particular case, they wished that they were working for the ACLU instead. Upon appeal to the High Court and because Defense Secretary Laird was replaced by Elliott Richardson, the case was subsequently appealed as *Frontiero v. Richardson* (1973). Finally, Frontiero Cohen attributed the climate as a factor that was a catalyst for the successful outcome of her case. She believed that the country was in a state of cultural change, having recently passed such landmark legislations as the Civil Rights Act of 1964, the Voting Rights Act of 1965, and punctuated by the likes of school desegregation. Accordingly, the time was ripe for such a challenge and had she not filed the lawsuit, Frontiero Cohen said, in time, someone else would have.

Following the success of her own lawsuit, Frontiero Cohen left the military after fulfilling her commission obligation and returned as a civilian to pursue the life that she desired, albeit one that many feminists believed was a betrayal of sorts and contradictory to their principles, in that she became a stay-at-home wife and mother. According to Frontiero Cohen, this lifestyle choice did not sit well with some of her fellow feminists, for which she was roundly criticized for choosing the path to be supported by a man. But Frontiero Cohen reasoned that whatever decision she made, there would always be others to criticize her for what she should have or should not have done.

Frontiero Cohen was more philosophical in nature though about the question of citizenship and was surprised that the question was not framed as one about patriotism instead. She replied that citizenship is related to group membership, giving what one reasonably can for the common good and involves taking responsibility. She provided the analogy of a fishing schooner in her hometown of Gloucester, Massachusetts, where each person was responsible for his own part in fishing and the amount of fish he caught would determine his wages at the end of the day, so to speak. Yet, she stated that this is only part of the story. She said that for the purpose of getting the vessel to be seaworthy, it was important that each person contributed to making the crew safe even though it was acknowledged that should the vessel sink each person was responsible for saving himself first. And so the same goes for democracy in the sense that at least in principle for it to work, it is important that we all work together for its survival while we each have the freedom and right to engage in those enterprising activities for self-gain. Yet, while as an American citizen, Frontiero Cohen does not necessarily see anything special that is to be attributed, she said that she feels proud of what the country has accomplished but does not believe that America is the greatest country on earth. What it does mean, however, is doing the things that are necessary to move the country in that direction in terms of justice, fairness, and tolerance, but not in terms of military might. She also believes that in addition to being an American citizen, she identifies herself as a citizen of the world as well as a feminist. When asked if her military service has sufficed in fulfilling her role as a citizen, Frontiero Cohen replied that being a citizen is like being in a family in that while you are obligated to the likes of civility, love, and respect and a reasonable support to one's family, it does not obligate you to being loyal to any family member. To be clear, Frontiero Cohen does not believe that having served in the military or being in the military for that matter makes you a better person than someone else who has not served in the military.

On whether or not the military has treated her as a citizen, Frontiero Cohen was less diplomatic, as the question appeared to have triggered old wounds, especially in light of her encounter with the sergeant in payroll that served as the spur for her landmark lawsuit. She stated that while in the military, on the one hand, she met many of the most upstanding people that she has ever known; on the other hand, she has also met some of the most "flaming assholes." Yet, she accepted the fact that the military is an environment, where like civilian society, it is one of policies and law that must be complied with. But, ironically, being barred from certain career fields as a woman did not by itself make Frontiero Cohen feel that she was less than a citizen while she was in the military, for as she stated, one cannot make another person feel less than a citizen given their assessment of who that individual is as a person because "Citizenship is a state of being." What irritated her more than anything was the fact that she was being compensated at a lower rate simply because of her gender. She remembered that prior to filing her lawsuit against the Department of Defense she was forewarned of the potential fallout from the act that would yield dire consequences, such as an assignment for outcasts, that is, Thule, Greenland. Yet, upon filing the lawsuit, Frontiero Cohen's experience was to the contrary. She only remembered receiving one death threat and some foul letters from civilians but none from anyone in the military. With regard to whether or not her treatment in the military has translated to similar treatment as a civilian, Frontiero Cohen was realistic. She said that despite the venue, that is, the military or civilian sector, sexism occurs in both.

About the combat exclusion policy, there was no question that Frontiero Cohen was direct in that women and men should be treated as equals. And, by barring women from certain career fields, she declared, the practice renders women either less qualified or disqualified for those jobs for which, by law, they cannot compete. Similarly, allowing one segment of the military's population to unnecessarily bear the disproportionate brunt of the risk of death and injury by using gender as the only proxy for exclusion, without such objective measures as performance, is without merit. She said that, it was in practice, for her at least during the 1970s when she served, although, the combat exclusion policy was not even a consideration. What was important then was the fact that married women and married men were compensated differently for dependent benefits with the onus on married women to prove that their husbands were indeed dependents. She continued that, in light of this *de facto* pay inequality, the law and in turn practice served as a discouragement for married women to remain in the military. Frontiero Cohen was quick to clarify though that at the outset she had no intention of making a career of the military, rationalizing that her independent streak made doing so an impossibility. Still, she believes that there is no room for the existence of the combat exclusion policy but is uncertain though about how repealing the policy would either impact the recruitment, promotion, and retention of women in the military or would improve the performance and thus the overall effectiveness of the military. Yet, whether or not the policy is repealed, women who are likely to be attracted to combat-oriented roles tend to share similar characteristics with men who do. That said, she believes that for the foreseeable future, repealing the policy may not change the performance of the military. Frontiero Cohen does envision though that given some of the pioneering moves that the military has made, repealing the combat exclusion policy will have similar consequences for the advancement of women in the civilian sector. She cites examples like equal pay and benefits for women and repealing the Don't Ask Don't Tell, Don't Pursue policy. While she said that the military does not necessarily operate that differently from the civilian sector, in many ways those changes that were enacted in the military provided powerful rippling effects for subsequent changes in the civilian sector.

Frontiero Cohen was more solemn yet angry in describing how repealing the combat exclusion policy may change the way in which military men will relate to military women. She stated that in the current climate women have seen a call for retrenchment of many of the gains that have been made during the past 40 years or so. She cites the backlash on women's reproductive rights in the defunding of Planned Parenthood as one such example. Yet, she was sanguine in light of the recent gains with homosexuals, for instance, who can now openly serve in the military. For even amidst the backlash she said, in quoting Martin Luther King, Jr., the "The arc of the moral universe is long but it bends toward justice."

Following her separation from the Air Force, Frontiero Cohen said that her military service has neither helped nor hindered her ability to secure employment or her compensation within the civilian sector, although it did accrue toward her pension from the municipality from which she retired in Gloucester, Massachusetts. Frontiero Cohen said finally that she is very proud of her service in the military and is occasionally asked by the Southern Poverty Law Center to appear at its press conferences to comment on the more recent *Cooper-Harris et al. v. the United States of America et al.* (2012) case filed by the Southern Law Poverty Center on behalf of litigants, Tracey Cooper-Harris and her partner, Maggie Cooper-Harris, where the former, a 12-year Army veteran, was denied benefits for multiple sclerosis even though their same-sex marriage is legally recognized by the State of California. However, according to Frontiero Cohen, for the most part, following her active duty service, the military has had a negligible impact on her life, marriage, and community. (Interview via questionnaire on July 13, 2012)

Chapter 8

Commanding the Sea: The Mariners

Dr. Darlene Iskra, U.S. Navy, Retired

First Woman to Command a Ship in the U.S. Navy

Darlene Iskra, Commander, USN (retired), PhD, holds the distinction of being the first woman in the U.S. Navy to command a commissioned ship. She hails from San Francisco, California, and while her family origins includes a rich ourstory (hers/history) of men in the military, Dr. Iskra is the first female in her family to have served in the military. She joined the military at a time in her life which she described as being at a crossroads; after responding to an advertisement in the local newspaper for mid-level managers she learned that the advertisement was courtesy of the Navy recruiting office. With an undergraduate degree in recreational studies in hand, Dr. Iskra was initially commissioned following officer candidate school (OCS) in the Naval Reserve.

When Dr. Iskra joined the Navy in the late 1970s, careers for women were still limited. After joining the Navy, but prior to OCS, a coworker at the swimming pool where she was working as an assistant manager told her about Navy diving and encouraged her to look into it. Ironically, the field had just opened for women officers. At OCS she took the physical tests, cleared it, and was sent to the Navy School of Diving and Salvage, then at the Washington Navy Yard. She was assigned to the USS *Hector* (AR-7) as a diving officer, and proceeded to pursue a very adventurous career.

While on the USS *Hector*, she obtained her warfare qualification as a surface warfare officer, and augmented to the regular Navy as a Navy special operations officer specializing in Navy diving and salvage. The Special Operations Community was very small, only about 500 officers, which included Diving and Salvage as well as Explosive Ordnance Disposal and Expendable Ordnance Management subspecialties. Out of about 500 officers, there were perhaps 25 women in the community. Iskra believes that the numbers of women in this specialty area has not changed much as women tend to self-select into these occupations at far less rates than men since the diving occupation is strenuous and requires personnel to remain in constant physical readiness. Dr. Iskra confided that the nature of the diving occupation is such that during training women were often called out and harassed by the diving instructors simply because of their gender. As a result, there is a high attrition rate of women in the diving career fields. Once the women completed training, they can become an integral part of the team depending on the officers in charge. In some instances, the requirement to prove oneself at each turn can become tiresome. This is another reason why women attrite at a higher rate than men in many of these types of occupations and do not remain for a full career.

Her career led her to roles of increasing responsibility starting at the rank of ensign as the Division Officer of two divisions on the repair ship USS *Hector* (AR7). The diving division comprised nine divers and the second division included personnel who made repairs to optical and other operational equipment, as well as draftsmen, journalists, and photographers.

She continued to pursue jobs in the special operations community, serving on three other ships before her historic selection and assignment as the Commanding Officer of the USS *Opportune*. Dr. Iskra took command of USS *Opportune* in December 1990, in Naples, Italy, as a Lieutenant Commander with only 11 years of service. Soon after taking command, the ship was deployed to the eastern Mediterranean Sea in support of Operation Desert Shield/Storm, serving as salvage assets with Explosive Ordnance Demolition (EOD) teams on board to sweep for and destroy any mines found in the eastern Mediterranean and the Suez Canal. Her ship and thus mission was one of combat support.

Dr. Iskra's military career took her all over the United States and overseas including a two-year tour to Guam. She was deployed three times overseas—first to the western Pacific on the USS *Hector* where the ship was temporarily deployed to Japan and the Philippines, the Indian Ocean, Kenya, New Zealand, and Australia and twice to the Mediterranean, first as Executive Officer of the USS *Hoist* (ARS-40) and then as Commanding Officer on the USS *Opportune*.

Following her Command tour, Dr. Iskra continued her career as a staff officer, earned a master's degree in National Security and Strategic Affairs from the Naval War College, and served in critical assignments at the Bureau of Naval Personnel, as Civil-Military Liaison Officer with the Commander Naval Forces Marianas in Guam, and finally as a Program Officer for the Naval Ordnance Command. It was during this last tour that Dr. Iskra grew increasingly weary of having to prove herself. Though a commander by this time, she felt that she was not given the respect nor the responsibilities of which she was capable. Dr. Iskra cited numerous occasions where she was taunted to engage in certain off-duty activities (i.e., tag football) with the men which were simply ploys on the men's part to prove what they could do and what she could not. She frequently declined such "invitations" to participate in what she considered to be puerile tactics to prove herself. Fed up and given the overwhelming pressure despite her pioneering achievements, she retired from the Navy after 21 years of service.

During her final year in the Navy, Dr. Iskra sought refuge through a Navy program for military professorship that offered the opportunity to earn a PhD at a reputable academic institution and subsequently return to teach at the Naval Academy. Although not selected for the program, she was admitted to the University of Maryland where under the direction of the famous duo scholars of military studies Mady Wechsler Segal and David Segal, she pursued and secured her PhD in Sociology, specializing in Military Sociology as well as Gender, Work, and Family.

Dr. Iskra's seagoing career was strenuous and entailed many months away from home. She married a fellow naval officer soon after her assignment to USS *Hector*, and with both of them on sea duty during the critical first few years of their careers, they were often separate. By the time she took command of USS *Opportune*, she had been separated from her husband for about five years in their 10 years of marriage. Being a dual military couple was an unknown circumstance at this early point of the women-at-sea program. As a senior officer on ships, her responsibility was to the command. Yet, she needed the support and friendship of her naval officer husband. It was a very difficult time, made more difficult by the constant scrutiny of being a woman in a man's world.

Even with the highs and lows of her career, Dr. Iskra would still have selected a career as a diver. She loved going to sea, loved diving, and was thrilled to combine the two. She is a believer in equal opportunity for those who are capable of performing the tasks at hand. Not all women can be divers, can be combat pilots, or serve in ground combat positions, she said. But if they are qualified, they should be given the opportunity to try. The culture of the Navy, said Iskra, is such that it is considered a man's world and women in general are often made to feel that they do not belong. The idea that women are not capable or good enough to do the most important things in the military is insidious but continues to this day.

Dr. Iskra relayed an incident that occurred in 1981 while the USS *Hector* was deployed to the Western Pacific. In planning for the latter stages of the United States' attempt to secure the release of the hostages in Iran, there were plans to send the USS *Hector* to the Persian Gulf for support. As the ship was to head into a war zone, the Captain of the ship was ordered to evacuate the women officers. At the time there were only six women officers on board the ship of 800 men, but all were in vital positions. The Captain refused the order citing that all six women possessed the complement of skills that were vital to the ship's mission and that the survival of the ship depended on their capabilities as divers, navigators, deck officers, engineering officers, and supply officers.

Even though women were assigned to noncombatant ships until 1994, the possibility of finding oneself in a combat zone was very real. During Operation Desert Storm, for example, the USS *Acadia* (AD-42), had women aboard and was stationed in the Persian Gulf. Yet, the women aboard had less protection than the all-male aircraft carrier that was also stationed there. The noncombat ships supported combat ships where needed in the war zone, but their capability was limited to self-defense.

The ARSs were in the same situation. The USS *Opportune* while deployed during Operation Desert Storm in the eastern Mediterranean had no ability to determine if an air-fired missile, a hostile aircraft, or torpedo was incoming, nor did it have the ability to fight it. The ship went to General Quarters daily, with the only hope that they could save the ship if hit. All on board were scared of the possibility, not just the women. Once the war was over, the Navy began opening combat ships and aircraft to women given the outstanding performance of women in that operation, both on land and at sea.

On citizenship, Dr. Iskra believes that as Americans we not only have the rights of citizenship, but also responsibilities. For example, voting is both a right and a responsibility, as is the responsibility to serve on juries pursuant to the right of a trial by one's peers. The right to a free education is tied to the responsibility to educate our children. Service in the military is considered a responsibility of citizenship, but many people, specifically women and some minorities, were forbidden from serving until the latter half of the twentieth century, and later with very specific restrictions on what they are allowed to pursue occupationally. Americans are blessed with many unique qualities, hence we cannot continue to exclude able-bodied and willing people from serving their country in the areas for which they are qualified. Dr. Iskra believes that the combat exclusion laws for women should be rescinded and combat jobs be opened for competition to both men and women. Some men will not be able to do some of the tasks just as many women will not be able to complete them; however, if capable they should be able to try. She sees the combat exclusion policy as unconstitutional, in that it denies equality under the Fifth Amendment; qualified and capable women should be allowed to pursue all military occupations.

Dr. Iskra believes that the younger generation of men in the military is likely to be receptive to women's integration into all career fields. She advised that these changes are already evident in Operations Enduring Freedom and Iraqi Freedom. And, as expected, while there will inevitably be push back from some men in the military, the pendulum will eventually swing in women's favor. However, for the assimilation of women into all career fields in the military to work, the military must first get a handle on the rate at which both gender and sexual harassment occur.

Dr. Iskra is proud of her service to the military, even if as a noncombatant. As a commander in a war zone, her ship would have fought to the end if it came to that and was prepared to do so. The line between combat and noncombat is only in the mission of the unit, not of the actions of the unit. By serving in the military she fulfilled her role as a citizen. In addition, despite some unpleasant challenges that she experienced during her Navy career, Dr. Iskra attributes these acts to individuals for which she cannot fault the military as an institution. And, though at the time of this interview the military continues to bar women from holding and pursuing certain occupations, she felt fortunate to pursue what she wanted despite limitations in the greater Naval and military establishment.

As a civilian and private citizen, Dr. Iskra believes that her career in the military has contributed to her stature as a civilian, and hence, she considers her tenure in the Navy beneficial. (In-person interview on July 9, 2012)

Maria "Zoe" Dunning, U.S. Navy, Retired

One of the First to Challenge the U.S. Navy and the Department of Defense Regarding Its "Don't Ask, Don't Tell, and Don't Pursue" Policy Barring Gays from Military Service
First and Only Openly Gay Person to Serve in the U.S. Military during the First 13 Years of the "Don't Ask, Don't Tell, and Don't Pursue" Policy
Sixth Class of Women to Enter the U.S. Naval Academy

This striking tall redhead with an authoritative voice and a deportment that implicitly conveys that she means business quietly lived in fear throughout her early career in the Navy that her secret, then illegal, would be discovered. At the time, as a gay woman, Commander Maria "Zoe" Dunning did everything that was humanly possible to not draw unnecessary attention to her sexual orientation, although unwittingly, there were a few close calls in the process. Commander Dunning was not only one of the first to challenge the U.S. Navy and as a consequence the Department of Defense over its "Don't Ask, Don't Tell, and Don't Pursue" policy that barred the service of gays in the military, but she was also the first and only openly gay person to serve in the U.S. military while the Navy determined the disposition of its proceedings given her precedent-setting challenge and status. Also, Commander Dunning comprised only the sixth class of women who entered the U.S. Naval Academy. Commander Dunning was born and raised in Milwaukee, Wisconsin, to a unique couple in that both of her parents served during WWII. Her father served in the Army Air Corps while her mother, whom she described as "a large, 5′10″ Iowan farm girl," heard that the military was accepting women for military service, and then, as a 19-year-old college student, heeded the call to enlist for the cause. As Commander Dunning put it, the military had plans for her mother and wanted her to fill the function of a butcher in the belief that she was big enough and strong enough to "carry around the quarter hinds of beef," but her mother who was not capable of this role denied the offer saying that she will think about it. But, upon return, her mother lied about her age to the recruiting officer, and became only the second cohort of women in the military to complete OCS at Ft. Des Moines in Iowa. After two years in the Women Army Corps (WAC) and at the rank of first lieutenant, her mother was forced to leave at the end of WWII as the men returned home from overseas.

Commander Dunning's sister too continued the family tradition with a commission in the U.S. Marine Corps. Interestingly enough, Commander Dunning found the Marines Corps to be impressive so much so that she convinced her sister to join in it, while Commander Dunning joined the Navy instead. She stated that in the Marines Corps one's occupational specialty dictates the type of training that would follow, because a marine is first an infantry officer and is therefore less identified by occupational specialty. She felt it was necessary for her sister to fully experience what it really meant to be a marine by not only completing OCS and training for her occupational specialty as a judge advocate general (JAG) officer, but the six-month panoply of required infantry training called the Basic School in Quantico, Virginia, the primary role of any marine. Her sister eventually pursued a successful career in the Marines Corps, subsequently retiring at the rank of Colonel.

Commander Dunning joined the Navy for a number of reasons. As the youngest of seven children, she was instinctively aware that to fund her college education, it was necessary to secure a scholarship. As a participant in Girls State, a program through the American Legion in each state designed to educate high school students about government, she represented her high school at the Wisconsin state capital. While there, a chance encounter with another female who was attending the U.S. Military Academy at West Point at the time became intriguing to the commander given the stories that she had heard about the academy. More importantly, this West Point student was admitted to the academy on a full scholarship, thus adding to the intrigue and about the possibilities of financing her college education through the military. But Commander Dunning was even more captivated by the school's holistic approach to preparing its graduates for their respective careers and life in general in terms of attaining leadership skills, physical fitness, athletics, and the values of the honor code of service in the military. Graduating from such an institution, the commander thought, seemed more than just about securing a degree and to her, was saying more about preparing oneself for service, integrity, and honor. To her surprise, upon returning home from Madison and though she had not initiated the process, she received an application package from the Naval Academy based on her test scores from her Preliminary Scholastic Aptitude Test (SAT). When asked why, despite the conversation with the West Point student that she chose the Navy over the Army, Commander Dunning jokingly replied that her decision was partly based on what each military academy displayed on its catalogue. The Army showed troops marching through the woods while the Navy's was in stark contrast with people sailing on the scenic Chesapeake Bay. Besides, this scenic view harkened back to her childhood days that she spent on Lake Michigan. So, she loves the water. Plus, the Navy seemed to offer more career opportunities for women than did the Army.

After serving as a midshipman for four years at the Naval Academy and following graduation, Commander Dunning remained on active duty for another six years, later choosing to transition to the Navy Reserve for another 16 years. However, Commander Dunning's departure from active duty service was motivated by two overriding factors. First, the Navy consistently stationed her on the East Coast while she envisioned residing on the West Coast. And, second, but more troubling as she found throughout her career, she served in the Navy in constant fear of being discovered that she is a lesbian. Yet, she wanted to continue her career in the Navy and so decided to do so in the Navy Reserve which she perceived as the less risky option of being exposed.

During her career, Commander Dunning served in the Supply Corps which she described as the business side of the military with oversight for such areas as logistics, finance, contracting, procurement, warehousing, distribution, and transportation. Although she was never a unit commander, immediately upon graduation from the Naval Academy, she served as a division officer with approximately 100 people under her supervision with a subsequent assignment as a department head. For a time though, Commander Dunning was stationed on the USS *Lexington*, then at the time, the only aircraft carrier on which women could serve as noncombatants since the vessel was an older ship without the capability to refuel at sea, and therefore the farthest that Commander Dunning remembered leaving the U.S. shores was to Guantanamo Bay in Cuba. As a reservist, however, she completed an amphibious assault exercise in the United Arab Emirates and a port security operation in Qatar and Bahrain. During Operations Desert Shield/Storm, she served in Washington, DC, where she worked with cryptology and with top secret agencies as a transportation point person for the procurement of equipment from destinations the agencies wanted to withhold from the various contractors who were working with them. While Commander Dunning had volunteered for overseas deployments, her requests were denied by citing the reason that her function was invaluable for she could not be replaced or back-filled with anyone else because she was the only contracting officer for the base and was also responsible for the budget. She was told that this was deemed an essential role that could not be left vacant. As a reservist, Commander Dunning volunteered and was active for a short period leading up to the initial stages of Operation Enduring Freedom. But with over 20 years of military service, the prospects for promotion to Captain (06) were dimming and so at the height of Operation Iraqi Freedom, a war in which Commander Dunning believed that the United States should not have become involved, she decided that this was the opportune time to retire from the Navy. And, at the time of her retirement, Commander Dunning had attained her graduate degree in business administration from Stanford University.

Yet, to understand Commander Dunning's inclusion in this research and book, it is important to highlight the series of events that led up to her designation as a pioneering, prominent, and/or elite former military woman. When then candidate Bill Clinton was vying for the Presidency of the United States in 1992, then as a second-year business school student at Stanford University while still in the Navy Reserve, Commander Dunning was moved by candidate Bill Clinton's campaign promise for the outright repeal of the ban on gays from military service. However, as the presidential campaign progressed, the resistance to such a promise became more vociferous including from the military itself, certain religious groups, and even many from the halls of Congress who vowed to block any effort at repealing the longstanding policy. A fellow veteran and classmate at Stanford University urged Commander Dunning to attend an upcoming rally outside of the Moffett Naval Air Station in Mountain View, California, which was approximately four days prior to President Clinton's inauguration in an effort to give visibility to the policy and to encourage the President to fulfill his campaign pledge. While Commander Dunning was supportive of the purpose behind the rally, she was understandably fearful for by attending the event she stood the risk of being caught on camera and "outed" and then of prematurely facing the ending of her military career as a result. Further, she had deliberately struck a compromise to remain in the military by not only transferring to the Navy Reserve thus reducing her exposure of the risks and duress that her sexual orientation would be revealed but that although she derived an income from the Navy, she rationalized that she was earning the largesse of her livelihood as a civilian. After securing additional information about the rally and introducing herself to its organizers, but following much pontification after being asked to speak at the rally, Commander Dunning concluded that the voices of lesbians, namely women gays, which too was gender based, was missing from the overall discourse about the issue of gays in the military. Consequently, she felt compelled to fill this void by offering herself as an exemplar, one with a stellar record of service in the military. Commander Dunning gave a brief speech at the rally that essentially changed her life. In her speech, she brought attention to the fact that as a Naval officer, the military's policy that banned the service of gays and lesbians was inherently contradictory to everything that she had been taught to uphold in the military such as honor, integrity, and telling the truth that then has forced a segment of the military's population to lie about their lives and thus their very existence.

However, upon reporting for reserve duty following the rally, Commander Dunning was immediately summoned to the installation's legal affairs office where she was advised that she was being placed on unpaid administrative leave pending discharge from the military. According to Commander Dunning, at that moment, she felt an immense sense of betrayal by an institution that repeatedly affirmed her value as a career Naval officer, yet, in the same vein, turned on her so easily by vowing her discharge from the military. During this interview, as Commander Dunning painfully relived the journey of her plight and spoke passionately of the dedication to an organization that betrayed her, the resurgence of the emotional feelings of hurt became evident in light of the rejection from an institution that she dearly loved. Left during that reserve weekend with nothing to do and still donned in her uniform, Commander Dunning showed up unannounced at an organizing campaign held in the Mission district of San Francisco by the National Gay and Lesbian Task Force to develop a strategy to encourage President Clinton to lift the ban on gays serving in the military. It was at that point in time, said Commander Dunning, in January 1993, that her activism work took traction, when she told the group that she had just been kicked out of the military and wanted to volunteer her services to help out. And, though falling short of the intended goal to repeal the ban on gays serving in the military, her efforts with key contacts in Washington, DC, led to President Clinton's compromise in the form of the "Don't Ask, Don't Tell, and Don't Pursue" policy.

It is equally important though to note the following. Before coming out as a lesbian, Commander Dunning consulted with her sister, then a JAG officer in the Marine Corps, on how to specifically frame her message. However, while her sister could offer off-the-record counsel, she could not legally advise or provide her with legal representation on the matter. Commander Dunning initially secured legal representation on a *pro bono* basis from the firm of Morrison and Foster for the military administrative hearings. The trial was conducted at Treasure Island, which is located on the outskirts of San Francisco. During the proceedings, despite the presence of several character witnesses, including her sister, who all spoke glowingly about her record as a Naval officer, the military panel unanimously voted to uphold the military's decision to discharge her. Yet, these proceedings were intended to provide the basis for challenging the constitutionality of the military's ban on gays serving in the military so Commander Dunning could file a lawsuit against the military in federal court. Nevertheless and ironically so, while the final decision upon recommendation of the Navy proceedings was waiting to be signed by the Secretary of the Navy, President Clinton's compromise policy in the form of Don't Ask, Don't Tell, and Don't Pursue was announced and created such ambiguity as to the actual meaning of the new policy that it resulted in a second administrative hearing by the Navy to rehear the case, but this time under the Don't Ask, Don't Tell, and Don't Pursue policy. Commander Dunning's attorneys were successful, however, in allowing her return to paid status while awaiting the second hearing and continuing to complete her reserve duty obligations until a decision was rendered.

What is most difficult though to understand and is in itself a conundrum is that during the time that the Navy twice held administrative hearings to discharge Commander Dunning and while she continued to complete her reserve duty, she received notice from the Navy that she had been selected for promotion to the rank of Lieutenant Commander. But it was both the novelty and ambiguity of the Don't Ask, Don't Tell, and Don't Pursue policy that led the Navy to overturn its initial decision to discharge her, thus allowing her to continue serving as a Navy reservist. But, unlike the first military panel that was constituted of two men and one woman, the panel for the second hearing consisted of two women and one man, to which Commander Dunning partially attributed her success. However, because Commander Dunning was successful in the second military hearing, the outcome prohibited her from challenging the constitutionality of the Don't Ask, Don't Tell, and Don't Pursue policy in federal court. And, therefore, she would have had no standing to file suit because she was subsequently retained in the Navy. Similarly, the Pentagon then issued a memorandum for the military services that was based upon the outcome of her second administrative hearing that any statement of sexual orientation presumes conduct and requires a recommendation for discharge. While this strategy, that is, basing the reason for consideration for discharge on conduct alone, proved to be successful for Commander Dunning, it further overshadowed her goal for the complete repeal of the policy on the ban on gays from military service, including the compromise Don't Ask, Don't Tell, and Don't Pursue policy. It, therefore, became necessary to work on crafting an alternative route to overturn the law.

At the time of Commander Dunning's commission, opportunities within the line officer occupation were still limited for women; she relished the idea of being a pilot and wanted to fly planes, although she admitted being airsick. She selected an occupation in Supply Corps, a field that appealed to her because its broad makeup would be transferable to skill sets within the civilian sector. When asked whether or not she would have selected the same occupation if all career fields had been opened to women at the time of her commission in the Navy, Commander Dunning replied that she did consider other career fields such as intelligence but concluded that the required top secret clearance and subsequent investigation could have jeopardized the potential revelation of her sexual orientation in the process. So, she abandoned that idea. Yet, because another officer was relieved of duty for cause, Commander Dunning was tapped for the very position that she feared and was subject to an investigation for a top secret clearance. During this investigation, it was speculated that there was cause for concern that she was a lesbian and during which time she was asked to undergo a polygraph, which she refused. It was because of Commander Dunning's refusal to take the polygraph, and following consultation with her sister, that she feared would result in her possible discharge from the Navy given her sexual orientation. But, Commander Dunning dodged this bullet as the Navy only suspected but lacked hard evidence for such allegations. In the end, Commander Dunning received a top secret security clearance for the position. Commander Dunning said that if women were allowed on combat ships at the time, she probably would have considered such occupations like surface warfare or even submariner as another career option as she longed for the real experience of being in the Navy. But, she would have also selected other career fields that would have increased the likelihood of her facing combat.

Commander Dunning credits the values that were instilled in her by her parents and feels fortunate in being an American citizen. As well, many members of her family pursued service-oriented occupations, given the importance of giving back to one's country and being grateful for being an American citizen. She believes that it is this cultivation that resulted in her own call to service and eventual service in the Navy. Commander Dunning is a proponent of mandatory service although such service she believed need not be through the military. She thus feels that it is both a privilege and a responsibility of being an American citizen. And, by serving in the military, she said that she has only partially fulfilled her role as a citizen and continues to serve her country in other ways. While she recognized that by serving in the military her rights were abridged, Commander Dunning felt that the military's exclusion of gays and lesbians in the military was not in keeping with one's ability to serve one's country or one's performance in serving one's country. Thus, this served as the basis and her underlying reasons for challenging the ban on gays from military service in the desire to move the military to be in keeping with the country's democratic ideals. As a result, given the military's actions, she believes that she was indeed treated as less than a citizen. Commander Dunning also believes that the military's use of gender as a qualification for exclusion from certain occupations was also wrong as such selection should be criteria and competency based. In effect, gender should never be used as a proxy for exclusion. Still, she described her overall experience in the military, the collegiality, and the ability to do unique things such as traveling to faraway places and the like as positive, although Commander Dunning regretted not having gained what she considered to be the full experience of what it means to be a Naval officer. Still, she believes that her experience has built character and as a result has heavily influenced how she goes about being in the civilian sector. As she continued, she said that she has become more sensitized to the cues of certain indiscretions such as sexual harassment that, given her experience as a midshipman in the Naval Academy and what occurs in the civilian sector under the guise of sexual harassment, pales in comparison. But, in many ways, she said, in dealing with these indiscretions in the military, it is much clear on what constitutes sexual harassment. In addition, given the infraction and with the support of the command and in light of the clarity of one's chain of command, it was more easily dealt with and rectified in the military.

On the combat exclusion policy, Commander Dunning believes that the policy creates two classes of service members where women suffer more discrimination as they are perceived to be unequal to men. As such, the qualifications for combat exclusion should be based upon competence and physical ability. Again, gender should never be the basis for which such decisions are made, she said. Further, the American public's dealing with the sight of body bags of deceased female service members should be just as disturbing as those body bags containing deceased male service members. Commander Dunning said that she would have pursued a line combat occupation had it not been for the existence of the policy. And, she chose to leave active duty because as a female she could not envision the opportunity to be promoted to the rank of Captain without having commanded a unit, which for the most part required completing combat duty. She soon realized that as a female there were just some career targets that she was unable to hit in order to achieve her career goals. Therefore, the combat exclusion policy should be repealed.

Commander Dunning is uncertain though as to how repealing the combat exclusion policy will impact the recruitment, promotion, and retention rates of women in the military. In some ways, she believes that the military will be left with those women with the desire to be involved in combat. Nonetheless, by repealing the policy, the way that military men relate to military women would improve as women would be seen as fulfilling their roles by vying for the same jobs, using the same criteria and qualifications as men and taking the same types of risks as men. Initially, she warned that the logistics challenges, that is, to accommodate women, will be evident and will no doubt result in resentment against the women by the men. But, over time, these challenges would be short-lived as men and women would learn how to work with each other, although this adjustment will depend upon the unit and the command climate, and how the new policy under the repeal is implemented, as there might be some backlash against women. For instance, Commander Dunning believes that the integration of women into the Naval Academy was poorly managed in the sense that, unlike the Air Force Academy whose integration of women was far more successful, there were no mentors for the women who were admitted to the Naval Academy, there was no reinforcement that women should be allowed to be there as professionals, and, as a result, and particularly as young midshipmen, she and her female classmates experienced nonstop sexual harassment.

Yet, this experience is to be contrasted with the implementation of the Don't Ask, Don't Tell, and Don't Pursue policy. Here, according to Commander Dunning, the Pentagon made it clear from the beginning to its senior leadership of the way in which the policy was to be implemented. Moreover, as Commander Dunning affirmed, this was the right thing to do. In this case, she continued, there was a clear message that was conveyed from and by the senior leadership and training was instituted for leaders as part of the implementation and reinforced even before repealing the Don't Ask, Don't Tell, and Don't Pursue policy. Consequently, gays and lesbians are now serving openly in the military. Likewise, this type of approach must apply in the event that the combat exclusion policy is repealed and where leadership will be forced to comply kicking and screaming or choose to be proactive by implementing the new policy as doing so will be the right thing to do. Similarly, repealing the combat exclusion policy will improve the overall performance and effectiveness of the military because the military will have a wider and more competitive pool from which to choose for recruitment, promotion, and in turn retention of the best qualified in the military. But, according to Commander Dunning, although repealing the combat exclusion policy will have a positive impact as well on the women within the civilian sector, she disputed whether or not this impact will be equal. Yet, the ripple effect of repealing the combat exclusion policy will be positive even for civilian women as those women who leave the military will be competitive for employment within the civilian sector.

Currently as a private citizen and when she has sought employment within the civilian sector, Commander Dunning said that people are frequently surprised that she served in the military because it is just not expected. Yet, as Commander Dunning pointed out, it is her military service that often distinguishes her from all other applicants. She said that on the one hand, there are actually positive stereotypes that emanate from being in the military such as neatness, discipline, and being organized. But, on the other hand, there are also negative stereotypes as well such as inflexibility, and being hierarchical and very structured. Commander Dunning has also been told that her military service can be intimidating to others and for this reason she sometimes deliberately withholds this information. So, she has become more strategic in how and when to disclose this information. She believes that her military service has facilitated her civilian employment as well as provided her with the opportunity to compete for roles that demand higher compensation. As a private citizen, who now resides in San Francisco, Commander Dunning described her overall experience as sometimes challenging as there is often a tenuous relationship between the military and the people of San Francisco, a very progressive city. When asked to identify what race and/or ethnicity she belongs to, Commander Dunning asserted that her status as a gay woman has helped her in understanding the sensitivities of other demographic groups in society as she constantly searches to understand the nature of the assumed privileges of being a Caucasian woman.

Ms. Rose Marie Jackson, Commander, U.S. Navy, Retired

First Female Cohort of Surface Warfare Officers in the U.S. Navy

Following the passage of the National Defense Authorization Acts (NDAA) of 1992, 1993, and 1994, marking Congress' willingness to formally open occupations that were previously closed to women in the military, Commander Rose Marie Jackson became one of the first cohorts of women and among the handful of African American women, at the time, to become surface warfare officers in the Navy. Jackson hails from a military family, having had her stepfather and an older brother serve in the Army and her oldest brother served in the Marine Corps. With two undergraduate degrees to her credit and at almost age 26, she joined the Navy after short circuiting her pursuit of graduate school as she no longer desired careers in economics and business that she had previously studied. Growing up as a military brat, Jackson found pursuing a military career to be a viable option and so following her acceptance to the delayed entry program for seven months, she secured a slot, completed OCS, served on active duty for eight years, and then continued in the Navy Reserve for almost 13 years until her retirement, the last five years of which she served as an inactive ready reservist (IRR).

After an initial stint as a line officer in an administrative category, Jackson had a choice as a female line officer to apply for and possibly be assigned to either a noncombatant aviation squadron or on surface ships. Although at the time she was already serving in an aviation squadron, she decided to apply for and was accepted to the surface warfare officer program when the field was initially opened to women following the Navy's successful experimentation of placing women in restricted capacity (auxiliary) on designated ships as surface warfare officers. Thereafter, Jackson moved from a general unrestricted line officer to that of a Division Officer on one ship, a split assignment to a second ship, where she served as the acting Chief of Engineering for decommissioning, supervising approximately five Division Officers. Her assignments included Rota, Spain; Auxiliaries Officer, Damage Control Assistant, and Acting Chief Engineer on two ships based on the Atlantic Coast; and a shore duty assignment as a Reserve Officer Training Corps (ROTC) instructor at Texas A&M University, during which time she left active duty to transfer to the Navy Reserve. Jackson's reserve assignment included Galveston, Texas; Seattle, Washington; and Portland, Oregon.

Because all Navy ships were deployed overseas, Jackson completed two Mediterranean deployments. She served during Operations Desert Shield/Storm on ammunitions and auxiliary fleet support ships that resupplied forward destroyers, aircraft carriers, and other combatant ships with weapons and supplies. Jackson's role while at sea was largely in combat support. When asked if at any time, especially during Operations Desert Shield/Storm, she experienced being in a combat zone or in a theater of operations where conflict occurred, Jackson replied that these distinctions were particularly ambiguous at the time in the sense that the ships on which she was assigned did cross into the Red Sea and the Arabian Gulf to resupply ships, which theoretically brought her ship into the combat zone and within the theater of operations.

Jackson eventually separated from the Navy as she was in line to return to sea duty again. Upon reflection, Jackson described her ship duty experience as not particularly positive. She had long decided that the military was no longer a viable career path for her as she was equally uncomfortable within the surface warfare community and there were other overriding factors that moved her to leave active duty. First, Jackson did not envision an acceptable work-life balance had she remained in the Navy as a surface warfare officer; there was already a high attrition rate within the career field even among male surface warfare officers and she did not desire to serve at sea given her especially negative experience. Moreover, in hindsight, Jackson is uncertain as to whether or not she would have selected the same career field, that is, as a surface warfare officer, if all career fields were opened to women. And, second, the military was experiencing a drawdown of its workforce and was offering monetary incentives for personnel to leave the Navy. This incentive provided the opportune time to make the transition to the reserve. Jackson separated from active duty and retired from the Navy at the rank of commander with master's degrees in international relations and English literature and information and library sciences.

On citizenship, Jackson defined the concept as a cooperative, collaborative, and dynamic situation, which at times requires one to either give or take more from society. She believes that being a citizen requires striking a compromise as a give and take relationship between oneself, one's society, and one's nation. Further, as an American citizen, this means having certain inalienable rights. As well, by serving in the military, Jackson believes that she has fulfilled her role as a citizen to her country. When asked however whether or not she believes that the military has treated her as a citizen, Jackson concedes that at times this was not the case. Yet, being in the military affords different levels of rights that are sometimes at odds with being a citizen. For example, one's ability to voice dissent is limited in the military, given the institution's hierarchical structure that requires unquestioned compliance as compared to that of citizenship. And being barred from certain occupations in the military on the basis of gender clearly created a caste system in the military's workforce.

Jackson cited her own experience, particularly as an African American woman, walking into an environment that was in its constitution at that time in excess of 90% white men, and one that created a constant and overwhelming need not only to prove oneself as a female but always doing so from a defensive stance. She spoke of the undue pressure of being an outlier in that as both a woman and an African American, she was different. Yet, in spite of this negative experience, Jackson lauds the positive examples of leadership and friendships that she developed in the process. As a civilian, however, she has found that unlike in the military where she consistently remained guarded, it was important as a civilian to let down those defenses. As for the combat exclusion policy, Jackson stated that the expectations for her generation joining the military were of a different mindset because she entered the military during a period of dormancy where the focus was more on readiness brought about by conducting exercises and training. And in all candor, given the times, she did not join the military to fight but for the opportunity that the institution provided to pursue a career. Moreover, in light of peacetime, it was unlikely that in the post-Vietnam period that combat would occur. However, women who entered the military following Operations Desert Shield/Storm faced a greater need to be involved in situations that called for combat, whereas her cohort did not. Jackson believes that selection to go to war should be based on one's career specialty, not gender. And, given the specialties, one would be more likely to be aware of the accompanying risks of combat, regardless of gender.

Jackson concedes that during her military service, the existence of the combat exclusion policy, then dubbed the risk rule, clearly limited her career options and in turn the types of ships and positions on those ships in which she could serve. Not only did this exclusion influence her career decisions, but she was barred from gaining the required experience for command at sea. Moreover, the ships on which women were assigned to at the time tended to be older auxiliary vessels, which prevented women from securing the necessary engineering experience, in her case, on the much newer ships. These restrictions on women only resulted in a domino effect that in turn confined their qualifications for assignment to only older ships. Therefore, said Ms. Jackson, the combat exclusion policy should be repealed. But while she does not believe that repealing the policy will dramatically increase neither the recruitment nor the retention of women, she foresees some improvement in their promotion rates with associated improvements in the ways that military men would relate to military women. The messaging and ensuing practice of exclusivity that says that only one gender gets to do certain things, which creates a structural barrier that also leads to promotional barriers for women because when someone, in this case a man, possesses an additional qualification that a woman is barred from even competing for, the man's record presented will be viewed more favorably by the promotion board that is most likely made up of men who have also attained the necessary qualifications and experience.

Jackson sees that repealing the combat exclusion policy would make men recognize that women are as capable and change their perceptions of women overall. In addition, the performance and overall effectiveness of the military would increase as a result. However, the manner in which the Navy initially began integrating women on ships, in a sense, created a quota system that inherently limited women's opportunities as well as even those of men's for assignments by removing especially younger men from assignment to auxiliary ships, for example, as given the restrictions, these slots were primarily reserved for women. This practice then created better opportunities for men, not women, to serve on combatant ships while devalued assignments to auxiliary ships by men. Thus, by opening additional positions to both men and women, everyone in the pool can compete for assignments on an equal footing. These structural changes in the military will be of particular advantage to civilian woman who work for the Department of Defense as repealing the combat exclusion policy may not immediately translate to similar advantages for women within the civilian sector. In fact, Jackson believes that the average civilian woman's life will be largely left untouched by such changes in the military.

Finally, securing employment within the civilian sector has been a positive experience for Jackson, which she attributes to her military service and experience. Additionally, having veterans' preference credited toward civilian employment consideration, to her knowledge, has resulted in increases in her compensation. However, though, as she sees it, unlike military men, military women in the civilian sector for the most part remain invisible as a group because it is less obvious that they have served in the military. For example, military men traditionally maintain a closer adherence to identification with the military in terms of haircut, attire, and language and similarly engage with the civilian community than military women. Jackson offers herself as a second example in that no one with whom she has worked as either recognized her service as a military officer or her unique and precedent-setting roles that she played in the military.

Rose M. Jackson is currently assigned as a Foreign Service Officer with responsibility for the eastern countries in the continent of Africa. (In-person interview on June 25, 2012)

Ms. Yona Owens, U.S. Navy

The First Cohort of Eight Women Accepted in the All-Male Occupation as Interior Communications Technicians in the U.S. Navy
*First Person to Challenge the Department of Defense's Restriction of Women's Assignment on Ships That Subsequently Led to Women's Integration on Ships (*Owens v. Brown *1978)*

This larger than life personality had the moxie to challenge the Department of Defense and by extension the Secretary of Defense Harold Brown over its policy that was a matter of law that barred women from assignment to ships (*Owens v. Brown* 1978). And though Owens did not personally benefit from its rescission for by then she had separated from the Navy before the court ruling, it was her legal action in challenging the constitutionality of this restriction that eventually led to women's assignments to shipboard duty. Owens was also in the first cohort of eight women to be accepted as interior communications technicians in the Navy. But in many ways, Owens's life before and during military service all represented mile markers along the road that pointed to her take-charge attitude. Born and raised in Charlotte, North Carolina, with a long tradition of military service in the U.S. military as far back as the Civil War when her great grandfather served—her grandfather served in the Spanish-American War at age 12 after lying about his age and subsequently served during WWI, and her father in WWII—Owens was raised in a family with a very strong Navy tradition. She emanates from a patriarchal family, one where 80% of the family members were male. Owens also came of age at a time when challenging the *status quo* was in vogue: Gloria Steinem, bra burning, and a time of consciousness raising about the Vietnam conflict coupled with the grim images of body bags from Vietnam on television. In essence, "being a wimpy woman at the time was not where we were headed," said Owens. So, the times were ripe for change. Owing to what Owens later learned was propaganda during WWII about women in the military, it was not until 1973 when at age 22 she joined the Navy and became the first female in her family to do so. She joined the Navy not only to continue her college education but also to secure viable skills for employment; however, she was desperately seeking her father's approval by continuing the family tradition.

Owens served on active duty in the Navy for four years with the remaining two years in the Navy Reserve and in the Navy's first cohort of women interior communication technicians, a formerly all-male occupation. While Owens did not intentionally select this occupation, she performed exceedingly well on the electronics portion of a battery of tests. And, incidentally, because she had been up early at 4:00 a.m. on the appointed morning of the tests, by 6:00 a.m. Owens said that she was in a hurry to eat breakfast and by a fluke took the electronics part of the tests by randomly selecting what she thought were the correct answers, although admittedly while she scored highly, she had no clue as to what she was doing. She subsequently attended both basic and advanced electronics school, where, given the broad range of occupations within the electronics field, she was often the only woman in attendance. For example, at one school, she was the only woman in a school of 650 men while in another school she was the only woman among 1200 men. As a result, Owens quickly developed a repertoire of quick-witted vocabulary to counteract the often rude encounters she experienced with fellow male students. However, according to Owens, once the male students learned that she knew what she was doing and received good grades as a result, they frequently wanted to team study with her.

Yet, as she described, there was always that one group of male students who were horrified at the sight of a woman in the Navy, much less in electronics school. Owens said that the verbal discrimination against women in the Navy at the time was fierce. She cites an incident where because women at the time were still wearing the uniform skirts that were designed for the WAVES (Women Accepted for Voluntary Emergency Services) or the WINS (Women in the Naval Services), to avoid the onslaught of sexually harassing remarks and unnecessarily calling attention to themselves, the WINS would deliberately wear their skirts below their knees. Owens described these scenarios as tantamount to walking through construction sites. But, because she came from a male-enlisted Navy background, one day when she encountered a similar situation, instead of ignoring the infraction, she decided to stop it head on by approaching the male who was leading the pack. She walked up to him directly and said "If I was your sister and you heard some guy say what you just said to me, what would you do to him?" He grew silent. And, by using this similar approach to quell such situations, she almost never encountered these problems again. While she served at many shore locations in the United States, at the time when her cohorts graduated from particular schools, only the men, not the women, could be assigned to ship duty which she desperately wanted to do. Owens then decided to question the reason for this practice and was told that because she is a woman they did not know exactly what to do with her upon graduation from each school or course even though given her career field, the equipment on which she needed to work were all to be found on ships. But, as a woman, she was barred from shipboard duty.

Incidentally, following this query, and while in queue with fellow classmates to use the telephone, Owens overheard one schoolmate attempting to convince the detailer that because his wife was very ill and in the hospital, he did not wish to be assigned overseas. Owens tapped her schoolmate on the shoulder and asked where he was being sent. He replied Negishi Microwave site in Japan. Owens asked, "Is this on land?" to which her schoolmate replied that it is. She demanded, "Give me the telephone!" and explained to the detailer to give her the assignment to Negishi and her school assignment to her male schoolmate. By then, Owens had simply grown tired of going from school to school without an official assignment to practice her job training. As a result of this unexpected request, Owens was deployed for 18 months to Japan in the Pacific Fleet and during the last months of the Vietnam era conflict.

While she never served shipboard duty, Owens received numerous calls from former male classmates who offered her opportunities to work on equipment on docked ships. Further, as she explained, this was the only way that she would have been able to hone her skills by working on the actual equipment on ships for which she had been trained. By today's standards, Owens stated, at that time doing so was a novel idea in that, because they liked her, she and her male cohorts concocted these plans as they wanted her to succeed. Besides, the interior communications field by then had become a small but close knit community of technicians. But Owens was actually the one who schemed to secure permission to work on the ships while they were dry docked for repairs. According to her then commander, there was nothing in the policy that barred her from doing so though no females had ever received such permission. During his appointment, the then Chief of Naval Operations, Admiral Elmo Zumwalt, was to many in the Navy, especially to women in the Navy, a feminist as he opened many positions that were formerly closed to women. However, while in 1972 and 1973, the Navy opened many schools to women, including the Naval Academy, according to Owens, it was not necessarily the Navy's policy that barred women from shipboard duty, it was the law that did. Unlike many women at the time, Owens continued to successfully pass test that resulted in successive promotions in rank to E-5. She said, however, that her stay and progression in the Navy confounded the powers that be in Washington, DC, as she was a statistical anomaly in that given the expectations for military women, she should have already separated from the military, preferring the roles of wife and motherhood.

Owens began to write letters to the leaders in Washington, DC, in an effort to challenge the law barring women from shipboard duty. Admiral Zumwalt had encouraged the enlisted corps to submit such "chits" or comments up the chain of command. His successor, Admiral James Holloway, encouraged this practice as well. Owens continued to utilize this medium to challenge the law but would in turn receive replies that nothing about the law could be changed and that she should not even think about securing orders for shipboard duty. Her actions preceded the passage of the risk rule, which was later replaced by the combat exclusion policy. What was also contradictory though, according to Owens, is that shore duty on which only females could be assigned was considered a plum assignment for men in the Navy and only following service after a specified period of time and shipboard duty, they could command such assignments. Besides, many of her male cohorts resented having to serve multiple shipboard duty assignments when she was always given shore duty assignments without paying the price, so to speak. Further, women were still under the 1948 and 1960 rules that barred them from also using firearms.

During her assignment in Washington, DC, Owens filed a class action lawsuit against both the Secretaries of Defense and the Navy citing that Title 10, Section 6015 of the U.S. Code, should be declared unconstitutional for the law barred women in the Navy from shipboard duty. She was joined by three other enlisted women and the case thus classifying the case for class action. Eventually, four female officers also joined the case. And, according to Owens, each female litigant in their own right had excelled in previously all-male occupations in the Navy. Apparently, the law was interpreted so narrowly that even a female helicopter pilot could not hover over a transport ship to deliver cargo. Owens decided that if the lawsuit had not been decided favorably by the end of her enlistment, there was no need for her to remain in the Navy as given the restrictions against women and where they could be assigned, she had advanced as far as she could in terms of job experience and would have remained at the same rank at E-5 for the next four years while her male peers would have advanced in both rank and experience in light of the range of assignments afforded to them. Owens's enlistment contract ended in 1977; the case of *Owens v. Brown* however was not decided until 1978.

Ironically, it was while she was stationed at Negishi Microwave site in Japan that Owens learned that the Navy Military Sealift Command operated oceanographic ships that were research vessels on which academic women served as researchers, which later became the impetus for the lawsuit. The Military Sealift Command also allowed the wives of the male captains aboard these vessels to live with them. Owens had befriended one of the detailers and asked him to try to secure orders for her on one of the ships in this command. Amazingly, the orders were approved but given her first name "Yona," no one at headquarters had scrutinized the orders closely enough even though such orders were dictated by gender. In essence, from her first name and perhaps occupation, it was not assumed that she was female. Owens was assigned to the USNS *Michelson*. Though she reported to the ship and received a warm welcome from the Captain's wife as well as the female researchers aboard, she was immediately contacted by the detailer and advised that the Admiral in charge of personnel had canceled her orders as he discovered that she is a female. The irony though at the time was that some in the Navy were actually seeking an exemplary female like Owens to challenge the law against women serving shipboard duty, for accordingly, there was always a supportive group of both women and men for the cause. The detailer said, however, that had she, Owens, been in the continental United States (CONUS), she could file a lawsuit. So, Owens began the process by doing just that. She requested that the detailer assign her somewhere in CONUS to facilitate this process and ended up at the National Military Command Center and of all places with the Joint Chiefs of Staff at the Pentagon. To Owens, this assignment could not have been more convenient.

While stationed at the Pentagon, she was asked on her own time, to research for the American Civil Liberties Union (ACLU) Women's Rights Project to locate documentation that provided the rationale for women's service on shipboard duty and why the law barring women was unconstitutional and should be repealed. The Women's Rights Project accepted the case and filed the complaint in federal court in Washington, DC. As more luck would have it again, John Sirica, who was more famously known as the presiding judge over the Watergate scandal, was selected for the only equal opportunity case of his illustrious career. He ruled that the law was unconstitutional at the district federal court level. Owens proclaimed that they nailed it right the first time avoiding any unnecessary appeal to either the appellate or the U.S. Supreme Court. But by then Owens had already separated from the Navy and did not directly benefit from the decision. Yet, in spite of the ruling, it was not until 1999, through a chance encounter, that Owens learned from a fellow female veteran that it was also not until 1992 that Congress actually repealed the law despite the 1978 court decision. And, it was not until the passage of the NDAAs in 1992, 1993, and 1994 that the risk rule was changed to the combat exclusion policy. Therefore, Owens is not only to be credited as the catalyst for helping to chip away at the law leading to its present iteration as the combat exclusion policy, she is to be forever memorialized as one of the Navy's first female interior communications technicians. As aforementioned, Owens did not knowingly select the electronics career field but later on realized that her college major where she was pursuing an undergraduate degree in arts and pottery and that required working in kilns and on similar equipment as in electronics actually helped to prepare her for an electronics career in the Navy. Besides, she was always mechanically inclined. And although she performed poorly in mathematics in high school, she credits the Navy with successfully moving her from basic mathematics to advanced calculus and trigonometry.

For Owens, citizenship means participating in government at some level and where one always votes. She believes that by serving in the military she has fulfilled her role as a citizen. She recalls an encounter with a Vietnam era veteran returning to the United States who said that if women want to demand equal rights, then they should also serve in the military. Believing this to be a logical argument, and determined to continue her family's legacy of military service, she joined the military. Yet, while in the military, Owens does not believe that she was treated as a full citizen. She said that for military service, until the law says any citizen without regard to gender can fully serve, only then can women be considered full citizens. And, by being barred from certain career fields in the military, women are treated as less than citizens. Job descriptions, not gender, should be the overriding criteria and qualification. But overall, Owens could not have imagined what her life would have been had she not joined the Navy, for what her military service ultimately taught her was how to act like a lady and think like a man.

In referring to the combat exclusion policy, Owens opines that unlike past wars that necessitated massive troop build up on the ground, future wars will be fought very differently. However, if the military fails to take advantage of the critical pool of women with the required skill sets at any time, it might find itself at a significant disadvantage. To lose the continuity of this expertise through failure to pass on these skills to the future generations of women will result in a real loss to the military overall. And, had it not been for the existence of the various iterations of the combat exclusion policy, Owens would have remained in the military. So, she is definitely a proponent of its repeal. However, the policy's successful repeal will be dictated by the efforts toward implementation by each branch of the military. And, while Owens does not anticipate drastic changes in the repeal of the policy in the rates at which women will be recruited, promoted, and retained in military branches like the Air Force and Navy, she believes that in light of the mission and culture of the Army and the Marines, achieving such rates will prove more challenging. Yet, as Owens was quick to note, this is not to say that women should not be given the opportunity to compete for any of these occupations. In fact, she believes that one approach for rescinding the combat exclusion policy would be to reinstate the draft which she supports as a better way of providing young people with the experience and maturity through boot camp as one of such avenues. Yet, she does not necessarily believe that repealing the combat exclusion policy will discernibly change the ways in which military men will relate to military women, although what she expects is that if women are trained in the ways of combat, the likelihood for the incidence of such indiscretions as sexual harassment and military sexual trauma will decline since women would not only be perceived as being on equal footing with men but will possess the assertiveness, skills, and confidence in themselves to counter such violations. Further, while she does not see a backlash in repealing the policy, Owens is hopeful that women will remain ever vigilant in the fight not only to retain the gains, particularly in light of the current political climate, but to keep moving forward for more gains. Repealing the combat exclusion policy will then result in the improved performance and the overall effectiveness of the military because women will be placed in a predominantly male environment that will move even men to improve their performance out of sheer competition in not exposing their deficiencies in the presence of women. However, it would be difficult to anticipate whether or not such advancements by women in the military would have parallel effects for women in the civilian sector, for like men, translating combat-related skills from the military to the civilian sector also poses a challenge, although such skills may be transferable to such public safety occupations as the police and firefighting.

Following military service in 1977, Owens was actually advantaged because of veterans' preference in hiring. She secured employment in corporate communications over a male applicant for the same position because she was a veteran and he was not. Owens said that she has never experienced any problems in securing employment in the civilian sector and has even established various businesses along the way. She has never shied away and has always made it a point though of mentioning that she is a veteran and also returned to school courtesy of Uncle Sam. And she discovered that when she disclosed that she is a veteran to male colleagues, there is always an instant rapport with them as she confessed that being in the military has certainly leveled the playing field for her. Yet, despite the veterans status advantage, Owens has also discovered, but not until age 45, that she experienced salary inequities simply because of her gender and has never missed the opportunity to bring this disparity to her male superiors' attention. Owens also made it a point of ending this interview on an optimistic note. She said that of the six or seven areas in which women were previously denied equal footing with men in accordance with the original Women Armed Services Integration Act of 1948, the denial of benefits to military women with dependents when military men with dependents automatically received such benefits as one example, these illegal and discriminatory acts against women were all successfully challenged by women through the court system. She credits the great courage that it took our foremothers to challenge these unfair systems. She bemoaned though, and as a stark reminder of the lengths to which women must go in order to make a difference, by invoking *Time Magazine*'s Women of the Year in 1976 when it took 10 women to grace its cover, a practice that is contrary to the magazine's usual portrayal of this coveted title reserved for singly the Man of the Year. (Interview via telephone on July 20, 2012)

Chapter 9

Commanding the Land: The Soldiers

Colonel Beverly "Sam" Stipe, U.S. Army, Retired

First Woman to Be Assigned to a Nike Hercules Battery Missile Unit
First Female Assigned to a Patriot Battery Missile Unit

It was after seeing her father's uniforms that were tucked away and long forgotten in the attic that first led to this senior Army officer's love for the military. Later, she developed a passion to become an Air Defense Artillery Vulcan platoon leader following her commission. During her formidable military career, despite her designation as a noncombatant simply because of her gender, she virtually spent all of her time in roles that reflected the opposite, or that of a combatant. In fact, one of this officer's initial functions following commission through the Reserve Officer Training Corps (ROTC) was the subject of Anne Mazur's (1998) work about the Cold War era when U.S. military women were placed in underground bunkers in geographically remote sites across the United States for the sole purpose of intercepting missiles from the Soviet Union that were headed toward the United States. Yet, Colonel Beverly "Sam" Stipe still managed to secure dual places in ourstory (history) that will forever identify her as not only the first woman to be assigned to a Nike Hercules battery missile system but the first woman to be assigned to the Patriot missile system, both during the Cold War era between the United States and the Soviet Union.

Colonel Stipe was born in Los Angeles, California. Her father's transfer with Litton Industries led to the family's relocation to Ocean Springs, Mississippi. While she remembers that her father was conscripted in the military during the Korean Conflict, Colonel Stipe is unaware of any other military service on either the maternal or the paternal side of her family. But, it was as an impressionable 14 year old when Colonel Stipe stumbled upon her father's footlocker containing his uniforms from the Korean Conflict that she became so enamored with the military and remembered making the decision to join the institution as a result. During college, she considered attending the U.S. Military Academy as one of the first cohorts of women and with her father's assistance and that of the then Congressman Trent Lott (R-MS) began to pursue this career route. However, instead, she decided to remain closer to home and secured a four-year ROTC scholarship through which she received her commission to active duty service in the Army with an undergraduate degree in athletic administration and coaching. Colonel Stipe became an air defense artillery officer, one of the Army's four combat arms occupations that is focused on air threats, one of those functions includes shooting down hostile aircraft from the sky. For four years during the 1980s, she was assigned as a platoon leader for the now extinct Nike Hercules missile defense system that included nuclear warheads. Her responsibility involved staving off the Russian Air Force should their aircraft or missiles cross into German airspace. Colonel Stipe remained in this Air Defense Artillery occupation throughout her military career that included multiple assignments in various leadership roles.

First, as a platoon leader in Germany with 81 male soldiers under her command, she became the first female to be assigned to the Nike Hercules battery missile system. Colonel Stipe described this period as a particularly cautious time especially as a female commanding an all-male force. Her second assignment also resulted in another first, this time as the first woman to be assigned to the Patriot missile battery of 150 male and female soldiers. As a Lieutenant Colonel and one of the few remaining women in the field who was promoted to that rank, she was selected to command a battalion of approximately 800 men and women. While one of the four women who was still in combat arms and promoted to the rank of Lieutenant Colonel retired from the military, the remaining three women were not only promoted to Colonel but then in an unprecedented move by the Army, all three women were subsequently selected to command brigades. Specifically, Colonel Stipe commanded approximately 3300 people who represented a panoply of mission support functions for Space and Missile Defense Command for the U.S. Army Kwajalein Atoll and the Ronald Reagan Ballistic Missile Test Center in the Marshall Islands. Here, she also served as a pseudo ambassador in her role working with the U.S. ambassador on Marshallese issues. In this capacity, Colonel Stipe described herself as "the roads and commodes Commander" in that the scope of her responsibilities were wide-ranging. She served in several domestic assignments and overseas in Germany, the Marshall Islands, Korea, and during Operations Desert Shield/Desert Storm in Saudi Arabia and Kuwait. She has served in a combat arms capacity throughout her career. And, to be clear, Colonel Stipe has always served in combat units but without the accompanying designation as a combatant. Her units, and particularly those during Operations Desert Shield/Storm, were Patriot units were used as defense against incoming scud missiles from Saddam Hussein's regime against targets in Saudi Arabia and Kuwait. In essence, Colonel Stipe, and many women under her command were in direct harm's way in an extended missile range. After 30 years of exemplary military service, Colonel Stipe retired from the Army with two graduate degrees, one in organizational management from the University of Phoenix, and one in strategy from the U.S. Army War College.

As a young cadet, Stipe was selected to fire artillery on the live firing range while attending the ROTC advanced camp at Fort Riley, Kansas, and learning about the various military weapon systems on air defense artillery day. It was at this point that she selected air defense artillery as her future field of study to pursue in the Army and as a distinguished graduate, Cadet Stipe's desire was to become a Vulcan platoon leader, although in the end, she was disqualified and assigned as a Nike Hercules platoon leader solely because she was not male. The short-range air defense artillery field was essentially closed to women because of their possible placement in direct combat while the larger missiles such as the Nike Hercules and the Hawk were permanently placed in remote locations and therefore were perceived as not placing those working on this mission in direct harm's way. Ironically, it was widely known at the time that the women routinely outperformed the men on these weapon systems. Cadet Stipe was assigned to the larger of the two missile systems, the Nike Hercules instead. Although she was barred from working with the Vulcan air defense missile system given her gender, Colonel Stipe said that even in retrospect, if all career fields in the Army were opened to women then, she would have still selected air defense artillery as her career in the Army.

To Colonel Stipe, being a citizen involves active engagement by making one's voice heard. And to her being an American citizen means protecting the rights of others in accordance with the Constitution, and by extension, through military service. Colonel Stipe received early civics lessons from her parents who were politically active to the point of having the U.S. Constitution as a reference point in their home. As a result of this upbringing, she takes her role as a citizen very seriously. Further, her mother was a natural ourstorian (historian). Having spent time in other countries, Colonel Stipe regards her role as an American citizen to be even more sacred. And, despite being barred from the system that she would have liked, that is, to work on the Vulcan missile defense system, she was still able to pursue air defense artillery and believes that she was given the choice to do so and was not treated as less than a citizen by the military. However, as a civilian, Colonel Stipe described her experience following military service as somewhat disappointing in the sense that in the Army she said that one's words was one's bond. Yet in the civilian sector as she later found, this is not the case. She felt that people take advantage of situations for the purpose of getting ahead and in turn getting something for nothing which appears to be the norm.

On the combat exclusion policy and the role of women in the military, Colonel Stipe used a very apt yet poignant analogy to explain the existence of this policy. As Colonel Stipe put it, the military in its role as "daddy" does not want its daughters to be in combat. According to Colonel Stipe, if women want to serve, then they should be allowed to do so providing that they have the capability. In fact, she believes that women react very differently to stressors than men do. And, with the exception of what she terms as a "small disappointment" in the scheme of things, she was placed exactly in the career field where she was supposed to have been in the first place. While this was the case for her, Colonel Stipe cautioned, however, that if the combat exclusion policy is repealed, women might be forced into positions that they may not be physically capable of handling. And, given the quota orientation of the Army, the women selected for certain positions might not make it. As a consequence, there may be a backlash against women as group. And, in effect, it would be setting them up for failure. This, Colonel Stipe declared, would be a form of forced integration. Colonel Stipe also believes that since the combat exclusion policy has now been repealed, it might deter women from joining the military. Forcing women into combat roles would come at an expense because they may not want to be placed into these roles. In light of her own military experience in being in positions of multiple firsts, and where she was forced to work with groups of men, women would have to consistently exceed the performance of men in order to be accepted in all career fields given the level of caution and potential distrust against them. Additionally, Colonel Stipe stated that she is uncertain whether or not the military would in turn benefit in recruiting, promoting, and retaining women as a result of the combat exclusion policy being repealed. Accordingly, women will only earn respect and acceptance through their actions. Colonel Stipe is equally uncertain as to whether or not repealing the combat exclusion policy will have similar effects on women in the civilian sector because, having retired recently, she is still very much in her infancy of becoming a civilian again. Similarly, she said that she would be unable to determine these potential effects for civilian women since there are virtually no occupations within the civilian sector, with the exception of some public safety occupations of course, that are on par with those involving combat in the military.

Following retirement from the military, Colonel Stipe has had almost no problems in securing employment within the civilian sector. Actually, in light of the reputation that she developed in the military, particularly in air defense artillery, she received unsolicited and lucrative offers from two defense contractors, which she subsequently declined. Colonel Stipe said that she has benefitted immensely, especially from the Veterans Administration (VA) from which she has received tremendous support, including training in entrepreneurship, to launch her own business. Her business involves boarding for the pets of deployed military personnel. Not only will her business be assisting veterans, but also including those no longer on active duty, she is also in a position to employ veterans, specifically wounded warriors with posttraumatic effects of war or traumatic brain injuries who have the desire to work with pets, and by extension, help in their healing. Colonel Stipe believes that her military service has been an advantage for her now that she is a private citizen. She stated that she is known by her reputation and is often addressed as "Colonel" as if she is still in the military. (Interview via telephone on August 30, 2012)

Command Sergeant Major Cynthia Pritchett, U.S. Army, Retired

First Female First Sergeant in a Combat Service Support Company in the First Infantry Division Forward Unit in Germany
First Female Command Sergeant Major of a Subunified Combatant Command at a Time of War
First Female Command Sergeant Major at Ft. Belvoir, Virginia
First Female Command Sergeant Major of the Combined Armed Center at Ft. Leavenworth, Kansas
First Female Senior Enlisted Advisor to the Commander for Operation Enduring Freedom
First Female Command Sergeant Major with Command for 30,000 U.S. and Coalition Enlisted Troops in Afghanistan

Command Sergeant Major (CSM) Cynthia Pritchett has always admired the military uniform. And, as a military brat she had repeated exposure to military life. But it was in defiance of her father who had other plans for his daughter that ultimately led to CSM Pritichett's pursuit of a successful career in the U.S. Army. Much of this success included becoming the first female First Sergeant of a combat service support in the First Infantry Division Forward Unit in Germany, the first female CSM of a subunified combatant command at a time of war, the first female CSM at the Ft. Belvoir military installation as well as the first female CSM at Ft. Leavenworth's Combined Armed Center with responsibility for all combat arms and combat support schools in the Army and for the leadership development education of the enlisted and commissioned officer corps, including warrant officers. Also, as an advisor to the three-star General and Commander and Commanding General in Afghanistan during Operation Enduring Freedom, she had the good fortune of advising the Commander on all matters concerning joint or combined force integration, utilization, and sustainment of over 30,000 U.S. and coalition enlisted troops stationed there. These numbers of firsts, together with the increasing leadership roles assumed, speak undeniably about CSM Pritchett's strength and depth of character.

Born in Concord, New Hampshire, but raised all over the United States given her father's career in the Navy, as a child, CSM Pritchett's father taught her how to shoot. So, she became enamored with the idea of hitting things down range, shooting things, and then blowing them up. Surprisingly though, CSM Pritchett was not the first female in her family to join the military. Her mother enlisted in the Navy to escape the routine of small town life. Yet, when her husband left for sea duty and she was pregnant, her mother returned to Concord, New Hampshire, to have her first child. However, the decision for CSM Pritchett to join the military came at the expense of an argument with her father about where she should attend college. While CSM Pritchett's desire was to attend college that was closer to home in light of the family dynamics that existed at the time, her father was insistent that she attend Purdue University. But she disobeyed him by visiting the local all services recruiting office, deliberately sidestepping the Navy, and at that point, opted to join the Army immediately upon graduation from high school and retired after 36 years, seven months, and 29 days of military service. Remarkably, CSM Pritchett quickly advanced through the ranks and the last 18 years of her almost 37-year career with the Army were spent as a CSM with increasing levels of responsibility from achieving technical prowess to the administration and leadership of troops. And, at the time of her retirement, she attained an undergraduate degree in administration and management.

CSM Pritchett progressed in the logistics career field in both rank and responsibility from supply clerk to various leadership positions including as squad leader, platoon Sergeant, unit First Sergeant, battalion CSM, task force CSM of multiple logistical units in Somalia, installation CSM, and battalion Commander of the United States' Sergeant Majors' Academy with her final assignment as the theater CSM of the U.S. and Coalition Forces in Afghanistan where she was responsible for approximately

30,000 soldiers during the 2004 through 2006 period. Throughout this impressive career, CSM Pritchett, in addition to assignments in Somalia and Afghanistan, also served in Korea with multiple tours in Germany. While in Somalia, as part of the mortuary unit which was part of her battalion, her responsibilities included overseeing the recovery of the remains of the bodies of the U.S. rangers who were in search of the outlaw General Aidid following the downing of the BlackHawk helicopters during the 1990s. Under her oversight was the processing of the remains of the 18 rangers who were killed during this mission. As the senior noncommissioned officer (NCO) and head of the logistical task force with eight locations in the capital of Mogadishu, Somalia, it was CSM Pritchett's charge to remain apprised of the progress of the task force. In doing so, she took to the streets of Mogadishu daily in a Humvee accompanied by a convoy to check on the health, welfare, and morale of her soldiers. Her task force was a combat support unit that supported the coalition, although the task force itself was not attached to any combat unit. Despite this distinction of only supporting coalition forces yet not attached to a combat support unit, according to CSM Pritchett, in delivering supplies and the like to remote units within the region in the field, she and the unit's convoy often came under attack to which she and her troops returned fire, remounted, and quickly exited the scene. For these occasions, CSM Pritchett was routinely armed with an M16A1 rifle and a 9 mm pistol.

While she traveled throughout Afghanistan during her two-year tour, CSM Pritchett always experienced narrow escapes, in that attacks had either occurred before her arrival or following her departure but fortunately never during her visit at any location. Because she was an advisor to the three-star General and Commander and Commanding General for the enlisted troops during Operation Enduring Freedom, she was personally asked by the four-star Commanding General at U.S. Central Command (CENTCOM) to extend her tour in Afghanistan for another year since the nation was at war. She agreed to do so.

When CSM Pritchett joined the Army in 1973, the career fields opened to women were limited. Consequently, she selected logistics in order to be able to drive a truck or any occupation that was physical in nature or required working outdoors, and, most important, to avoid sitting at a desk doing administrative work. CSM Pritchett admitted though that if at the time of her enlistment in the Army, there was a broader range of career fields from which to choose, she would not have chosen logistics. Had she had her druthers, she would have selected a career field like armor that would have increased the likelihood of her direct involvement in combat as she enjoys shooting weapons for, as she stated, "Everybody serves to be in the fight." When asked though, given this orientation, that is, her desire to shoot things and blow them up, if she resented that she was barred from pursuing certain career fields simply because she is a woman, she replied that at the time, she did not think about it until as time progressed, she remembered completing double duty when she returned to Ft. McClellan, Alabama, where she had completed basic training. She ended up in the same company where she completed basic training and as a former trainee, her former drill instructor involved her in the training of new recruits. Then, at the rank of corporal, when the career field for drill sergeant was opened to women, CSM Pritchett volunteered to attend drill sergeants' school. With less than two years in the Army and at the tender age of 20, she was already a drill sergeant and secured a waiver because she was a female, and got the opportunity unlike others, to fire weapons at the range. Yet, she has harbored no ill feelings for being excluded from certain career fields, given gender, because her life's work has facilitated the opening of doors for other women to follow.

In 1996, CSM Pritchett secured the unique opportunity to serve as an advisor to the Defense Advisory Committee on Women in the Services (DACOWITS). At the rank of E-9, she was the Army's advisor to the Committee. She said that it was following her promotion to this rank that she realized how women were excluded from all of the occupations, for in her words, "you don't know what you don't know."

CSM Pritchett's notion of citizenship means giving back to society and, specifically as an American citizen, having the opportunity to dream to "Be all that you can be" which, she said, was to be attributed to Eleanor Roosevelt in describing what it means to be an American. CSM Pritchett thus views her military service as fulfilling her role as a citizen. And, even given the exclusion of women from certain career fields by the military, she still does not believe that she was treated as less than a full citizen for as she described, her overall experience with the military was a "blast." When asked if she believes that her experience in the military has translated to similar experiences within the civilian sector now that she is a private citizen, CSM Pritchett bluntly replied, "I didn't take crap then and I don't take crap now!" She said that, in essence, the military teaches one to develop a tough skin.

CSM Pritchett views the combat exclusion policy as simply outdated and recalled her assignment in Somalia, for instance, where the battlefield was asymmetrical in nature. Though not sanctioned, women may not have been in combat units but were in combat nonetheless. Therefore, the combat exclusion policy should be repealed. She does not see how repealing the policy will adversely impact the recruitment of women and since the military is merit based, she also sees the minimal impact of repealing the policy on women's promotion and retention rates as well. Regarding how military men will relate to military women in a postcombat exclusion environment, CSM Pritchett was of the opinion that the military has sorely learned some lessons from past mistakes such as those made when integrating women into the military academies because you had men preparing men on how to accept women in this new environment. In fact, particularly men who have served in theaters of war like Operations Enduring and Iraqi Freedom probably would have no problems in accepting women alongside them in the battlefield. Further, there are already commanders who have called for the repeal of the policy given their overriding need to comply by placing the best qualified troops in the theater. She said that the policy imposes restrictions and places undue limits on where troops can be deployed. Moreover, this way of thinking on whether or not women should serve in combat is partly generational, she believes, especially given the ire of the Vietnam era conflict. CSM Pritchett sees that this acceptance by men of women in combat has a great deal to do with the way in which men and women have been acculturated in the same sense that certain segments of society, such as minorities, are not accepted for one reason or another. For this reason, given one's value system and despite the inculcation by the military, these beliefs and value systems can remain largely unchanged for some segments of the population. But, by repealing the combat exclusion policy, the performance and overall effectiveness of the military would certainly increase. And because the military sometimes serves as a trailblazer for change, women in the civilian sector could see similar gains given the repeal.

CSM Pritchett believes that her military service has served to facilitate both her employment and increased compensation within the civilian sector. However, despite living in a locale that is within close proximity of a military installation, she is considered an anomaly in her neighborhood as she is one of the few female residents who have served in the military. She said that people are constantly fascinated by her military service as well as her advancement to the rank of E-9. (Interview via telephone on August 24, 2012)

Ms. Sandra Intorre, U.S. Army, Retired

First Uniformed Woman to Be Assigned at Camp Zama, Japan, Following WWII

This petite yet spry and quick-witted 92 year old celebrates her birthday on July 4. Sandra Intorre was born and raised in Monvue Gallatin, Pennsylvania, and hails from a family with an ourstory (history) of military service having had two brothers who served in the Army and her father served in the Italian Army—she surmised that it was probably during WWI. To her knowledge, Intorre was the first female in her family to have ever served in the U.S. military. As an undergraduate at Pennsylvania State University, she wanted to follow the career path of her friends at the time. However, at 4'11" tall, she was initially turned down for military service. She returned home dejected but, at the taunting of an older sister, requested and was granted a waiver for entry. Yet, with an obstinate streak to boot and bruised from the initial decline by the military, Intorre vowed never to return to the recruiting office to accept the offer under the waiver. But determined to demonstrate to her sister that she had the hutzpah to follow through, Intorre returned to the Army recruiting office and officially enlisted in the military in June 1943 as she waited until the end of the academic year to complete college. But, in November 1945, she was separated from the Army when the War Department suspended the Women's Army Corps (WAC). Intorre subsequently reenlisted one year later in November 1946 and served in the Army until her retirement in November 1967.

In her youth, Ms. Intorre remembered reading storybooks about the military and fantasized about how exciting pursuing that life would be even though she was acutely aware that at the time, as a female, it would have been an unusual career to pursue. But to join the war effort during WWII, all of her friends, both male and female, were enlisting in the military. This need to join was reinforced by the widely advertised commercial that "Uncle Sam wants you!" Ms. Intorre recalled, while babysitting her niece and watching the television, the imposing finger of the character pointing at her and others to galvanize this call to action for the war. As others did, though she short-circuited her college education for this purpose, she heeded the call for military service in the enlisted corps of the Army. Ms. Intorre's duties were administrative in nature and progressed in both responsibilities and rank from clerk typist to stenographer then to First Sergeant of a 450 women company under her charge at Ft. Sam Houston, Texas, at the rank of E-8. She advised that prior to this assignment, and as an E-7 or Sergeant Major at Ft. McClellan, Alabama, the Army instituted two additional higher ranks as E-8 and E-9 known then as "super grades." Ironically, Ms. Intorre was first offered the opportunity to meet the board for promotion to E-8 but thinking that it would have been necessary for her to have more years of college to be competitive, she declined the opportunity despite the urging of a Major for whom she worked and who advised her that she was already in the position and performing its functions.

Still, true to her obstinate character, Ms. Intorre dug in her heels by rationalizing that it was not necessary for her to meet a board for her previous promotions, so why should she be required to do so at this point of her career? Her refusal to vie for the promotion resulted in a transfer to a Basic Company in Ft. McClellan, Alabama. But, within six months, her position was upgraded to an E-8. Again, Ms. Intorre was asked to meet the board and for a second time she declined to do so opting instead to volunteer for what she considered as a plush assignment to Hawaii. It is important to note that this plush assignment at the time was still a foreign country that had not yet become a part of the United States. But, in so doing, there was a method to her madness, so to speak. Because Ft. McClellan was the second assignment following her initial refusal to meet the board, Ms. Intorre feared that if she met the board and succeeded, she would have been stuck there in the assignment. She wanted to travel and so travel became the overriding motivation for remaining in the Army; being stationed at Ft. McClellan would have markedly limited that opportunity. But, while this decision thwarted a potential promotion in rank, Ms. Intorre was of an adventurous spirit and the cost–benefits analysis weighed more heavily in favor of travel and assignment elsewhere.

While Ms. Intorre took much grief for this decision as others believed that her assignment to Hawaii was undeserved, she held on to her decision, accepted the assignment, and completed a successful three-year tour, even receiving a six-month extension as a result. As Ms. Intorre described this story, it was evident that she still relishes the feat. But it was during her final assignment as First Sergeant of a small group of women at Ft. Lawton, Washington, that she was called into the Colonel's office. However, Ms. Intorre was under the impression that perhaps she was going to be reprimanded for something of which she was unaware but upon entry to the Colonel's office she noticed that not only was the Major to whom she reported present but so were some of the personnel from her company. This time, though, she was called into the Colonel's office for a promotion to the rank of E-8 and without ever having to meet the board. With the Colonel on one side and the Major on the other, they simulated the pinning of her new rank, albeit with scotch tape on each side of her arm and in unison said "Congratulations." Ms. Intorre also received a three-year extension in the Army as a result of the promotion. In retrospect, according to Ms. Intorre, her rationale for not meeting the board to vie for the promotion to E-8 was that if she deserved it, she would receive it. And, she did in the end; to her, money, rank, and prestige were all of secondary concerns. For Ms. Intorre, being in the Army was about the adventure.

During her 23-year career, Ms. Intorre's overseas assignments took her to places such as England, Belgium, France, Germany, Japan, and Hawaii (then not a part of the United States) and many locations within the continental United States (CONUS) including Governor's Island, New York, then a military installation. But, she considered that her most memorable assignment was at Camp Zama, Japan, in the legal office as a stenographer. Ms. Intorre became the first WAC to be assigned there while the prisoners of war (POWs) were being interrogated about the torture that they had endured during WWII. And, as the only uniformed female, she was forbidden from fraternizing with the officers who were all males. Therefore, donned in her civilian attire, it was during the evenings that she visited the hospital where the soldiers were housed to simply talk with them and to find out what kind of food they desired. She would often beckon the "grey ladies" as they were called or elderly women who worked with the nurses on staff or the Red Cross to fulfill these requests. Ms. Intorre remembers that the POWs did not have much to eat during the war due to desperation, where, for instance, one soldier offered another $80 for a bowl of rice to eat. At any length, they were overseas and could not spend the money since the currency there was worthless. She said that despite her travels and particularly these experiences, she always looked forward to returning to the United States in light of the deprivation that she witnessed in other countries. Ms. Intorre served during two major campaigns, WWII and the Korean Conflict while in Japan.

Yet, by today's standards, Ms. Intorre's assignments would have been considered in combat support roles, albeit administrative in nature as her responsibilities involved the procurement of supplies for the various deployment efforts. Then as she recalled, these duties were simply under the guise of administrative support. Ms. Intorre left military service because her mother wanted her to return home. She had a disabled sibling in her mother's care and her mother was concerned that there would be no one to care for her sister in the event of her death. When her mother died, Ms. Intorre assumed sole guardianship for her sister. While her desire was to remain in the military for 25 years, Ms. Intorre continued to work as a civilian for the Department of Defense for another 10 years and specifically for the ROTC.

Ms. Intorre recalled that when she first enlisted in the military, she wanted to drive a jeep, be in the motor pool or as she termed "be with the cooks and bakers." But considering her height, and particularly as a woman in those days, the Army found none of the careers suitable as size dictated what occupation one pursued. Consequently, Ms. Intorre was placed in the administrative field for which she has no regrets. She is actually grateful to the Army for this selection for when asked if more career fields were opened to women at the time would she have selected another career and more importantly, one that would place her directly in combat, Ms. Intorre said she would not have selected such occupations that placed her in direct harm's way. And, because she described herself as a person of the time, at the time of this interview, she reflected upon such questions as "What would people think?" and "Given such close quarters, how would you separate the men from the women?" Ms. Intorre acknowledged this cognitive dissonance, where, despite her desire for adventure and being in the military, there were boundaries on what men and women could do as she did not believe that it was culturally appropriate. And, as she stated, even today, her view has not changed about such issues.

With regard to citizenship, Ms. Intorre said that she is very happy to be an American. More importantly, while she is happy to have the freedom as an American, she conceded that Americans are in jeopardy of losing that freedom. Yet, as an American, she also believes that it is important to obey the laws of the land. And, by serving in the military, she has fulfilled her role as a citizen. On being barred from certain career fields because she is a female, during military service, Ms. Intorre has never felt that she was treated as if she was a second-class citizen by the military. She summed up her experience in the military in this way—the military has provided her with opportunities that she would not have been able to do otherwise as well as to witness how people in other countries live. Given this experience, she said that it makes her appreciate what it means to be an American even more. She poignantly illustrated the importance of being an American while stationed in Japan where she volunteered at an orphanage and following a bus trip in which they took 22 children to a Christmas party to receive age-appropriate gifts. However, upon return, two children were missing despite repeated counts by the volunteers. The volunteers were confounded because they were certain that all of the children were accounted for. However, upon physical inspection of the bus, they discovered two children who were crouched under the bus seats. The children did not want to the return to the orphanage. They wanted to accompany the American volunteers home.

While Ms. Intorre's tenure with the military, especially during WWII, preceded what later became the combat exclusion policy, when asked about the policy, and despite her belief that the sexes should be separated, she views combat as a duty that should be voluntary. In other words, for those women who desire to secure occupations that increase the likelihood of being in combat, Ms. Intorre believes that it should be their prerogative in a voluntary force to do so. As a matter of fact, she said that the same choice should be afforded to men as well. Ms. Intorre admitted though that the military must change with the times and if the need exists for everyone to be called to combat duty, then both men and women must make it their duty to do so. But, if this need does not exist, she said, then the combat exclusion policy should not be repealed. But should the policy be repealed, Ms. Intorre is aware that parents will forbid their daughters from joining the military even though that is exactly what their daughters will want to do. Ms. Intorre recalls her own experience when she decided to join the military. She disobeyed her parents' wishes by doing just that. She remembered that upon knowing her decision, her mother cried and her father was so disappointed that, according to Ms. Intorre, his looks could kill, "I would have been dead on the spot." Yet, in the end, her father came to recognize that as a 21-year-old, she could do whatever she wanted. However, he forewarned that she would regret her decision to join the military.

Given this premonition from her father, and upon completion of basic training, Ms. Intorre had the opportunity to visit home on leave but was reluctant to do so. She along with a fellow female soldier, who was in the same predicament, consulted with the Army chaplain for fear that their fathers would not allow them into their homes. The chaplain advised the women that, despite their fears, if they wanted to return home, especially to visit their mothers and siblings, then they should do so. Ms. Intorre, on returning home in uniform to visit her family, received a pleasant yet welcome surprise from her father who paraded her throughout the town by ensuring that she visited all of her relatives. Her father had finally embraced the reality that his daughter was in the military and was very proud of her even though his idea of a woman's place, and especially that of his own daughter, was in the home. Her uncle, her father's brother, further warned that since his niece had begun a new tradition for future female members of the family to join the military, his brother must be prepared for the changes that will ensue. In broaching the question of whether or not repealing the combat exclusion policy would result in a difference in the ways that military men would relate to military women, Ms. Intorre offered this sage advice that it would depend upon the men. She related her own experience when she first arrived at the military retirement home where she now resides. She said that the male veterans who were already in the home resented the intrusion of the female veterans, to which Ms. Intorre countered that the women veterans are just as entitled to residence in the retirement home as the men are for they had also served their country through military service.

Of note is that the interview with Ms. Intorre took place during August 2012. She said that regrettably there are still many male veterans in the retirement home who still resent the female veterans living there. I asked Ms. Intorre if she views her experience in the retirement home as akin to women's predicament with the combat exclusion policy. She concurred. She continued that there is even one male veteran in the home who refuses to enter the elevator with any female veteran. But, according to Ms. Intorre, even if the combat exclusion policy is repealed she sees many men as still never accepting women for as she stated, "Men … they just want to be king" because they still see themselves as protectors. Still, while Ms. Intorre believes that repealing the combat exclusion policy would improve the performance and thus the overall effectiveness of the military, she believes that repealing the policy should be needs based and that because civilian women want the same rights, they will be similarly affected by the elevation of military women. In fact, Ms. Intorre believes that her military service has definitely benefited her in securing employment within the civilian sector. And to her knowledge, her military service has helped in her civilian compensation as well. (In-person interview on August 22, 2012)

Mrs. Tiffany Kravec-Kelly, U.S. Army Reserve

First Female PSYOP Team Chief in the U.S. Army Reserve
First Woman Known to Unofficially Serve in the Designated 37F "I" Indicator Position (Male-Only Designation) in Iraq and in Direct Ground Combat
Recipient of the Combat Action Badge

A patriot to the core who was fortuitously born on the fourth of July in Escadon, California, but raised in Portland, Oregon, Mrs. Tiffany Kravec-Kelly is the first female in her family to have ever served in the military, although male members of her family such as an uncle on her mother's side preceded her. Already married with two children, Mrs. Kravec-Kelly wanted to challenge herself by doing something different. So, she decided to join the Army Reserve at the age of 28. And, with some college courses to her credit, she decided to join the enlisted corps and pursue the psychological operations (PSYOP) military occupational specialty (MOS), which among the many requirements in the field included relaying information from and to foreign populations through print and other forms of media, one of which may include face-to-face distribution, all for the purpose of targeting certain audiences and speaking with select communicators in villages given the demographics by determining who the key communicators are. PSYOP teams in turn would take back information to commanders in the theater on how to achieve certain objectives for the mission by sustaining the least number of casualties in the process. According to Mrs. Kravec-Kelly, this is deemed as an alternative form of warfare. For example, during Operation Iraqi Freedom, she was assigned to a cavalry troop where her responsibilities included advising and cooling hostilities on divergent sides by encouraging the parties to communicate directly with each other.

As an Army reservist, Mrs. Kravec-Kelly received rapid promotions in rank until her separation from the military as an E-6 (Staff Sergeant/SSG). And, as a SSG or noncommissioned officer, she was exposed to multiple high level for a such as battle staff meetings that under normal circumstances, would have been attended by a commissioned officer. She was also involved in various battalion and brigade mission training to include morning meetings about the plans for the day and evening meetings to debrief as an after action report on what was accomplished. She even had the opportunity to twice brief at the divisional level in Baghdad CENTCOM. Originally assigned to a unit in Portland, Oregon, upon relocation, Mrs. Kravec-Kelly was assigned to a second unit in Cleveland, Ohio, a four-hour one-way commute from her home in Ft. Wayne, Indiana. Mrs. Kravec-Kelly had no idea of what occupation she wanted to pursue in the military. She scored so well on the Armed Services Vocational Aptitude Battery (ASVAB) that the recruiter advised her that she could basically pursue any career that she wanted. The recruiter then pushed what amounted to be the size of two telephone books in front of her and asked that, upon review, she select a career field from the innumerable offerings. Almost simultaneously, Mrs. Kravec-Kelly noticed a poster behind the recruiter of a paratrooper and immediately announced to the recruiter that "I want to do that!" to which the recruiter scoffed, "Anything but that!" because only males can be paratroopers. But, the recruiter advised her that there is only one MOS in which a female could do something similar, that is in PSYOP.

According to Mrs. Kravec-Kelly, basic training proved to be only the second in a series of reminders along the way that as a female in the military, she was barred from pursuing certain careers. She remembered having three drill instructors, namely, an airborne ranger with multiple jumps in Panama to his credit; a ranger; and another in administration. While during training, the other platoons were inordinately staffed by drill instructors from the administrative MOS, those destined for PSYOP and thus more rigorous training, included rangers and the like but who were men. Then, Private First Class (PFC) Warner (also known as Kravec) proved to be the "best shot" at the qualifying range and she mentioned to the airborne ranger, whom she later learned was also a sniper, that she wanted to attend sniper school. The airborne ranger replied that women were not accepted into sniper school. For Mrs. Kravec-Kelly, this was yet another frustrating reminder that even if you are best at something, for the military, and in this case the Army, it is your gender that is the determining factor on whether or not you get to do something. Yet, these experiences only strengthened her resolve in proving to the Army that she was the best at doing whatever she pursued. These experiences also proved instrumental in preparing her for the subsequent battles that she was to encounter as a female in her unit and her personal life.

Mrs. Kravec-Kelly was deployed for one tour from 2004 through 2005 during the follow-up phase of Operation Iraqi Freedom. PSYOP, as a component of Special Forces, personnel in that MOS were not deployed to Iraq as traditional Army units in that PSYOP teams were farmed out as part of platoons, where in many cases these teams found themselves in isolated situations on the battlefield. Mrs. Kravec-Kelly's team was loaned out by a division but utilized by whomever they were farmed out to by the forward operating base (FOB). In essence, PSYOP teams were all farmed out at high command levels yet worked at the lowest levels on the ground in the theater of war in an advisory capacity through orders for their dispatch that emanated from the highest levels of command where they served in combat support roles, albeit directly in ground combat. But to understand the predicament that Mrs. Kravec-Kelly faced as a female soldier and particularly in a time of war where as a designated noncombatant she was frequently placed in situations involving direct ground combat, it is important to understand how and why this situation was created in the first place.

But the designation of combat support was a moving target. Mrs. Kravec-Kelly said that she often ran missions by herself among the Iraqi population during her yearlong deployment where she found herself in the thick of real-time activities as they occurred on the ground, that is, during this period, her duties took her directly into the combat zone despite her designation by the military as a noncombatant. Mrs. Kravec-Kelly said that missions leaving the FOB were required to have a total of three vehicles. Given this mandate, the Army fell short of both people and vehicles. So, she achieved and carried out her missions by utilizing the Iraqi Army soldiers to fill in where possible, as she had developed a good relationship with the soldiers in the Iraqi Army as well as the Iraqi people. But, as she put it, the challenge with this "I" designation, however, was not as it seemed in the sense that everyone who was assigned to the career field had the same designation number, in this case 37F. The teams that were attached to the combat units all have an "I" indicator that is the designation for "male only." However, females as noncombatants would not have this designation and would be assigned in any other capacity within a unit. But, there were only few positions or in the positions with E-6 slots, almost all of which were on teams with an "I" indicator. Further, as females, the opportunities for promotion within the units become even more limited given the "I" restriction. And, at the higher unit ranks, that is, E-7, competition becomes intense as there are even fewer slots for which everyone can compete. This scarcity of positions, exacerbated by the restriction given the "I" designation, often resulted in women's premature attrition from the PSYOP MOS in search of promotional opportunities to higher ranks unless the incumbents in these few high-ranking positions either retire or die.

The slot that Mrs. Kravec-Kelly held, however, as a noncombatant despite her actual duties on the ground did not have an "I" indicator on the roster of record. She was in an open slot that could either be held by a female or male but the actual duties that she performed in the theater of operations were that of a male or one with an "I" indicator. Yet, although she was more than qualified for the position, the unit wanted to place a much less qualified male, an E-4, simply because he was a male, and not based upon his qualification for the position. As a result, and given her qualifications, she was already performing the job of a male, but had also trained many of the male members on the PSYOP teams, then Kravec-Kelly became visibly irate at the prospect of not only this nonsensical selection based solely on gender but that doing so could potentially lead to jeopardizing the lives of the team members by assigning a less qualified member in a slot for which she was more than qualified. Moreover, in the process, doing so could have also adversely impact the mission. According to Mrs. Kravec-Kelly, she had worked tirelessly to be the best in order to compete for this position, particularly since she was already performing the job, that is, the male or "I" indicator's job without the designation. She was finally placed on the team following one moth of demanding to be placed in the position as well as to thwart possibly jeopardizing the lives of team members, but still without the "I" indicator where she performed more missions above and beyond the teams in the unit that immediately preceded her. In fact, according to Mrs. Kravec-Kelly, at one point, there was talk of transferring her to another location to quell the issue. However, given her reputation and prowess for successful mission completion, the members of the cavalry troop to which she was attached were so outraged about the possibility of her removal, that they mounted a barrage of complaints that advanced to the division level. In the end, Mrs. Kravec-Kelly was not transferred to another unit.

When Mrs. Kravec-Kelly submitted her initial SIT REPS (situational reports detailing what had been accomplished during any given day), she was instructed by her superiors never to disclose any indication of her gender on these reports. Yet, it was her gender that played a crucial role in securing much of the information, which she believed led to confusion at the division level on how a male on the PSYOP team was able to secure this information. Likewise, as a female in Iraq, said Mrs. Kravec-Kelly, she was not perceived as a threat, so consequently unlike her male counterparts on her team as well as the other teams, she was able to secure information that foreign male soldiers simply could not. As a matter of fact, these Arab men would regularly engage her in conversations by asking questions, something that they would not have done with the male soldiers. She recalled an incident when she worked with the Iraqi Army and a wahabi ("bad guy") was identified. Because no one could disembark the vehicle quickly enough at the time, Kravec-Kelly jumped out of the vehicle and tackled the wahabi to the ground in the open marketplace, zip tied, and placed him into the van to the point of garnering the attention of a highly respected Iraqi Army General, with whom she had previously had a difficult encounter. Owing to her actions in the incident, this Iraqi Army General placed his arm around her in the marketplace in full view of onlookers while uttering the words that she is his sister. The Iraqi General declared in the marketplace that anyone who touches Kravec-Kelly will have to account to him for such gaffe. This was just one of the many experiences that defined her deployment in Iraq, where she also recalls being shot at and narrowly escaped being the casualty of a bomb at least three times. So, most definitely, Mrs. Kravec-Kelly considers herself a combat veteran as a result.

Kravec-Kelly became team chief and was to remain in the previously designated male "I" indicator position. She was also assigned the responsibility in an area in northern Iraq that was reputed for its disproportionate supply of IEDs. Yet, as team chief during her tenure in the region, when she left briefly on leave in February 2005 for the United States, one of the biggest car bombs detonated. She attributed this lapse in oversight to her absence because upon return, no such devices were found nor had such incidence occurred under her team's watch.

Following an extension of another three years in the Army Reserve after her tour in Iraq, Kravec-Kelly returned to the United States, this time to face some unanticipated battles of her own. Her then spouse, who was also in the Army National Guard but was stationed in Kuwait, grew increasingly weary and unappreciative of his wife's achievements for as the male of the couple, these experiences were to be his. Essentially, Kravec-Kelly's sharing of her experiences became a major source of conflict in their marriage, so much so, that her then husband prematurely severed ties with her as he was visibly threatened by her accomplishments. These ongoing issues with him over the custody of their two-year-old daughter became too overwhelming for Kravec-Kelly to continue serving in the military. And, despite her love for the Army, and the special meaning and worth that she derived from her career in PSYOP, the love and stability that she sought for her daughter took precedence and center stage in her life. As Mrs. Kravec-Kelly put it, when a man who is the father goes off to war, he is labeled a hero. But when a woman who is the mother goes off to war, she is abandoning her child. And, given the ensuing custody battles and because she was again approaching the end of reconsideration for another term of enlistment, Mrs. Kravec-Kelly decided to short-circuit her career by separating from the military. Additionally, as a consequence of the custody proceedings, the courts were considering her in poor light because of her military service, for which, as she stated, she was being penalized. Regrettably, in many ways on returning home from Operation Iraqi Freedom, Mrs. Kravec-Kelly paid the ultimate price when she eventually lost custody of her daughter.

While citizenship means to her being accepted into a group, Mrs. Kravec-Kelly questioned the level of patriotism that she has seen being displayed by Americans in recent years. She sees herself as an American citizen in not just being responsible to and for the United States but taking larger responsibility for the world. However, she believes that the military has failed in its responsibility to treat her as a citizen because the Army has never treated her fully as a soldier. Further, her experience in being barred from serving in certain career fields simply because of her gender is yet another reminder that the military did not treat her as a full citizen. But, by serving in the military, she has witnessed a profound change in herself that she is not the same person as she was before she enlisted and despite her negative experiences, she will be forever grateful to the military for challenging her in the ways that had never been done before. Now as a civilian, and particularly as a college student, the military forced her to think differently in that she has been exposed to different cultures, as one of the many examples. Mrs. Kravec-Kelly even believes that the military's "suck it up and take it" mentality had actually prepared her for the challenges of her divorce and the custody battle for her daughter that ensued. Without this acculturation through the Army, Mrs. Kravec-Kelly admits that she would have been a basket case by not possessing the intestinal fortitude that was needed.

Mrs. Kravec-Kelly reminisces fondly about her military career and is saddened that it was short-circuited. She does not believe though that her experiences in the military have translated to her life as a civilian in that given her gender, the military continues to be ambiguous about the roles that men and women should play, whereas in the civilian sector, political correctness takes precedence in the roles that women are allowed to pursue, although the inequities in how women are treated in society as a whole still persist. Accordingly, as she sees it, the combat exclusion policy is still a reflection of an American society that does not want to witness women being shot because as men they are taught to protect women. And, likewise, women are taught to allow men to protect them. For this reason, Mrs. Kravec-Kelly believes that the combat exclusion policy should be repealed as men are never going to accept women in certain fields until those criteria are standardized across the board. While she understands the divergence in criteria given age, the same should not hold for gender as doing so creates unnecessary animosity between the sexes. And, even should the combat exclusion policy be repealed, adaptation will be slow. For, as she stated, despite the repeal of the policy, some recruiters will continue to persist by recruiting women and men to specific occupations and behaviors by some will be slow to comply with the new law. The military is also male in character and full acceptance of females as partners will be intimidating and/or uncomfortable for some military men. Thus, these will just be some examples of the backlash that women will experience as a result of repealing the policy. In asking whether or not the number of sexual harassment or sexual trauma cases will increase against women in light of repealing the policy, Mrs. Kravec-Kelly thinks that elevating these issues for debate will be oppressing as similarly situated men do not react in kind. In fact, such experiences against men largely go unreported. Female victimization thereby becomes oppressive. Finally, repealing the combat exclusion policy will not reveal the discernible effects given the slow learning curve. But, eventually, the performance and overall effectiveness of the military will improve as a result. Such benefits will also translate to the general advantage of women in the civilian sector.

Now that Mrs. Kravec-Kelly has resumed her academic studies in college to pursue an undergraduate degree in anthropology, she has established a group at her university called Military Students' Services (Indiana–Purdue University) given her own observation of soldiers' struggles with transitioning back into civilian life and in light of her personal struggles. Ironically, this effort at the university was funded in part by an affluent donor, himself a Korean Conflict veteran. Still, as a female veteran in a civilian society, Mrs. Kravec-Kelly again finds that she is having to prove herself all over again. As a case in point, at a Veterans' Day parade, she is often the only female veteran. As a consequence, she has deliberately begun engaging her four daughters as part of these activities believing that as females, they too have the right to be recognized and be involved in such activities as the Veterans' Day parade.

Mrs. Kravec-Kelly recalls while on deployment in Iraqi, she experienced another disconcerting blow, yet another reminder of what it means to be a woman in the military. For her exemplary performance during her tour, her package was submitted for a Bronze Star Medal. While the necessary paperwork was signed and advanced to the division level with countless laudatory remarks as evidence of her stellar performance, the award was downgraded because as a female she should not have been on the mission that called attention to this outstanding performance. Instead, she received a Medal of Achievement. Yet, the male officer who was in charge of the detachment, but who largely remained behind the safety of the green zone, was submitted for this very award, the Bronze Star, using the merits of her work. He, in turn, received the Bronze Star and thus the credit for her work. While gravely disappointed to justifiably bitter, Mrs. Kravec-Kelly continues to seek ways as a civilian to make a difference for veterans, particularly women veterans. Fortunately, she now has a partner and husband, himself a veteran of Special Forces, who takes every opportunity to recognize her work as a veteran such as when they are seen together in a restaurant, he is quick to seize the opportunity to advise those who recognize his efforts, that like him, his wife is a veteran. As part of her husband's work in the ROTC program at Ball State University, Mrs. Kravec-Kelly was successful in leading the only female ranger team to their unprecedented win. This win is a *fait accompli* in the sense that the cadets were repeatedly told of the impossibility that as females they could neither rise nor exceed the challenge, which, of course, they did. (Interview via Skype on July 13, 2012)

Sergeant Michelle Wilmot, U.S. Army Reserve

Member of the All Woman Combat Force "Team Lioness," the First Known Embedding of Female Soldiers and Marines in Operations Enduring and Iraqi Freedom and Any U.S.-Led Engagement in Combat

To say that this NCO was fighting simultaneous wars, one in Iraq, the other in her unit to which she was assigned in Iraq, would be an understatement. To say that this NCO displayed an immense level of resilience given the adversities she encountered would be an understatement. And, to say that this Sergeant was not the epitome of a profile in courage would be an understatement. Her performance under relentless duress was nothing short of amazing. What was even more remarkable yet inexplicable at best is that she recounted this nightmare and perilous journey all the while maintaining a sense of humor. Sergeant (Sgt.) Michelle Wilmot, an Army reservist, told a riveting tale of her experience while deployed during Operation Iraqi Freedom and who unexpectedly became part of the now famous all-female soldiers and Marines force dubbed "Team Lioness." Her story is emblematic of the early years of the war, the associated confusion, and the organized chaos that ensued and defined her yearlong tour in Iraq. This outspoken, feisty, and not-to-be-taken-lightly service member was dually assigned as a combat medic and combat stress control or mental health NCO with additional duties that required qualification in a third skill set as the unit's retention officer. While assigned to a combat stress control unit, Sgt. Wilmot was also attached to a Marines unit as one of the 18 all-female team members embedded with the Marines or Team Lioness during Operation Iraqi Freedom, for the purpose of frisking Iraqi civilian personnel, conducting house raids, and completing searches and the like with their male soldier and Marine Corps counterparts, the first-ever known such effort by the U.S. Department of Defense.

As a military brat but who was born in New York City, Ms. Wilmot was raised all over the United States given the military tradition on both her maternal and paternal sides of the family. For instance, two of her aunts on her mother's side served in the Army. Aunt Dianne served as an X-ray technician during the late 1970s while her Aunt Joanne served in communication during the early 1980s. As such, it was not unusual then that both aunts joined the military. While Ms. Wilmot was in Encinal High School in Alameda located on the East Bay side of San Francisco, California, at age 17 when she joined the military to the chagrin of her teachers who encouraged her to go to college, even though she had applied to several universities and was even accepted to the University of California–Berkeley. However, given the exorbitant costs of tuition despite the availability of state grants and other loans to help offset the costs, according to Ms. Wilmot, to qualify, one's socio-economic status had to be near abject poverty. Ms. Wilmot's family was just above the poverty line, and as a result, she was offered only $2000 per month in Stafford loans, which by no means is enough to live on in California. But, what she found ironic is that in her high school, it was mandatory that all students took the ASVAB to qualify for entry into the military. Ms. Wilmot surmised that this was not the case for students who resided in affluent communities. Yet, the reality she faced was that there was simply no money to attend college and so she was forced to take an alternative route via the military. She said that her teachers were extremely upset given this decision for they believed that she was throwing her life away. Ms. Wilmot enlisted in the Army Reserve during the senior year of high school and because of her age, this required her parents to sign a waiver allowing her to do so. Upon graduation from high school in 1999, she was sent to and completed basic training and remained in the military until her separation in 2006.

While in the military, Sgt. Wilmot was trained for qualification in dual MOS of 91B as a combat medic and 91X in mental health. Technical training for both specialties took one year. She also served in the role as her unit's retention NCO with responsibilities for assisting in the retention of fellow Army reservists. Sgt. Wilmot was initially assigned to the Oakland Army Base in Oakland, California; then onto Jacksonville Naval Air Station (NAS); from which she was subsequently deployed to Ramadi, Iraq, as part of Operation Iraqi Freedom for a one-year tour from late 2004 through late 2005. She served with a combat stress control unit that, unlike a combat support hospital, served as a detachment to a large hospital. Her attachment with the combat stress control unit out of Indiana was based on a lottery system of sorts, whereby one's selection was a condition of MOS skill level and rank. From her unit of 500 members in Jacksonville, Florida, she was one of two members who were selected for immediate deployment to Iraq. Unfortunately, the other unit member, whom Sgt. Wilmot knew, a border patrol agent in civilian life, literally passed away on the day that he received orders for deployment to Iraq, although his death was unrelated to his impending deployment. Sgt. Wilmot was thus the sole service member from her unit to be deployed and cross-leveled with a reserve unit from Indiana. However, her arrival to Indiana and to her newly attached unit as she attempted to navigate her way to the commander and first sergeant offices was inhospitable from the start and in many ways set the stage for her tumultuous journey in Iraq as well. Upon entrance to the unit, a senior NCO blurted out, "Who's the raghead?" "Raghead" is a derogatory term for a Middle-Easterner whom they thought fit Sgt. Wilmot's appearance and despite her donning of the American military uniform, her experience thereafter with this unit was one of open hostility. She faced tremendous odds from her own American service members despite the fact that they all wore the American military uniform.

As a combat stress control unit, Sgt. Wilmot's unit was considered one of combat support. The personnel in the unit were dispersed upon arrival to Iraq. While the majority of the unit's members remained in the heavily fortified Green Zone in Baghdad, another group was sent to a large base known as Balad, and a few personnel were sent to Rustamiyah which was close to Sadr city, near the Iranian border. Sgt. Wilmot and her team of four people were dispatched to Ramadi, the capital of Anbar Province to Camp Ar Ramadi, a military installation of approximately 4000 personnel of which there were only 30 women, many of whom were tasked with conducting civilian searches, house raids, and check point operations. However, it was apparent that more women were needed to assume many of these roles. Sgt. Wilmot and her team discovered that the main 16 women who were being rotated in and out for these duties were not getting much relief. Only the male soldiers and Marines were receiving their required time off. As a result and given the overriding need to provide the women with downtime, Sgt. Wilmot and her female team member by default and out of need became participants in what she later learned was Team Lioness. She said that she was unaware that she was now part of this unprecedented effort by the Department of Defense. Initially, and as part of this venture, Sgt. Wilmot did not see her participation as anything special. She only knew that the women who were participating were not getting any days off while the men did. She said that she and her female teammate continued to assume their responsibilities as combat medics and combat stress control NCOs even as they executed their responsibilities in Team Lioness. However, the frequency of their participation increased to every week. And, now with a total of 18 women instead of the original 16 women, Sgt. Wilmot, along with her teammate, were assigned to a very dangerous post and for a duty for which she was not originally tapped. She thus became a member of Team Lioness out of necessity.

Sgt. Wilmot said that the number of women and teams varied and was contingent upon where they were needed each day. For example, sometimes two women each were assigned to Northbridge, the entrance to Ramadi, two women at Southbridge not far from Northbridge in the city, and sometimes they were assigned at government centers. At times, however, she served in these dangerous roles by herself or with another team member. Incidentally, despite the existence of the combat exclusion policy, and thus the need to prevent women from being in direct ground combat, the actual needs on the ground at any given time trumped the policy.

It was evident that she and her female cohorts were in direct ground combat and so were in direct harm's way. According to Sgt. Wilmot, to avoid noncompliance with the combat exclusion policy, she and her fellow female teammates were attached, but not assigned, to a Marines infantry unit and to her knowledge these personnel were all active duty soldiers and Marines. However, the women were attached to the Marine Corps units based upon need and deployed to the streets to conduct house raids, personnel searches (women and children), check point operations, and other assigned duties. According to Sgt. Wilmot, "Lionesses were out there every day. Not just when we were needed. We were always needed." However, for Sgt. Wilmot and her teammate, when not performing missions that were connected to their roles in Team Lioness, they were performing missions that directly involved their career fields of combat stress control/mental health outreach, suicide and homicide prevention dealing with deaths, grief counseling, and dealing with the wounded. As Sgt. Wilmot put it, given her capacity, there was always something to do. However, she advised that her scope of responsibilities within those missions for her career fields but outside of her responsibilities on Team Lioness were only to be provided to U.S. military personnel. However, she said that the functions and services were, for the most part, disorganized at this period of the war.

Sgt. Wilmot said that she was assigned to the ourstorically (historically) poorest part of Iraq and where the population was the angriest. She described the situation, albeit comically, that the position in which she frequently found herself and which could not have been more dire as after all it was in a war zone was akin to fanatically devoted Oakland raiders fans who were always angry because the raiders often lost the games and the fans would set cars on fire yet there was nothing that anyone could do about it. Sgt. Wilmot said that the situation was similar in Ramadi, but magnified. She continued using the Oakland Raiders analogy, that while the fans went home, in Ramadi, she would have to jump into her Humvee to investigate given the losses of life that were to be tolled. Sgt. Wilmot said that to compound an already very complex situation, hardly anyone spoke English in Anbar, Baghdad Province. And, to add fuel to an already burning fire, she never received any language or cultural preparation before deployment. So the only remedy that she had was to purchase a basic CD and book set that she listened to and read repeatedly until she was able to learn the basic phrases. However, much of the information was couched in modern standard Arabic which she said was closer to an Egyptian dialect. She also practiced the language in the Iraqi streets when dealing with the Iraqis, although sometimes people became confused and frequently asked her if she was Egyptian. Consequently, Sgt. Wilmot said, even if she could, she could not offer counseling to any Iraqis as 99.9% of them did not speak English. She also said that things were disorganized as to who should service whom, although she was advised that her primary responsibility was to the American military when not conducting her duties as Team Lioness.

It is interesting to note that Sgt. Wilmot described these sometimes seemingly comedic scenes despite their gory content. Yet, she very effectively used humor to convey her message and to a great degree the feeling of what seemed to have been the sense of learning of all involved by muddling through in an effort to make sense of an intensely hostile environment. Still, in her role as part of Team Lioness during house raids and searches, Iraqi women were more likely to approach them and voluntarily provide intelligence or offer information about their husbands that there might be a bomb in the car, for instance, than had they been male soldiers or Marines in the same role. Sgt. Wilmot said that, in many respects, the women saw them as allies. Further, because the women were uncertain as to her race and/or ethnicity, they trusted her more as in many ways she appeared to be a Middle Easterner but in an American uniform. Her teammate on the other hand fit what Iraqis understood as typically European, therefore, a Westerner and thus was not to be trusted. Sgt. Wilmot, who said that she is of mixed race and so her skin has an olive hue, was more likely to be approached by Iraqi women to advise her when something was wrong. She was always mistaken for being from various ethnic and racial groups. In fact, Sgt. Wilmot stated that sometimes there was a game among the Iraqis to discern what her racial and/or ethnic group was. She said that she was in an American uniform but confounded many Iraqis as she did not fit the typical description of what Iraqis understood to be the portrayal of a Westerner given what they had seen via the movies and/or television. She represented many contradictions—as a woman in uniform and one who appeared to be from that region. Some would even ask if she was Iraqi. Most often though she said that she was identified as being Turkish. Sgt. Wilmot attempted to explain to the Iraqis that America was heterogeneous in makeup and there are many different groups in the country including Native Americans. To Sgt. Wilmot, as a mixed race woman, it served as a great ice breaker in dealing especially with the Iraqi women.

While Sgt. Wilmot said that she was ill-prepared for the language and cultural challenges in Iraq, she was grateful for the training that the Army provided in school to secure her skill qualifications, especially in mental health. In this career field, students were routinely advised that they should expect to find themselves in situations where it would become necessary to go into battle to seek out patients instead of waiting for patients to come for help. However, Sgt. Wilmot said regrettably, that during her tour in Iraq, this was not the case. Despite conditions on the ground and in light of the mindset of those in the chain of command, their belief was that they should wait for the patients to come to them. Nonetheless, and particularly for mental health, those who required such services were the least likely to seek them out. Therefore, according to Sgt. Wilmot, it became important to "go outside the wire" as she termed it as it was necessary to leave the confines of the secured area or site to find them. She said that failure to seek mental health was attributed to two things. First, the stigma attached in the military for self-identification with mental health issues. And, second because the clinic hours were unreasonably scheduled between 9:00 a.m. and 5:00 p.m. daily and closed during the lunch period that did not accommodate those who needed these services, and, even if they sought out these services, they were unavailable. Sgt. Wilmot provided a poignant example. Camp Victory in Baghdad had relatively safe-housed military personnel who remained in their comfortable air-conditioned offices and waited for people who required assistance to come by rather than the personnel with the skill sets going outside the wire to locate people with these needs. In fact, she said that after 5:00 p.m., the military personnel who were there to support those in the field simply would return to their respective trailers and play video games.

On the other hand, where Sgt. Wilmot was located, the operations tempo (ops tempo) was extremely high and consequently, the mental health people were always on the go. For example, when someone was on the verge of committing suicide, she and her team would immediately get into their Humvee and race to wherever the situation was to attempt to thwart such an effort. In essence, according to Sgt. Wilmot, the situations dictated that she and her teammates sought out who was in need of help, not the converse, and they were on schedule 24 hours per day, 7 days per week. And, though her responsibility was primarily to serve the needs of the American military, she and her teammates had to be equally available to Iraqi interpreters as well, including others regardless of national origin who required assistance whenever the need arose. They could not turn anyone away, although it was common knowledge that there were some units that failed to serve those who needed assistance such as if someone did not possess a social security number or one could not be found, that individual was simply not serviced.

Sgt. Wilmot was promoted to the rank of Sgt. (E-5) in 2002. From 2002 through 2006 or until her separation, she served as the NCO in charge (NCOIC) of the Neuropsychology Department of a combat support hospital at the Jacksonville NAS. Upon deployment to Iraq, she assumed the position as the NCOIC of the Ramadi Clinic, although there was a mental health officer who was in charge of mental health but who was never around choosing instead to spend most of his time at the gym. Sgt. Wilmot separated from the Army Reserve because it was the end of her term of enlistment. However, her departure from the military also hinged on a number of factors that served as a catalyst, although she originally had plans to remain in the Army Reserve as long as she could.

For Sgt. Wilmot, the unit to which she was assigned and that was based out of Baghdad "were a bunch of racists." "Let's just cut to the chase," she said. The personnel in the unit, particularly its leadership, "persecuted" her, as she put it, including a Jewish officer in the unit. Sgt. Wilmot said that anyone who did not fit the white Anglo-Saxon mold was equally persecuted. She went on to clarify that this behavior was reflected in the unit's leadership. She described the situation as simply "awful" and as she was about to state what was so disheartening about the situation, she interrupted the thought that she was about to articulate by saying that the combat exclusion policy is "ridiculous" as women, unlike men, and specifically, she as a female, handled combat stress significantly better than many of her male counterparts. Why? Sgt. Wilmot said that she felt grief, she expressed grief, she talked about grief, and did not have a problem admitting it to herself even when she returned home to the CONUS because she was still dealing with grief.

She said, however, that this was really not the problem. She then returned to her original point and stated that what she found most disheartening was that the leadership in her unit was so entrenched in racial discrimination that she decided to leave the Army. But, Sgt. Wilmot also said that she became tired of giving to the Army. Her experience with the unit in Baghdad conveyed to her that it was all about one's color. So she decided that she was no longer willing to remain in this toxic environment. I, the interviewer, interjected that it is regrettable that these acts occurred despite the fact that the Army is the largest of the military branches and the most diverse yet to have this occur is reprehensible. Sgt. Wilmot replied that in light of this fact, there are still pockets of racism in the United States. She was equally fervent about pointing out that this reserve unit to which she was assigned while on deployment in Iraq was out of Indiana which she jokingly referred to as the birthplace of the Ku Klux Klan. I again mentioned to Sgt. Wilmot that it was unfortunate that the members in the unit simply brought their biases with them. Sgt. Wilmot replied that while some unit personnel were from states like Iowa and Wisconsin others who were nonwhite and came from Kentucky were equally attacked with racist behaviors. She said that unfortunately the few nonwhite members in the unit were "questioned into submission," yet all but two, that is she and the Jewish officer, outright refused to succumb to this level of intolerance.

The unit members verbalized their disdain for minorities and when she, Sgt. Wilmot, spoke out about it, she was told in so many words that she was too sensitive and should just deal with it. The challenge though, as Sgt. Wilmot saw it, was that she could not stand for such nonsense. As she put it, "Call it culture, upbringing … I don't care!" but "I'm not a person who shuts up for anything." I brought up the point that given the animus that these unit members felt against their fellow unit members who were Americans that one cannot then imagine the level of animus against the Iraqis whom they were there to help. Sgt. Wilmot mentioned that she actually wrote a manuscript in which she described the situation as "the neo-colonialistic mindset" of the members of the unit. The unit, she said, reminded her of watching old black-and-white films of when the British occupied India in that although it was their country, the Indians were relegated to servitude to the British simply because of the color of their skin. But, what is most despicable is that "we are oppressors in American uniform" and that even she and her fellow unit members who were nonwhite became victims of this oppression. She saw it as reliving the depictions of this gone by era all over again. There was, for instance, when the American military was assigned Iraqi aides who essentially cleaned up after them. To Sgt. Wilmot, this was in contradiction to everything that she was taught in the Army that everyone should clean up for themselves. She said that the Army used the Iraqis as a maid service and she saw this practice as "just wrong" for a people whom we, as Americans, vowed to help.

Sgt. Wilmot was emphatic as she related the situation. She said that this was not the behavior that the American military should have been portraying simply because this was a country of brown people therefore their role was to clean up after the white American. She repeated that this behavior was in direct contradiction to how she was trained in the Army and so much so that she held on to her beliefs and made it a point of vocalizing her displeasure to the unit as the Iraqi aides should not have been used in this manner. This practice by the American military, and specifically her unit, caused Sgt. Wilmot so much consternation that she held on to her beliefs and to her detriment throughout her assignment in Iraq. She was incensed by this practice. The military in turn, as she pointed out, gave every indication that they were above the Iraqis. I interjected by stating that given the animus that her unit members levied against fellow Americans in the unit who were different then it was unimaginable to think of the level of animus that they directed toward the Iraqis. Sgt. Wilmot concurred that the Americans who were serviced by the Iraqi civilian were cordial for the most part but upon learning the plight of one Iraqi woman, who was a maid for her unit in Baghdad, when Sgt. Wilmot returned to Baghdad, she said that she was startled to learn that no one in the unit even knew the woman's name. And, yet, Sgt. Wilmot said that within one week of her return to Baghdad, she already knew the woman's name. Sgt. Wilmot said that she became even more incensed given the level of disrespect, especially after reading about the rich ourstory of the Iraqis and that they constituted one of the world's oldest civilizations. But, she said that the Iraqis were treated as if "they had just crawled out from under a rock" despite their rich culture.

No one engaged Widad, the Iraqi woman, about what she thought about the war or anything for that matter and Sgt. Wilmot said that her weeklong visit to Baghdad resulted in multiple conversations with this woman. She learned that Widad was a widow and her daughter was involved in a car accident; but because Widad is a woman, she was mugged. Further, no one in the community came to her assistance though she sought help. She could not secure help because she was a woman and more importantly she was by herself and did not have a husband. As a result, she was dismissed. This treatment, or one of being dismissed, was equally apparent, by the unit members. As Widad related her story, Sgt. Wilmot said that she sobbed uncontrollably, further Sgt. Wilmot said that she asked how much it could cost for her daughter's health care. When Widad replied she required 40 American dollars, Sgt. Wilmot said she gave Widad 80 American dollars out of her own money.

Thinking that she was assisting Sgt. Wilmot, Widad went and thanked the unit's commander profusely for the gift and for Sgt. Wilmot's good deed. However, according to Sgt. Wilmot, she was instead verbally chastised by her commander and told never to give money to these "terrorists." In essence, her commander referred to the Iraqi woman who cleaned up after the American uniformed personnel in the unit a terrorist. Sgt. Wilmot said that despite her commander's rank as a colonel, she simply "went off" by citing to the commander that it was alright for the Iraqi civilians to clean up after the unit's members but that they were "terrorists" when they asked for something. As she detailed the story, Sgt. Wilmot sarcastically mentioned that it is even more regrettable that as a civilian in the United States her commander is a psychiatric nurse with a federal health-care institution in the Midwestern United States. Basically, she displayed no empathy whatsoever.

Prior to her one-year deployment in Iraq, Sgt. Wilmot had every intention of remaining in the Army. Besides, while in Iraq, her packet for promotional consideration to E-6 was submitted. However, inexplicably and more so mysteriously, after submitting her promotion packet seven consecutive times, she was told that each time the packet got lost. Sgt. Wilmot went onto explain the series of events that led up to, during, and after the seven time mysterious loss of her promotion packet. Further, she said that there were indications along the way that served to reinforce the biased behavior toward her and others in her unit. As a case in point, Sgt. Wilmot said that funds that were earmarked for such equipment as a radio for her Humvee were never provided. Instead, she and her team members were forced to ride around the dangerous Iraq countryside without the aid of any form of communication with either the unit or each other. She said that her unit commander misappropriated these funds for the purchase of such appliances as gaming consoles, television, and luxury furniture for her office that according to Sgt. Wilmot were clearly not mission-related items. In addition, the commander succeeded in sending the surplus to CONUS. Sgt. Wilmot said that this stealing of federal dollars constituted a felony. She said that as a result she sought the counsel of the judge advocate general (JAG) that was located in Ramadi because as she stated "they all got away with it." Moreover, both she and the Jewish officer who were subjected to much grief by her unit's leadership reported the racial bias that was being hurled at them. To Sgt. Wilmot, every derogatory term for being Jewish that could be directed toward the Jewish officer was levied by the unit's leadership. Yet, Sgt. Wilmot said that the irony was that her unit was made up predominantly of white women. But, to Sgt. Wilmot, she said that it was all about leveraging power by putting others down in order to feel better about themselves in light of "their poor mediocre lives." According to Sgt. Wilmot, the situation became unbearable during the final weeks of her deployment.

Sgt. Wilmot and the Jewish Colonel who reported the untoward behavior of mistreatment by their unit's leadership were advised by the JAG officer that they have a bona fide case against the commander for the relief of command. However, during the time that the case made its way to Baghdad to the Office of the Inspector General (IG), Sgt. Wilmot and her fellow complainant discovered that their commander had befriended powers be at the IG. Consequently, their case, previously considered solid enough for relief of command action, was suddenly dismissed. Even more disconcerting was that Sgt. Wilmot was called upon charges for mutiny. Sgt. Wilmot said that upon learning of the charge, she simply "lost it" mentally and that following this incident she was as she put it "done." As Sgt. Wilmot retold the details of this hellish story, she periodically laughed during the interview which in many ways spoke volumes of her coping ability in dealing with this grim subject matter by interjecting humor. She said that she found the absurdity of her own plight after having dealt with charred bodies, smelling charred bodies, dealing with peoples' medical and mental health issues, picking up dead bodies off the sides of roads, being shot at all of the time, dealing with others who were being shot at and where she was dealing with a sucking chest wound in one minute and called to rescue others by jumping into her Humvee in another minute. In essence, Sgt. Wilmot was bewildered by the whole event. It also became evident that she visibly became overwhelmed as she relived every agonizing detail during this interview. She admitted that upon receipt of the news, at that point, she was so rattled that she became abnormally calm. Yet, she likens the way that she felt then as tantamount to "the whole Ft. Hood thing" except as she said, imagine the situation on a much larger scale and involving a female. And, en route to Baghdad, Sgt. Wilmot said that she could not help but contemplate about her predicament and the charges that she was facing but accompanied by the need to act upon her desire at that point in time. Further, she said that no one came to her defense as no one wanted to get involved.

Incidentally, Sgt. Wilmot said that the Army decided to take this action while the Jewish officer was on rest and recuperation (R and R). And, quite coincidentally, the Jewish officer returned just in the nick of time when she was facing charges in Baghdad. At the commander's office, the Jewish officer sat next to her and broke down in tears about the situation. Yet, with a steely resolve, Sgt. Wilmot said to herself of her commander that she "never wanted to put a bullet into somebody so bad." And, as she was en route to Baghdad, she had every intention as she recounted of "making going to jail worthwhile." Sgt. Wilmot mentioned that she was the subject of the book by Kirsten Holmstedt *The Girls Come Marching Home: Stories of Women Warriors Returning from the War in Iraq* but believed that the information about her experience in Iraq was sanitized so much so that the story was not a true portrayal of what actually went on. She said that she thought of doing some "horrible, horrible things" given her predicament. She said though that unfortunately, yet in some ways fortuitously, her helicopter was grounded in Fallujah for one week; she contacted her uncle who was in the Navy and attached to a Naval construction battalion with the Marines in Fallujah. She confided in him about the situation. Again, Sgt. Wilmot told him that she was "losing it" for at that point she no longer even cared about living. She admitted to her uncle that she did not know what to do. Ironically, and of all the events, Sgt. Wilmot celebrated, without the accompanying celebration, of course, was her 24th birthday during that week in Fallujah. Her uncle offered this advice—to take advantage of the downtime by collecting all of the evidence for court and march into her commander's office with the information. He advised her though that it was important that she not do anything against her commander, for even though she was still traumatized, that is exactly what they wanted her to do. Sgt. Wilmot likened her experience with what her unit's leadership was doing to "wiggling a stick into a lion's cage" as a way of provoking her. She said that you would think that it is something that they would not even think of doing. I advised Sgt. Wilmot that I found it befitting that she would use the aforementioned analogy to describe her situation as a former member of Team Lioness. She concurred given the irony.

Sgt. Wilmot continued that this is exactly what the commander was doing to her, for she was sent to a combat zone where she was turned into a wild animal and was further being constantly taunted with a stick. She said that most of the people in the unit who were being harassed simply folded to the pressure. She felt that the unit's leadership considered this kind of harassment as a kind of sport in that they enjoyed it. While Sgt. Wilmot was grounded in Fallujah, she said that she compiled a 39-page report detailing her experience, which she had prepared to present to the court, and, with her uncle's assistance, made several copies. She subsequently marched into her commander's officer, threw a copy of the report on her desk, and in so many words said, "If you're taking me down for mutiny, I'm taking you all down too! I'm going to send a copy to the *New York Times*, the *Washington Post*..." and basically every major media outlet including MSNBC detailing the kind of people who were at the helm in the unit. Essentially, Sgt. Wilmot's intent and message was that if she was illegally being charged with mutiny, then she was not above exposing the illegal activities of the unit's leadership. According to Sgt. Wilmot, this was the kind of verbiage she used when she marched into her commander's office. Further, at that point, she could not have cared less about her commander's rank given what the Colonel had done to her. In Sgt. Wilmot's view, she had far more integrity as a Sergeant than her commander had as a Colonel.

As a result of this act, Sgt. Wilmot said that by the time that she arrived in Baghdad, she felt much more composed and emboldened in her ability to mount an affirmative defense against the mutiny charge. In her words, "I was ready to rock!" But, quite coincidentally, the charge of mutiny was significantly downgraded to an Article 15 for threatening an officer, a charge that Sgt. Wilmot said amounted to a slap on the wrist. In effect, her threat to expose those who were conducting illegal activities in the unit worked to which she concurred confidently that it did so "big time!" Following the hearing, and for what Sgt. Wilmot considered for unknown reasons, she and the Jewish officer were separated and reassigned; the Jewish officer was assigned to Ramadi while she was sent to West Baghdad. Sgt. Wilmot joked that having these two forces combined, referring to herself and the Jewish officer, would have made the world "a blur." Sgt. Wilmot said that being in West Baghdad, albeit isolated, was like being in a tent city but she was happy as she did not have to deal with the people in her unit. And, owing to her exemplary performance there while attached to an explosives ordinance unit, she was nominated for a combat action badge by an active duty Marines Corps Master Sergeant. Unfortunately, according to Sgt. Wilmot, her company commander at the unit to which she was still assigned in Baghdad deliberately disposed of her nomination packet. Additionally, Sgt. Wilmot also discovered that the commander conveniently misplaced the paperwork for other awards for which she was nominated and should have received while in theater. And Sgt. Wilmot was told that because she had disrespected an officer, her promotion packet was withdrawn from consideration. Sgt. Wilmot said that she then questioned what actually happened to the previous six submissions of her promotion packets. I recommended that her story is so fascinating that it has the making of a book and encouraged her to follow through for it to be realized. Ironically, this recommendation was timely as Sgt. Wilmot said that at the time of this interview, she was seated at her computer in preparation to craft a book proposal to a prospective publisher. She said that at first she was reluctant to do so. But she envisioned that her book, unlike many that have been written about Operations Enduring and Iraqi Freedom, will delve into the racial nonsense that she experienced while deployed in Iraq and the abuse of power in the process. Sgt. Wilmot said that one does not have to be in the military to understand the effects of racism and hurting someone to the extent of driving that person to the desire to kill.

Before deployment to Iraq, Sgt. Wilmot said that she was attending the University of North Florida pursuing an undergraduate degree in psychology but then transferred to Orlando, Florida, and had to disrupt her studies given her deployment. Upon return to CONUS from Iraq, she said that she wanted nothing to do with mental health so she changed her major to political science and also became as interested in Middle Eastern ourstory, culture, and international relations. As Sgt. Wilmot began discussing what she found about U.S. foreign policy, she immediately abandoned the idea she wanted to articulate and said "Well, that's another conversation." She continued though by saying that she simply wanted to become involved. At the end of her enlistment in 2006, she secured the David L. Boren NSEP Scholarship which precluded her employment in the federal government. Choosing the scholarship though came with the condition to relocate to Europe for one year and terminate her enlistment with the Army Reserve. Upon returning to her home reserve unit in Florida, she said that she was so broken that despite the Army's offer of $30,000 to reenlist, she declined the offer, for as she stated, there was no amount of money that could make her choose to endure another round of what she had experienced in Iraq. Sgt. Wilmot explained that it was not the combat per se that she was exposed to while in Iraq as this was an expectation prior to deployment there. What she found to be deplorable was the betrayal of trust by her unit which to Sgt. Wilmot simply signaled "the continuation of neocolonialism." She said that as she saw it, she was simply there to perform her job, not to put up with what she was forced to put up with and to be treated as if she was "garbage." She said that no one should have ever had to deal with this type of treatment because of religion or someone's "skin color" that someone does not like. During her encounter with the new retention NCO at her home unit in Florida who kept prying Sgt. Wilmot's to discuss her experience in Iraq, Sgt. Wilmot told the NCO that she neither wanted to discuss the matter nor reenlist in the Army. What Sgt. Wilmot did disclose to this NCO, however, was that the matter was not combat related as she earlier explained but had everything to do with people who wanted to destroy or "was constantly out to get you." This retention NCO even recommended that Sgt. Wilmot be submitted for a promotion to which Sgt. Wilmot retorted that she did not need to receive a promotion out of pity. Sgt. Wilmot said that she lost the promotion that she deserved while in Iraq even though she deserved it and that they took everything away from her. Moreover, Sgt. Wilmot's overriding rationale for not reenlisting in the Army was that the institution failed to protect her.

Sgt. Wilmot said that she selected the mental health field and thus combat stress control as an occupation to pursue in the military because it seemed to be an interesting career field. Further, as she stated, it was something that she also wanted to pursue in college. She said that the Army promised to train her. In fact, Sgt. Wilmot lauded the training that she received in the Army as excellent. Her problem though was not with the training but its lack of enforcement. In her opinion, an 18-year-old who was trained in mental health in the Army was far better prepared than one who had earned an undergraduate degree after four years of college as the Army's training prepared its soldiers by undergoing the intake and clinical work for psychiatrists and psychologists for actual practice in the field. However, Sgt. Wilmot said that if upon enlistment in the Army all career fields were opened at the time, she would have loved to have been an 18D or special forces medic. She said that she even got the opportunity to work with the Special Forces in Iraq. Sgt. Wilmot found this elite force to be unidimensionally focused on its work at hand and was unencumbered by the political concerns of the military. She said that the forces would get in, doing what they were charged to accomplish and get out. She even began collecting Special Forces training manuals or anything having to also do with ranger training. However, at the time she was barred from pursuing this career because of her gender. Now that she has a five-month-old daughter, Sgt. Wilmot said that she will encourage her to pursue such fields as a ranger or combat arms, as two examples. She said that her mother had no idea that women could perform the type of work that Sgt. Wilmot was performing in the Army for she was under the belief that this was the sole province of men. And, ironically, one of her mother's brothers, her uncle, was a ranger in the Army. She said that she wished that she could have pursued that field as well but unknowingly did so by becoming a part of Team Lioness.

For Sgt. Wilmot, being a citizen means not being limited to contributing to one's country but to one's community as well. While she believes that people have this naïve notion that when one thinks of citizenship it is simply about embracing Western culture, as an American citizen and despite the country's horrible past, it constitutes a diversity of languages and people. While she has visited many other parts of the world, Sgt. Wilmot believes that there is no other place like America that she would rather be as she does not believe that other countries are as open to immigrants as America is. When asked if by serving in the military she believes that she has fulfilled her role as a citizen and especially in light of the grueling and unique experiences she had especially as a female soldier, Sgt. Wilmot candidly replied "Hell yeah. And, then some." In fact, she fulfilled this role to the point of the willingness to sacrifice her life for it.

Given the mistreatment to which she was subjected to by her unit's leadership in Iraq, Sgt. Wilmot said that it would be unfair to generalize her experience as a problem in the military, and specifically the Army; however, she believes that the military is not yet doing a good-enough job of enforcing its existing regulations. Further, as she clearly points out, "The military did not give me a fair share at all." Sgt. Wilmot said that regardless of how she was treated, she had never felt less than citizen given her treatment in Iraq. What she did feel, however, was insulted. Yet, undoubtedly, Sgt. Wilmot said that the way that she was treated by her unit in Iraq is not surprising as the military represents a microcosm of the United States. She said that there are still problems including racial discrimination and sexual assault, to name a few. Plus, she continued that being in close quarters in the military exacerbates the problem. For instance, she sees people in the civilian sector who resemble the character traits of those of her commander in Iraq and she believes that if given the opportunity, these people would abuse their power and authority in the same manner as well. She said that sometimes when people in the civilian sector learn that she is a combat veteran they turn it around and attempt to use it against her because people are intimidated and/or have certain negative perceptions about women in the military. For some people she said, it is all about a power struggle for as soon as they either find out what you did in the military or see her on a poster, people will begin to contrive that you are a ring leader who is trying to influence other women to do certain things. She said that especially men are intimidated by her. And, in effect, from what Sgt. Wilmot explained that regardless of how the information is framed about you, given the perceptions about women in the military, rightly or wrongly, military women will forever find themselves in an untenable situation as a result.

On the combat exclusion policy, Sgt. Wilmot said that if women can perform the job as she has repeatedly demonstrated, then women should be allowed to do so. To Sgt. Wilmot, if a certain segment of the military's population is barred from performing those jobs simply because they have "ovaries," it becomes a matter of practicing open discrimination against that group. She said that she witnessed in Army combat and Marines units men who are either smaller in size or weigh less or are even taller than her in some cases and are unable to even change a 50-caliber machine gun. She said that she can do it so why should she not be allowed to perform that type of job. It was evident that Sgt. Wilmot holds the Marine Corps in the highest esteem. She said that while working with the Marines in Iraq, she found them to be extremely disciplined, having undergone rigorous training and working with them she said "they never gave me crap about being a woman." Incidentally, Sgt. Wilmot was quick to point out that this was the active duty Marines. She said that the Army, however, is a completely different animal and if she could have done it all over again, she would have joined the Marine Corps instead. Sgt. Wilmot said that the existence of the combat exclusion policy has certainly affected the career decisions that she has made because first and foremost she would have pursued such occupations as a Special Forces medic or as a ranger. She remembered being in Ramadi at a small military hospital when a badly burned Marine required a skin graft and the only person on that military installation with the equipment to perform the technique was a Special Forces medic. In addition, Sgt. Wilmot believed that the Marines were so much better prepared for Iraq having completed such activities as advanced weapons and language training, although Special Forces (Army) routinely receive this type of training and as a result were able to adapt to any kind of environment.

Sgt. Wilmot had always fantasized about the Special Forces career field if only it were opened to women. She said that not only should the combat exclusion policy be repealed but as a combat veteran, unlike her male counterparts, she does not receive credit for this kind of service and it is not reflected on her DD Form 214 for having done so. She also stated that without this proof of credit, she cannot secure the associated benefits as a man can that comes with being a combat veteran. Further, men more than women are the first to report to the VA to claim their benefits despite the misnomer that women are the weaker sex. Why is it then, Sgt. Wilmot asked, that men are the first ones who rush for their benefits? She said that unfortunately when women visit the VA to claim their benefits, they are less likely or not treated with the same regard as male veterans. Particularly in the absence of the combat veteran information on the DD Form 214, even if a combat veteran, a female will not be given the same level of respect as their male counterpart. She, the female combat veteran, is thus left wanting and must be content with the level of benefits, if any, that she receives.

Should the combat exclusion policy be repealed, Sgt. Wilmot said that she is uncertain as to whether or not doing so, at least in the foreseeable future, will have a positive impact on the recruitment, promotion, and/or retention levels of women. In fact, she said that she envisions some backlash against women as there will still be the old school or misogynistic men who believe that women just do not belong in the military and who will erect veiled barriers to make the situation unbearable for women to prevent them from pursuing certain positions. Yet, there will be men who will be more accepting of women and embrace the repeal of the policy. As well, there are even women who may not be receptive given their negative experiences. Sgt. Wilmot mentioned Captain Katie Petronio who claimed that she was a member of Team Lioness. However, Sgt. Wilmot said that while she was deployed in Iraq as a member of the Team, she did not see any female officers who were associated with the effort. She said, however, that this officer wrote an article railing against women in combat and Sgt. Wilmot questioned the legitimacy of this officer's claim that she was a part of Team Lioness in 2008. But, according to Sgt. Wilmot, the 2003 through 2006 period represented the height of the Team's work. And, even if the Captain did participate in the Team, Sgt. Wilmot said, by the time that she did, the scale of violence in Iraq had significantly decreased.

Sgt. Wilmot stated that as long as women can perform the jobs, this is what should take precedence over the existence of the combat exclusion policy. Besides, as she continued, in Middle-Eastern countries where given culture men cannot touch women, as one example, women function exceptionally in these countries as diplomats and the like. She complained that the United States should not find itself in situations where it is preaching one thing in terms of its foreign policy yet its actions are contradictory with regard to the treatment of its own women in the military. Sgt. Wilmot believes that should the combat exclusion policy be repealed, women in the civilian sector will be equally affected. Interestingly enough, she said that many women in the civilian sector do not believe that they would be able to perform in certain occupations, whereas if provided the opportunity, civilian women can definitely benefit from the advances made for military women. Sgt. Wilmot said that women are unfortunately socialized to believe that they are weaker and are therefore less competent than men and have in turn internalized these myths about themselves. They are taught that they are not as strong and/or as intelligent as men. Sgt. Wilmot provided an apt analogy that it becomes irrelevant as to whether someone has a vagina or testicles, if your home is being burglarized it is your prerogative to protect yourself by utilizing whatever means at your disposal to do so. She continued that duty, loyalty, and strength are not exclusive to being male. Females possess these same traits.

As a former military woman, Sgt. Wilmot described her ability to secure employment in the civilian sector, particularly in the nonprofit sector, as "okay," although she believes that some people are leery of her once they learn that she is a combat veteran. She said that to some people the term is synonymous with "crazy." She likens her state of mind as not crazy but as simply very aware. She said that she is currently pursuing her graduate degree and disclosed that she had undergone a series of interviews with the FBI. The final interview consisted of a polygraph examination. As was anticipated, the man who was performing the polygraph explained what the process would entail and gave a brief synopsis of his background and an explanation of the accompanying rules. What was interesting though about this final interview was that the man began asking her a series of questions, a mini-interview of sorts, about her experiences in Iraq. However, the man, she believes, inappropriately asked her the following question, "Don't you believe that your combat experience would be detrimental to office morale?" She surmised that he only posed that question because she is a woman. Not one to be outdone, Sgt. Wilmot replied "So, I'm good enough to die on the battlefield but I'm not good enough to work in one of your offices." Her quick-witted response caught the man conducting the polygraph off guard and he tried to play it off by stating that she had misinterpreted his question and, in essence, she was being too sensitive. I told Sgt. Wilmot that in Iraq she faced the problem of race and now that she has returned home to the United States, she now faced the problem of being a woman. Sgt. Wilmot said that believe it or not, her military service only served as a hindrance when she applied to the FBI. Yet, in a bizarre way, her experiences have helped her to develop and craft very effective resumes.

On the question of compensation and whether or not her military service has facilitated or hindered her civilian employment compensation, Sgt. Wilmot replied that she was unaware of her compensation being affected either way. However, she stated that she learned that while male veterans are advantaged in their civilian compensation by military service, female veterans experienced the opposite. I then asked Ms. Wilmot whether or not she believed that this is the case because automatically men in the military are designated as combatants and therefore they receive combat pay while women despite their service in war zones like Iraq are legally designated as noncombatants and as a result do not receive the accompanying pay. Sgt. Wilmot said that while in Iraq, she and all who were assigned in Iraq received hostile fire pay. I asked if there was any distinction between hostile pay and combat pay. She was unaware of any distinction but advised that she would investigate. Sgt. Wilmot provided an apt example of the entrenched ignorance that exists even among the women who are in positions to determine the benefits of veterans at the VA. She said that when the woman who attended to her learned that she was a combat veteran, she was startled and so much so that Sgt. Wilmot felt insulted. At that point, Sgt. Wilmot proceeded to leave. However, the woman coaxed her into remaining seated. Sgt. Wilmot said that she proceeded to educate the female VA counselor. Sgt. Wilmot was adamant and said that no VA counselor should speak to any female veteran in that manner as doing so, she explained, is the primary reason why women veterans do not visit the VA to claim their rightfully earned benefits. I advised Sgt. Wilmot that this action also reinforces why women do not voluntarily identify themselves as veterans. But, as Sgt. Wilmot said, given her family tradition, she had always identified herself as a veteran. She said that for her, this has always been a strong sense of her identity.

Sgt. Wilmot said that she also proudly displays that she is a combat veteran on her car. Yet, unfortunately I pointed out that onlookers probably believe that the display relates to either her significant other or husband. Sgt. Wilmot concurred. Similarly, she cited the story of another veteran in Arizona who is both Native American and Hispanic and despite his bumper sticker on his truck that proudly identifies him as an Army ranger and the recipient of a Purple Heart, few, if any, believe that he has earned either of these accolades. As a civilian, Ms. Wilmot said that her experience has been mixed, one of admiration and resentment as both a woman and a minority for she believes that when an American thinks of the military what immediately comes to mind is still that of a white male. Ms. Wilmot described herself as an anomaly that sets in motion a series of contradictions. She said that in many ways, she represents an "HR nightmare" as she does not fit into a given race and/or ethnic group. However, as part of the interview, when asked what she would identify as her race and/or ethnicity, Ms. Wilmot replied that her father's side is a mixture of English and Irish, while her mother's side is Chamorro, or people from the Mariana Islands in the North Pacific. Ms. Wilmot described herself as simply "herself." (Interview via Skype on July 18, 2012)

WOMEN AT WAR   III

Toward Full Agency

The highly acclaimed documentary film *The Invisible War* effectively underscores the morally reprehensible experience that some military women are forced to confront and bear as a consequence of being in the military. Regrettably, this treatment is only one in myriad of biases with which they must contend. This is not to say, however, that women have not successfully pursued careers in the military as is evidenced by many of the women portrayed in this book and the steady, albeit trickle of, advancements that have been made in recent years in the selection of more female general and flag officers, increasing roles of leadership such as the appointment of the first female fighter pilot in the Air Force to command a combat fighter wing, the opening of formerly off-limit positions closed under the guise of categorization as combat and combat related and, most significantly, the repeal of the combat exclusion policy. One cannot then help but be optimistic about women's continued trajectory as key players in the military. But, lest we forget, a note of caution must be interjected. Women's growth in the military has been sporadic, characterized by ebbs and flows, and tainted with convenient memory lapses that fostered the inculcation of selective amnesia by the various decision makers who while recognizing women as an invaluable resource for deployment during times of war, otherwise choose to engage in a form of "cultural amnesia" (Segal 1995, p. 761) during peacetime and with little acknowledgment as to the roles and the sheroic performance of women.

Herbert (1998) characterizes this phenomenon as a constant juxtaposition between gender and sexuality where the appropriateness of women's pursuits, particularly in organizations like the military, is continually being judged as not in keeping with what it means to be a warrior. Culturally, it is then inappropriate for women to assume roles, especially in the military, that are perceived as inherently male. Thus the uneven advancement of women in the military has been typically depicted as an unholy coupling of progression and retrenchment. As Herbert (1998) describes, the military and in turn this notion of the warrior spirit are a rite of passage or "finishing school" (p. 9) for men, not women. While women, say in the Marine Corps, were once dubbed as women Marines because they are perceived first as women and then as Marines, this ensured that part of the training included ensconcing recruits in the art of applying makeup and attending etiquette classes, two among the multiple examples provided that being woman and being in the military are simply incompatible.

Based on a series of questions that were posed to the 17 women portrayed in this book, Section III addresses some menacing yet overriding issues that formed the basis for the combat exclusion policy. These include issues such as gender and the perceived role of women as citizens in a democratic society, the real prospects for implementation following the repeal of the combat exclusion policy, what will be the impact of repealing the policy on the future recruitment, promotion, and retention of women; and in a post–combat exclusion environment, will the repeal of the combat exclusion policy facilitate the promise for women's full agency in the larger American society?

Chapter 10

On Gender and Citizenship

On Gender

In many ways, gender has served as a proxy, if not the defining yardstick, for women's treatment as a collective in American society. Gender is a status characteristic (Ridge and Correll 2004). In the workplace, gender is a determinant of the behaviors and expectations of individuals. For example, because men on the one hand are perceived as fathers and protectors, this dual role is self-reinforcing (Deutsch and Saxton 1998) and increases their asymmetric status in society. Women on the other hand, and by extension motherhood, another status characteristic, lose status in competence and worth even as their role as mothers is valued by society, yet their worth as mothers is devalued in the workplace (Ridgeway and Correll 2004). And, while single professional women are perceived as competent (Fiske et al. 2002), once they adorn the role of motherhood, they are underevaluated in the workplace (Deutsch and Saxton 1998). In fact, Pazy and Oron (2001) found that female military officers were underevaluated simply as a consequence of gender, not their performance. To Snitow (1990) though, once women enter any male-dominated organization or profession for the purpose of achieving equality and gender neutrality, they become "conceptual men" (p. 26).

As such, we find gender to be an integral part of how power is distributed as well as in how we concoct practices, processes, ideologies, and images for use in life (Herbert 1998). More importantly, because the military is about war, it becomes synonymous with manhood. And, given the distribution of power, the roles that are established and the occupations we hold are dictated along the boundary of gender.

These practices, processes, ideologies, and images are reinforced through the denigration of women, or what Burke (1996) refers to as ways of demonstrating even more maleness. According to Goffman (1977), much of what men do is fundamentally an affirmation of not just what manly men do but what women cannot do or is at least ineffective at doing. Hence, to Hopfl (2003), the Tailhook convention was the mother (ironically) of all displays of male prowess by upholding a time-honored naval tradition. This constituted a "free-fire zone" where men could be men "without regard to rank or reprisal" (Hopfl 2003, p. 20).

So, to join the military is perceived as counterintuitive for women, as the institution is ultimately the place where men exude their manhood or expect to achieve manhood. Yet, the military is reflective of the larger society and only by having women in the military in limited roles can the notion of manhood be reinforced (Herbert 1998). Further, military service not only confirms a man's masculinity, the need for training in applying makeup, etiquette, and the like reinforces a gender polarization that is designed to keep specific gender roles intact (Herbert 1998). Andrews (1992) and Pearson (1985) believe that this polarization is accomplished through socialization and cultural processes where women and men learn to conform to socially appropriate behaviors. Essentially, the internalization of desirable accepted behaviors for men together with the rejection of those by women embodies behaviors of male orientation (Pearson 1985). Similarly, women internalize desirable behaviors that are associated with femininity while rejecting those that are defined as masculine to affirm their femaleness. Masculinity is believed to be correlated with such characteristics as dominance, assertiveness, leadership, and competitiveness. Those that are feminine in nature and suit the female sex role orientation include compassion, sensitivity, yielding, and cooperation (Bem 1993; Nadler and Nadler 1990). This view aligns with perceived sex role congruency theory where women and men project traits that are congruent with their sex role orientations and are viewed more favorably than those who are not (Stewart et al. 1990). Women are followers since their sex role orientation is congruent with what is believed to be the traits that characterize being female. Therefore, women cannot be leaders. And, when either women or men display behaviors that are culturally regarded as inconsistent with their corresponding sex role orientations, they are "judged harshly" (Stewart et al. 1990). This results in polarization when given sex role orientations are aligned with physiological sex which is female or male.

Likewise, Bem (1993) sees a dichotomy in the degree to which social life is organized between the sexes. This, too, creates gender polarization where there are clearly delineated feminine and masculine traits for women and men. Women and men who deviate from what is considered normal for one's gender are abnormal. For instance, military women are regarded as deviant (Ellefson 1998). West and Zimmerman (1987) also believe that beyond these sex role orientations is the interaction of the sexes that elicits certain responses by assigning meaning to certain behaviors. Gender then becomes symbolic of our actions or what we do rather than simply what we are, that is either female or male. Any woman in a male-dominated organization may execute behaviors differently from a woman in an organization that is not deeply steeped in male ideology. The conundrum then for military women occurs when they are perceived as displaying behaviors that are also perceived as skewed toward characteristics that are culturally held as male while still expected to hold fast to those characteristics that are fundamentally defined as female. This phenomenon is attributed to the role of sexuality, values, and norms that, according to Herbert (1998), imposes boundaries on established gender roles.

It is interesting to note that the integration of women in the military just prior to WWII in the United States elicited a prompt response from the then Director of the Women's Army Corps, Oveta Culp Hobby, that women were neither "Amazons rushing into battle" nor "butterflies fluttering free" (Freedom of Press 1942—see Holm 1992). However, it became necessary to clarify, at least to the American public, how women, who for the most part would be performing traditional men's work as well as dressing like men, would not bring about underlying changes in their femininity as women (Honey 1984, p. 3). In an effort to quell these fears, the Office of Emergency Management said:

> There is an unwholesomely large number of girls who refrain from even contemplating enlistment because of male opinion. An educative program needs to be done among the male population to overcome this problem. Men-both civilian and military personnel-should be specifically informed that it is fitting for girls to be in the service. This would call for copy ... which shows that the services increase, rather than detract from, desirable feminine characteristics. (Honey 1984, p. 113)

Specifically, Army advertising showed a woman standing by her helicopter donned in a flight suit and helmet but wearing lipstick and mascara. Below the advertisement depicted another woman, this time in civilian attire, with large earrings and with a ring on her finger (symbolizing marriage, I suppose) while in the company of a male with his arms around her (symbolizing her husband or a significant other, I suppose). The purpose of the advertisement was, of course, to reassure women that though they would be performing traditional men's duties, doing so would in no way change their sexual orientation. Essentially, they would remain as women who just happen to perform men's jobs and in men's clothes.

At the heart of these campaigns, it seems though, was the military's attempt to control how gender roles were being perceived, particularly in light of the large-scale deployment of thousands of women in support of WWII. Herbert (1998) refers to this practice as "doing gender" (p. 14) where the perceptions of women are controlled, even as soldiers. Yet, they are liable as both women and soldiers. Here, gender is defined and redefined not only as feminine and masculine but as structural. But the military, at least prior to the 1970s, was largely defined as a male institution that reinforced "maleness" and "soldiering" (Herbert 1998, p. 15). And in integrating women into this inherently male institution resulted in a state of conflict for the institution.

In response, the military employed multiple mechanisms to downplay the role of gender and correspondingly sexuality in its continual effort to portray the military as innately male. This was achieved through actual and illusory ways of segregating women and men in the military. For example, from the latter part of the 1970s through the early 1980s, the Army tested the viability of sex-integrated basic training (Herbert 1998). While there were always separate sleeping quarters for women and men, the actual training of troops was integrated. But, in 1983, the Army reverted to segregated training because of the fear of potential fraternization between female and male troops, not that this decision was made based on actual reports of fraternization during this period of experimentation. Publicly, the Army held that sex integration of basic training was purported to lower the training standards of men given the presence of women, thus creating easier training for men.

Beyond basic training, the military enforces stern policies against fraternization and adultery between heterosexual women and men by segregating the sexes (Herbert 1998). Prior to repealing the Don't Ask, Don't Tell, and Don't Pursue policy, the military employed a similar practice under the guise of segregating lesbians and gay men from potential fraternization by banning them from military service (Herbert 1998; Holm 1992). The rationale provided by the military was that, like heterosexual women and men, dispensation should not be given to homosexuals, especially since heterosexuals were not being afforded these privileges (Herbert 1998). But, as observed by Herbert (1998), at no time did this ban against homosexuals from military service prevent homosexuals from entering military service. What this policy did succeed in accomplishing, though, was to reinforce the defined boundaries for behavior in terms of femininity and masculinity, or normative behaviors for women and men. Says Herbert (1998), these policies were perhaps less based on maintaining "good order and morale" (p. 18) and more about maintaining perceived cultural norms of gender. As related by Gross (1990), the following statement by the then Vice Admiral Joseph Donnell of the U.S. Navy in July 1990, is emblematic of the military's need to control conceptions of gender amid blatant contradictions about the fallacy of such policies. The Admiral described women in the military who are perceived as lesbians as generally to be "hardworking, career-oriented, willing to put in long hours on the job, and among the command's top performers" (Gross 1990, p. 24), which he continued to contribute to commanders' half-hearted attempts in pursuing these investigations (Herbert 1998). Moreover, according to Herbert, this constituted a mischaracterization of heterosexual sailors. As one female drill instructor at Parris Island put it, given the attempts to uncover lesbian Marines, "The qualities and traits that we demand and are supposed to be training our recruits are the same traits that make us look homosexual" (Shilts 1993, p. 56).

Herbert (1998) invokes Pharr's (1988) homophobia as a weapon in sexism that is used against and affects all women. This occurs when reported sex-inappropriate behaviors are committed such as those displayed by women who are perceived as male in nature and consequently become suspect. Actually, regardless of marital status, where a woman is perceived as masculine, she will be perceived as a lesbian. She becomes subject to censure and her sexual orientation in question (Herbert 1998). Lowe's (1993) study of female bodybuilders highlights how beliefs about femininity and masculinity are used to curb women's participation in nontraditional jobs and occupations. As an illustration is Herbert's (1998) citation of the film *Pumping Iron II: The Women*, where values about femininity and masculinity resulted in penalizing a female bodybuilder for not projecting the musculature of a female. And, ironically, Kite and Deaux's (1987) work revealed that lesbian characteristics such as short hair, donning masculine clothes, and being athletic are often attributed to military women. The researchers concluded that homosexual stereotypes are the consequences of gender. Shilts (1993) supported the following finding: "Although clerk typists were as likely to be lesbians, they were rarely suspect; mechanics almost always were. Husky women were suspicious; petite women were not" (p. 496).

To Herbert's (1998) question then "What happens when the same attributes (e.g. masculinity) that are seen as desirable for success in the occupation or industry (e.g. military/soldiering) are also those that lead a group (e.g. women) to be labeled with a characteristic (e.g., lesbian) deemed unacceptable for participation in the occupation?" (p. 21). More so than other predominately male institutions, the military is an institution which apart from being male-oriented is central to its core. As a result, men are more desirable than women as is masculine over feminine. Said one Army female police officer, "It's still a male-oriented military, and no matter how hard you work, or how good your reputation is, you're a woman, and you get slighted for being one" (Barkolow 1990, p. 251). Essentially, women in the military have consistently faced the quandary of attempting to achieve a modicum of balance between being feminine and being masculine (Herbert 1998). Sheppard (1989) says that, for women, this includes the delicate management of being feminine yet businesslike. For to be perceived as too feminine risks the reputation of incompetence while being perceived as too masculine risks being classified as a lesbian. For Bevans (1960, p. 69), despite the time of his research, the belief unfortunately still holds true, "A woman in business is supposed to be a woman, not one of the boys. On the other hand, you must avoid being so female that you embarrass your co-workers." Women in male-dominated organizations like the military are then forced to contrive strategies to negotiate what Herbert (1998) hails as "hostile terrain" (p. 22).

These strategies may include minimizing their femininity, on the one hand, to facilitate kinship with the boys by defeminizing themselves to avoid bringing attention to themselves (Herbert 1998). Yet, on the other hand, women deliberately distance themselves from one another and unidimensionally focus on the work at hand. In contradiction though, some women may even capitalize on their femininity as a way of demonstrating to male cohorts that they should not be perceived as a threat. Doing so may also include estrangement from other women who are not perceived to be feminine enough. But these challenges and the need for corresponding strategies are only visible to those who experience them (McElrath 1992). But, according to Probert et al. (1998), the only way for women to succeed is to act like men. These normative ways of thinking and believing are holdovers from childhood that are constantly subject to cultural reinforcement as to what is feminine and what is masculine (Herbert 1998).

As important is the naturalness of what is considered to be gender-role appropriate that dictates. These cultural roles and expectations play out in the workplace. Gutek et al. (1986) refer to this phenomenon as sex-role spillover where jobs or occupations are divided as female and male with the associated gender expectations of these jobs and occupations. Jobs and occupations then become gendered (Acker 1992). With this comes the notion that only men should serve in the roles as warrior, protector, and defender. These are the inherent domains of men. Besides, war is the prerogative of men; this includes protecting women and children. To do otherwise is to "disrupt the natural order of things" (Herbert 1998, p. 29). Yet, to refute these conceptions is ill-advised. It then becomes more important to determine its roots. Resistance and hence beliefs about women in the military and the naturalness of men only to the avocation of the military are exposed in two forms. Anecdotally, there is no evidence to refute this claim. And, even in the face of scientific evidence that contradicts this natural affinity of men to war and the military, to accept this evidence as fact would be tantamount to question one's own existence. There is an alternative viewpoint though that men's naturalness to the military is the result of a social construct (Herbert 1998), wherein our values and beliefs about gender are socially and culturally determined. Proponents on both sides of the aisle fervently argue, for instance, that women do not belong to the military, not because they are ill-suited but because of socialization. Others contend that some, but not all women are ill-suited for military life and defy these dogmas that only exist to confine women. So, women reside in a world of contradictions that, at least in the military, is borne of women's initial induction into the institution (Herbert 1998). Women must be prudent in embellishing their femininity while simultaneously being perceived as competent enough to carry out their military duties. As one respondent in Herbert's (1998) study remarked, "It is a perception that military women who may be too feminine get the good, high visibility jobs on admirals' or generals' staffs" (p. 33). But to one's chagrin, these women are simply viewed as "sex objects" who are "not able to show their brains work" (Herbert 1998, p. 33).

Still, to be masculine in the military is to be revered and women must be particularly careful in not overly exuding such traits or at least being perceived as masculine (Herbert 1998). Nevertheless, for women who are perceived to display these traits (i.e., direct, disciplined, and aggressive), while they may be undermined by their reputation as "castrating" bitches, overall, they are respected and accomplish their jobs (Herbert 1998, p. 33). Yet, the demands of the military are such that women are forced to navigate the tightrope of traits and whether or not they are being perceived as portraying "good" or "real," women that are gender appropriate, says Herbert (1998, p. 34), while displaying those traits that result in good performance or perceived to be masculine. For accordingly, maintaining this fragile balance hinges on sexuality. As good soldiers and thus good stewards in the military, unlike men, women must possess both perceived feminine and masculine traits. No such demands are made of men in the military. Herbert's (1998) results yielded some interesting, yet not surprising, although still inconclusive, results about the extent to which the sample of women from four branches of the military (Army, Air Force, Navy, and Marine Corps) believed that they are being penalized for portraying traits that are perceived to be either feminine or masculine.

Ironically, at the aggregated level, Herbert (1998) found a wide range between the services in the degree to which the respondents felt pressured to act as either feminine or masculine, from 42% in the Air Force to 56% in the Marine Corps, a finding that is especially contradictory given the branch's practice of indoctrinating its female recruits first as women and second as Marines. Herbert cautions, however, that this finding was only based on a small sample of 11 women Marines. While these results are followed closely by those who were in the Army and the Navy, only 20% of Air Force veterans believed that these pressures existed. This finding though for the Air Force is not surprising, as the service continues to be reputed as the most female friendly in the military as well as the most effective in integrating women (Holm 1992).

Herbert (1998) speculated whether or not this reputation was also based upon the combination of the Air Force's emphasis of "brains over brawn" (p. 39) that attracts even men with more technical skills or is it as a result of self-selection that causes both women and men to be attracted to the Air Force that in turn reduces the need for any resistance to women. Yet, this overall finding for the pressure of women in the services to display either feminine or masculine traits was also inconclusive. But, the findings on the penalties enforced for failure to exude the traits of one gender or another were stark. At 66%, Army women were the most likely to believe that there were associated penalties with being too masculine, with the Navy, Air Force, and Marine Corps at 64%, 50%, and 41%, respectively. The latter is again inconsistent with the Marine Corps' practice of producing women first and Marines second. When controlled for other variables, officers and enlisted respondents diverged in the extent to which they perceived that penalties existed for exuding such traits. Officers were more likely than enlisted respondents to view that these penalties existed for femininity and were only somewhat more likely to view that similar penalties existed for masculinity. Junior ranking officers were more prone to believe that penalties existed for femininity and masculinity while more than 50% of the respondents who were senior in rank held similar beliefs, although overall, 66% of junior ranking respondents were more likely to say that these penalties existed for masculinity compared to slightly over 50% for senior ranking respondents.

In the study (Herbert 1998), sexual orientation was highly correlated with perceptions of such penalties. For example, self-identified lesbian and bisexual women tended more often than not to believe about the existence of these penalties for women than were heterosexual women (25% versus 60%). And 81% of lesbian and bisexual women believed that there were consequences for being too masculine versus a rate of slightly higher than 50% for being heterosexual women. Three additional findings that were important to the study cannot be overlooked. Race and/or ethnicity, the time of separation from active duty, and the level of education served as predictors of women's perceptions about the likelihood of being penalized for femininity or masculinity. Women of color were purported to have had these experiences both on gender and race and/or ethnicity. Thus, the need to conform to perceived normative behaviors was more burdensome for them, although Herbert (1998) surmised that the sample of 28 was also too small to deduce more robust conclusions. Incidentally, Herbert concluded that, at the time of the study, women who separated from active duty perhaps experienced a "less tolerant" (p. 50) military for femininity than their earlier cohorts when expectations were such that women were expected to be more feminine. Herbert also concluded that less educated women were more likely to be found in occupations with less tolerance for femininity whereas those with higher levels of education were in occupations that called for more brain than brawn such as military intelligence. Yet, what the study concluded was that by virtue of tenure, women who remained in the military were less likely than those who prematurely separated to experience the tensions or pressures of negotiating the paths between femininity and masculinity. Besides, high tenure or the propensity to remain longer in the military was also an indication that even where women encountered these tensions and pressures, they were more likely to learn to adjust to avoid such unpleasantries. However, the foregoing points are gender management strategies or what is referred to as doing gender (West and Zimmerman 1987) that many military women must employ to survive and thrive in military life. "One of the hardest parts of being a military woman is just the constant scrutiny and criticism. Act 'too masculine' and you're accused of being a dyke; act 'too feminine' and you're either accused of sleeping around, or you're not serious; you're just there to get a man" (Lieutenant, Navy in Herbert 1998, p. 112).

Many of these same frustrations were echoed by some of the women chronicled in this book who cited the constant and overwhelming pressure to keep proving themselves even after they had already surpassed multiple precedent-setting roles. It will be interesting then to observe whether or not women will have similar experiences in a post–combat exclusion policy environment, particularly with regard to those occupations that will be opened to them under the semblance of combat and combat-related designations.

On Citizenship

All the women chronicled in this book spoke to having very strong feelings about the notion of citizenship. They were each posed a series of questions on the topic that delved into the following: What is your concept of citizenship? What does it mean to you to be an American citizen? Do you believe that by serving in the U.S. military you have fulfilled your role as a citizen? Do you believe that the military has treated you as a citizen? Does being barred from certain career fields in the military make you feel less than a citizen? And, what was your experience in the military?

While each woman defined citizenship uniquely, the overriding theme was clear; citizenship is neither a role that should be taken frivolously nor one that can be filled through military service alone. Being a citizen is a responsibility that is lifelong in nature and as Mrs. Anna Monkiewicz, the oldest interviewee, whom I dub as one of the original fly girls, put it, citizenship transcends time, as doing so begins from the cradle and never ceases until one goes to the grave. Many of the women also realized the unique endowment of being American citizens. Major General Marcelite Harris remarked that, despite all of its faults as she came of age at the height of racial tensions during the civil rights era in the United States that culminated in the assassination of Reverend Dr. Martin Luther King, Jr., she is still blessed to be in a country where overcoming seemingly intractable odds can be achieved provided that one is dogged in their determination to pursue their goals. Nevertheless, for some, the question as to whether or not the military has treated them as less than citizens revisited and exposed the depth of old wounds that appeared to have only been superficially healed. While the women did not blame the military per se, they abhorred the injustice of many of its policies, chief among them, combat exclusion, that intentionally and openly discriminated against certain segments of its population and with, as they saw it, no rational basis whatsoever. Consequently, some of the women believed that they were indeed treated as less than full citizens or second-class citizens at best which deprived them of not only exercising and experiencing the full complement of what it means to be in the military, but a point that many made was that doing so was detrimental to the country. Yet, none of the women hesitated in their zeal to join the military even knowing that the military was an inherently different institution from its civilian counterparts. In other words, the women enlisted with the expectation that, though the military is a subset of a democracy, being in the military is an undemocratic endeavor as dissent is limited, if not discouraged altogether. With this perspective in mind, they believe that they have benefited immensely from their military experiences. And, the majority of the women, in one form or another, were able to leverage and translate their military experiences by successfully launching opportunities within the civilian sector as private citizens, although, admittedly, some believed that they fell far short of some of their personal and professional milestones as compared to what many of their male, particularly white male, counterparts have achieved in the civilian sector following military service.

But in spite of their precedent-setting successes, their experiences as women, together with the dual tribulation as women in the military, are a path on which women, even those who reside in the world's model of democracy, have been forced to sojourner. Neither the enactment of the U.S. Constitution, the Nineteenth

Amendment to the Constitution that granted women universal suffrage for the right to vote, nor the failed appeal to ratify the Equal Rights Amendment (ERA) that has since been introduced at every session in Congress since 1923 and subsequent laws since, including most notably the Civil Rights Act of 1964, nor the Glass Ceiling Act of 1991 has fundamentally changed the cultural schemas that continue to prevent women from being all that they can be despite myriad advancements. Only one woman, Hillary Rodham Clinton, has come close to realizing the full personification of achieving full citizenship. According to Schwarzenbach (2003), these results should come as no surprise, as nowhere in the original draft of the Constitution are the pronouns "woman" or "women" explicitly mentioned. Truth be told, the document was explicit in its reference of men, at least 30 times. Further, as Schwarzenbach (2003) explains, this was deliberately not expected since the document was unidimensionally drafted by a cadre of men. Any enumeration of rights with regard to citizenship rights were not inclusive of women for they did not have the right to vote, to be property owners, and were banished from public view unless, of course, such publicity was approved by their husbands and fathers.

Others like Morris (1987), Hoff (1991), Gunderson (1987), and Smith-Rosenberg (1992) are of the same mindset believing that women's explicit exclusion from the Constitution was no accident. It is by way of exemption from serving in juries and in the military, said Kerber (1998), that has rendered women as second-class citizens. Horrigan (1992) concurs, for where the combat exclusion policy is concerned, women have been denied equal protection under the Fourteenth Amendment of the Constitution, particularly in the Navy, because unlike the Air Force, it is steeped in 150 years more of tradition. Even the U.S. Supreme Court has been less disturbed by the disparate treatment of women, yet is more uneasy about providing legislative relief for African Americans. This statement by the High Court encapsulates the indifference toward women: "The natural and proper timidity and delicacy which belongs to the female sex evidently unfits it for many of the occupations of civil life ... The paramount destiny and mission of woman are to fulfill the noble and benign offices of wife and mother. This is the law of the Creator" (Horrigan 1992, p. 242). Notice the not-so-subtle reference to women as "it," an object in the first and knowing her place in the second. For after all, it is not just a matter of law but is as interpreted by men that it has been ordained as such by the Creator. Therefore, it must be so.

It was only sometime later through legal challenges against the military, in this case against the Air Force (*Frontiero v. Richardson* 1973) and the Navy (*Owens v. Brown* 1978), both of whom as the primary plaintiffs are also profiled in this book, did the U.S. Supreme Court move to strike down in part, or in whole, practices and policies on the part of the military that resulted in adverse impact on its female workforce. In *Frontiero v. Richardson* (1973), the Court held that it was not interfering in military matters when it struck down a discriminatory policy requiring that female members of the Air Force had to prove that their spouses were their dependents in order for them to receive benefits, a status and right that were automatically bestowed upon the spouses of male members of the military (Horrigan 1992). The Court struck down a portion of the Navy's interpretation of Section 6015 of one of the iterations of the combat exclusion policy in *Owens v. Brown* (1978). While women continued to be barred from ships designated as combat or combat related, they were allowed, albeit relegated, to serve on repair and salvage ships. Similarly in *Schlesinger v. Ballard* (1975; Horrigan 1992), the High Court denied the Navy plaintiff, a male officer, relief against a Navy policy that allowed female officers more time for promotion before they could be affected by the military's "up or out" rule (Horrigan 1992, p. 247). The plaintiff argued that he was as similarly situated as female officers, and that therefore he should be given more time before falling victim to the up or out rule. The Court fired back that, "The different treatment of men and women naval officers ... reflects, not archaic and overbroad generalizations, but, instead, the demonstrable fact that male and female line officers in the Navy are *not* similarly situated with respect to opportunities for professional service. Appellee has not challenged the current restrictions on women officers' participation in combat and in most sea duty." (From *Schlesinger v. Ballard* 1975, p. 508 in Horrigan 1992, p. 247). The last statement referred to the fact that the appellant failed to challenge the Navy's policy that similarly situated women and men were not subject to the restrictions of the combat exclusion policy (Horrigan 1992). Horrigan's (1992) contention of the High Court's reticence to decide in matters of gender-based discrimination surrounds the notion that, as held in *Reed v. Reed* (1971), on the grounds of equal protection, such legal challenges, in this case dealing with gender, and as cited by Justice Brennan, are "inherently suspect" (*Reed v. Reed* (1971), p. 682 in Horrigan 1992, p. 245). Likewise, as ruled in *Craig v. Boren* (1976, pp. 197 and 198), "Classifications by gender must serve important government objectives and must be substantively related to achievement of those objectives" (Horrigan 1992, p. 250).

Nonetheless, there are those like Lewis (2003), Belz (1992), and Goldwin (1990) who believe that the Constitution's failure to explicitly include women in no way means that women were not considered. In fact, some like Belz (1992) see the document as simply gender-neutral. Lewis (2003) adamantly insists that women were part and parcel of the document under the guise of such terms like "free person," "person," or "persons" (p. 24). It was thus implied that women were specifically addressed. In addition, because women, as were children, the young, and the infirmed, were to be protected from an overreaching government, their exclusion from the Constitution and in turn from government was for their very protection given that government was suspect during the early days of the American republic (Belz 1992; Goldwin 1990). Evidently, Charles Sumner, a staunch abolitionist and senator from Massachusetts, attempted to craft the Fourteenth Amendment in such a manner as to make it gender-neutral. As stated, "he wrote over nineteen pages of foolsap to get rid of the word 'male' and yet keep 'negro suffrage' as a party measure intact, but it could not be done" (Siegel 2002, p. 58).

But, the language in the Fourteenth Amendment proved to be a bone of contention. Under "natural rights," the Amendment would have not only made the case for providing blacks full citizenship but women as well (Buescher n.d.). Retaining this language would have bolstered the women suffragists' case for the right to vote, though the Amendment was based on the need for full citizenship. But, natural rights would have provided them with both the political and practical cover in that the Constitution was implicit in its granting of full citizenship to women. However, it is believed that such a practice was not upheld because of outmoded conventions about women at the time. Section 1 of the Amendment, for example, states that "All persons born or naturalized" are afforded citizenship of the United States, and as such, these rights cannot be abridged. But, while explicit, in that it can only be assumed that women meet this criterion for citizenship, the law was not explicit enough. According to Herrmann (2008), if this is the case and that all citizens have equal protection, given the Fourteenth Amendment, then why is it that the second section of the Amendment, in its reference to the criteria for U.S. Representatives in Congress, specifically employs such language as "male citizens" (p. 7), thus excluding women altogether from the Constitution? And yet again, while the Fifteenth Amendment was passed only two years later or in 1870, while it rallied women to seek and fight for suffrage, nowhere in the Constitution are women included, despite its verbiage that the Amendment guarantees all U.S. citizens the right to vote. Moreover, although women eventually gained suffrage, there was no equal right to be achieved in the Fourteenth Amendment, hence the rationale for crafting the ERA in an attempt to fill this void.

Even so, Young (2005) frames the argument for women to have full citizenship in terms of what a good or bad woman would do. A "good" woman (p. 25), on the one hand, willingly submits herself and without question to the protection of a man, be it her father or her husband. A "bad" woman (p. 25), on the other hand, secures the status either because of her unwillingness to be protected by a man or the claim that she should or given the misfortune of not having a man to do so. Either situation, says Young (2005), puts women at risk as vulnerable to male domination. For, this so-called male protection, women are then forced to surrender to this kind of protection or should they refuse this protection, and are attacked, they will not be protected. While Young was using this analogy to describe the United States as a new security state in light of the times, she believes that this language of fear or that of "good citizen" and "bad citizen" likens them to good women and bad women that forces us to kowtow in fear by subordinating our rights as democratic citizens who are neither above nor below our government that is acting as our protector. But Young (2005) says that "Subordinate citizenship is incompatible with democracy" (p. 27). Besides, in a democracy, the legitimacy of citizenship comes with the relationship of equality in terms of the rights and responsibilities for both the citizens and the leaders who represent them must be accountable. Therefore, whether we are to accept or dispute the premise that women were originally mentioned in the Constitution is moot.

The fact of the matter is that women now comprise over 50% of the country's population (U.S. Census 2010) and 16% of the military's force (Population Report FY 2011; 2011 Demographics Profile of the Military Community November 2012), points that were also made by Horrigan (1992) over 20 years ago as justification to repeal the combat exclusion policy. Still, the irony of the Constitution and specifically the Fourteenth Amendment is being utilized as the basis for giving and legitimizing the polity of a democratic society, its rights of full citizenship while simultaneously denying those same rights of full citizenship to women in the military, a segment of that same society that constitutes more than 50% of its civilian population. Even more ludicrous are people of the same ilk, that is, other women, who are ardent opponents of women in the military like Gutman (1997) without realizing that their positions needlessly subordinate their sisters, and themselves, I might add, to that of second-class citizenship through such slights as "What no one is publicly saying (but what everyone in the military knows) is that incidents like these (Referring to sexual assault at the Army's Aberdeen Proving Ground) are bound to recur. In a military that is dedicated to full integration of women and to paring over the implications of that integration as best it can, sex and sexual difference will continue to be a disruptive force" (Titunik 2000, p. 18). Implicit in this statement, and regrettably from a woman, is that women in the military not only "insert their ill-mannered selves to thwart the efforts of men off to battle" but "in the same vein … women's mere presence induces grown rational men to view them as temptresses ready to lead them astray" (Harris 2009, p. 71). Yet, nothing could be further from the truth.

Using agency theory, Mazur (1998) emboldens women to overcome this perceived novelty effect and one of victimization such as to be protected by taking responsibility for one's own actions for to not do so would be equally perceived as being irresponsible. This action (i.e., being responsible) thus becomes one of women's own volition in order to shed this perceived status of victimhood. Says Snyder (2003), the exclusion of women in exercising certain roles in the military, for example, weakens and goes against the democratic values of the citizen–soldier tradition. And, if the primary purpose of a military is to uphold and protect those democratic ideals, then denying the rights of one half of the country's citizens is a hostile act that is subterfuge to women's rights, not entitlement to military service. As Snyder (2003) suggests, it is important then to purge the military of sexism by focusing less on gender and more on military effectiveness to give women, like men, opportunities for contributing to the mission of the institution. The American Civil Liberties Union (ACLU) was more direct in its drive to set the stage of equality for women in the military by saying that "Men do not have a monopoly on patriotism, physical ability, desire for adventure, or willingness to risk their lives. Until both the responsibilities and rights of citizenship are shared on a gender-neutral basis, women will continue to be considered less than full-fledged citizens."

Consequently, the outright exclusion of one segment of the military's population from the opportunity to engage in combat, a right to which men in the military are inherently entitled, makes the definition of citizenship suspect, despite the Fourteenth Amendment. As well, while in theory women's full citizenship is recognized, in practice it is not. Then to say that women in the military as do women in the general society are entitled to the same rights as men in the military and in turn men in the general society is to ignore the conditions of reality on the ground to invoke a military analogy. If this was the case, that is, that women are entitled to full citizenship as men, then such subsequent legislations as the Civil Rights Act of 1964, Title VII, and the Voting Rights Act of 1965, to name a few, for the purpose of addressing the limitations in both the recognition and practice of the law as per the Fourteenth and Fifteenth Amendments for certain groups would have been for naught. But, this is not the case. These subsequent legislations were necessary to fill the gaping chasms between the Amendments, that is, the laws, and their implementation. And given these blaring deficiencies, the late Major General Jeanne Holm, the first female woman in the military to be so elevated, affirmed that women's struggle in the military is about achieving the rights and responsibilities of full citizenship (GenderGap 2000). Further, women have struggled and have earned the right to be all that they can be. Simply put, women's struggle in the military is about realizing full agency (Harris 2009). Repealing the combat exclusion policy is only one of the milestones toward this journey.

Chapter 11

Repealing the Combat Exclusion Policy: Prospects for Implementation

While the mounting lawsuits by current and former service members against Department of Defense (DoD), including those by the American Civil Liberties Union (ACLU), perhaps served as the final and overpowering weight that forced the combat exclusion policy over the precipice to its demise, the ACLU struck a cautionary note in light of this unprecedented news. Said the ACLU, it will be imperative to bring the forces to bear by continuing the pressure on DoD and the military branches to open all closed positions to women in the military given the repeal (ACLU). Yet, in spite of the recent repeal of the combat exclusion policy, many schools, positions, and career fields remain closed to women. Failure to honor the conditions of the repeal, as earlier suggested by Harris (2009), means that not only will the military diminish in its ability to compete for the best and brightest that society has to offer but will also concurrently lose women with the requisite skills, talents, and experience (aclu.org) as well as in retaining those who are highly qualified, amid the troop drawdown from Operations Enduring and Iraqi Freedom (DACOWITS 2012) and New Dawn. The ACLU's cautionary note is hardly one to be discounted as the hope is that the repeal of the combat exclusion policy is neither purely symbolic nor is to function as a delay tactic to keep forces at bay from continuing the fight in ensuring that the issue remains at the forefront of the conscience of the American psyche. This is a point of significance, not one of paranoia, as the ourstory of women's progress in the military, despite the advances, has been rife with a steady pattern of promises only to be followed by a series of inaction, much of which usually devolves into studying the issue to no end.

All but 2 of the 17 women profiled in this book are the first females in their families to join the military. Fifteen of the women operated under various iterations of the combat exclusion policy and although the two exceptions were under some form of restrictions for women in the military, both served, prior to and during WWII, when women's service in combat was, in effect, a nonissue. But despite the generational differences, the 17 women were unanimous in their call for repealing the combat exclusion policy, many citing it as outdated; a policy whose time has come; one that inherently creates a caste system of women and men together with the undue burden for the risk of death on one segment of the military's population that is not based on performance but gender, an implicit proxy for exclusion. Many also described the policy as ridiculous in its intent, for like it or not, women have already been serving in combat and being placed at greater risks than their male counterparts simply because they lack the required protection against such risks and without the repeatedly proven recognition for their valiant acts. Many of the women bemoaned the fact that the existence of the policy restricted their choices of career fields and where they could and could not be assigned. Both actions amounted to the stifling of career growth, and as as discussed in this section, not being afforded the opportunity to experience the full range of what it means to be in the military. When asked should the combat exclusion policy be repealed do they anticipate a backlash against women, some of the interviewees conceded that the first cohort of women in any traditionally male-dominated occupation will unwittingly encounter the brunt of the burden for their successors. Others reiterated the pivotal role of leadership in guiding with clear goals for implementation and transition if the full integration of women throughout the military is to be successful. Not surprisingly, the women advised that had they had their druthers and had it not been for the combat exclusion policy, they would have knowingly selected to pursue different career fields from those that they ultimately pursued as careers in the military and that would have placed them directly into situations of combat, ground, and otherwise. Few of the women were lucky enough to pursue their first love as a career. And, ironically, although the oldest interviewee who was one of the first in this sample to join the military did not make a career of the military, she was fortunate in pursuing her first love for flying to become one of the first cohorts of women before the buildup to WWII to fly for the military.

So, what are the tangible plans in store for implementation in a post–combat exclusion policy environment? Following the announcement of the repeal of the combat exclusion policy, the then Secretary of Defense Panetta called for each service to formulate plans for its full integration of women into all positions and units in the military by January 2016 (Evans 2013) lest those services can justify why women would be considered inappropriate and/or not yet ready for such assignments (Sutton 2013). In a memorandum dated May 21, 2013, Defense Secretary Chuck Hagel (2013) acknowledged the receipt of the plans for proposed implementation for the integration of women into the remaining positions in the military services that are still closed to them and which are classified under the 1994 definition of direct ground combat. In this memorandum, the Secretary acknowledged that these proposed plan submissions by each military service is intended to "methodically and deliberately remove gender restrictive barriers" (Memorandum from Secretary of Defense Chuck Hagel, p. 1). According to Secretary Hagel, the decision for full implementation is anticipated in January 2016. Proposed plans for the full integration of women into the military were submitted by the Army, Navy, Air Force, Marine Corps (USMC), and the U.S. Special Operations Command (USSOCOM) (U.S. Department of Defense Implementation Plans in Memorandum from Secretary of Defense Hagel 2013). Each plan is said to detail how, when, and to what extent integration will be implemented. It is the understanding that the full integration of women into all positions and occupations will proceed incrementally for full implementation by January 2016. However, there are already signs of concern, a holding back, if you will, on whether or not such plans will be followed through and/or if all positions will be opened. It also appears that some of the military branches and commands, that is, USMC and SOCOM, are holding fast to the notion that they reserve the right to not adhere to guidance under the repeal of the combat exclusion policy. The following represents a snapshot of what each service plans to accomplish toward full integration.

Army[*]

According to the Army, as early as 2011, it was being proactive in assessing barriers that it considered unnecessary to its female workforce's success. In response, the Army opened 14,000 positions as a result of abolishing the collocation restriction and assigning women at the battalion level in nine Brigade Combat Teams (BCTs). In employing a phased-in approach, the Army said that it notified the Office of the Secretary of Defense of its intentions to open up another 6000 positions to women under the auspices of 17 Active Component (AC) BCTs, nine National Guard BCTs, and Special Operations Aviation. Surveys, assessments, and interviews were completed as a part of this process to discern the prospects for expanding women to other positions and career fields. Supposedly, plans are also underway for opening the remaining areas of concentration (AOCs) comprising units, positions,

---

[*] http://www.defense.gov/news/ArmyWISRImplementationPlan.pdf

and AOCs with 76 corps, 35 AOCs for the commissioned corps, and 19 military occupational specialties (MOSs) for warrant officers. This phased-in approach to implementation is scheduled to adhere to the following:

1. Development and validation of gender-neutral accession standards for still closed occupations to be opened in succession by branch, first with the Army Engineer Branch by July 2012 which, by far, constitutes the largest force of women soldiers and leaders. This accession will be followed by those occupations in Field Artillery which contain a small contingent of women soldiers and leaders to be accomplished by March 2015. Apparently, the Army will utilize the lessons learned in three Field Artillery occupations opened to women in 2012.
2. By no later than September 2015, the Army plans to apply data from the aforementioned to apprise how next to proceed. Armor and Infantry units will follow those of the completion of Field artillery. The Army anticipates working with the U.S. Army Research Institute for Environmental Medicine (USARIEM) to collect data for this endeavor. Doing so will include coordinating with various other entities, including USSOCOM and U.S. Army Special Operations Command (USASOC), for Ranger School.
3. The Engineering Branch plans to open 10,281 positions that were previously closed to women.
4. Field Artillery Branch will open a total of 15,941 positions that were previously closed to women.
5. Armor and Infantry Branches will result in the opening up of 90,640 positions for women (84,594 for the enlisted corps; 6,046 for the commissioned corps).
6. Special Forces. While the Army promises occupations, skill identifiers, and skill qualification identifiers by working with USSOCOM, it did not specify the number of positions that will be opened to women.
7. The Army plans to engage its Training and Doctrine Command (TRADOC) Analysis Center (TRAC) in an effort to identify those institutional and cultural factors involved with integrating women into formerly closed MOSs and units. Results of this study will be used to inform the development of strategies to mitigate implementation. As well, soldiers and leaders will be sought for their feedback through focus groups and interviews at various active duty, Reserve, and National Guard installations.

Migdal and Leveille (2013) of ACLU's Women's Rights Project and Washington Legislative office laud the Army's comprehensive approach for plans to fully integrate women into its formerly closed positions. However, they eagerly await greater details into how the Army plans to inform those already tried and true women currently in the Army who are already qualified and are waiting to compete for these positions.

Air Force[*]

As the youngest of the military branches and reputed as the most female friendly, 99% of the Air Force's positions are currently open to women. Only seven fields or Air Force Specialty Codes (AFSCs) spanning 4686 positions remain closed to women (3470 active duty; 178 Reserve; 1038 Air National Guard [ANG]). Most of the AFSCs and positions still closed to women encompass such areas as combat rescue officer, special tactics officer, special operations weather officer, enlisted combat controller, enlisted tactical air command and control party, enlisted pararescue, and enlisted special operations weather officer. As with the Army, those positions and AFSCs for which coordination with USSOCOM is necessary remain indeterminate as to how women will be integrated. In making the case for integration into the seven remaining career fields, the Air Force provided schematics of the career progression for each as well as the timelines for reviewing, modifying, coordinating with other military departments, developing and validating for the establishment of gender-neutral physical performance tests and standards, and strategies for integrating women into these formerly closed AFSCs and positions. These strategies will include recruiting, assessing, selecting, and training and developing for the purpose of career development in each field. Anticipated timelines through 2019 are also provided for each AFSC with flexibility based on such variables as accession source, application process timelines, selection of qualified candidates, and course schedules and availability, among others. However, many questions still remain unanswered, for example, on how women will be integrated into those career fields that require coordination with USSOCOM.

Navy[†]

The Navy acknowledged that although 88% of its billets are opened to women, the remaining 12% of positions and occupations are cost prohibitive. For instance, many of the positions having to do with retrofitting for berthing and privacy for women on ships and SEAL (sea, air, and land) and submarine occupations are currently closed to women. However, according to the plan, the Navy endeavors to leave no stones unturned by opening all closed positions to women by January 2016. The plan is to implement integration by executing five decision points in specific timelines as follows:

Decision Point 1

Integration of women into the four enlisted and one officer designator that span the Coastal Riverine Force Small Craft with initial assignments of incumbents by October 2013.

---

[*] http://www.defense.gov/news/Air_%20ForceWISRImplementationPlan.pdf
[†] http://www.defense.gov/news/NavyWISRImplementationPlan.pdf

Decision Point 2

Under the USMC Ground Combat Support Element, plans will be in motion or as of March 2013, to begin integrating women into closed position, including those within the reserve component (RC) into noninfantry, infantry, and reconnaissance units and battalions through January 2016.

Decision Point 3

It appears that the implementation of this decision or of USSOCOM/Naval Special Warfare Integration is being preceded by a series of studies, with an expected completion date of July 2014, to determine the impact of integration, requirements, standards integration, cadre development, and personnel processes. The Navy anticipates that the initial cohort of women officers for SEAL/SWCC (special warfare combatant-craft crewmen) training will occur in 2016.

Decision Point 4

While the Navy's integration of women into the submarine career field began in Fall 2011, the first cohort of women was selected for training (Mount 2010; Weber 2010) and the first female graduates in Fall 2012 (Friedrich 2012), the Navy still has some way to go toward the full integration of the enlisted women. Likewise, eight enlisted ratings on submarines are still closed to women. With habitability studies, conducting cost estimates, engaging the submariner community, adherence to decommissioning and commissioning schedules, and modifying timelines as a backdrop, the Navy hopes to use the success of the first officer cohort of women as a model of integration for women in the domain. Here, ironically, the Navy was less certain as to its intent on going forward. In effect, despite its commitment at the outset of its plan to fully integrate women into the remaining 12% of its occupations and positions still classified as combat and/or combat related that were subject to the restrictions of the now repealed combat exclusion policy, the Navy has now placed conditions on fully integrating women even into the submarine community under the pretext of "if decision is made to integrate" (Slide 12 of the Plan).

Decision Point 5

It also appears that the decision to integrate women onto Frigates, Patrol Coastal Crafts, and Mine Countermeasure ships like Decision Point 4 will be subject to the results and determination of habitability studies, cost estimates, career impact, decommissioning/commissioning schedules, and modification timelines despite the rhetoric of commitment to the full integration of women into all occupations and positions and for "All new classes of surface ships are designed as gender-neutral" (Slide 13 of the Plan). It is then hopeful that the Navy will neither continue nor return to its suspicious practice of preventing the integration of women on ships following the passage of the the National Defense Authorization Act (NDAA) of 1994 lifting the restrictions of women's assignments on ships or combatant vessels and the rescission of the risk rule that redefined ground combat, but where especially enlisted women were prevented from serving on combatant ships because of the limitations of berthing accommodations (Harrell et al. 2002). Admittedly, this is a point that the Navy recently described as still being cost prohibitive even after almost 20 years of its refusal to honor the mandate to accommodate women by retrofitting these ships.

Marine Corps[*]

As the smallest of the military branches, the USMC comprises the smallest female workforce of its sister branches, at 6.8% (Women in the Military Services of America [WIMSA], as of November 30, 2011). The USMC perhaps holds the dubious distinction of being the staunchest and most reticent of the services against the full integration of women into combat occupations and positions. According to the results of a survey of 53,000 Marines, 17% of male Marines admitted that they would consider leaving the Corps if women were placed into combat positions (Watson 2013). Among the respondents' primary concerns were that they could be falsely accused of sexual harassment or worse yet, sexual assault; the preferential treatment for some Marines; or fraternization given the mixing of the sexes. Another less-known survey that was commissioned by the USMC indicated that one out of four men would voluntarily separate from the Corps if women were integrated into combat units and positions (Kredo 2013). Of the female and male respondents, 23% said that they would separate if women were required to be placed in combat occupations and units. Yet, 31% of the women surveyed said that they welcomed placement into combat roles, but 43% stated that had it not been for the restrictions under the combat exclusion policy when they joined the USMC, they would have selected to pursue combat arms. Another 13% said that they would be interested in entering the USMC Ground Combat Element (GCE), also known as the first attack land force that includes combat arms and communications.

More unfortunate though, this time from the institution's top, USMC Commandant General James Amos prematurely and publicly expressed his uncertainty about female Marines' ability to perform in infantry units (Watson 2013) even as he cited that the USMC was in full support of repealing the combat exclusion policy. Supposedly, General Amos was simply expressing the doubt of the service chiefs that women will be able to withstand the austere conditions of the commando environment. Further, given the institution's all-male history, he continued, this revelation should not be surprising. This comment is reminiscent of the ire that former Air Force Chief of Staff General McPeak suffered after he prematurely injected his personal and irrational opinion into his testimony to the Senate on

---

[*] http://www.defense.gov/news/MarineCorpsWISRImplementationPlan.pdf

why women should not be selected to fly in combat even if a female pilot is far more qualified that a male pilot (Holm 1992). And, the Commandant did not help the situation when he implied that the USMC would not lower its standards by placing women into combat units with men (Associated Press 2013) suggesting that for women to assume these positions, it would require that the USMC lower its standards for placement. Unfortunately though, previous research by Harrell et al. (2002) supports this finding of the earlier survey with regard to male Marines' fear of the accusation of sexual harassment/assault and fraternization. For instance, one commander became so obsessed with avoiding, being accused of these indiscretions, that he refused to have a female driver or aide.

According to the USMC, a total of 70,000 billets in the active (54,000) and reserve (16,000) components are closed to women. These billets span 32 primary MOSs (PMOSs) and 16 additional MOSs. There are currently 335 PMOSs opened to women. However, what is disturbing is that the USMC made no commitment to fully integrate women into these closed billets (MarineCorpsWISRImplementationPlan.pdf; Migdal and Leveille 2013). Instead, following research and testing, it intends to retain its prerogative to open closed positions to women as it deems necessary. Nevertheless, the USMC plans to address the integration of women into closed billets via what it dubs as following a pillar system to be conducted over a three-phase and three-year timeline. Pillar One is designed to assess the manner in which closed MOSs will be opened and classified for women while Pillar Two will assess and classify the assignment of women into MOSs that are opened but housed in units closed under the combat exclusion policy. These units include 13 battalions, regiments, and platoons/teams in the AC and nine battalions or regiments in the RC. It is estimated that phase 1 of Pillar One will occur during calendar year (CY) 2013 to validate gender-neutral occupational standards for performance. Part of this process will include collecting data from research on the physical performance of 800 Marines (400 women and 400 men). Research data underway for 165 women Marine lieutenants since 2012 will determine the standards for completion of the Basic Officer Course (BOC) and required Infantry Officer Development (IOD) courses upon commission. Phase 2 of Pillar One, to be completed during CY 2014, will seek to establish the conditions under which women will be assigned to newly opened MOSs, including consideration for schoolhouse cadre, integration education for faculty delivery of the education such as training recruiters to administer physical screening tests in accordance with the requirements for each MOS, facilities review, and access processing for both the enlisted and commissioned corps.

Finally, phase 3 of Pillar One, scheduled for execution during CY 2015, seeks to deploy the assignment of accessed and trained women Marines in a sequenced fashion to the newly opened MOSs and units. Apparently, this approach is devised in a manner that makes sense and that "maintains combat effectiveness" (p. 5, MarineCorpsWISRImplementionPlan.pdf). Also, because its mission includes collaborating with some of its sister branches, namely the Army, Navy, and USSOCOM, the USMC plans to do so for the purpose of training, berthing accommodations, and billeted assignments according to units and MOSs.

U.S. Special Operations Command[*]

There is little in the way of a plan per se by USSOCOM that details its intent for the full integration of women into its operation despite its laudatory remarks about the intent surrounding the repeal of the combat exclusion policy. If anything, the language is couched as not wanting to outright appear not to be in line with adhering to the policy, essentially, coopting language, at least in public, that is either one of placation or to escape criticism. The Command concedes that, in light of its mission, it does have concerns about the complexities owing to its assignments in "austere, politically-sensitive environments for extended periods" (p. 1, U.S. SOCOMWISRImplementationPlan.pdf), citing "cultural ramifications" (Migdal and Leveille 2013). These trepidations appear to encompass its Special Forces Groups, SEAL Teams, Ranger Regiments, 160th Special Operations Aviation Regiment, Special Operation Forces (SOF) Battlefield Airmen, and Marine Special Operators. Without making any commitment to integrating women into its Command, SOCOM has promised to engage its Center for Operations Studies and Research and the RAND Corporation to determine the feasibility at Levels 1 (by unit) and 2 (by specialty) on whether or not to move forward with such integration or to request an exception. For Level 1 (by unit), for work with the Air Force Special Operations Command (AFSOC), all 331 billets remain closed to women. For work with the Army (USASOC), of the 15,086 billets, 47.7% are open to women, but still leaving another 7,191 closed to them. For work with the USMC Forces Special Operations Command (MARSOC), of the 773 billets, 57.1% are open to women, still leaving 332 closed to women. And, for work with the Navy (NAVSPECWARCOM), of the 16,577 billets, while 55% are open to women, 7,191 remain closed. At Level 2 (by specialty), the picture for the full integration of women into USSOCOM is grim. None of the 15,497 positions are open to women and coupled with Level 1, this leaves 22.4% of all positions/billets in the Command that are strictly off limits to women.

Overall and not surprisingly, Migdal and Leveille (2013) are skeptical as to the services' commitment, especially with regard to the USMC and USSOCOM to fully integrate women into closed occupations, positions, and units despite the combat exclusion policy repeal. They remain troubled; a position that I believe is justified given the ourstory of unfulfilled promises in the past where the execution, implementation, follow-through, and accountability for such efforts have fallen flat. Moreover, failure to implement has been mired with calls for perpetual studies when it has been proven time and time again that not only have women been ready to perform these tasks, but which for the most part, women have been performing for many years, if not from the beginning, under the various iterations of their exclusion from combat. Congressionally directed studies requested by the Under Secretary of Defense for Personnel and Readiness have commissioned RAND to

---

[*] http://www.defense.gov/news/SOCOMWISRImplementionPlan.pdf

ascertain the readiness of women for combat (i.e., Harrell and Miller 1997; Harrell et al. 2002). Each unbiased study has only served to quell doubts about women's ability and capacity to perform in combat. For instance, Harrell and Miller (1997) found that the effect of women's integration on military readiness, and cohesion to be negligible, if not a moot point. Men confirmed that women performed as well as men. Both women and men attribute such characteristics as leadership and training in making the difference. Many preferred integrated to segregated training. And, regarding combat at the time, although more men (66%) in the Army and USMC were more likely to concur with restricting women from combat, then under the risk rule, over 80% of the female respondents said that they would welcome the opportunity to serve in ground combat positions with their male comrades. The Army, itself, found that mixed-gender units proved superior in performance over that of single-gender ones (U.S. Army 2002). Again, leadership was salient as a moderating variable as well as the levels of commitment, motivation, confidence, and ability of soldiers. The subsequent study by Harrell et al. (2002), also commissioned by the Office of the Secretary of Defense, pointed to women's ability to endure the austere and harsh living conditions of certain occupations (i.e., engineering and air support), neither of which deterred women's desires for such jobs.

Thus, while the concerns by USSOCOM and the other services may have some merit, even the studies commissioned by the military have shown otherwise. And, as stated by Migdal and Leveille (2013), the time has come to abolish these categories that exclude women. As is a pressing concern for both the MLDC (2011) and DACOWITS (2012), failure for the military to remove these exclusions will be dire, the cumulative effect of which will be the premature exodus from the military by women who are denied from competing for combat positions (Migdal and Leveille 2013) and the institutional brain drain of qualified women, particularly as the forces draw down from Afghanistan and Iraq (DACOWITS 2012). So, the prospect for the full integration of women in the military under a post–combat exclusion policy environment is mixed with hopeful promises but guarded optimism. Women have already proven their worth and with the intestinal fortitude of what it takes to endure future challenges. It is now time for both the civilian and military leadership to uphold public rhetoric with bold action by fully integrating this invaluable constituency, without whom wars cannot be won and missions cannot be achieved. In the process, the American public is being ill-served as military readiness and in turn national security will be imperiled. To do otherwise, would be to intentionally flout the law and carry on the disservice to women in the military through their illegal exclusion as combatants.

Chapter 12

Impact of the Combat Exclusion Policy on the Recruitment, Promotion, and Retention of Women in the Military

Overwhelmingly, the 17 women profiled in this book stated at the time of their interviews that repealing the combat exclusion policy would be a positive move for the recruitment, promotion, and retention of women in the military, although some cautioned that, given the implementation of policy changes of this magnitude, its success will be hinged on leadership to convey a clear and consistent message. Some, like Brigadier General Wilma Vaught, also warned that the effects of repealing the combat exclusion policy on the recruitment, promotion, and retention of women might not be immediate. For example, Brigadier General Vaught remarked that traditionally the military has experienced challenges in retaining women, especially for promotion to higher ranks. Some women leave the military, she said, because they are simply tired of military life, while others realize that the passing of time leaves them with even less time to spend with their children and so separate to be with their families. Others, like Dr. Rita Sumner, believed that leadership in preparing the groundwork to facilitate the recruitment, promotion, and retention of women is key, as is helping the culture to adapt to these ensuing changes.

And, Chief Warrant Officer (5) Trish Thompson acknowledged that the policy's repeal will take some time to change the behaviors of some men, in that there would be growing pains ahead in adopting the changes that over time will eventually bear fruit by yielding positive changes for the future.

As the military branches, including U.S. Special Operations Command (USSOCOM), ponder how they plan to fully integrate women into their respective services, the message from watchdog groups of the Department of Defense (DoD), like the Defense Advisory Committee on Women in the Services (DACOWITS), the American Civil Liberties Union (ACLU), and Service Women's Action Network (SWAN), is clear. Inaction is not an option, as DoD will face the ire of repercussions through increasing lawsuits and the like. The aim is to consistently hold DoD's feet and those of the military branches to the fire for the full integration of women throughout the military. The findings of the congressionally mandated Military Leadership Diversity Commission (MLDC, 2011), as a result of the National Defense Authorization Act (NDAA) of 2009, was stark. Specifically for women, the Commission found that, overall, the military's top leadership was not representative of the women they led. This void is the result of four overriding factors: minimal representation of women in the early accession stage to the commissioned corps, under representation by women officers in career fields such as those that are combat and combat related would facilitate advancement to general and flag rank, high attrition among women at the mid-level ranks within both the enlisted and commissioned corps, and a decline in the progression of female commissioned officers. The Commission also recognized that lower rates in advancement for women are due to the structural and institutional barriers that are directly attributed to the combat exclusion policy. Most significant, the Commission called for a leveling of the playing field for women in the military by way of removing the policies under combat exclusion.

Following the MLDC's (2011) report, DACOWITS (2012) published its own findings partly in response to the Commission's recommendations for additional investigation into the matter given its concern for lower retention rates among women in the military. Further, the military is not being perceived as a viable career option by women, a finding also by Harris (2009a), in this case for white women, based on the unpublished work on this demographic by Moskos (January 2005 email). DACOWITS (2012) also concluded that taking into account the troop drawdown from Afghanistan and Iraq, attrition rates for women will be exacerbated. For this foreseeable gender gap, the Committee recommended that strategies be developed to combat this challenge. Similarly, the Committee was equally concerned about the resultant loss of qualified women and talent within the ranks. More directly though, the Committee concurred with the MLDC (2011) by recommending that the ground combat restrictions of the combat exclusion policy be abolished to provide career, training, and schooling opportunities that are close to women through the "Full integration of women into Ground Combat Units, including through the development of gender-neutral physical standards"

(DACOWITS 2012; Executive Summary, p. v). But, as the ensuring plans for the services take center stage, of foremost concern is how the drawdown of troops will impact the already growing retention chasm among military women and how to mitigate the drain in talent by staving off the attrition of highly qualified women.

For example, between fiscal year (FY) 2011 and FY 2012, both the Army and Marine Corps plan to drawdown their active workforces by roughly 80,000 and 25,000 troops, respectively (DACOWITS 2012). The Army is keenly aware of this challenge and prior to the repeal of the combat exclusion policy was actively taking steps toward remediation such as opening up more military occupational specialties (MOSs) to women. It has long been determined, however, that surprisingly, female soldiers prematurely separate from the Army for the same reasons that male soldiers do. Still, the attrition rates for Army women are much higher than those for Army men. Although as Harris (2009a) noted, increasing deployments is a fact of military life; the problem has been intensified by the exponential increase in the operations tempo (OPSTEMPO) (DACOWITS 2003) even before the back-to-back deployments of personnel under Operations Enduring and Iraqi Freedom began (Burns 2007; GAO January 2007; National Security Advisory Group 2006). As early as 2001, a survey of military personnel revealed that first-term enlistees were more likely to be dissatisfied with military life than those at the midpoint of their careers (GAO December 2001). The report showed that only 14% of those surveyed had planned to make a 20-year career of the military. Multiple deployments were at the core of many personnel and family issues (DACOWITS 2003). Says Nataraj-Kirby and Naftel (2000), especially for the National Guard and Reserve, it is important to understand how such deployments affect their families and employers. Consequently, this knowledge will inform us about the impact of deployments on the recruitment and retention of personnel and thus the future shape of the force. DACOWITS (2005) identified that post-September 11, 2001, changed the landscape for deployments. And, specifically for military women with children, the situation was magnified by longer and more frequent deployments that brought about adjustment challenges for their children (Joint Economic Committee 2007). Moreover, as concluded by Hosek et al. (2001), when these situations become acute, women at much higher rates are far more likely than their male partners to forsake their careers by leaving the military. These trends were as likely for female officers as they are for females within the enlisted corps (DACOWITS 2003).

Interestingly enough, although where family programs existed, they were deemed effective in helping with the difficulties of separation and reunions before and following deployments (National Military Family Services [NMFS] 2005); the Army's attempt to utilize such programs have not been as successful, partly due to the unawareness of such programs (Burrell et al. 2003). The Army is also examining to what degree do medical maladies such as fractures and injuries influence female attrition and is devising steps to prevent these injuries. Moore (2002) observed, for instance, that in excess of 71% of women separated from the military during the seventh and 48th month of enlistment because of medical reasons or lack of good physical conditioning. Studies on women physicians, chaplains, and attorneys uncovered abnormally high rates of attrition, particularly between the *fifth and eighth years* of military service (DACOWITS 2006; Smith 2006). Of equal note is that women officers were less likely than their male peers to complete a 20-year career in the military (DACOWITS 2003) as well as not remain in the military long enough between promotion cycles. This premature exodus reverberates throughout by creating lower promotion rates for especially white female officers (Hosek et al. 2001).

The Navy has instituted the Career Intermission Pilot Program (CIPP) to help alleviate some of the challenges that its personnel experience with work–life conflicts (DACOWITS 2012). Among the array of available arrangements, personnel may temporarily transfer to the Individual Ready Reserve (IRR) from active duty to sort out their affairs. During this limited time of absence, Sailors are still entitled to medical and dental benefits as well as military exchange and commissary privileges. However, the Navy mandates that personnel on the CIPP must remunerate the Navy at a 2:1 ratio of active duty service for each month in the program. The program was launched in 2009 with the availability of 20 slots for officers and 20 slots for the enlisted corps, although since its inception the program has had altogether only 20 service members who have taken advantage of the program for a number of reasons, including to pursue higher education, care for a dependent, or simply to travel. While it is indeterminate as to the CIPP's impact on retention, data from the Navy's pregnancy and parenthood survey look optimistic in that respondents believe that the program demonstrates the importance of work–life issues to the Navy.

For the Marine Corps, its 2012 and 2011 officer and enlisted surveys indicate that women and men separate from the Corps for similar reasons as well (DACOWITS 2012). Officers cited pay and benefits, job satisfaction, and opportunities for advancement as the top reasons for remaining in the Marine Corps, while they listed seeking opportunities in the civilian sector to begin a second career and family as primarily the reasons for wanting to leave. Enlisted personnel pointed to the opportunity to lead others, choice in duty stations, and pride of being in the Marine Corps as the reasons for staying in the Corps and the desire to seek other opportunities within the civilian sector and work hours as the top two reasons for wanting to leave the Corps. The Marine Corps currently offers a number of avenues, all aimed at improving the retention rates of especially women, by encouraging them to transfer from the enlisted to the commissioned corps in the hope of making a career of the Corps. Between FY 2010 and FY 2012, the Marine Corps experienced an increase in the accession rates of women from the enlisted corps to the commissioned corps. The Corps also offers the opportunity to transfer from active duty to the Selective Ready Reserve through monetary incentives as a way of increasing retention among highly qualified women who may be influenced to make a career of the Marine Corps. Additionally, like the Navy's CIPP, the Marine Corps is considering the launch of an initiative called CIPP in those occupations with the highest attrition rates. There are similar retention programs offered by such professional organizations as the Women Marines Organization.

During peacetime, the Coast Guard falls under the auspices of the U.S. Department of Homeland Security (DHS) but under the Department of the Navy during wartime (Population Report FY 2011). But, unlike its sister services, the Coast Guard, which has never been subject to the combat exclusion policy, has been the most bullish, beginning with its Commandants, in promoting women and fully integrating them into all of its occupations (Holm 1992). And, ironically, perhaps in light of this designation, its status as more of a peacetime arm unless activated for war, the Coast Guard has been jokingly reputed by the other military branches as not really being a military service. In a 1979 testimony before the House Subcommittee regarding DoD's policies on women in the military, the then chief of Personnel for the Coast Guard proudly acknowledged the performance of women on ships that:

> There are times when obviously a 200-pound pump may not be lifted by women; however, that same pump may not be lifted by all of the male population of a particular unit as well. We have exposed women to the gamut of our missions: law enforcement, marine environmental protection; aids to navigation; all of the other missions that we have. I can categorically state, air, that their performance has been outstanding. (Tilley 2013, p. 18)

And, according to Tilley (2013), the women whom he consulted with for input for his article unanimously declared that the Coast Guard is a cut above its sister services in the treatment of its female workforce. This is not to say, however, that along the way there have not been challenges in discrimination against women. In addition to DACOWITS's advising the military about the concerns of women in the Coast Guard, the Coast Guard has its own Women's Advisory Council to address such concerns. The Coast Guard also has a range of programs with foci on women, parents, and the whole Coast Guard population (DACOWITS 2012). Women-centric programs include those that provide affiliation and mentoring through various symposia, for instance. A Women's Afloat Coordinator is also available in ensuring that women are afforded the same ship duties as men. And, like the Navy and under consideration by the Marine Corps, the Coast Guard instituted the Care for Newborn Children (CNC) program for women and men to separate for up to two years from the service to care for a child who is less than one year old. Its equivalent, the Temporary Separation Policy, is available to personnel without children. This program provides leave for a maximum of two years as well. Other retention programs in the Coast Guard include helping new mothers to regain physical conditioning for passing the physical fitness test, a 30-day leave policy for both women and men, and childcare development centers that offer subsidies for a family with an income of less than $100,000 per annum.

The Air Force has had several programs underway for retaining women in both the enlisted and commissioned corps in the forms of Special Duty Assignment pay, Selective Reenlistment Bonus (enlisted corps), and Critical Skills Retention Bonus (DACOWITS 2012). Two studies are also in progress. The first, with RAND, will help determine the retention patterns of women and men. The second, a Career Decision Survey, is designed to ascertain those factors that influence the retention decisions of women and men. The intent is to utilize the results of these studies to develop retention strategies for targeted groups and occupational specialties that have traditionally experienced abnormal rates of attrition.

According to the National Guard Bureau, both the Air National Guard (ANG) and Army National Guard (ARANG) have created strategic plans to focus on the retention challenges of underrepresented groups, for the commissioned officers, and enlisted corps (DACOWITS 2012). The Bureau has experienced though a discernible increase in the recruitment, promotion, and retention rates of women over the past years. In light of these positive trends, it is then anticipated that over time more senior commissioned and noncommissioned women officers will become visible. And, unlike its active duty and reserve counterparts, the Bureau does not forecast a negative effect on the impact of its workforce in either the ANG or ARNG. As a matter of fact, quite the contrary, with the opening of positions for women due to the repeal of the combat exclusion policy, it will experience a net positive gain in its overall representation of women while the ANG will continue in its efforts to recruit and retain professional women, especially in rated positions like aviation.

While none of the services addressed the issue of promotion directly as part of their retention programs, and particularly for women, the goal was implicit in their efforts. The resultant and premature attrition rates for women in the military undoubtedly and adversely impact the promotion rates of women, especially for promotion to the senior ranks and even to provide viable cadres of highly qualified women to compete for promotion consideration at each level. As Harris (2009a) observed based on her analysis of Moskos's unpublished data, white women are a demographic that is especially at risk for premature attrition from the military, although this, too, is a condition of the changing demographics in the larger society and in turn the military. Another consideration though is that the current numbers of highly qualified women for the military may not be sustainable and will be a function of the economy, for as the economy improves, it will become increasingly more difficult for the military to not only attract the desired cohorts of women (Population Report FY 2011) but also provide steady pools of qualified candidates of women for promotion and to improve the overall promotion rates of women in the military.

According to a DoD report (2004), the promotion rates of female officers do not diverge from those of male officers, especially at the junior levels. Yet, Hosek et al. (2001) found that white female officers, for example, are less likely than other segments of the military's population to remain for the necessary promotion cycles for promotional consideration to the next levels. Remaining long enough between promotion cycles would result in enhanced promotion chances. And, while DoD (2004) showed no divergence in promotion rates for women and men, the same report pointed to marked declines in the promotion of women to the senior field grade officer and command levels (05 and 06). As well, in the Navy and worst off in the Marine Corps, women were less than 50% as likely as men to be promoted to senior field grade and senior officers, although DACOWITS (2005) showed no differences in these rates from the senior enlisted to field grade and senior officer levels. Baldwin (1996) said that although the Air Force has been the best at attracting a female force, and thus the rates of promotion in it are more positive than those in its sister services, female attrition rates in the Air Force negatively impact the promotion rates of women to the field grade and senior officer ranks. Baldwin attributes this finding to characteristically male-dominated organizations, but Ellefson (1998) blames these problems on the barriers that prevent women's accession to higher ranks in the military.

The MLDC (2011) found that the promotion rates to the field grades (04 and 05) for women officers in the Navy and Coast Guard were below average relative to the promotion rates of men. And, for the enlisted corps, women in the Marine Corps reflected below average rates of promotion to the highest enlisted rank (E-9), although better rates of promotion to E-7 in comparison to their male counterparts. Enlisted women in the Army also showed lower than average promotion rates to both E-8 and E-9. Here, the MLDC offered four recommendations to improve the promotion rates of underrepresented groups in the military. This includes women. First, the MLDC stated that it is important to significantly improve the transparency of the expectations for performance, the criteria for promotion, and the associated processes for each. Second, given the anemic representation of women who are general or flag officers and senior noncommissioned officers, it becomes imperative to specify the required knowledge, skills and abilities, and developmental opportunities to position oneself for potential promotion to these ranks. Additionally, the MLDC recommends the institution of a more flexible career development system, particularly for officers, for core competencies that should segue into broader skill development as one ascends the ranks. Candidates for promotion must also bear the responsibility for their own promotion packages to meet the Board. Finally, in the absence of a systematic analysis to determine the extent of its occurrence, the Commission found that certain demographic groups in the military are disproportionately placed into certain assignments for the purpose of recruitment and equal opportunity.

However, the Commission cautions that officers should not be penalized for assuming such assignments. Although this finding was speculation on the Commission's part, it has been validated by the likes of Hosek et al. (2001) and Harris (2009b) that certain groups, that is, women and underrepresented minorities, are disproportionately placed in the so-called minority jobs (Harris 2012) or support occupations like support and health care. Unfortunately, these assignments, even if perceived as career broadening ones, merely set up the already marginalized groups to be perceived as not being competitive for promotion to higher ranks given these assignments. Instead, the Commission (2011) recommends that promotion boards become enlightened in that should a candidate's package reveal this kind of assignment, particularly if taken at the behest of one's leadership, then these opportunities should serve as part of the institution's overall goal toward diversity. Similarly, Harris (2009b) recommends that to offset this negative perception of these assignments, a complement of white males should be placed into these assignments as well as part of their overall professional development.

Harris (2009a) ascribes the general challenge of the recruitment, promotion, and retention of women in the military, notwithstanding then the existence of the combat exclusion policy, to a confluence of factors that conspire against women, in this case, white women, from viewing the military as a worthwhile career endeavor. These factors include but are not limited to increasing, multiple, and back-to-back deployments, especially during Operations Enduring and Iraqi Freedom; problems experienced in the service academies that still constitute "vestiges of resistance" (GAO 1994, p. 52), which the DoD's Inspector General validated after 10 years; the consequences of gender, many of which include the disproportionate burden for childcare; low promotion rates; women's poor performance on the technical components of the Armed Forces Vocational Aptitude Battery (AFSVAB) and the Air Force Qualifying Test (AFQT); perceived problems of unit cohesion, which has been repeatedly invalidated (Harrell and Miller 1997; Harrell et al. 2002); and sexual harassment/sexual assault.

The MLDC (2011) also found across all services and for both the active duty and reserve components that women were more likely than men to prematurely leave the military by not remaining for at least a 20 years of service. But, for active duty, at least for women in the Air Force (up to the mid-2000s) and the Marine Corps, women who were early in their careers showed either higher or comparable reenlistment rates to men. Still, for female officers, according to the Commission, and as borne out by other research, including those by Hosek et al. (2001) and Harris (2009a), the picture is less rosy. It is at the fourth year mark for officers that retention rates for women and men begin to diverge (MLDC 2011). And, as the years advance, this rate of divergence only widens between both groups in each of the services. In essence, as the years increase, female officers were more likely than male officers to prematurely separate and at much higher rates. Ironically though, after the 20-year mark, the retention rates for both groups begin to converge again. These patterns were mirrored in the reserve component across all services. But, while women prematurely separate for dissatisfaction with the military, men did so most likely for the failure to be promoted.

Using longitudinal data on women from 1988 to 2010, a recent and more comprehensive study by Asch et al. (2012) exposed an even more troubling prospect of retaining women in the military. Because female officers are less likely to be promoted from the junior to first field-grade officer ranks (02, 03, and 04) than their white male counterparts (Asch et al. 2012), it stands to reason that they will be more likely to prematurely separate. Likewise, the overall retention rate for women at the highest company grade rank (03) is lower than that for men (Asch et al. 2012). But, while the majority of female officers experience lower rates of retention than white men, an anomaly, nonblack women defy this trend with higher rates of promotion to the senior officer rank (06) than men. Asch et al. (2012) attributes this to higher retention rates for nonblack women once they overcome this hurdle. Yet, black women are the least likely of any group to be promoted to the senior officer rank given the low retention rates at the senior field grade officer level (05) compounded by even lower promotion rates to 05 and 06. Consequently, the MLDC (2011) made its principal and sole recommendation that due to its limited mandate as a Commission, the DACOWITS address the gender gap issue through further investigation of the reasons for women's abnormal attrition rates from the military.

In keeping with the MLDC's (2011) recommendation that women's retention in the military be investigated by DACOWITS but before reaching its own conclusion to call for the definitive repeal of the combat exclusion, DACOWITS (2012) relied on the findings and recommendations from the MLDC (2011) to further investigate the matter; engaged in consultation with ICF International, a research contractor; conducted 42 focus groups with 397 participants at 8 military installations in 2012; and garnered the perspectives of militaries within the international community such as the Australian Defence Force and the Canadian Armed Forces about their respective programs for retaining women. The DACOWITS (2012) focus groups, like the findings of the MLDC (2011), found that 68% of female respondents versus 81% of male respondents did not plan on remaining in the military past their current enlistment obligation (DACOWITS 2012). Both women and men who were planning to leave the military cited work–life balance as the primary concern and conceded that this issue was more likely to adversely impact a disproportion number of women than men. Even the secondary issues cited were related in some manner to work–life balance. For example, many respondents pointed to the additional challenge of dual military marriages and in dealing with the pressures of military life. And, as is frequently the case, the wife more so than the husband is more likely to sacrifice her military career for the sake of keeping her family unit intact (Harris 2009a). Other concerns include the high OPSTEMPO, work hours, lack of satisfaction with one's occupational specialty, and the desire to seek other opportunities within the civilian sector. Surprisingly, most respondents did not see the force drawdown as influencing their decision to leave the military but believed that the impact would be equally detrimental for the military in those jobs and occupations where women (i.e., administrative) and men (i.e., combat MOSs) are disproportionately concentrated. The more recent RAND study confirmed the consistent retention patterns of women in the military (Asch et al. 2012). The study found that the highest retention rates for women were between the junior ranks of the commissioned corps (01–03) and the enlisted corps (E1–E4), though there was a decline in the promotion rates for women in the commissioned corps between the 02 and 05 ranks.

DACOWITS (2012) recognizes that retention and thus the premature attrition of women remains a gnawing issue for the military. Notwithstanding women's exemplary ourstory of performance in the military, the Committee continues to be concerned about the ensuing troop drawdown together with the manner in which the military is carrying out the troop drawdown that may potentially exacerbate the existing retention problems for women in the military by losing the diversity and highly qualified women in the process. Along with its recommendation to repeal the combat exclusion policy by fully integrating women into combat units, occupations, and positions coupled with establishment of gender-neutral physical standards, the Committee recommends that the military continue to create and install novel mechanisms to facilitate the retention of highly qualified women. It is, therefore, hopeful that DoD, and by extension the military, will be committed to the conditions of repealing the policy by implementing the recommendations of the MLDC (2011) and DACOWITS (2012), which unanimously call for the full integration of women throughout the military. These actions should be carried out in a thoughtful, calculating, and deliberate fashion to ensure the successful performance of both women and men in rising, meeting, and achieving the highest call to service, that is, the profession of arms.

Chapter 13

Women in a Post-Combat Exclusion Environment: The Promise for Full Agency

It is yet to be determined as to how the implementation of the repeal of the combat exclusion policy and the full integration of women throughout the military will be realized. The prospects are hopeful but restrained. And, while no such behemoth like repealing the combat exclusion policy given present and future generations of military women legal and unprecedented access that their forbearers could only dream about has never been slain before, as repeatedly mentioned, the ourstory of women's progress in the military has been fraught with inconsistent movement given unfulfilled promises, time and time again. Yet, the potential for this monumental feat, if properly executed, is endless. Most important, if successfully orchestrated, unlike ever before, military women will be on a level playing field with military men. One could say, finally, as partners at last. Yes, true partnership between military women and military men is soon to become a reality. But, in the scheme of things, or at least for the foreseeable future or until January 2016, when each of the services launches its respective plans, how would women's status in a post-combat exclusion environment look like? Even more indeterminate is whether or not the policy's repeal can ultimately serve as the long elusive elixir to women's full agency in American society for which we have been pining? Here, the irony, as Holm (1992) rightly complained, is that during the period of the feminist movement of the 1960s and 1970s, civilian women never remotely considered their sisters-in-arms as part of the overall fight for women's equality. It is therefore now fitting that I should envision the repeal of the combat exclusion policy for military women as the potential launching pad for attaining equality for women in the larger American society.

The steady drumming of the calls for dismantling the corrosive effects of the combat exclusion policy has been beating for decades. Many effects include how sexism is played out in the military, most notably in the forms of sexual assault and the like. Consequently, women have suffered unnecessarily under a repressive system and like all such systems, they create an underclass through asymmetric patterns of behavior even once the structure of oppression has been removed, for in the absence of the physical structure of oppression, these ways of behaving and relating to each other persist. Racism in America comes to mind. The system of slavery has long been demolished. Yet, its presence and destructive effects still informally reside and in many ways structurally in American society, for even as we vociferously declare its absence, the remnants are apparent. And, more debilitating despite the presence of laws to counteract, if not deter it, those who have traditionally stood to benefit from this injustice, quietly and deliberately work tirelessly to undermine the effectiveness of such laws through surreptitious means, all to ensure that things never change. This vicious cycle of oppression is self-reinforcing, causing the traditionally oppressed or marginalized to simply act in kind. In the case of racism, DeGruy Leary (2005) refers to this malady as posttraumatic slavery syndrome (PTSS). In the case of women in American society, while the roots of marginalization are different, especially say for white women, as one example, the affliction is no less incapacitating as this attempt at depersonalization strikes at the very core of one's identification as either a person or as a group. For women in the military, the underlying message throughout their journey has been that they can never measure up to the performance of men when the evidence consistently proves otherwise.

Many of the women in this book speak of this constant badgering by male cohorts for them to prove their worth despite repeated demonstrations. Some have not only short-circuited their military careers for this very reason but after and illegally so under combat exclusion performed jobs that males should have been performing and, where in many cases, the women were the very ones who trained their male cohorts for such jobs, but are essentially told to pretend that what they did never occurred. And, to add insult to injury, not only did these women never received credit for performing the jobs of combatants, but less qualified males were not only acknowledged for performance but were also formally recognized, recognition that will no doubt make them more competitive for promotion and/or for highly critical assignments. This seemed to have been the scenario, particularly for women who served more recently during Operations Enduring and Iraqi Freedom. One woman figured out that since she cannot outcompete her male peers given the uneven playing field, she creatively found legal ways to circumvent the system by being the very best at the jobs for which she was competing; she discovered that the only way that she could leverage her talents was to out educate her competition. In the end, her strategy paid handsome dividends. Contrary to popular belief, at no time, particularly when faced with adversity, did these women retreat. Instead, they either employed tactics to mitigate the situation or confronted it head on via legal challenges to the system. Yet, while all of the women are proud of both their achievements and military service, with many parlaying that service to succeed in their civilian professional endeavors as private citizens, some consciously either choose not to disclose their status as veterans, or when such information was disclosed, were encountered with disbelief as if their stories about military service, especially that of combat, were fabricated.

In one situation, the veteran visited a local Veterans Administration (VA) facility only to be made to feel as if she did not belong and by a fellow woman nonetheless. In another case, the veteran chose to directly challenge the female worker at another local VA facility through whom it was necessary to apply for benefits but who did not believe that the female veteran was the recipient of the combat badge that she earned in combat. And, still another female veteran stated that while her husband proudly volunteers this information about his military service, she has found it best not to do so for as she put it, the military has beaten the love of it (flying) out of her. Women's propensity then to either discuss and/or disclose information about their military service is predicated upon the manner in which they were either treated in the military and/or by those within the civilian sector. But, for all their struggles, for all their achievements, for all women have endured in the American military, they still lack full agency that only repealing the combat exclusion policy, while in principle has a fighting chance, it will be its deployment of troops on the ground, an apt metaphor, for implementation to fully integrate women throughout the military or its practice, that will make the difference in how women as a group will be perceived.

To achieve full agency then is to undo the asymmetry and thus the marginalization of women through their full integration throughout all occupations, positions, levels, and units of the military. The employment of studies to determine how best to seamlessly integrate women into formerly closed positions is appropriate in ensuring that, as far as possible, women's integration will be a resounding success. However, to employ these studies as a delay tactic is to eschew previous gains, prolong healing by re-festering still gaping wounds, falsify the true intent of repealing the combat exclusion policy not as a genuine tool for women's integration into the military but as a ploy to emasculate, for lack of a better term, such efforts to in the end alienate an invaluable constituency without whom wars can never be won and the military can never function even during peacetime given this void in talent. For as Harris (2009) correctly postulates, women will not only begin to shun the military but women in support of all women in the military will dissuade their male partners as well in pursuing the military as an endeavor. This will be especially pronounced during economic times of robust civilian employment when the military has been traditionally challenged at not only attracting the highly qualified but convincing those already within its ranks from prematurely separating. In essence,

DoD's and the military's failure to genuinely honor the conditions that call for the repeal of the combat exclusion policy will have grave, if not catastrophic, implications for the armed forces. It therefore seems that the only logical strategy to stave off this hemorrhaging in the current and future attrition of women and potentially of other groups is to comply with the conditions that called for repealing the combat exclusion policy. U.S. Special Operations Command's (USSOCOM) "reserves the right" stance and those of its fellow services with which it coordinates to carry out its various operations is indeed worrisome, at best. To be fair though to USSOCOM, some of its considerations in placing women in some assignments are valid and therefore cannot be dismissed. But, for example, placing female colleagues in certain countries and/or regions where there are cultural and religious mores about women can be feasibly accomplished on a case-by-case basis and, in all candor, as any such operation would require. As well, such factors, including consideration for the political instability of the country and/or region where the assignments are already dangerous and may even be imprudent for placing any U.S. military personnel, female or male, in harm's way cannot be overlooked. However, these considerations are not unresolvable. Such is the case of the military's strategic and by all indications successful embedding of female engagement teams during Operations Enduring and Iraqi Freedom to overcome any fear of violating the cultural and religious norms of the regions. For these reasons then, USSOCOM's posture will unquestionably warrant close scrutiny and under the watchful eyes of women's interest groups, for any departure from the full integration of women throughout its operations must be rendered in the least as unacceptable.

In accordance with Mazur's (1998) agency theory and as advanced by Harris's (2009) theory of attrition will help to dispel the novelty effect that women in the military in still so-called nontraditional occupations are liable to experience given their absence in critical mass in these career fields. Kanter (1977) estimates that in order for this critical mass to be achieved, women must constitute at least 15%, in this case of a given occupation, or otherwise those women present will be reduced to the status of mere tokens. However, the more prestigious the jobs, and for the military combat and combat-related jobs from which the preponderance of general and flag officers are selected (Kennedy-Pipe 2000; Putko 2008), the less the likelihood that women will be advanced to those positions (Kanter 1977). This homo social reproduction ensures that only men and hence men will continue to favor men who in turn are elevated to key positions of authority and power (Kanter 1977; Schneider 1987). Schneider (1987) calls this need to promote one's own as attraction-selection attrition where situations are always controlled by the majority (men in the military) as a strategy for retaining power by keeping outgroups (women in the military) from sharing in the bounty. But, as Blalock (1967) views this situation, it is simply a matter of pure economics or protecting perceived valuable resources from being squandered on perceived minority or outgroups. Essentially, it is the competition for these limited resources that forces the traditionally advantaged (the ingroup/majority/men) to act in kind. These dynamics also play themselves out in the military.

Nevertheless, the die has been cast as per the repeal of the combat exclusion policy which mandates that combat and combat-related positions, like all resources from January 2016 on, must be opened and shared between women and men in the military. However, any increase in the minority or outgroup may correspondingly result in a like level of prejudice against them, given the fight for these scarce resources (Blalock 1967; Friesbie and Neidert 1977). Doing so will also determine the degree to which both minority and majority groups interact (Reskin et al. 1999), although depending on the extent to which women are integrated into combat and combat-related occupations, positions, and units will dictate this level of interaction. If fully integrated into the military, bias against women, again, particularly into those occupations that have been disguised or protected under the façade of combat, may, too, occur since women are judged as other (Patterson 2000) or deviant (Ellefson 1998; Law 1999), words that connote marginalization or subordination to the majority. In effect, women are not seen as a natural part of the combat or combat-related landscape and as Grimes (2002) suggests, like race, in this capacity, women are forced to overcome unwarranted hurdles to justify full citizenship, unlike the American or perceived mainstream white male, to consistently prove their worth to the military.

So, for now, while professing publicly to support the repeal of the combat exclusion policy, the holdouts, USSOCOM and its like operations with the military branches, despite the law, want to reserve the right, at least as long as possible, under the guise of feasibility studies, to assess the situation for the full integration of women when there may be no such intent at all. The real intent, it can be surmised, is then yet another stall tactic in the hope that the integration of women into USSOCOM will never come to fruition. Why? Because USSOCOM represents the most prized of resources, the last stronghold of manhood, in a manner of speaking. And, only the exclusive, even among men, can secure the privilege of being elevated into this domain. Further, women, as the perceived minority (Blalock 1967; Kanter 1977; Rosen et al. 1996) and low-status outgroup (Yoder 1991), have never been part of this equation, much less vie for consideration for such elevation. For when all is said and done, the fight for such resources, especially when scarce, is really about power. Where groups are represented and how they are distributed (Reskin et al. 1999) speak volumes of how their power is leveraged within organizations. This balance of power is based upon the perceived share of organizational resources to the minority/outgroup by the majority/ingroup. And, if the share of these resources to the minority/outgroup is perceived as a credible threat to the viability and economic well-being of the majority, then the majority will resort to any means necessary, including attempts to outright thwart, sabotage, or undermine distributions to follow (Frederico and Sidanius 2002a, 2002b; Kravitz et al. 2000; Renfro et al. 2006).

We see like struggles for women within the civilian sector in achieving gender parity and thus full agency. These disparities play themselves out in many media. In recent years, in government, at least in the United States, women have achieved a modicum of standing as the country's chief diplomat as Secretary of State and even more recently as the first female director to head the Secret Service (U.S. Secret Service n.d.). For the private sector, for 2013, 21 of the Fortune 500 companies or 4.2% are led by women (Catalyst 2013) and 4.5% of the Fortune 1000 companies are led by women (Catalyst). Ironically, these data actually signify improvements from previous years yet are woefully wanting when one considers that women comprise 50.8% of the general civilian population in the United States (U.S. Census 2010, Age and Sex Composition) and 58.1% of the labor force (U.S. Bureau of Labor Statistics (U.S. BLS) 2013). While there is encouraging news, for instance, in that women's earnings have increased from 62% of men's in 1979 to 82% of men's in 2011 and 51% in all positions classified as management, professional, and related, their absence is still stark in such industries like agriculture, manufacturing, transportation, utilities, and mining (U.S. BLS 2013). According to a report on women, women were more likely than men to live in poverty, and this rate has been increasing between the two groups since 1966 (White House Council on Women and Girls 2011). For example, 7% of men compared to 11% of women, who are at least 65 years of age, fell below the poverty line of $11,161 for a single person who resides alone. An astonishing 28% of women who are unmarried and with children live below the poverty threshold of $17,285 compared to the poverty levels for women and men of 8% and 6%, respectively.

Worse yet is the plight of black and Hispanic women with poverty rates of 28% and 27%, respectively (White House Council on Women and Girls 2011). These data confirm the findings of a 2010 study to reveal that across all racial groups, although white women outearned their sisters of color, when compared to especially white men, women earned much less (Insight 2010). But for black women, the state of affairs is most dire. When all variables have been controlled, their earning power is equated at just $5 per annum. Women outpace men in college enrollment and the number of degrees earned, including graduate degrees (White House Council on Women and Girls 2011). This includes the unprecedented number of women who are attaining doctoral degrees (West and Curtis 2006). The academic fields that women pursue, for example, in science, technology, engineering, and mathematics (STEM), are underrepresented (White House Council on Women and Girls 2011). And the earnings gap between women and men is exacerbated as a result. According to the Insight (2010) study, women's net worth or wealth becomes an invaluable asset to be passed down from one generation to the next in terms of financing children's college education as well as in passing on such wealth to future generations. Research shows that wealth and income are linked. Chang's (2012) book highlights the depth of this inequality between women and men and why it has economic consequences for women's overall well-being. A 2007 report by the U.S. General Accountability Office (GAO) cites how the disproportionate burden for care during women's most productive years puts them at a grave disadvantage in their later years as many lose out on maximizing their earnings by forsaking career aspirations for childbearing, childcare, and/or eldercare. As a consequence of low lifetime earnings, the propensity to pursue part-time employment, self-selected career choices that lead to low pay, and equally lower contributions to social security, women's income amount to 70% of that of men's. Women also experience more frequent interruptions from the workforce, but because they also outlive men, they face an uncertain outlook in lacking the wherewithall to shore up their financial future. In her review of Blau et al.'s (2009) work on the significance of gender in the American workplace, Harris (2011) invokes Ridgeway's (2009) scholarly appraisal by impugning that to build financial equity between women and men, both must be willing to make a shift in entrenched cultural paradigms. Women must be willing to relinquish many domestic responsibilities while men must be willing to assume more of these responsibilities (Ridgeway 2009). And, only by reviewing past lessons, including those learned about division of labor in other countries, can they become instructive for the future (Harris 2011).

That said, women in the larger American society face a daunting financial future if not for these life-altering interruptions. They not only disproportionately bear but cumulatively lose ground over time given such mediating effects as gender bias in employment, low earnings, and career choice, among others, to result in diminishing returns and at a time in life when they are least positioned to recover. As Blau et al. (2009) see it, the problem has been an undue credence placed on equal opportunity versus equal outcomes. Women's continual wage disparities for similar jobs are a case in point because even the emphasis on comparable worth for women, which has been inconsistent, has proven to be unsuccessful for them. At the heart of the matter then have been wage disparities between women and men. Seemingly, such gauges determine what Blau et al. dub an "economic well-being" (p. 38) over time, the fair and equitable distribution of wages to predictably evaluate status and is a component of the division of labor decisions that women and men make.

But other factors play an important role in regulating the economic well-being of women. Less credentialing, the practice of discrimination that penalizes women to assume nontraditional jobs and how women are socialized early in their development influence their career choices or gendered roles (Blau et al. 2009). Incidentally, during the 1980s, women experienced substantial wage convergence with men owing to enhanced job experience and skills that were favored by the labor market; speculated decline in gender discrimination given human capital investments in education, skills, and experience; changing attitudes by society about gender roles; the increased need for technology; and the decline in manufacturing that adversely impacted men in brawn or blue-collar jobs while calling for an increase in brain or white-collar jobs that favored women. However, the subsequent 1990s resulted in a marked decline in earnings between women and men, which, while unclear, may have been attributed to the trend in decreased credentialing by women entering the workforce along with a spike in the number of low-skilled single women who were heads of households also entering the labor market at the time (Blau et al. 2009).

Goldin (2009) ascribes these divergences in the earnings of women and men to institutional biases by employers and industries. And, even where women and men entered the labor force with comparable earnings, men, particularly married men over married women's earnings, consistently outperformed that of women's overall. As previously described in Chapter 5 of Section I and Chapter 13 of Section III of this book, the phenomenon called pollution theory ensured that women either remained out of traditionally male-dominated fields such as firefighting or severely constrained the rates at which they entered these career fields. Asymmetry in earning power and thus status between women and men, says Polachek (2009), has everything to do with the incentives that are provided by employers that predict the costs and benefits of entering and remaining in the workforce over one's lifetime. Division of labor, perceived or otherwise, has costs, not benefits for women, as it is assumed that women will undertake the largest of domestic work at home and even when employed, are still not perceived as assuming the burden for outside employment. Interestingly enough, the earnings power of married women with and without children still lags behind that of married men with or without children even when the women deliberately space their births apart to not negatively impact their earnings power. Polachek (2009) calls this institutional bias "motherhood penalty," (p. 112) which is supported by multiple studies (Baum 2002; Berger et al. 2003; Budwig and England 2001; Ridgeway and Correll 2004).

But, while Polachek (2009) is optimistic that women can overcome and even surpass this earnings lag with men, Hartman et al. (2009) are less sanguine about such prospects. They envision women's disproportionate rate of job segregation due to an overconcentration in low-paying occupations during their most productive years and which they spend raising families. At this point, their earning potential and power becomes contingent upon that of their respective male partners, not their own. The result? Women will not have invested enough years as participants in the workforce to yield comfortable lifestyles during their retirement years. Hartman et al. (2009) do not quibble about this assessment for they view that it is the decisions that women make during their work lives that render them vulnerable to such gloomy ends. In other words, these life decisions are self-perpetuating and impact lifetime earnings regardless of marital status, with or without children. Moreover, even when women do not follow this traditional path in an attempt to challenge cultural paradigms, they encounter structural barriers like the glass ceiling. While Jackson (2009) does not see the need for this gloom and doom in terms of the earnings potential for women, he believes that women must simply reject these paths to domination.

England (2009) recognizes, at least in part, that women's lapse in earnings worth is not being compensated for, such necessities as childcare. Additionally, since the 1970s, because women's overall participation in the labor force has increased, particularly among married women, while the rate of men has decreased, women have been moved to compensate for what men have lost in order to maintain their standards of living. But England concedes that this incentivized movement of women into the workforce has not necessarily resulted in an aggregated increase in women's earnings power because of their propensity to be situated in low-paying jobs despite some wage convergence with women entering managerial positions. And to her chagrin, she doubts that women's increased participation in the labor force has resulted in a commensurate assumption of men's domestic responsibilities at home. Still, like Jackson (2009), England (2009) shares an optimistic outlook for women's earnings power trajectory and in gender equality as a result in that, unlike the past, men are less interested in subordinating women. She attributes this modern day way of thinking and ideology, that is, in the form of such employment laws as the Family and Medical Leave Act, that force men to think otherwise, although such variables as division of labor decisions still unfairly penalizes women to result in a disparate impact on their lifetime earnings.

Abolishing the combat exclusion policy can then serve as a catalyst, or a springboard, if you will, for getting not only women in the military into what are still considered nontraditional career fields for women but in encouraging civilian women into pursing more technical and scientific career fields as well. I see this goal as having a tripartite purpose. One, to encourage women to pursue still categorized nontraditional jobs such as those in the STEM. Two, by doing so, women will begin to amass higher earnings during their most productive years, not necessarily to compensate for earnings lost by their male partners but to shore up their own quality of life and in turn their financial future that will become less dependent upon the earnings of men. And, three, women's pursuit of still nontraditional careers together with an increase in earnings, will help to leverage women's power in American society, for with money comes prestige and access and with access comes the power to influence public policy in society as an electorate. The repeal of this single illegal policy, that is, the combat exclusion policy, among others, can mark the beginning of infusing calculated mechanisms to close the earnings gap between women and men, and especially so for women of color, particularly underrepresented minority women who are African American, Native American, and Hispanic. As Harris (2009) proposed, given her estimation as to the multifaceted reasons for the premature attrition of white women from the military, girls, like boys, should be introduced at their early stages of development, preferably at the elementary and secondary levels of education or even earlier, for that matter, to increase the likelihood that girls, at higher rates, will want to pursue those subjects in school that will lead them to technical (technology, engineering, and mathematics) and scientific careers in the military. The same should hold true for all girls whether or not they choose to pursue the military route as a career. This approach, says Harris (2009), will have a domino effect where targeted recruitment by the military can facilitate a proliferation in the number of enlistees' and officer candidates' exposure to and representation in these still nontraditional career fields for women. Especially important at this juncture will be the selection of a cadre of female recruiters in the military who, on special assignments from their respective career fields, can function as exemplars for prospective female recruits and/or for the importance of having female recruiters as the face of the military to choose the military as an employer of choice as well as to encourage women to pursue these career fields.

Likewise, the greater this representation of women in the military who are pursuing both technical and scientific careers, the greater will be their stabilization rates and consequently their retention rates over time (Harris 2009). Particularly for white women, since they are the group least likely to remain in the military, doing so would enable the completion of the minimum 15 year cycles within these career fields to increase retention. Correspondingly, increased completion of an average 15-year cycle in these technical and scientific career fields would not only create a critical mass of women but their increased visibility in these career fields as well. And, because previous actions beget subsequent ones, more women in the military, together with their civilian sisters, will aspire and pursue these career fields to become commonplace for women throughout all occupational and professional arenas. Incidentally, Harris's (2009) theory of attrition contends that it is the need for full agency that drives white women's premature attrition from the military. And, while white women, unlike other groups in the military, are the most supportive of gender equity and thus women in combat and combat-related roles (Wilcox 1992), it appears that they do not necessarily benefit in the civilian sector from military service (Cooney et al. 2003). In fact, multiple research support this penalty given their civilian earnings following military service (Mehay and Hirsch 1996; Segal and Segal 2004). Further, white women prematurely leave the military since unlike other segments of the military, including especially underrepresented minorities and particularly African Americans who traditionally utilize the military as a conduit for leveling the playing field, they do so because they simply can in order to pursue what they perceive as greener pastures for employment within the civilian sector. Says Harris (2009), it, therefore, behooves the military to not alienate this group that is the staunchest about women's equality in that they may view the military as most hostile to women.

The pursuit of women in these still nontraditional career fields would potentially reverberate, whereby those in the civilian sector will begin to populate those industries (i.e., mining and agriculture) where women's presence has been acute, if at all. And, as more women in the military pursue these careers, including even those who prematurely separate or retire from the military along with those in the civilian sector, the likelihood of women's earnings potential and capacity for building wealth over time can only be advanced and cultivated into the mindset of future generations of women. With earnings potential and the accumulation of wealth comes power and with power comes a renewed respect for women as a constituency, and so powerful as a voting bloc that they become a force in influencing public policy, including those that affect the military. Politicians and aspiring politicians alike, as women and men of all persuasions, ideologies, and ilk, will be compelled to succumb to the will of this polity. To do otherwise would be to risk obsolescence.

For women in the military, like men in the military, service means the subordination of self to that of country (Baker 2006). However, women, like men, demand to be treated not as second-class citizens but as fully functioning members of a democratic society with all of the rights and responsibilities of citizenship, including the right to bear arms. Therefore, the path to full citizenship for women and in turn full agency as members of a democratic society like the United States is ultimately the path to amassing power. Kanter (1979, p. 320) describes power as "America's last dirty word." Yet, power is a mechanism that women must strategically wield and exploit to demand and command the attention and resources that they deserve. Though today power is not an often-invoked word that is used alongside such pronouns as "she" and "her" or nouns like "woman" and "female," concentrated power or power en masse can prove as a credible threat. So, for women to be powerful and to be perceived as a viable and credible threat, they must be among the brokers in making and influencing those decisions that impact or potentially will impact their constituencies. For military women, in particular, although repeatedly acknowledged as an invaluable resource, regrettably they have never been perceived by the predominantly male decision makers as partners to be consulted on matters that impact them. As a consequence, up to now, military women's voice as a force has been largely silenced. And, without their presence in critical mass as general and flag officers, women's views in the military have not been fully represented.

According to Kanter (1979), to be effective, controlling the sources of power is essential. Sources of power come as lines of supply (i.e., people, money, materials, resources for distribution as awards, and prestige), lines of information (i.e., the purveyors and receivers of privileged information through formal and informal networks), and lines of support (i.e., coalescing necessary formal and informal support). The more access to these channels of power, the greater the leverage and influence that the holders of these lines of power have over decision making. But, as Kanter points out, women experience certain power failures that produce powerlessness. And for all intents and purposes, women in the military have been repeatedly marginalized as victims of this powerlessness. As Fenner (2001) and others like Holm (1992) have justly argued, policies like combat exclusion and the outright ban of women from combat only serve as artificial and indeed arbitrary barriers to ensure women's continual exclusion. I also argue that such policies are so designed to ensure the powerlessness of military women as a collective.

Since its commission by Secretary of Defense George Marshall in 1951 (dacowits.defense.gov), Defense Advisory Committee on Women in the Services (DACOWITS) has effectively functioned as a proxy for women in the military by providing sage counsel to DoD and the military branches on policies that impact women in the military. And fortunately in retrospect was the foresight of Secretary Marshall in appointing this civilian body, each member carrying with them the equivalent military rank and thus the authority of a two-star general (Holm 1992). DACOWITS has been a steady drumbeat, a force to be reckoned with in championing the issues of military women that undoubtedly struck the defining blow that led to the repeal of the combat exclusion policy together with the recommendations of the Military Leadership Diversity Commission (MLDC, 2011). To this end, DACOWITS must continue in this vital role. But while DACOWITS regularly solicits the input of women representatives from the various branches of the military, a like body, that is internal to the military, is necessary in helping to advance the issues of military women, similar to the governing body on women's issues in the Coast Guard. This body, to be composed of women general and flag officers, should operate as the first line of defense for military women that would work in tandem with DACOWITS in the capacity of perpetual inspector generals per se with reporting responsibility to DACOWITS, the civilian body. This second official and specifically high-ranking military layer will ensure that the issues that impact military women are addressed to reduce the likelihood of falling through the cracks of routine inaction. But more importantly, because this second tier or governing body will share the same uniform and culture as their high-ranking male peers, it is more likely that while there will be expected disagreements, this will be largely a body of military women who are influential and well respected by those within the military community. In essence, military men would now have the opportunity to engage in substantive discourse with their female partners across the table in strategizing and developing solutions for the good and effectiveness of the institution as a whole. This move will be imperative as the services mull over their respective plans on how to best achieve full integration of women throughout the military. If women are to be all that they can be, as Major General Mary Clarke, the then highest-ranking woman in the Army, said in 1982, then "The duty performance of the average woman soldier is a solid, quality performance—too good ever to return to an all-male force, or a force with only a few token women" for:

> The bottom line for the Army is the mission. Do women mission really contribute to mission readiness? Anyone who asks that question seriously, man or woman, needs to question his or her assumptions and prejudices, and instead face the facts. It is the quality of women's service which gives an affirmative answer to the readiness question. (Letter published in the *Army Times*, September 21, 1981, in Holm 1992, pp. 401 and 402)

It is then unfair, says Fenner (2001), to put men at risk even during peacetime and sanction their mandatory participation in the military in the Selective Service rolls as a duty of citizenship when young women yearn for the same calling and are slighted when they, too, put themselves at similar risks as young men do but under the pretext as noncombatants and without the equal protection should they sustain injury or worse yet death. Fenner, herself a senior officer and Vice Wing Commander of an Intelligence Wing in the Air Force, then went as far as advocating that for women to achieve equality and thus the rights and responsibilities that come with the civic duty of citizenship, women, like men, should be expected to register for Selective Service once they reach the age as required by law to make this decision.

Bhagwati (2013) is publicly concerned though about the prospects of success for implementation based on the repeal of the combat exclusion policy for as she fears, little has changed for women on the ground, it is only more of the same, as she puts it "Pentagon rhetoric" (p. 4). Further, as proven from the epidemic rates of sexual assault against women in the military, the few women who are promoted to the ranks of prominence like Lieutenant General Susan Helms are more likely than not to go the way of the culture for the survival of their own careers. As Bhagwati (2013) notes, one is rewarded for remaining silent. This, of course, neither ameliorates the situation nor helps to bring the depth of its pathology to light. If anything, the problem is more likely to intensify as the message conveyed to all throughout the ranks is to go the way of the culture and you will be rewarded. Basically, the few women who are elevated to ranks of prominence will only fail to exercise the authority bestowed upon their positions and rank that are required in order to effect much needed change. Yet, had it not been for the collective push back from the still few women in Congress, the issue of sexual assault, for instance, might not have been elevated to the level of urgency that it deserves. It is this critical, albeit fledgling, mass of women who are needed, says Bhagwati (2013), to significantly increase the number of women in the military. She calls for a 25%–33% goal for the recruitment of women to make women visible throughout the institution. And, like Fenner (2001) and others, competition for positions should be based upon a system of meritocracy, not gender. Most important, because there is a severe dearth of women in senior leadership positions in the military, there is an urgency of need to fill this chasm, a finding twice identified by the MLDC (2011) and DACOWITS (2012).

The substance of the services' implementation plans and how they are to be orchestrated will be of note, as each plan will require careful calibration to facilitate success. Who is appointed to the helm of these efforts will therefore be crucial, as those who stand to lose will not be complicit in ensuring women's success at all. Actually, if the selection of those to lead these endeavors is not strategic, this misstep alone will stymie, undermine, or even thwart successful implementation. Timed, regular, and phased reporting to Congress for the purpose of oversight, monitoring, and accountability by the individual service chiefs must be part and parcel of the process. Similar to the straw that broke the camel's back of the Government Performance and Results Act of 1993, the perceived stealth legislation, which did not take root until 12 years later or in 2005, it was the threat of the loss of prized resources, in this case funding, that eventually fueled change in the principals' behaviors to comport with the law. Similar machinery must be installed by Congress as a means of instilling budgetary or resource penalties when targeted milestones by DoD and the military have not been reached as planned. And, to overcome any unforeseen vulnerabilities, if unavoidable, as part of regular reporting to Congress, service chiefs must specifically provide sound rationale for the lapse in meeting these timelines.

This type of reporting to Congress by the service chiefs on a regular basis should be conducted in public by way of televised proceedings or testimonies to enable the public, from which the military force is drawn, to become a participant in the process by being informed on the military's treatment of half of the country's population as well as half of its electorate. This modality can equally serve as yet another layer of accountability in that the military's work on behalf of a grateful nation cannot be achieved in a vacuum. Likewise, it compels DoD and the military to cede to the will of its civilian constituency from which it derives its support. Leveraged with public reporting, accountability, oversight, monitoring, and follow-up via evaluation at each stage of the integration of women in the services process will go a long way in conveying the gravity and political will galvanized as well as in improving the civil–military divide, not to mention to boost the diminishing reputation of a much wounded Congress and the renewed need for transparency.

IV

WOMEN, WAR, THE MILITARY, AND BEYOND

It is no secret that women have been instrumental in successfully guiding many of the world's great nations into wars for innumerable reasons but for which the scant literature has not given them credit though war is a phenomenon in which and to which women have been an integral part, if not the driving force. Yet, despite this rich legacy, women's roles in modern day wars have been marginalized to one of support even as they actively partake in virtually every conceivable function for the successful execution of wars, including those in combat. The American experience, and by extension the military, is a symbol of what has regrettably become the cultural modern day norm, albeit an invidious and ourstorical contradiction. American women's progress in the military has constantly been held in check under the bondage of the repressive combat exclusion policy. The following section is essentially a call to action for the military to take heed in the treatment of its female workforce and what it must do to redeem itself from the continuing adverse impact of the policy, particularly as it relates to the recruitment, promotion, and retention of women (and men) in the military.

Chapter 14

In Conclusion: The Revolution Continues!

As of this writing, the federal government shutdown was settled in a cease-fire between the opposing forces, but despite said agreements, they may be temporary, as we may again experience or at least be on the verge of the threat of another government shutdown. For now, a new continuing budget resolution will fund the federal government's activities. The political fallout though in hindsight might prove detrimental as no political party in Congress wants to be attributed to this debacle. However, this shutdown of the federal government brought with it new and unforeseen realities from which new priorities will likely emerge. It is estimated that continuing the government shutdown would have cost the U.S. economy approximately $200 million per day or approximately $1.3 billion per week. The actual cost of the 16-day shutdown inflicted a whopping $24 billion to the economy (Dockterman 2013).

But with the $16.7 trillion debt ceiling and the reality of the adverse impact in how it would have reverberated throughout the country and the rest of the world, the situation could not have been ignored or taken lightly. So, too, under much consideration was the pressure from some European leaders in how the shutdown would impact their own internal economies coupled with the overarching need that neither political party wanted to be reputed for the shutdown that broke the stalemate of wills in Congress especially in light of the upcoming midterm elections. And, after all of this posturing, the crisis was averted when the principals agreed to increase the debt ceiling (McCarthy and Newell 2013). But, lest we forget, 800,000 federal employees were either furloughed or deemed essential, and in some cases, for that reason, were forced to work without compensation to meet their livelihood, not to mention the negative outcome on morale and the unintended effects to the subordinate levels of government that rely on the resources of the federal government. Even with retroactive pay and a 1% increase to boot that federal employees have not witnessed since 2010 (Jamieson 2013), memories will be long this time around in living down this period in infamy, one that has not occurred since 1993 and certainly not on the likes of this scale.

This new state of affairs, that is, the federal government shutdown, has brought with it new urgencies for Department of Defense (DoD) and its respective military branches pertaining to military readiness and national security. Consequently, the conditions under which the repeal of the combat exclusion policy were based may now be imperiled, for yet again for military women, as new priorities surface to possibly call for another compromise that would no longer rise to the level of prominence that it once commanded only months before the government shutdown. And, with much loss in productivity, including to the Pentagon to the tune of $600 million (Serbu 2013), the fear is that plans for implementing the full integration of women throughout the military—most specifically in combat and combat-related occupations, positions, assignments, units, and levels—will be delayed, usurped by other perceived and more imminent priorities in light of budgetary constraints, or worse yet, forgotten altogether due to inaction characterized by the instrument of choice, more delay tactics. The follow-through will then demand galvanizing the forces in Congress, chief among them the small yet vociferous cadre of female politicians, who must coalesce key constituents to ensure that this issue remains at the forefront of the Congress' agenda. No doubt though that watchdog groups like DACOWITS, the ACLU, and SWAN will keep up the pressure to compel DoD's and the military branches' compliance with the conditions of the repeal. The hope is that this compliance will not needlessly take the form of more lawsuits against DoD to pummel it into action. These actions, notwithstanding those that helped to fuel the debate surrounding the prevalence of sexual assault in the military, must be kept visible for public scrutiny if DoD and the military are to move beyond this malaise.

As Harris (2009) contends, if women continue to experience such indignities as sexual assault and like crimes in the military, they may conclude that their presence is unwanted. She asserts that, for instance, the reason for white women's premature attrition from the military is basically a struggle for full agency. In turn, because the military may be perceived as a hostile work environment, parents may discourage their children, female and male, from pursuing this route as a viable career, particularly following the damning comments by two ranking senators in Congress that parents should beware of putting their children into the line of fire given the prevalence of sexual assault; the spouses of military men in support of military women will encourage their husbands to leave the military and more so as the economy improves; and even civilian women who are employed by DoD and the military branches may follow suit. And, as Harris suggests, and a point that has been validated in surveys conducted by DACOWITS (2012), the military may be equally challenged in filling those occupations that women in the military traditionally pursue. But this perfect storm is to be avoided at all costs for particularly when there is an uptick in the economy, as is expected, the military may find itself stranded and eating crow for an unforgiving public will be in no mood to be trifled with as one of its most precious resources, women, are being sidelined and abused. The civilian–military rift will only widen and the military may be in jeopardy of losing much needed support and funding to retain its reputation as the best in the world. Moreover, because unlike in the past when the Congress was comprised of a disproportionate number of white male veterans-turned-politicians, the military could potentially lose allies in Congress as well. However, by ensuring that present and future generations of women and men not only flock to the military as a preferred employer, but also the military can position itself to better compete with the civilian sector for the best and brightest that the society has to offer.

Undeniably, many of the military's offspring will have aspirations of their own for the Congress as have generations of veterans before them, who, it is hoped, will comprise a critical mass of women. But, only by valuing its human resources, many of whom are women, can DoD and by extension the military reclaim its once-stellar reputation. Full compliance that called for the repeal of the combat exclusion policy is its only savior. Therefore, anything short of full compliance for the full integration of women throughout all positions in the military will be unacceptable, if not the ultimate insult. According to renowned anthropologist Margaret Mead, in some societies, men have an overriding need to subordinate women by ensuring that they are barred from certain activities which men consider as their dominion (Margaret Mead 1949 as cited by Francke 1997). More importantly, as the verbal exchange in the Senate between former Air Force Chief of Staff General McPeak and former Senator Cohen revealed, such decisions like the combat exclusion policy and the desire to protect those positions classified as combat and combat related are primarily motivated, as one would say, to prevent women from showing men up, for in many cases women simply outperform men in these very activities. For as Mead (1949, p. 160) notes, "Their maleness, in fact, has to be underwritten by preventing women from entering some field or performing some feat" (in Francke 1997, p. 260). And, says Major General Gail Reals of her beloved Marine Corps, "We [women] were kind of handy for someone making a speech who would showcase their woman general. They tolerated us but they didn't accept us" (Francke 1997, p. 260). Besides, as Francke (1997) and others (i.e., Holm 1992) have found and has been repeatedly borne out, because women as a group are judged as not having what it takes as a man, the right stuff as one would say, then they are forced to endure the unnecessary obstacle course of undergoing a series of testing, studying and the like, all ludicrous delay tactics that have been employed *ad infinitum*. I would argue that by now we should have evolved as a specie beyond the limitations of these basic instincts, which for men, and especially for the white male, solely translates to a fundamental need to conceal his innate insecurities.

The 17 women chronicled in this book and others like them have sacrificed in blood, sweat, tears, and tragically in death, and stand as exemplars of overcoming adversity. And, no less is to be expected of their present and future generations of sisters-in-arms as they carry forth this legacy. But, as a collective, women in the military have reached the brink of intolerance and their patience has worn thin. They will wait no longer for the promised long overdue recognition that they deserve as equal players and partners in America's military. And, to what end will this charade continue? But the confluence of the premature exodus of women (and men) from the military, the unforeseen yet anticipated challenges of recruiting women (and men) into the military, and the call for the conditions that the repeal of the combat exclusion policy has set in motion serve as wake-up calls to bring the military to the precipice of redemption. Even for selfish means, if only to protect perceived prized resources, for to do otherwise would prove disastrous for a military that will be pushed into paying an irrevocable price, one that will not likely be forgotten and should not be forgotten by future generations of women and men as it struggles to shore up an anemic workforce.

America's military has been the envy of the world, so much so, that many immigrants have joined its ranks in an attempt to give back in the way of patriotism. As Fenner (2001) states, women like men have this same call to patriotism and yearn to be treated in kind as full citizens in a democratic society with all the rights, privileges, and trappings that accompany civic duty. This includes the right to bear arms (Snyder 2003). Why deny women in the military this endowed right? Why deny any American citizen, for that matter, of this right only to be relegated to second-class citizenship? This deliberate act of exclusion is unconstitutional and smacks of flouting the equal protection clause under the Fourteenth Amendment of the U.S. Constitution even with the recognition that the military is inherently an undemocratic institution. But, the military emanates from a civilian democratic society upon which its very existence depends and from which its resources are drawn. While repealing the combat exclusion policy will result in women in the military as the most direct beneficiaries, its impact will be far reaching beyond those of military women toward the path to full agency for their civilian sisters as well. Women as a constituency can amass power and prove to be an invaluable voting bloc in all walks of American life to noticeably influence public policy, including those that impact the military.

Repealing the combat exclusion policy then represents only one in a long line of mechanisms toward achieving this central goal, for even when women are successfully integrated throughout the military, when women begin to populate those industries and occupations within the civilian sector where their presence is still wanting, and when women's actual earnings finally begin to gain parity by converging with those of especially white men, women (and enlightened men as allies) must never rest upon their laurels for the path to full agency is never static. So is the path to democracy, for according to President Franklin Roosevelt, "It is an everlasting march" (October 1, 1935, as cited by Peters and Woolley n.d., the American Presidency Project). And, if we pride ourselves in being the model and steward of democracy for which we are reputed, then we must be the first to live it, honor it, cherish it, and do all that we can to protect it. Therein lies the work ahead as the journey toward equality, full citizenship, and hence full agency for military women and correspondingly for American women in general will no doubt be rife with unforeseen trials, much of which have largely defined the arduous road already traveled. So, in conclusion, for all of these reasons and more, the revolution must continue.

Bibliography

Chapter 1

2011 Demographics. Profiles of the Military Community. 2012. November. http://www.militaryonesource.mil/12038/MOS/Reports/2011_Demographics_Report.pdf. Retrieved January 22, 2013.

Alvarez, L. 2009. G.I. Jane Breaks the Combat Barrier. *The New York Times*. August 16, AI.

Armour, D.J. 1996. Race and Gender in the U.S. Military. *Armed Forces & Society*, 23, 1, 7–27.

Associated Press. 2012. Air Force Picks 1st Woman to Command Fighter Wing. *Air Force Times*. May 23. http://www.airforcetimes.com/article/20120523/NEWS/205230328/AF-picks-1st-woman-command-fighter-wing. Retrieved February 21, 2013.

Bachman, J.G., Segal, D.R., Freedman-Doan, P., and O'Malley, P.M. 2000. Who Chooses Military Service? Correlates of Propensity and Enlistment in the U.S. Armed Forces. *Military Psychology*, 12, 1, 1–30.

Baker, H. 2006. Women in Combat: A Culture Issue? ADA449305. U.S. Army War College. March.

Baldor, L.C. 2007. Decline for Military in Black Recruits. *Huffington Post*. June 24. http://www.huffingtonpost.com/huff-wires/20070624/military-recruits-blacks/. Retrieved April 27, 2008.

Bernard, M. 2013. With Women in Combat, Will Military Finally Address Epidemic of Sexual Assault? *The Washington Post*. January 24. http://www.washingtonpost.com/blogs/she-the-people/wp/2013/01/24/with-woman-in-combat-will-military-finally-address-epidemic-of-sexual-assault/. Retrieved January 25, 2013.

Burnes, T. 2008. Contributions of Women to U.S. Combat Operations. Strategy Research Project. U.S. Army War College. March 15.

Burrelli, D.F. 2012. Women in Combat: Issues for Congress. Congressional Research Service (CRS). May 9.

Bynum, R., and Jelinek, P. 2009. Navy Moves to Put Women on Submarines. *Associated Press*. October 13. http://www.msnbc.msn.com/id/33297422/ns/38027577. Retrieved July 12, 2010.

Christensen, S. 2013. Ban on Women in Combat Ends. *My San Antonio*. January 24. http://www.mysanantonio.com/news/article/Ban-on-women-in-combat-ends-4218940.php. Retrieved January 24, 2013.

Cohn, C. 2000. How Can She Claim Equal Rights When She Doesn't Have to Do as Many Push-Ups as I Do? The Framing of Men's Opposition to Women's Equality in the Military. *Men and Masculinities*, 3, 2, 131–151.

Coleman, K. 2012. President Obama Nominates First Woman as Four-Star U.S. Air Force General. *National Public Radio (NPR)*. February 7. http://www.npr.org/blogs/thetwo-way/2012/02/07/146518211/president-obama-nominates-first-woman-as-four-star-u-s-air-force-general. Retrieved January 21, 2013.

Cooney, R.T., Segal, M.W., Segal, D.R., and Falk, W.W. 2003. Racial Differences in the Impact of Military Service on the Socioeconomic Status of Women Veterans. *Armed Forces & Society*, 30, 1, 53–86.

Dawley, K. 2012. Gen, Wolfenbarger Receive Fourth Star, Assumes Leadership of AFMC. *Aerotech News/Desert Wings*. June 8. http://www.aerotechnews.com/edwardsafb/2012/06/08/gen-wolfenbarger-receives-fourth-star-assumes-leadership-of-afmc/. Retrieved January 21, 2013.

DeCew, J.W. 1995. The Combat Exclusion and the Role of Women in the Military. *Hypatia*, 10, 1, 56–73.

Defense Advisory Committee on Women in the Services (DACOWITS). 2003. Status Report. dacowits.defense.gov/portals/48/Documents/Reports/2003/Annual%20Report/dacowits2003report.pdf. Retrieved May 12, 2004.

Defense Advisory Committee on Women in the Services (DACOWITS). 2005. Status Report. dacowits.defense.gov/portals/48/Documents/Reports/2005/Annual%20Report/dacowits2005report.pdf. Retrieved September 8, 2006.

Defense Advisory Committee on Women in the Services (DACOWITS). 2006. Status Report. dacowits.defense.gov/portals/48/Documents/Reports/2006/Annual%20Report/dacowits2006report.pdf. Retrieved April 27, 2007.

Defense Advisory Committee on Women in the Services (DACOWITS). 2009. Status Report. dacowits.defense.gov/portals/48/Documents/Reports/2009/Annual%20Report/dacowits2009report.pdf. Retrieved January 24, 2013.

Defense Advisory Committee on Women in the Services (DACOWITS). 2012. Status Report. http://dacowits.defense.gov/Portals/48/Documents/Reports/2012/Annual%20Report/dacowits2012report.pdf. Retrieved January 26, 2013.

Delmore, E. 2013. Senator Gillibrand's Sexual Assault Bill Gets Tea Backing. *MSNBC*. July 16. http://tv.msnbc.com/2013/07/16/sen-gillibrands-military-sex-assault-bill-gets-tea-party-backing/. Retrieved March 23, 2013.

Department of Defense. 2004. Report on the Status of Female Members of the Armed Forces. Office of the Under Secretary of Defense for Personnel and Readiness. June.

Ellefson, K.G. 1998. *Advancing Army Women as Senior Leaders—Understanding the Obstacles*. U.S. Army War College. AD A344984.

Ellison, J. 2012. Panetta, Gates, Rumsfeld Face New Suit over U.S. Military Rape "Epidemic." *The Daily Beast*. March 6. http://www.thedailybeast.com/articles/2012/03/06/panetta-gates-rumsfeld-face-new-suit-over-u-s-military-rape-epidemic.html. Retrieved December 18, 2012.

Enloe, C. 1983. *Does Khaki Become You? The Militarisation of Women's Lives*. London: Pluto Press.

Evans, B. 2013. Defense Department to Remove Female Combat Exclusion Policy. *Brandpoint Online Journalism*, Ohio University. January 28. http://www.ivn.us/2013/01/28/military-to-remove-female-combat-exclusion-policy/. Retrieved January 29, 2013.

Evertson, A., and Nesbitt, A. 2004. The Glass Ceiling Effect and Its Impact on Mid-Level Female Officer Career Progression in the United States Marine Corps and Air Force. ADA422296. Navy Postgraduate School. March.

Fischer, H. 2013. U.S. Military Casualty Statistics: Operation New Dawn, Operation Iraqi Freedom, and Operation Enduring Freedom. Congressional Research Service (CRS). February 5. http://www.fas.org/sgp/crs/natsec/RS22452.pdf. Retrieved March 12, 2013.

Fox, L., and Brown, M.H. 2013. Women in U.S. Military Fight for Right to Serve in Combat. Gaithersburg Soldier among Those Suing Panetta over Exclusion. *The Baltimore Sun.* http://articles.baltimoresun.com/2013-01-05/news/bs-md-women-in-combat-20130105_1_combat-exclusion-policy-direct-combat-women/. Retrieved January 24.

French, S.J. 2000. Analyzing Personnel Retention Utilizing Multi-Agent Systems. ADA386919. Naval Postgraduate School. December.

Friedrich, E. 2012. Navy Pins First Nuclear-Qualified Female Submariners. December 5. http://www.kitsapsun.com/news/2012/dec/05/navy-pins-first-nuclear-qualified-female/#axzz21.ay2FBLh. Retrieved February 21, 2013.

Garamone, J. 2011. Don't Ask, Don't Tell Repeal Certified by President Obama. U.S. Department of Defense American Forces Press Services. July 22. http://www.defense.gov/news/newsarticle.aspx?id=64780. Retrieved January 23, 2013.

Goldstein, J.S. 2003. *War and Gender: How Gender Shapes the War System and Vice Versa.* New York, NY: Cambridge University Press.

Grosskruger, P.L. 2008. Women Leaders in Combat: One Commander's Perspective. In *Women in Combat Compendium.* M. Putko and D.V. Johnson III (Eds.). Carlisle, PA: U.S. Army War College. January, 43–52.

Harrell, M.C., Beckett, M.K., Chien, C.S., and Sellinger, J.M. 2002. *The Status of Gender Integration in the Military: Analysis of Selected Occupations.* Santa Monica, CA: National Defense Research Institute (NDRI), RAND Publications.

Harrell, M.C., and Miller, L. 1997. *New Opportunities for Military: Effects upon Readiness, Cohesion, and Morale.* Santa Monica, CA: National Defense Research Institute (NDRI), RAND Publications.

Harris, G.L.A. 2009. The Multifacted Nature of White Female Attrition in the Military. *Journal of Public Management & Social Policy*, 15, 1, 71–93.

Hlad, J. 2013. Women Already Proven in Combat, Lawsuit Says. *Stars and Stripes.* http://www.stripes.com/news/officials-panetta-depmsey-to-remove-ban-on-women-in-combat-1.205053. Retrieved February 18, 2013.

Hlad, J., and Shane, L. 2013. Officials: Panetta, Dempsey to Remove Ban on Women in Combat. *Stars and Stripes.* January 23. http://www.stripes.com/news/us/official-panetta-dempsey-to-remove-ban-on-women-in-combat-1-205053. Retrieved February 18.

Hosek, S.D., Tiemeyer, P., Kilburn, R., Strong, D.A., Duckworth, S., and Ray, R. 2001. *Minority and Gender Differences in Officer Career Progression.* Santa Monica, CA: National Defense Research Institute (NDRI), RAND Publications.

Independent Lens. 2008. *Lioness.* November. http://www.pbs.org/inependentlens/lioness/film.html ; http://lionessthefilm.com/about_the_film/. Retrieved July 14, 2010.

Iskra, D. 2012. More Navy Women Joining the Silent Service. October 3, 2012. http://nation.time.com/2012/10/03/more-navy-women-joining-the-silent-service. Retrieved February 21, 2013.

Jeffreys, S. 2008. Double Jeopardy: Women, the U.S. Military and the War in Iraq. *Women's Studies International Forum*, 30, 16–25.

Joint Economic Committee. 2007. Helping Military Moms Balance Family and Longer Deployments. Senator C. Schumer (Chair) and Congresswoman C. Maloney (Vice Chair). May 11.

Katz, B. 2012. Two Women Say Were Raped, Punished at U.S. Military Academies. *Reuters*. April 20. http://www.reuters.com/article/2012/04/20/us-usa-military-rape-idUSBRE-83J1DB20120420. Retrieved December 18, 2012.

Keenan, J.O. 2008. The DoD Combat Exclusion Policy: Time for a Change? In *Women in Combat Compendium*, M.M. Putko and D.V. Johnson III (Eds.). Carlisle, PA: U.S. Army War College. January, pp. 21–26.

Kennedy-Pipe, C. 2000. Women and the Military. *Journal of Strategic Studies*, 23, 4, 32–50.

Lindon, M.R. 2008. Impact of Revisiting the Army's Female Assignment Policy. In *Women in Combat Compendium*. M. Putko and D.V. Johnson III (Eds.). Carlisle, PA: U.S. Army War College. January, pp. 37–42.

Lioness Report. 2012. Cultivating Change: Lioness Impact Report. Based on *Lioness*, A Feature Documentary directed by M. McLagan and D. Sommers. Room 11 Productions.

Maninger, S. 2008. Women in Combat: Reconsidering the Case Against Deployment of Women in Combat-Support and Combat Units. In *Women in the Military and Armed Conflict*. H. Carreiras and G. Kummel (Eds.). Wiesbaden, Germany: VS Verlang fur Sozialwissenschaften, pp. 9–28.

Mazur, D.H. 1998. Women, Responsibility, and the Military. *Notre Dame Law Review*, 74, 1, 1–45.

McLagan, M., and Sommers, D. 2010. Introductions: How We Came to Make "Lioness." July. http://www.pbs.org/pov/regardingwar/conversations/women-at-war/introductions-how-we-came-to-make-lioness.php. Retrieved July 14, 2010.

Mehay, S.L., and Hirsch, B.T. 1996. The Post Military Earnings of Female Veterans. *Industrial Relations*, 35, 2, 197–217.

Migdal, A. 2013. Women in Combat: Policy, Meet Reality. American Civil Liberties Union (ACLU) Women's Rights Project. January 24. http://www.aclu.org/blog/women-srights/women-combat-policy-meet-reality. Retrieved January 24, 2013.

Military Leadership Diversity Commission (MLDC). 2011. From Representation to Inclusion: Diversity Leadership for the 21st-Century. March 15. http://www.hsdl.org/?view&did=715693. Retrieved January 26, 2013.

Miller, L. 1998. Feminism and the Exclusion of Army Women from Combat. *Gender Issues*, Summer, 33–64.

Moore, B. 2002. The Propensity of Junior Personnel to Remain in Today's Military. *Armed Forces & Society*, 28, 2, 257–278.

Morris, M. 1996. By Force of Arms: Rape, War, and the Military Culture. *Duke Law Journal*, 45, 4, 652–781.

Moulton, K., and Peterson, G. 2012. Nineteen Veterans, Servicemembers Sue over Military Sexual Assault. *Denver Post*. September 28. http://www.americanhomecomings.com/news/2012/09/28/nineteen-veterans-sue-over-military-sexual-assault/. Retrieved December 18, 2012.

Mount, M. 2010. Women to Begin Serving on Navy Submarines, Officials Say. April 29. http://www.cnn.com/2010/US/04/29/women.submarines/index.html. Retrieved August 22, 2010.

Nantais, C., and Lee, M.F. 1999. Women in the United States Military: Protectors or Protected? The Case of Prisoner of War Melissa Rathburn-Nealy. *Journal of Gender Studies*, 8, 2, 181–191.

National Security Advisory Group. 2006. The U.S. Military: Under Strain and At Risk. http://thinkprogress.org/wp-content/uploads/2006/01/NSAG%20report%20012406.pdf. Retrieved April 27, 2008.

Park, S. 1999. White Women Lead Military in Dropping Out. *USA Today*. March 26.
Parker, A. 2011. Lawsuit Says Military is Rife with Sexual Assault. *New York Times*. February 15, http://www.nytimes.com/2011/02/16/us/16military.html?_r=0. Retrieved December 18, 2012.
Parrish, K. 2012. DoD Opens More Jobs, Assignments to Military Women. American Forces Press Service. U.S. Department of Defense. February 9. http://www.defense.gov/news/newsarticle.aspx?id=67130. Retrieved November 28, 2012.
Patten, E., and Parker, K. 2011. Women in the U.S. Military: Growing Share, Distinctive Profile. Pew Social and Demographic Trends. http://www.pewsocialtrends.org/files/2011/12/women-in-the-military.pdf. Retrieved January 30, 2013.
Petronio, K. 2012. Get Over It! We're Not All Created Equal. *The Marine Corps Gazette*. http://www.mca-marines.org/gazette/article/get-over-it-we-are-not-all-created-equal. Retrieved May 22, 2013.
Population Representation in the Military Services. 2006. Office of the Under Secretary of Defense for Personnel and Readiness. http://prhome.defense.gov/portals/52/Documents/POPREP/poprep2006/pdf. Retrieved July 14, 2010.
Population Representation in the Military Services. 2011. Office of the Undersecretary of Defense, Personnel and Readiness. http://prhome.defense.gov/portals/52/Documents/POPREP/poprep2011/links/links.html. Retrieved February 27, 2013.
Putko, C. 2008a. USAWC Women in Combat Survey Interpretation. In *Women in Combat Compendium*. M. Putko and D.V. Johnson III (Eds.). Carlisle, PA: U.S. Army War College. January, pp. 1–20.
Putko, M. 2008b. The Combat Exclusion Policy in the Modern Security Environment. In *Women in Combat Compendium*. M. Putko and D.V. Johnson III (Eds.). Carlisle, PA: U.S. Army War College. January, pp. 27–36.
Putko, M.M., and Johnson, D.V. (Eds.). 2008. Women in Combat Compendium. http://www.StrategicStudiesInstitute.srmy.mil/pdffiles/pub830.pdf.
Regan, T. 2005. Blacks, Women Avoiding U.S. Army. http://www.csmonitor.com/2005/0309/daily/Update.html. Retrieved May 31, 2008.
Rodgers, J. 2013. Major General Michelle Johnson First Woman to Lead Air Force Academy. *The Denver Post*. March 1. http://www.denverpost.com/breakingnews/ci_22698627/air-force-ac. Retrieved March 4, 2013.
Schroeder, P. 1991. The Combat Exclusion Law Should Be Repealed. In *Women in the Military*. C. Wekesser and M. Polesetsky (Eds.). San Diego, CA: Greenhaven Press, pp. 73–74.
Segal, M.W. 1982. The Argument for Female Combatants. In *Female Soldiers: Combatants or Noncombatants?* N.L. Goldman (Ed.). Westport, CT: Greenwood Press, p. 267–290.
Segal, M.W. 1993. Women in the Armed Forces. In *Women and the Use of Military Force*. R. Howes and M. Stevenson (Eds.). Boulder, CO: Lynne Rienner Publishers, p. 81–93.
Segal, M.W. 1995. Women's Military Roles Cross-Nationally, Past, Present, and Future. *Gender & Society*, 9, 6, 757–775.
Segal, M.W. 1999. Gender and the Military. In *Handbook of the Sociology of Gender*. J.S. Chafetz (Eds.). London: Springer.
Segal, D.R., and Segal, M.W. 2004. America's Military Population. *Population Bulletin*, 59, 1, 1–42.
Shanker, T. 2006. Young Officers Leaving Army at a High Rate. *New York Times*. April 10. http://www.nytimes.com/2006/04/10. Retrieved May 31, 2008.
Sheppard, C. 2007. Women in Combat. Strategy Research Project. Carlisle, PA: U.S. Army War College. March 30.

Simons, A. 2000. Women Can Never "Belong" in Combat. *Orbis*, Summer, 451–461.
Snyder, R.C. 2003. The Citizen-Soldier Tradition and Gender Integration of the U.S. Military. *Armed Forces & Society*, 29, 2, 185–204.
Sohn, D.S. 2013. Kirsten Gillibrand Gains on Chain of Command Changes. *POLITICO Pro*. August 13. http://www.politico.com/story/2013/09/kirsten-gillibrand-sexual-assault-military-reforms-97530.html. Retrieved September 13, 2013.
Stiehm, H.J. (Ed.). 1982. The Protected, the Protector, the Defender. In *Women's Studies International Forum*. Oxford, UK: Pergamon, pp. 5, 3–4, 367–376.
Stiehm, H.J. 1988. The Effects of Myths about Military Women on the Waging of War. In *Women and the Military System*. E. Isaksson (Ed.). New York, NY: Simon & Schuster, pp. 94–106.
Sutton, J. 2013. Ending U.S. Combat Ban Will Even Career Playing Field, Servicewomen Say. January 23. *Reuters* and the *Chicago Tribune*. http://www.chicatribune.com/news/politics/sns-rt-us-usa-military-women-reactionbre90n046-20130123,0,6408329.story. Retrieved January 24.
Tilghman, A. 2013a. Lawsuit Takes on Combat Exclusion for Women. January 7. http://www.thetowntalk.com/article/20130108/NEWS01/301080309. Retrieved January 20, 2013.
Tilghman, A. 2013b. Pentagon Advisory Panel: Strip Commanders' Ability to Prosecute Sexual Assaults. *Army Times*. September 30. http://www.armytimes.com/article/20130930/NEWS06/309300029/Pentagon-advisory-panel-Strip-commanders-ability-prosecute-sexual-assaults. Retrieved October 2, 2013.
Titunik, R.F. 2000. The First Wave: Gender Integration and Military Culture. *Armed Forces & Society*, 26, 2, 229–257.
Titunik, R.F. 2008. The Myth of the Macho Military. *Polity*, 40, 2, 137–163.
Twitchell, R.E. 2008. The 95th Military Police Battalion Deployment to Iraq—Operation Iraqi Freedom II. In *Women in Combat Compendium*. M. Putko and D.V. Johnson III (Eds.). Carlisle, PA: U.S. Army War College. January, pp. 69–70.
U.S. Army. 2002. Women in the Army: An Annotated Bibliography. U.S. Army Research Institute for the Behavioral and Social Sciences. Special Report 48. May.
U.S. General Accountability Office (GAO). 1987. Combat Exclusion Laws for Women in the Military: Testimony. GAO/T-NSIAD-88-8. November 19.
U.S. General Accountability Office (GAO). 1998a. Gender Issues: Information on DoD's Assignment Policy and Direct Ground Combat Definition. GAO/NSIAD-99-7. October
U.S. General Accountability Office (GAO). 1998b. Gender Issues: Information to Assess Servicemembers' Perception of Gender Inequities is Incomplete. GAO/NSIAD-99-27. November.
U.S. General Accountability Office (GAO). 1999. Gender Issues: Trends in Occupational Distribution of Military Women. GAO/NSIAD-99-212. September.
U.S. General Accountability Office (GAO). 2001. Military Personnel: First-term Personnel Less Satisfied with Military Life than Those in the Mid-Career. GAO-02-200. December.
U.S. General Accountability Office (GAO). 2005a. Military Personnel: Financial Costs and Loss of Critical Skills Due To DoD's Homosexual Conduct Policy Cannot Be Completely Estimated. GAO-05-299. February.
U.S. General Accountability Office (GAO). 2005b. DoD Needs to Conduct a Data-Driven Analysis of Active Duty Military Personnel Levels Required to Implement the Defense Strategy. GA0-05-200. February.

U.S. General Accountability Office (GAO). 2005c. Military Personnel: Preliminary Observations on Recruiting and Retention Issues with the U.S. Armed Forces. GAO-05-419T. March.

U.S. General Accountability Office (GAO). 2005d. Military Personnel: Reporting Additional Servicemember Demographics Could Enhance Congressional Oversight. GAO-05-952. September.

U.S. General Accountability Office (GAO). 2007. Military Personnel: Strategic Plan Needed to Address Army's Emerging Officer Accession and Retention Challenges. GAO-07-224. January.

Weber, C. 2010. Women to Begin Serving on Navy Submarines for the First Time. April 29. http://www.politicsdaily.com/2010/04/29/women-to-begin-serving-on-navy-submarines-for-the-first-time/. Retrieved August 22, 2010.

Whitlock, C. 2012. Female Service Members Sue over U.S. Combat Exclusion Policy. *The Washington Post*. http://www.independent.co.uk/news/world/americas/female-service-members-sue-over-us-combat-exclusion-policy-8363339.html. Retrieved January 23, 2013.

Wilson, B.A. 1995. Women in Combat—Why Not? http://userpages.aug.com/captbarb/combat.html. Retrieved July 14, 2009.

Women in the Military Services of America (WIMSA). 2011. Status of Women in the Military. As of November 30. http://www.womensmemorial.org/PDFs/StatsonWIM.pdf. Retrieved December 18, 2012.

Chapter 2

Abbott, N. 1941. Pre-Islamic Arab Queens. *American Journal of Semitic Languages and Literature*, 58, 1–22.

Alpern, S.B. 1998. *Amazons of Black Sparta: The Women Warriors of Dahomey*. New York, NY: New York University Press.

Crim, B. 2000. Silent Partners: Women and Warfare in Early Modern Europe. In *A Soldier and a Woman: Sexual Integration in the Military*. G.J. DeGroot and C.M. Peniston-Bird (Eds.). Essex, UK: Pearson Publishing, pp. 18–32.

Davis-Kimball, J. 1997. Warrior Women of the Eurasian Steppes. *Archaeology*, 50, 1, 44–48.

DeGroot, G.J., and Peniston-Bird, C.M. 2000. *A Soldier and a Woman: Sexual Integration in the Military*. London: Longman Press.

DePauw, L.G. 1998. *Battle Cries and Lullabies: Women in War from Prehistory to the Present*. Norman, OK: University of Oklahoma Press.

Eads, V. 1986. The Campaigns of Matilda of Tuscany. *MINERVA: Quarterly Report on Women and the Military*, 4, 1, 167–181.

Elshtain, J.B. 1987. *Women and War*. New York, NY: Basic Books, Inc. Publishers.

Fraser, A. 1990. *The Warrior Queens: The Legends and the Lives of Women Who Have Led Their Nations in War*. New York, NY: Vintage Books.

Gibb, H.A.R. 1973. *The Life of Saladin: From the Works of Imad ad-Din and Baha ad-Din*. Oxford, UK: Clarendon Press.

Goldstein, J.S. 2003. *War and Gender: How Gender Shapes the War System and Vice Versa*. New York, NY: Cambridge University Press.

Grant, M. 1972. *Cleopatra: A Biography*. New York, NY: Barnes & Noble.

Jones, D.E. 1997. *Women Warriors: A History*. Washington, DC: Potomac Books, Inc.

Kelly, A. 1950. *Eleanor of Aquitaine and the Four Kings*. Cambridge, MA: Harvard University Press.
Ludwig, E. 1937. *Cleopatra*. New York, NY: Viking Press.
Mazur, D.H. 1998. Women, Responsibility, and the Military. *Notre Dame Law Review*, 74, 1–45.
Miles, R. 1988. *The Women's History of the World*. New York, NY: Harper & Row Press.
Newark, T. 1989. *Women Warlords: An Illustrated History of Female Warriors*. London: Blandford Press.
Vaughan, A.C. 1967. *Zenobia of Palmyra*. New York, NY: Doubleday.

Chapter 3

Allen, T.B. 2006. *Harriet Tubman, Secret Agent: How Daring Slaves and Freed Blacks Spied for the Union during the Civil War*. Washington, DC: National Geographic Children's Books, Scholastic Book Club Edition.
Bellafaire, J. 2010. *Women in the United States Military: An Annotated Bibliography*. Hoboken, NJ: Routledge Press.
Bellafaire, J. n.d. America's Military Women—The Journey Continues. Women in the Military Services of America (WIMSA). http://womensmemorial.org/Education/WHM982.html.
Burrelli, D.F. 2012. Women in Combat: Issues for Congress. Congressional Research Service (CRS). April 5. http://www.fas.org/sgp/crs/natsec/R42075.pdf. Retrieved April 20, 2013.
Chandler, R. 1967. Our Military Women. *Air Force Times*. May 17.
Corum, R. 1996. Soldiering: The Enemy Doesn't Care If You're Female. In *It's Our Military Too! Women in the U.S. Military*. J.H. Stiehm (Ed.). Philadelphia, PA: Temple University Press. pp, 3–23.
Curphey, S. 2003. 1 in 7 U.S. Military Personnel in Iraq Is Female. *WeNews*. March 22. http://womensenews.org/story/military/030322/1-7-us-military-personnel-iraq-female#.UnrYneI1lGM. Retrieved May 22, 2013.
DeCew, J.W. 1995. The Combat Exclusion and the Role of Women in the Military. *Hypatia*, 10, 1, 56–73.
Defense Manpower Data Center (DMDC). U.S. Military Casualties and Wounded in Action for Operations Enduring and Iraqi Freedom and New Dawn. http://www.dmdc.osd.mil/dcas/pages/casulaties.xhtml. Retrieved October 30, 2013.
DePauw, L.G. 1998. *Battle Cries and Lullabies: Women in War from Prehistory to the Present*. Norman, OK: University of Oklahoma Press.
Drake, K. 1967. Our Flying Nightingales in Vietnam. *Readers' Digest*, December, p. 75.
Enloe, C.H. 1993. *The Morning After: Sexual Politics at the End of the Cold War*. Berkeley, CA: University of California Press.
Faust, D.G. 1990. Altars of Sacrifice: Confederate Women and the Narratives of War. *Organization of American Historians*, 76, 4, 1200–1228.
Fischer, H. 2013. U.S. Military Casualty Statistics: Operation New Dawn, Operation Iraqi Freedom, and Operation Enduring Freedom. *Congressional Research Service*. February 5.
Francke, L.B. 1997. *Ground Zero: The Gender Wars in the Military*. New York, NY: Simon & Schuster.
Fritze, J. 2013. Obama to Sign Off on Tubman Monument on Eastern Shore. *The Baltimore Sun*. March 22. http://articles.baltimoresun.com/2013-03-22/news/bs-md-tubman-monument-20130322_1_tubman-monument-designation-eastern-shore. Retrieved July 14, 2013.

Goldstein, J.S. 2003. *War and Gender: How Gender Shapes the War System and Vice Versa.* Cambridge, UK: Cambridge University Press.

Haas, M. 1991. *Women's Perspectives on the Vietnam War.* Pittsburgh, PA: Center for Social Studies Education.

Hall, R. 1994. *Patriots in Disguise: Women Warriors in the Civil War.* New York, NY: Marlowe & Company.

Harris, G.L.A. 2009. The Multifacted Nature of White Female Attrition in the Military. *Journal of Public Management & Social Policy*, 15, 1, 71–93.

Holm, J. 1992. *Women in the Military: An Unfinished Revolution.* Revised Edition. Novato, CA: Presidio Press.

Iraq and Afghanistan Veterans of America (IAVA). n.d. Women Serving in Iraq, Afghanistan and Beyond. http://iava.org/content/women-military#learnmore. Retrieved September 20, 2013.

Mazur, D.H. 1998. Women, Responsibility, and the Military. *Notre Dame Law Review*, 74, 1, 1–45.

Monahan, E.M., and Neidel-Greenlee, R. 2010. *A Few Good Women: America's Military Women from World War I to the Wars in Iraq and Afghanistan.* New York, NY: Anchor Books, Division of Random House, Inc.

Moskos, C. 1998. The Folly of Comparing Race and Gender in the Army. *The Washington Post*, C1. January 4.

Patten, E., and Parker, K. 2011. Women in the U.S. Military: Growing Share, Distinctive Profile. *Pew Social Trends.* December 22. http://www.pewsocialtrends.org/2011/12/22/women-in-the-u-s-military-growingshare-disctinctive-profile. Retrieved December 22, 2012.

Population Representation in the Military Services. 2012. FY 2011.

Priest, D. 1997a. A Trench between Women Jobs. *The Washington Post*, A1 and A14. December 28.

Priest, D. 1997b. Engendering a Warrior Spirit. *The Washington Post*, A1 and A14. March 3.

Priest, D. 1997c. In a Crunch, Ban on Women Bends. *The Washington Post*, A1. December 30.

Sanchez, R., and Phillips, D.T. 2008. *Wiser in Battle: A Soldier's Story.* New York, NY: Harper Collins e-books, Kindle Edition.

Segal, M.W. 1995. Women's Military Roles Cross-Nationally, Past, Present, and Future. *Gender & Society*, 9, 6, 757–775.

Service Women's Action Network (SWAN). 2011a. Women in Combat. *The Facts.* February. http://servicewomen.org/wp-content/uploads/2011/01/97-WIC-fact-sheet.pdf. Retrieved January 23, 2013.

Service Women's Action Network (SWAN). 2011b. Women Vets Health Facts, Facts and Statistics, Office of Public Health and Environmental Hazards. February. http://www.publichealth.va.gov/womenshealth/facts.asp. Retrieved January 23, 2013.

Smith, W. 1992. *American Daughter Gone to War: On the Front Lines with an Army Nurse in Vietnam.* New York, NY: William Morrow.

Soderbergh, P. 1992. *Women Marines: The World War II Era.* Westport, CT: Praeger Press.

Solaro, E. 2006. *Women in the Line of Fire: What You Should Know about Women in the Military.* Emeryville, CA: Seal Press.

Synder, R.C. 2003. The Citizen-Soldier Tradition and Gender Integration of the U.S. Military. *Armed Forces & Society*, 29, 2, 185–204.

Titunik, R. 2000. The First Wave: Gender Integration and Military Culture. *Armed Forces & Society*, 26, 2, 229–257.

Treadwell, M.E. 1954. *United States Army in World War II, Special Studies: The Women's Army Corps*. Washington, DC: Office of the Chief of Military History, Department of the Army.

U.S. Army OneSource. n.d. The Invisible Wounds of War. http://www.myarmyonesource.com/syn/article/id/e4f259e309462310VgnVCM100000381e0a0aRCRD. Retrieved May 20, 2013.

U.S. Coast Guard. 2013. http://www.hagertygrain.com/spar/. Retrieved April 3, 2013.

U.S. Department of Veterans Affairs. Military Service History and VA Benefit Utilization Statistics. National Center for Veterans and Statistics. November 23. http://www.va.gov/VETDATA/docs/SpecialReports/Final_Womens_Report_3_2_12_v_7.pdf. Retrieved May 23, 2013.

Van Devanter, L., and Morgan, C. 1983. *Home before Morning: The True Story of an Army Nurse in Vietnam*. New York, NY: Warner Books.

Vietnam Women's Memorial Foundation. n.d. http://www.vietnamwomensmemorial.org/vwmf.php. Retrieved July 2, 2013.

Walker, K. 1985. *A Piece of My Heart*. New York, NY: Ballantine Books.

Walsh, P.L. 1982. *Forever Sad the Hearts*. New York, NY: Avon Books.

Women in the Military Services of America (WIMSA) Foundation. 2011. Statistics on Women in the Military. As of November 30. http://www.womensmemorial.org/press/stats.html. Retrieved May 5, 2013.

Wright, A. 1984. The Roles of Army Women in Grenada. *MINERVA: Quarterly Report on Women and the Military* 2, 2, 103–113.

Zunes, S. 2003. The U.S. Invasion of Grenada. October. http://www.globalpolicyforum.com. Retrieved April 22, 2013.

Chapter 4

Alvarez, L. 2009. G.I. Jane Breaks the Combat Barrier. *New York Times*, August 16, p. A1.

Barnes, S. 1995. Sibling Rivalry in the Navy: Tom Cruise Meets His Little Sister. *Minerva Bulletin Board*, Winter, p. 11.

Bird, J. 1989. Special Report. *Air Force Times*, December 4.

Boudreau, V.G. 1995. Corazon Aquino: Gender, Class, and the People Power President. In *Women in World Politics: An Introduction*. F. D'Amico and P.R. Beckman (Eds.). Westport, CT: Bergin & Garvey/Greenwood Publishing Group, pp. 71–80.

Breuer, W.B. 1997. *War and American Women: Heroism, Deeds, and Country*. Westport, CT: Praeger Publishing.

Bush, T. 1986. Watkins: Navy Has All the Women It Needs. *Navy Times*, June 23, p. 1.

Campbell, D. 1995. Servicewomen and the Academies: The Football Cordon and Pep Rally as a Case Study of the Status of Female Cadets at the United States Military Academy. *Minerva*, Spring, p. 8.

Carras, M.C. 1995. Indira Gandhi: Gender and Foreign Policy. In *Women in World Politics: An Introduction*. F. D'Amico and P.R. Beckman (Eds.). Westport, CT: Bergin & Garvey/Greenwood Publishing Group, pp. 45–57.

Center for Military Readiness (CMR). 2002. Demise of the DACOWITS. April 15. http://cmrlinl.org/content/women-in-combat/page-12/34447/demise_of_the_dacowits. Retrieved January 15, 2006.

Chavez, L. 1995. Did Navy Policy Cost Pilot Her Life? *USA Today*, May 10.

Defense Advisory Committee on Women in the Services (DACOWITS). 2009. Status Report. http://dacowits.defense.gov/Portals/48/Documents/Reports/2011/Documents/DACOWITS%20September%202011%20Committee%20Meeting/16%20USMC%20WISR%20DACOWITS%20Brief.pdf. Retrieved September 15, 2012.

Defense Advisory Committee on Women in the Services (DACOWITS). 2012. Status Report. http://dacowits.defense.gov/Portals/48/Documents/Reports/2012/Annual%20Report/dacowits2012report.pdf. Retrieved January 26, 2013.

DePauw, L.G. 1975. *Founding Mothers: Women of America in the Revolutionary Era*. Boston, MA: Houghton Mifflin Publishing.

DePauw, L.G. 1998. *Battle Cries and Lullabies: Women in War from Prehistory to the Present*. Norman, OK: University of Oklahoma Press.

Eltshain, J.B. 1987. *Women and War*. New York, NY: Basic Books, Inc.

Eskind, A. 1991. Women Soldiers—Prisoners of Army Discrimination. Military: In Saudi Arabia, Yet Another Excuse for Keeping Women from Showing They Can Do the Job—Like Guarding Iraqis—Too. *Los Angeles Times*, April 28, p. M2. http://articles.latimes.com/1991-04-28/opinion/op-1299_1_women-soldiers.

Fenner, L.M. 2001. Moving Targets: Women's Roles in the U.S. Military in the 21st Century. In *Women in Combat: Civic Duty or Military Liability?* L.M. Fenner and M.E. deYoung (Eds.). Washington, DC: Georgetown University Press, pp. 3–104.

Finer, J., and Partlow, J. 2006. Missing Soldiers Found Dead in Iraq. *Washington Post Foreign Service*. June 20. http://www.washingtonpost.com/wp-dyn/content/article/2006/06/20/AR2006062000242.html. Retrieved February 8, 2013.

Firestone, J.M., and Harris, R.J. 2008. The Impact of Sexual Harassment on Likelihood of Reenlisting in the Military, 2002. Defense Equal Opportunity Management Institute (DEOMI) Research Directorate. Internal Report No. 18-08. Summer.

Francke, L.B. 1997. *Ground Zero: The Gender Wars in the Military*. New York, NY: Simon & Schuster.

Fraser, A. 1989. *The Warrior Queens*. New York, NY: Knopf Press.

Garrison, B. 1995a. Deployed and Pregnant. *Navy Times*, April 3, p. 6.

Garrison, B. 1995b. Internal Report Confirms Hultgreen's Error. *Navy Times*, April 3, p. 6.

Garrison, B. 1996. The Grounding of Morale at Air Wing 11. *Navy Times*, March 18, p. 6.

Goldstein, J.S. 2003. *War and Gender: How Gender Shapes the War System and Vice Versa*. Cambridge, UK: Cambridge Press.

Gordon, M.A., and Ludvigson, M.J. 1991. A Constitutional Analysis of the Combat Exclusion for Air Force Women. Reprinted in *MINERVA: Quarterly Report on Women in the Military*, IX, 2 (Summer), 1–34.

Harrell, M.C., Beckett, M.K., Chien, C.S., and Sollinger, J.M. 2002. *The Status of Gender Integration in the Military: Analysis of Selected Occupations*. Santa Monica, CA: RAND Publications.

Harrell, M.C., and Miller, L. 1997. *New Opportunities for Military: Effects upon Readiness, Cohesion, and Morale*. Santa Monica, CA: National Defense Research Institute (NDRI), RAND Publications.

Harris, G.L.A. 2003. The Impact of Monetary Strategies on Organizational Commitment in the Military. Ph.D. Dissertation, Rutgers University, New Brunswick, NJ. May.

Harris, G.L.A. 2009a. The Multifaceted Nature of White Female Attrition in the Military. *Journal of Public Management & Social Policy*, 15, 1, 71–93.

Harris, G.L.A. 2009b. Women, the Military and Academe. Navigating the Family Track in an Up or Out System. *Administration & Society*, 41, 4, 391–422.

Harris, K. 1995. Prime Minister Margaret Thatcher: The Influence of Her Gender on Her Foreign Policy. In *Women in World Politics: An Introduction.* F. D'Amico and P.R. Beckman (Eds.). Westport, CT: Bergin & Garvey/Greenwood Publishing Group, pp. 59–67.

Herbert, M.S. 1998. *Camouflage Isn't Only for Combat: Gender, Sexuality, and Women in the Military.* New York; London: New York University Press.

Holm, J. 1992. *Women in the Military: An Unfinished Revolution* (Revised Edition). Novato, CA: Presidio Press.

Hosek, S.D., Tiemeyer, P., Kilburn, R., Strong, D.A., Ducksworth, S., and Ray, R. 2001. *Minority and Gender Differences in Officer Career Progression.* Santa Monica, CA: RAND Publications.

Inkeep, S., and Bowman, T. 2008. Army Documents Show Lower Recruiting Standards. *National Public Radio (NPR)*, April 17.

Jeffreys, S. 2007. Double Jeopardy: Women, the U.S. Military and the War in Iraq. *Women's Studies International Forum*, 30, 16–25.

Jones, M. 1986. Women Marines Doing Better Than Expected on Rifle Range. *Navy Times*, January 27, p. 3.

Kaplan, J. 2008. Dumb and Dumber. The Army Lowers Recruitment Standards. January 24. http://www.slate.com/articles/news_and_politics/war_stories/2008/01/dumb_and_dumber.html. Retrieved July 8, 2013.

Letters to the Editor. 1986. *Navy Times*, August 4.

Lioness Report. 2012. Cultivating Change: Lioness Impact Report. Based on *Lioness*, A Feature Documentary directed by M. McLagan and D. Sommers. Room 11 Productions.

Maninger, S. 2008. Women in Combat: Reconsidering the Case Against Deployment of Women in Combat-Support and Combat Units. In *Women in the Military and Armed Conflict.* H. Carreiras and G. Kummel (Eds.). Wiesbaden, Germany: VS Verlag fur Sozialwissenschaften, pp. 9–28.

Mazur, D.H. 1998. Women, Responsibility, and the Military. *Notre Dame Law Review*, 74, 1, 1–45.

McElrath, K. 1992. Gender, Career Disruption and Academic Rewards. *Journal of Higher Education*, 63, 3, 269–281.

McLagan, M., and Sommers, D. 2010. Introductions: How We Came to Make "Lioness." July. http://www.pbs.org/pov/regardingwar/conversations/women-at-war/introductions-how-we-came-to-make-lioness.php. Retrieved July 14, 2010.

Military Leadership Diversity Commission (MLDC). 2011. From Representation to Inclusion: Diversity Leadership for the 21st-Century. March 15. http://www.hsdl.org/?view&did=715693. Retrieved January 26, 2013.

Mitchell, B. 1997. *Women in the Military: Flirting with Disaster.* Washington, DC: Regnery Publishing, Inc.

Monahan, E.M., and Neidel-Greenlee, R. 2010. *A Few Good Women: America's Military Women from World War I to the Wars in Iraq and Afghanistan.* New York, NY: Anchor Books, a Division of Random House, Inc.

Moore, M. 1988. Top Marine Bars Widening Women's Roles. *Washington Post*, April 26, p. 1.

Moskos, C. 1993. From Citizens' Army to Social Laboratory. *Wilson Quarterly*, Winter, pp. 83–95.

Petronio, K. 2012. Get Over It! We're Not All Created Equal. *The Marine Corps Gazette*. http://www.mca-marines.org/gazette/article/get-over-it-we-are-not-all-created-equal. Retrieved May 22, 2013.

Pexton, P. 1995. Women Rise, Tension Reigns. *Navy Times*, January 2, p. 22.
Purcell, R. 1987. Weinberger Thaws Freeze on Adding Women. *Navy Times*, February 16, p. 30.
Randal, M. 1981. *Sandino's Daughter: Testimonies of Nicaraguan Women in Struggle*. Vancouver, Canada: Star Books.
Randal, M., and Yanz, L. 1995. *Sandino's Daughters: Testimonies of Nicaraguan Women in Struggle*. New Brunswick, NJ: Rutgers University Press.
Reed, F. 1999. Recruiting and Gender. *Armed Forces News*, 18 November. http://www.armedforcesnews.com. Retrieved March 23, 2013.
Richardson, J.A., and Howes, R.H. 1993. How Three Female National Leaders Have Used the Military. In *Women and the Use of Military Force*, R.H. Howes and M.R. Stevenson (Eds.). Boulder, CO: Lynne Rienner Publishers, pp. 149–166.
Rosen, L.N., Bliese, P.D., Wright, K.A., and Gifford, R.K. 1999. Gender Composition and Group Cohesion in U.S. Army Units: A Comparison across Five Studies. *Armed Forces & Society*, 25, 3, 365–386.
Rosen, L.N., Durand, D.B., Bliese, P.D., Halverson, R.R., Rothberg, J.M., and Harrison, N.L. 1996. Cohesion and Readiness in Gender-Integrated Combat Service Support Units: The Impact of Acceptance of Women and Gender Ratio. *Armed Forces & Society*, 22, 4, 537–553.
Rosen, L.N., Knudson, K.H., and Fancher, P. 2003. Cohesion and the Culture of Hypermasculinity in U.S. Army Units. *Armed Forces & Society*, 29, 3, 325–351.
Rosen, L.N., and Martin, L. 1998. Psychological Effects of Sexual Harassment, Appraisal of Harassment, and Organizational Climate Survey among U.S. Army Soldiers. *Military Medicine*, 163, 2, 63–67.
Sagawa, S., and Duff Campbell, N. 1992. Recommendation in the Presidential Commission on the Assignment of Women in the Armed Forces Regarding Parents in Military Service. National Women's Law Center, Washington, DC, November 14.
Saywell, S. 1985. *Women in War*. New York, NY: Viking Press.
Scott, K. 2006. Interview with Sergeant Connie Rose Spinks, U.S. Army Reserve. Women in the Military Services of America (WIMSA) Oral History Project. January 26. Arlington, VA.
Segal, M.W. 1995. Women's Military Roles Cross-Nationally, Past, Present, and Future. *Gender & Society*, 9, 6, 757–775.
Sheppard, C. 2007. Women in Combat. Strategy Research Project. U.S. Army War College. 30 March.
Simons, A. 2000. Women Can Never "Belong" in Combat. *Orbis*, Summer, pp. 451–461.
Solaro, E. 2006. *Women in the Line of Fire: What You Should Know about Women in the Military*. Emeryville, CA: Seal Press.
Thomas, P.J., and Thomas, M.D. 1992. *Impact of Pregnant Women and Single Parents upon Navy Personnel Systems*. San Diego, CA: Navy Personnel Research and Development Center, Women and Multicultural Research Office [Report TN-92-87]. February.
U.S. Army. 1996. Update on Gender-Integrated Basic Combat Training. U.S. Army Research Institute for the Behavioral and Social Sciences. http://www.ari.army.mil/110504.html. Retrieved March 12, 2008.
U.S. Army. 2002. Women in the Army: An Annotated Bibliography. U.S. Army Research Institute for the Behavioral and Social Science. Special Report 48. May.
U.S. Government Accountability Office (GAO). 1987. Combat Exclusion Laws for Women in the Military. Testimony. GAO/T-NSIAD-88-8.
Van Creveld, M. 2000. The Great Illusion: Women in the Military. *Millennium: Journal of International Studies*, 29, 2, 429–442.

Van Creveld, M. 2002. *Men, Women & War: Do Women Belong in the Front Line?* London: Cassell Publishing, a Division of Barnes & Noble.

The Vindication of Navy Pilot Lt. Kara Hultgreen. *Nightline.* February 28, 1995.

Women's Research and Education Institute (WREI). 2005. *Women in the Military: Where They Stand* (7th Edition). Washington, DC: WREI.

Chapter 5

Adams-Roy, J., and Barling, J. 1998. Predicting the Decision to Confront or Report Sexual Harassment. *Journal of Organizational Behavior*, 19, 329–336.

Archard, D. 1998. *Sexual Consent.* Boulder, CO: Westview Press.

Becker, E., and Hennenberger, M. 1999. Disgraced General, Now Redeemed, Resurrected, Rewarded. *Pittsburgh Post-Gazette.* August 5.

Berdahl, J.L. 2007a. The Sexual Harassment of Uppity Women. *Journal of Applied Psychology*, 92, 425–437.

Berdahl, J.L. 2007b. Harassment Based on Sex: Protecting Social Status in the Context of Gender Hierarchy. *Academy of Management Review*, 32, 641–658.

Bhagwati, A. 2013. Why the Military Needs to Recruit and Promote More Women. *Washington Post.* May 24. http://articles.washingtonpost.com/2013-05-24/opinions/39492232_1_two-women-more-women-anu-bhagwati. Retrieved May 27, 2013.

Bowser, B.A. 2004. Rape in the Ranks. *PBS NewsHour Online.* April 26. http:www.pbs.org/newshour/bb/military/jan-june04/bab_04_26.html. Retrieved April 2, 2013.

Briggs, B. 2013. McCain Cannot Give "Unqualified Support" for Women Joining the Military Until Crisis Resolved. *NBC News.* June 4. http://usnews.nbcnews.com/_news/2013/06/04/18729878-mccain-cannot-give-unqualified-support-for-women-joining-the-military-until-crisis-resolved. Retrieved June 6, 2013.

Briggs, R.V. 1997. Comment: Old v. [sic] New Morality and Sexual Harassment. March 20. *Humanities and Social Sciences (H-NET) Online.* http://www.h-net.msu.edu/cgi-bin/logbrowse.pl?trx=vx&list=h-minerva & month=9703&week=d&msg=TKiX8iELg8vQyFrL1G%2B8g&user=&pw=. Retrieved May 29, 2013.
TKiX8iELg8vQyFrL1G%2B8g&user=&pw=. Retrieved May 29, 2013.

Brownmiller, S. 1975. *Against My Will: Men, Women, and Rape.* New York, NY: Bantam Books.

Burns, R. 2013. Military Assault Cases Put Pentagon Under Fire. *Huffington Post Politics.* May 15. http://www.huffingtonpost.com/2013/05/16/military-sexual-assault_n_3283666.html. Retrieved June 6, 2013.

Butler, J.S. 2000. Militarized Prostitution: The Untold Story (USA). In *War's Dirty Little Secret: Rape, Prostitution, and Other Crimes against Women.* L. Barstow (Ed.). Cleveland, OH: Pilgrim Press, pp. 204–232.

Cassata, D. 2013. Kirsten Gillibrand Targets Military Sexual Assault Law. *Huffington Post Politics*, July 29. http://www.huffingtonpost.com/2013/07/29/kirsten-gillibrand-military-sexual-assault_n_3669914.html. Retrieved August 12, 2013.

Chamberlain, L.J., Crowley, M., Tope, D., and Hodson, R. 2008. Sexual Harassment in Organizational Context. *Work and Occupations*, 35, 262–295.

Chang, I. 1997. *Rape of Nanking: The Forgotten Holocaust of World War II.* New York, NY: Basic Books.

Cicoca v. Rumsfeld et al. 2013. American Association of University Women (AAUW). http://www.aauw.org/resource/cioca-et-al-v-rumsfeld-et-al/. Retrieved December 28, 2013.

Clift, E. 2013. Air Force Blames Increase in Military Rape Hookup Culture. *U.S. News Report.* May 8. http://www.thedailybeast.com/articles/2013/05/08/air-force-general-blames-increase-in-military-rape-on-hookup-culture.html. Retrieved May 19, 2013.

Cohn, M. 2006. The Fear That Kills. Appalling New Evidence Reveals that Female Soldiers Serving in Iraq Made Fatal Decisions in their Attempts to Avoid Rape. January 31. http://www.alternet.org/story/31584/the_fear_that_kills. Retrieved. March 23, 2013.

Connell, R.W. 1987. *Gender and Power: Society, the Person, and Sexual Politics.* Stanford, CA: Stanford University Press.

Cooney, R.T., Segal, M.W., Segal, D.R., and Falk, W.W. 2003. Racial Differences in the Impact of Militry Service on the Socioeconomic Status of Women Veterans. *Armed Forces & Society,* 30, 1, 53–86.

Copelon, R. 1994. Surfacing Gender: Reconceptualizing Crimes Against Women in Times of War. In *Mass Rape*: The War Against Women in Bosnia-Herzegovina. A. Stiglmayer (Ed.). Lincoln, NE: University of Nebraska Press, pp. 197–218.

Cruz, L. 1999. Retired General Fined, Reprimanded for Affairs. *Associated Press.* March 18.

Culbertson, A.L., Rosenfeld, P., Booth-Kewley, S., and Magnusson, P. 1992. Assessment of Sexual Harassment in the Navy: Results of the 1989 Navy-wide Survey. Report No. NPRDC TR 92-11. Navy Perseonnel Research Development Center, San Diego, CA.

Dansby, M.R., and Landis, D. (1998). Race, Gender, and Representation Index as Predictors of an Equal Opportunity Climate in Military Organizations. *Military Psychology,* 10, 2, 87–105.

Dansby, M.R., and Landis, D. 1998. Race, Gender, and Representation Index as Predictors Military Officers. *Journal of Organizational Behavior,* 22, 689–702.

Dansky, B.S., and Kilpatrick, D.G. 1997. Effects of Sexual Harassment. In *Sexual Harassment: Theory, Research, and Practice.* W. O'Donohue (Ed.). Boston, MA: Allyn & Bacon Press, pp. 152–174.

Day, K. 1994. Conceptualizing Women's Fear of Sexual Assault on Campus: A Review of Causes and Recommendation s for Change. *Environment and Behavior,* 26, 6, 742–765.

Defense Advisory Committee on Women in the Services (DACOWITS). 2012. Status Report. http://dacowits.defense.gov/Portals/48/Documents/Reports/2012/Annual%20Report/dacowits2012report.pdf. Retrieved January 26, 2013.

Dekker, I., and Barling, J. 1998. Personal and Organizational Predictors of Workplace Sexual Harassment of Women by Men. *Journal of Occupational Health Psychology,* 3, 7–18.

Department of Defense (DoD). 2005. Report on the Service Academy Sexual Assault and Leadership Survey. Office of the Inspector General. Project No. 2003C004. March 4.

Department of Defense. 2012. Annual Report on Sexual in the Military. Sexual Assault Prevention and Reponse, Vol.1. FY 2012. http://www.sapr.mil/index.php/annual-reports. Retrieved May 19, 2013.

DeSousa, E., and Solberg, J. 2004. Women's and Men's Reactions to Man-to-Man Sexual Harassment: Does the Sexual Orientation of the Victim Matter? *Sex Roles,* 50, 623–639.

Editorial Board. 2012. Predators in the Ranks. *Washington Post.* July 4. http://articles.washingtonpost.com/2012-07-04/opinions/35488039_1_female-soldier-cases-of-sexual-assault-criminal-case. Retrieved May 15, 2013.

Ellison v. Brady. 1991. Columbia Law School. http://www2.columbia.edu/faulty-franke/Torts/Ellison.pdf; Brigham Young Law School. lawreviewbyu.edu/archives/1993/1/pin.pdf; and Sexual Harassment Training. sexualharassment.biz. Retrieved February 27, 2013.

Enloe, C. 1989. *Bananas, Beeches and Bases: Making Feminist Sense of International Politics.* Berkeley, CA: University of California Press.

Enloe, C. 1996. Spoils of War. *Ms. Magazine.* March/April, p. 15.

Faragher v. City of Boca Raton. 1998. Cornell University Law School. http://www.law.cornell.edu/supct/html/97-282.ZO.html. Retrieved February 27, 2013.

Firestone, J.M., and Harris, R.J. 2008. The Impact of Sexual Harassment on Likelihood of Reenlistment in the U.S. Military, 2002. Defense Equal Opportunity Management Institute (DEOMI), Research Directorate. Internal Report No. 18-08. Summer.

Fitzgerald, L.F., Drasgow, F., and Magley, V.J. 1999. Sexual Harassment in the Armed Forces. A Test of An Integrated Model. *Military Psychology*, 11, 3, 329–343.

Forell, C.A., and Matthews, D.M. 2001. *A Law of Her Own: The Reasonable Woman as a Measure of Man.* New York, NY: New York University Press.

Francke, L.B. 1997. *Ground Zero: The Gender Wars in the Military.* New York, NY: Simon & Schuster.

General Loses Command. 1995. June 27. *The New York Times.* http://www.nytimes.com/1995/06/27/us/general-loses-command.html. Retrieved July 25, 2013.

Goldin, C. 2006. The Rising (And Then Declining) Significance of Gender. In *The Declining Significance of Gender?* F.D. Blau, M.C. Brinton and D.B. Grusky (Eds.). New York, NY: Russell Sage Foundation, pp. 67–101.

Goldstein, N. 2013. The Military Can't Handle the Truth. *The American Prospect.* May 10. http://prospect.org/article/military-cant-handle-truth. Retrieved June 22, 2013.

Grossman, D. 1995. *On Killing: The Psychological Cost of Learning to Kill in War and Society.* Boston, MA: Little, Brown and Company Books.

Gruber, J.E., and Bjorn, L. 1982. Blue Collar Blues: The Sexual Harassment of Women Autoworkers. *Work and Occupations*, 9, 3, 271–298.

Gruber, J.S.E. 1998. The Impact of Male Work Environments and Organizational Policies on Women's Experiences of Sexual Harassment. *Gender & Society*, 12, 3, 301–320.

Gutek, B.A. 1985. *Sex and the Workplace.* San Francisco, CA: Jossey-Bass Publishers.

Gutek, B.A., Cohen, A.G., and Konrad, A.M. 1990. Predicting Social-Sexual Behavior at Work: A Contact Hypothesis. *Academy of Management Journal*, 33, 3, 560–577.

Gutman, A. 2005. Unresolved Issues in Same-Sex Harassment. *The Industrial Psychologist*, 42, 3, 67–75.

Harkins, G. 2013. It's Time for a UCMJ Overhaul. *Army Times.* June 29. http://www.armytimes.com/article/20130629/NEWS/306290004/-s-time-UCMJ-overhaul-. Retrieved July 2, 2013.

Harrell, M.C., and Miller, L. 1997. *New Opportunities for Military: Effects upon Readiness, Cohesion, and Morale.* Santa Monica, CA: National Defense Research Institute (NDRI), RAND Publications.

Harris v. Forklift Systems. 1993. Cornell University Law School. http://www.law.cornell.edu/supct/html/92-1168.ZO.html. Retrieved February 27, 2013.

Harris, G.L.A. 2009. The Multifaceted Nature of White Female Attrition in the Military. *Journal of Public Management & Social Policy*, 15, 1, 71–93.

Hersh, S.M. 1970. *My Lai 4: A Report on the Massacre and Its Aftermath*. New York, NY: Random House.
Hosek, S.D., Tiemeyer, P., Kilburn, R., Strong, D.A., Ducksworth, S., and Ray, R. 2001. *Minority and Gender Differences in Officer Career Progression*. Santa Monica, CA: RAND Publications.
Howard, J. 1999. Pilot Dismissed from Air Force: Childhood Dreams End in Court-Martial. *Associated Press*. April 29.
Hunter, M. 2007. *Honor Betrayed; Sexual Abuse in America's Military*. Ft. Lee, NJ: Barricade Press.
Janda, L. 2002. *Stronger Than Custom: West Point and the Admission of Women*. Westport, CT: Praeger Publishers.
Johnson v. Transportation Agency, Santa Clara County. 1987. Cornell University Law School. http://www.lw.cornell.edu/supremecourt/text/480/616. Retrieved February 1, 2013.
Jones, K. 2006. Fort Hood-Based Soldier "Loved People, and They Knew It." *Associated Press/ Temple Daily Telegram*. March 21.
Kanter, R.M. 1977. *Men and Women of the Corporation*. New York, NY: Basic Books, Inc.
Katz, E. 2012. Repored Sexual Assault at Military Academies Continue to Rise. *Government Executive*. December 27. http://www.govexec.com/defense/2012/12/reported-sexual-assaults-military-academies-continue-rise/60361/. Retrieved March 13, 2013.
Katz, R.C., Hannon, R., and Whitten, L. 1996. Effects of Gender and Situation on the Perception of Sexual Harassment. *Sex Roles*, 34, 1/2, 35–42.
Kempster, N. 1993. What Really Happened at Tailhook Convention Scandal: The Pentagon Report Georgraphically Describes How Fraternity-Style Hi-Jinks Turned into Hall pf Horrors. *Los Angeles Times*. April 24. http://articles.latimes.com/1993-04-24/news/mn-26672_1_tailhook-convention. Retrieved March 23, 2013.
Kernoff-Mansfield, P., Barthlow Koch, P., Henderson, J., Vicary, J.R., Cohn, M., and Young, E.W. 1991. The Job Climate for Women in Traditionally Male Blue-Collar Occupations. *Sex Roles*, 25, 12, 63–79.
Kim, E. 1997. Sexual Harassment Alleged Against Admiral, Top Army Official. *Associated Press*. May 31.
Kimes, P. 2011. Troops' Sexual Assault Lawsuit Dismissed. December 13. *Army Times*. http://www.armytimes.com/article/20111213/NEWS/112130326/Troops-sexual-assault-lawsuit-dismissed. Retrieved May 22, 2013.
Klay and Hellmer v. Panetta et al. 2013. U.S. Government Printing Office. http://www.gpo.gov/fdsys/pkg/uscourts-dcd-1_12-cv-00350/pdf/USCOURTS-dcd-1_12-cv-00350-0.pdf. Retrieved December 20, 2012.
Lardner, R., and Cassata, D. 2013. Lawmakers Press Forward on Sexual Assault Bill. *Associated Press*. June 6. http://bigstory.ap.org/article/lawmakers-press-forward-sexual-assault-bill. Retrieved July 7, 2013.
Lawrence, Q., and Penaloza, M. 2013a. Off the Battlefield, Military Women Face Risks from Males Troops. *National Public Radio (NPR)*. March 20. http://www.npr.org/2013/03/20/174756788/off-the-battlefield-military-women-face-risks-from-male-troops. Retrieved May 13, 2013.
Lawrence, Q., and Penaloza, M. 2013b. Sexual Violence Victims Say Military Justice System is "Broken." *National Public Radio (NPR)*. March 21. http://www.npr.org/2013/03/21/174840895/sexual-violence-victims-say-military-justice-system-is-broken. Retrieved May 13, 2013.

Lehr, D.M. 1993. Madwoman in the Military's Attic: Mental Health and Defense Department Policy in the Lives of U.S. Air Force Wives. Ph.D. Dissertation, Union Institute, Cincinnati, OH.

LeShan, L. 2002. *The Psychology of War: Comprehending Its Mystique and Its Madness*. New York, NY: Helios Press.

Lisak, D. 2002. Rape Fact Sheet. U.S. Army. http://www.sexualassault.army.mil/files/RAPE_FACT_SHEET.pdf. Retrieved March 26, 2013.

Lunney, K. 2013. Military Ditches Racy Magazines. *Government Executive*. July 31. http://www.govexec.com/defense/2013/07/military-services-ditch-racy-magazines/67835/. Retrieved August 3.

MacKinnon, C. 1982. Feminism, Marxism, Method, and the State. An Agenda for Theory. *Journal of Women in Culture and Society*, 7, 31, 515–544. http://www2.law.columbia.edu/faculty_franke/Certification%20Readings/catherine-mackinnon-feminism-marxism-method-and-the-state-an-agenda-for-theory1.pdf. Retrieved January 24, 2013.

Magley, V.J., Waldo, C.R., and Fitzgerald, L.F. 1999. The Impact of Sexual Harassment on Military Personnel: Is it the Same for Men and Women? *Military Psychology*, 11, 3, 283–302.

Malovich, N.J., and Stake, J.E. 1990. Sexual Harassment on Campus: Individual Differences in Attitudes and Beliefs. *Psychology of Women Quarterly*, 14, 63–81.

Marquet and Kendzior v. Gates et al. 2012. http://www.mdd.uscourts.gov/opinions/12-cv-2184 kendzior MTD.pdf.

Marquis, C. 2000. Army Confirms Officer's Claim of Harassment. *New York Times*. May 11. http://www.nytimes.com/2000/05/11/us/army-confirms-officer-s-claim-of-harassment.html. Retrieved March 23, 2013.

McDonald, N. 2013. The U.S. Military Surge in Sexual Assaults. *CBC News*. May 13. http://www.cbc.ca/news/world/neil-macdonald-the-u-s-military-surge-in-sexual-assaults-1.1330526. Retrieved May 27, 2013.

McDonough, K. 2013. Petraeus Apologizes for Affair with An Eye Toward What's Next. *Salon News*. March 27. http://www.salon.com/2013/03/27/petraeus_apologizes_for_affair_with_an_eye_toward_whats_next/. Retrieved May 19, 2013.

McHugh, J. 2004. Congresswomen Urge Punishment for Sexual Assaults. *Army Times*. April 12.

McLaughlin, H., Uggen, C., and Blackstone, A. 2012. Sexual Harassment, Workplace Authority and the Paradox of Power. *American Sociological Review*, 77, 4, 625–647.

Mehay, S.L., and Hirsch, B.T. 1996. The Post Military Earnings of Female Veterans. *Industrial Relations*, 35, 2, 197–217.

Meritor Savings Bank, FSB v. Vinson. 1998. http://www.caselaw.lp.findlaw.com/script/getcase.pl?court=US&vol=477&invol=57. Retrieved February 1, 2013.

Military Leadership Diversity Commission (MLDC). 2011. From Representation to Inclusion: Diversity Leadership for the 21st-Century. March 15. http://www.hsdl.org/?view&did=715693. Retrieved January 26, 2013.

Miller, L.L. 1997. Not Just Weapons of the Weak: Gender Harassment as a Form of Protest for Army Men. *Social Psychology Quarterly*, 60, 1, 37–51.

Mitchell, B. 1989. *Weak Link: The Feminization of the American Military*. Washington, DC: Regnery Publications.

Mitchell, B. 1997. *Women in the Military: Flirting with Disaster*. Washington, DC: Regnery Publishing.

Monahan, E.M., and Neidel-Greenlee, R. 2010. *A Few Good Women: America's Military Women from World War I to the Wars in Iraq and Afghanistan*. New York, NY: Anchor Books, a Division of Random House, Inc.

Montagne, R., and Lawrence, Q. 2013. What Does It Mean To Be a Woman in the U.S. Military? *National Public Radio (NPR)*. March 22. http://www.npr.org/2013/03/22/175014364/what-does-it-mean-to-be-a-woman-in-the-u-s-military. Retrieved May 13, 2013.

Moon, K. 1997. *Sex among Allies: Military Prostitution in U.S.-Korean Relations*. New York, NY: Columbia University Press.

Murdoch, M., Bradley, A., Mather, S.H., Kelin, R.E., Turner, C.L., and Yano, E.M. 2004. Women and War: What Physicians Should Know. *Journal of General Internal Medicine*, 21 (Supplement), S5–S10.

Murnane, L.S. 2007. Legal Impediments to Service: Women in the Military and the Rule of Law. *Duke Journal of Gender Law and Policy*, 14, 1061–1096.

Niebuhr, R.E. 1997. Sexual Harassment in the Military. In *Sexual Harassment: Theory, Research, and Treatment*. W. O'Donohue (Ed.). Boston, MA: Allyn & Bacon Publishers, pp. 250–262.

Norris, J., Nurris, P.S., and Dimeff, L.A. 1996. Through Her Eyes: Factors Affecting Women's Perception of and Resistance to Acquaintance Sexual Aggression Threat. *Psychology of Women Quarterly*, 20, 1, 123–145.

O'Hare, E.A., and O'Donohoe, W. 1998. Sexual Harassment: Identifying Risk Factors. *Archives of Sexual Behavior*, 27, 561–580.

Oncale v. Sundowner Systems. 1998. Cornell University Law School. http://www.law.cornell.edu/text/523/75. Retrieved July 30, 2013.

Orloff v. Willoughby, 345 U.S. 83, 94, 1953. Cornell University Law School. http://www.law.cornell.edu/supremecourt/text/345/83. Retrieved February 23, 2013.

Park, S. 1999. White Women Lead Military in Dropping Out. *USA Today*. March 26.

Parrish, N. 2012. The Pentagon Is Camouflaging the Truth about Rape in the Military. *Huffington Post*. April 20. http://usmvaw.com/2012/04/23/the-pentagon-is-camouflaging-the-truth-about-rape-in-the-military/. Retrieved January 26, 2013.

Pateman, C. 1988. *The Sexual Contract*. Stanford, CA: Stanford University Press.

Pazy, A., and Oron, I. 2001. Sex Proportion and Performance Evaluation among High Ranking. Military Officers. *Journal of Organizational Behavior*, 22, 6, 6, 689–702.

Pinkston, D.L. 1993. Redefining Objectivity: The Case of the Reasonable Woman Standard in Hostile Environment Claims. *Brigham Young Law Review*, 1993, 1, 12, 363–383.

Priest, D., and Spinner, J. 1997. Army Misconduct Probe Digs Deeper, Aberdeen Commander's Departure May Become Issue in Courts-Martial. *Washington Post*. June 4.

Pryor, J.B. 1995. The Phenomenology of Sexual Harassment: Why Does Sexual Behavior Bother People in the Workplace? *Consulting Psychology Journal: Practice and Research*, 46, 3, 160–168.

Pryor, J.B., and Fitzgerald, L.F. 2003. Sexual Harassment Research in the United States. In *Bullying and Emotional Abuse in the Workplace: International Perspectives in Research and Practice*. S. Einarsen, H. Hoel, D. Zapf, and C. Cooper (Eds.). London; New York: Taylor and Francis Group, pp. 79–101.

Pupovac, J. 2005. Sexual Assaults Up 40% in 2005. *Army Times*. March 27.

Pupovac, J. 2008. Silenced in the Barracks. *In These Times*. March 3. http://inthesetimes.com/article/3541/silenced_in_the_barracks. Retrieved March 23, 2013.

Pynes, J.E. 2009. *Human Resources Management for Public and Nonprofit Organizations* (3rd Edition). Jossey-Bass Press. San Francisco, CA.

Reinders, L. 1992. A Reasonable Woman Approach to Hostile Environment Sexual Harassment: *Ellison v. Brady*, 924 F.2d 872 (9th Cir. 1991). *Journal of Urban and Contemporary Law*, 41, 227–242.

Ricks, T.E. 2004. Top Air Force Lawyer Steps Aside, Investigators Examine Alleged Sexual Conduct with Subordinate. *Washington Post*. September 30.

Rosen, L.N., Durand, D.B., Bliese, P.D., Halverson, R.R., Rotherberg, J.M., and Harrison, N.L. 1996. Cohesion and Readiness in Gender-Integrated Combat Service Support Units: The Impact of Acceptance of Women and Gender Ratio. *Armed Forces & Society*, 24, 4, 537–553.

Rospenda, K.M., Richman, J.A., and Nawyn, S.J. 1998. Doing Power: The Confluence of Gender, Race and Class in Contrapower Sexual Harassment. *Gender & Society*, 12, 40–60.

Sadler, A.G., Booth, B.M., Nielsen, D., and Doebbeling, B.N. 2000. Health-Related Consequences of Physical and Sexual Violence: Women in the Military. *Obstetrics & Gynecology*, 96, 3, 473–480.

Sanchez, R., and Phillips, D.T. 2008. *Wiser in Battle: A Soldier's Story*. New York, NY: Harper Collins e-books, Kindle Edition.

Schneider, K.T., Swan, S., and Fitzgerald, L.F. 1997. Job-related and Psychological Effects of Sexual Harassment in the Workplace: Empirical Evidence from Two Organizations. *Journal of Applied Psychology*, 82, 404–415.

Schulz, V. 2003. The Sensitized Workplace. *Yale Law Journal*, 112, 2061–2193.

Schutt, E. 1995. Navy Kills Promotion of Two to Admirals. *New York Times*. October 13, p. A25.

Segal, D.R., and Segal, M.W. 2004. American Military Population. *Population Bulletin*, 59, 4, 1–44.

Segal, M.W., Bachman, D.R., Freedman-Doan, P., and O'Malley, P.M. 1998. Gender and the Propensity to Enlist in the U.S. Military. *Gender Issues*, 16, 3, 65–87.

Seifert, R. 1994. War and Rape: A Preliminary Analysis. In *Mass Rape: The War against Women in Bosnia-Herzegovina*. Lincoln, NE: University of Nebraska Press.

Shear, M.D. 2012. Petraeus Quits, Evidence of Affair was Found by F.B.I. *New York Times*, November 9. http://www.nytimes.com/2012/11/10/us/citing-affair-petraeus-resigns-as-cia-director.html?pagewanted=all. Retrieved March 27, 2013.

Shenon, P. 1997. Military Morality: The Overview; Cohen Criticized for His Support of a Top General. *New York Times*. June 6.

Shin, A. 2013. Women Accusing 3 from Naval Academy of Rape "Didn't Want Anyone Else to Get in Trouble." *Washington Post*. August 28. http://articles.washingtonpost.com/2013-08-28/local/41521370_1_accuser-young-woman-alleged-assault. Retrieved August 30, 2013.

Skinkman, P.D. 2013. Army Investigates Sexual Assault Prevention Worker Accused of Sexual Assault. May 15. *U.S. News and World Report*. http://www.usnews.com/news/articles/2013/05/15/army-investigates-sexual-assault-prevention-worker-accused-of-sexual-assault. Retrieved May 16, 2013.

Snyder, R.C. 2003. The Citizen-Soldier Tradition and Gender Integration of the U.S. Military. *Armed Forces & Society*, 29, 2, 185–204.

Sochting, I., Fairbrother, N., and Koch, W.J. 2004. Sexual Assault of Women Prevention Efforts and Risk Factors. *Violence against Women*, 10, 1, 73–93.

Solaro, E. 2006. *Women in the Line of Fire: What You Should Know about Women in the Military*. Emeryville, CA: Seal Press.

Stiehm, J.H. 1989. *Arms and the Enlisted Woman*. Philadelphia, PA: Temple University Press.

The Invisible War. 2012. Directed by Kirby Dick. Los Angeles, CA: Cinedigm, Documentary/film.

Tucker, E. 2012. 8 Women File Lawsuit, Accuse Military of Having "High Tolerance for Sexual Predators in Their Ranks." *Huffington Post*. March 6. http://www.huffingtonpost.com/2012/03/06/military-rape-lawsuit_n_1324899.html. Retrieved January 26, 2013.

Uggen, C., and Blackstone, A. 2004. Sexual Harassment as a Gendered Expression of Power. *American Sociological Review*, 69, 64–92.

United States v. Cisler, 33 M.J. 503 (A.F.C.M.R.), 2000.

United States v. Cisler. 1991. In Strite Murmane, L. 2007. Legal Impediments to Service: Women in the Military and the Rule of Law. *Duke Journal of Gender Law and Policy*, 14, 1061–1096. http://scholarship.law.duke.edu/cgi/viewcontent.cgi?article=1134&content=djglp. Retrieved January 28, 2013.

United States v. Hebert, No. ACM 29622, 1993 WL, 430214, at 1-10 (A.F.C.M.R.).

United States v. McCreary, No. ACM 30753, 1995 WL 77637 (A.F. Ct. Crim. App. February 15, 1995), review denied, 43 M.J. 157 (C.A.A.F), 1995.

United States v. Reeves, 61 M.J. 108 (C.A.A.F.), 2005.

United States v. Shober, 26 M.J. 502 (A.F.C.M.R.), 1986.

United States v. Simpson, 58 M.J. 368 (C.A.A.F.), 2003.

U.S. Census. 2010. Age and Sex Composition. 2010 Census Briefs. http://www.census.gov/prod/cen2010briefs/c2010br-03.pdf. Retrieved January 29, 2013.

U.S. General Accountability Office (GAO). 2011. Preventing Sexual Harassment. DoD Needs Greater Leadership Commitment and an Oversight Framework. GAO-11-809. September 11.

U.S. General Accountability Office (GAO). 2013. Military Personnel: DoD Has Taken Steps to Meet the Health Needs of Deployed Servicewomen, But Actions Are Needed to Enhance Care for Sexual Assault Victims. GAO-13-182. January.

U.S. Merit Systems Protection Board (USMSPB). 1981. *Sexual Harassment in the Federal Government: Is It a Problem?* Washington, DC: U.S. Government Printing Office.

U.S. Merit Systems Protection Board (USMSPB). 1987. *Sexual Harassment of Federal Workers: An Update*. Washington, DC: U.S. Government Printing Office.

U.S. Merit Systems Protection Board (USMSPB). 1994. *Sexual Harassment in the Federal Workplace: Trends, Progress and Continuing Challenges*. Washington, DC: U.S. Government Printing Office.

Van Creveld, M. 2000. The Great Illusion: Women in the Military. *Millennium: Journal of International Studies*, 29, 2, 429–442.

Van Creveld, M. 2001. *Men, Women & War: Do Women Belong in the Front Line?* New York, NY: Cassell Publishing, a Division of Barnes & Noble, Inc.

Vistica, G.L. 1995. *Fall from Glory: The Men Who Sank the U.S. Navy*. New York, NY: Touchstone Books.

Waldo, C.R., Berdahl, J.L., & Fitzgerald, L.F. 1998. Are Men Sexually Harassed? If So, By Whom? *Law and Human Behavior*, 22, 59–79.

Watkatsuki, Y., and Shaughnessy, L. 2013. Two U.S. Servicemen Imprisoned for Rape in Japan. *CNN*. March 1. http://www.cnn.com/2013/03/01/world/asia/japan-u-s-rape-sentencing/index.html. Retrieved April 2, 2013.

West, C., and Zimmer, D.H. 1987. Doing Gender. *Gender & Society*, 1, 125–151.

Whitlock, C. 2012. Air Force Investigates Growing Sex-Abuse Scandal. *Washington Post*. June 28. http://articles.washingtonpost.com/2012-06-28/news/35461886_1_sexual-misconduct-sexual-assault-female-recruits. Retrieved March 23, 2013.

Whitlock, C. 2013a. General's Promotion Blocked Over Her Dismissal of Sexual-Assault Verdict. *Washington Post.* May 6. http://articles.washingtonpost.com/2013-05-06/world/39060954_1_sexual-assault-jury-commander. Retrieved May 12, 2013.

Whitlock, C. 2013b. Obama Delivers Blunt Message on Sexual Assaults in the Military. *Washington Post.* May 7. http://articles.washingtonpost.com/2013-05-07/world/39078504_1_sexual-assault-offenders-kirsten-gillibrand. Retrieved May 16, 2013.

Whitlock, C. 2013c. Sordid Details Spill Out in Rare Court Martial of a General on Sex Charges. *Washington Post.* May 14. http://articles.washingtonpost.com/2013-08-14/world/41408586_1_army-ranger-sinclair-military-law. Retrieved May 15, 2013.

Whitlock, C. 2013d. Some in Congress Want Changes in Military Law as a Result of Sex Crimes. *Washington Post.* May 15. http://www.washingtonpost.com/world/national-security/some-in-congress-want-changes-in-military-law-as-a-result-of-sex-crimes/2013/05/672a2a8a_bd8b-11e2-a31d-a41b2414d001_story.html. Retrieved May 16, 2013.

Whitlock, C. 2013e. Hagel Orders Retraining of Sex Assault Prevention Officers; Army Sergeant Investigated. *Washington Post.* May 14. http://www.washingtonpost.com/world/national-security/hagel-orders-retraining-of-sex-assault-prevention-officers-army-sergeant-investigated/2013/05/14/38473bc8-bcfg-11e2-9b09-1638acc3942e_story.html. Retrieved May 15, 2013.

Whitlock, C. 2013f. Air Force General's Reversal of Pilot's Sexual Assault Conviction Angers Lawmakers. *Washington Post.* March 8. http://www.washingtonpost.com/world/national-security/air-force-generals-reversal-of-pilots-sexual-assault-conviction-angers-lawmakers/2013/03/08/f84b49c2-8816-11e2-8646-d5742/6d3c8c_story.html. Retrieved May 13, 2013.

Wilcox, C. 1992. Race, Gender, and Support for Women in the Military. *Social Science Quarterly,* 73, 2, 310–323.

Williams, J.H., Fitzgerald, L.F., and Drasgow, F. 1999. The Effects of Organizational Practices on Sexual Harassment and Individual Outcomes in the Military. *Military Psychology,* 11, 3, 303–328.

Wright, A. 2008. Is There An Army Cover-Up of Rape and Murder of Women Soldiers? *Common Dreams News Center.* April 28. https://www.commondreams.org/archive/2008/04/28/8564. Retrieved March 23, 2013.

Zimmerman, J. 1995. Tailspin: *Women at War in the Wake of Tailhook.* New York, NY: Doubleday Press.

Chapter 6

Major General Marcelite J. Harris, in person at her home on August 28, 2012 and via telephone on August 31, 2012.

Brigadier General Wilma L. Vaught (with Marilla Cushman, Director of Public Relations for the Women in Military Service for America Memorial [WIMSA] Foundation present), in person at her office on August 23, 2012.

Chapter 7

Ms. Sharron Frontiero Cohen, via questionnaire on July 13, 2012.

Msgt. Judith Hatch, in person at her home on September 8, 2012.

Mrs. Anna Flynn Monkiewicz, in person at her home on July 11, 2012.

Colonel Pamela Rodriguez, in person on September 8, 2012.
Dr. Rita F. Sumner, in person at her place of employment on June 21, 2012.
Chief Warrant Officer (CWO) 5 Trish Thompson, in person on September 7, 2012.
Probert, B., Ewer, P., and Whiting, K. 1998. *Gender Pay Equity in Australian Higher Education*. Melbourne National Tertiary Education Union. South Melbourne, Australia.

Chapter 8

Ms. Maria "Zoe" Dunning, in person on September 9, 2012.
Dr. Darlene Iskra, in person at her home on July 9, 2012.
Ms. Rose Marie Jackson, in person on June 25, 2012.
Ms. Yona Owens, via telephone on July 20, 2012.

Chapter 9

Ms. Sandra Intorre, in person at her home on August 22, 2012.
Mrs. Tiffany Kravec-Kelly, via Skype on July 13, 2012.
Command Sergeant Major (CSM) Cynthia Pritchett, via telephone on August 24, 2012.
Colonel Beverly "Sam" Stipe, via telephone on August 30, 2012.
Ms. Michelle Wilmot, via Skype on July 18, 2012.

Section 3

Herbert, M.S. 1998. *Camouflage Isn't Only for Combat: Gender, Sexuality, and Women in the Military*. New York; London: New York University Press.
Segal, M.W. 1995. Women's Military Roles Cross-Nationally, Past, Present and Future. *Gender & Society*, 9, 6, 757–775.

Chapter 10

Acker, J. 1992. Gendered Institutions. *Contemporary Sociology*, 21, 565–569.
American Civil Liberties Union (ACLU). Combat Exclusion Policy for Women. https://www.aclu.org/combat-exclusion-policy-women. Retrieved September 8, 2013.
Andrews, P.H. 1992. Sex and Gender Differences in Group Communication: Impact on the Facilitation Process. *Small Group Research*, 23, 1, 74–94.
Barkolow, C. 1990. *In the Men's House*. New York, NY: Poseidon Press.
Belz, H. 1992. Liberty and Equality for Whom? How to Think Inclusively about the Constitution and the Bill of Rights. *The History Teacher*, 25, 3, 263–277.
Bem, S.L. 1993. *The Lens of Gender: Transforming the Debate on Sexual Inequality*. New Haven, CT: Yale University Press.
Bevans, M. 1960. *McCall's Book of Everyday Etiquette*. New York, NY: Golden Press.
Buescher, J. n.d. Voting Rights and the 14th Amendment. http://teachinghistory.org/history-content/ask-a-historian/23652. Retrieved January 27, 2013.

Burke, C. 1996. Pernicious Cohesion. In *It's Our Military Too! Women and the U.S. Military*. J. H. Stiehm (Ed.). Philadelphia, PA: Temple University Press, pp. 205–219.
Demographics Profile of the Military Community. 2011. November. http://www.militaryonesource.mil/12038/MOS/Reports/2011_Demographics_Report.pdf. Retrieved September 8, 2013.
Deutsch, F.M., and Saxton, S.E. 1998. Traditional Ideologies, Nontraditional Lives. *Sex Roles*, 38, 516, 331–362.
Ellefson, K.G. 1998. *Advancing Army Women as Senior Leaders—Understanding the Obstacles*. Carlisle, PA: U.S. Army War College.
Fiske, S.T., Cuddy, A.J.C., Glick, P., and Xu, J. 2002. A Model of (Often Mixed) Stereotype Content: Competence and Warmth Respectively Follow from Perceived Status and Competition. *Journal of Personality and Social Psychology*, 82, 878–902.
Frontierro v. Cohen, 1973.
GenderGap.com. 2000. Women and the Military. July 4. http://www.GenderGap.com/military.htm. December 13, 2005.
Goffman, E. 1977. The Arrangement between the Sexes. *Theory and Society*, 4, 301–331.
Goldwin, R.A. 1990. *Why Blacks, Women, and Jews Are Not Mentioned in the Constitution*. Washington, DC: Aei Press.
Gross, J. 1990. Navy Is Urged to Root Out Lesbians Despite Abilities. *New York Times*. September 2, p. 24.
Gunderson, J.R. 1987. Independence, Citizenship, and the American Revolution. *Signs*, 13, 1, 59–77.
Gutek, B., Larwood, L., and Stromberg, A. 1986. Women at Work. In the *International Review of Industrial and Organizational Psychology*. C.L. Cooper and I. Robertson (Eds.). New York, NY: Wiley Press, pp. 217–234.
Gutman, S. 1997. Sex and the Soldier. *The New Republic*. February 24, pp. 18–22.
Harris, G.L.A. 2009. The Multifaceted Nature of White Female Attrition in the Military. *Journal of Public Management & Social Policy*, 15, 1, 71–93.
Herbert, M.S. 1998. *Camouflage Isn't Only for Combat: Gender, Sexuality, and Women in the Military*. New York; London: New York University Press.
Herrmann, J. 2008. *The National Organization for Women and the Fight for the Equal Rights Amendment*. Frankfurt; Munich, Germany: GRIN Verlag Publishers.
Hoff, J. 1991. *Law, Gender, & Injustice: A Legal History of U.S. Women*. New York, NY: New York University Press.
Holm, J. 1992. *Women in the Military: An Unfinished Revolution* (Revised Edition). Novato, CA: Presidio Press.
Honey, M. 1984. *Creating Rosie the Riveter: Class, Gender, and Propaganda during World War II*. Amherst, MA: University of Massachusetts Press.
Hopfl, H.J. 2003. Becoming a (Virile) Member: Women and the Military Body. *Body & Society*, 9, 4, 13–30.
Horrigan, C. 1992. The Combat Exclusion Rule and Equal Protection. *Santa Clara Law Review*, 32, 1, 229–263.
Kerber, L.K. 1998. The Paradox of Women's Citizenship in the Early Republic: The Case of *Martin v. Massachusetts*, 1805. *American Historical Review*, April, 349–378.
Kite, M.E., and Deaux, K. 1987. Gender Belief Systems: Homosexuality and the Implicit Inversion Theory. *Psychology of Women Quarterly*, 11, 83–96.

Lewis, J. 2003. Representation of Women in the Constitution. In *Women and the United States Constitution: History, Interpretation, and Practice*. S.A. Schwarzenbach and P. Smith (Eds.). New York, NY: Columbia University Press, pp. 23–32.

Lowe, M.R. 1993. Beauty, Strength, and Grace: A Critical Analysis of Female Bodybuilding. Paper presented at the annual conference of the American Sociological Association. Miami, FL.

Mazur, D.H. 1998. Women, Responsibility, and the Military. *Notre Dame Law Review*, 74, 1, 1–45.

McElrath, K. 1992. Gender, Career Disruption and Academic Rewards. *Journal of Higher Education*, 63, 3, 269–281.

Morris, R.B. 1987. *The Forging of the Union, 1781–1789*. New York, NY: New American Nation Series/HarperCollins Children's Books.

Nadler, L.B., and Nadler, M.K. 1990. Perceptions of Sex Differences in Classroom Communication. *Women's Studies in Communication*, 13, 46–65.

Owens v. Brown, Leagle. 1978. http://www.leagle.com/decision/1987746455FSUPP291_1702.xmL/OWENSv.BROWN. Retrieved January 25, 2013.

Pazy, A., and Oron, I. 2001. Sex Proportion and Performance Evaluation among High Ranking Military Officers. *Journal of Organizational Behavior*, 22, 689–702.

Pearson, J.C. 1985. *Gender and Communication*. Dubuque, IA: William C. Brown Press.

Pharr, S. 1988. *Homophobia: A Weapon of Sexism*. Inverness, CA: Chardon Publishers.

Population Representation in the Military Services. FY 2011. Office of the Secretary of Defense, Personnel and Readiness. http://prhome.defense.gov/rfm/MPP/ACCESSION%20POLICY/PopRep2011/. Retrieved January 29, 2013.

Ridgeway, C.L., and Correll, S.J. 2004. Motherhood as a Status Characteristic. *Journal of Social Issues*, 60, 4, 683–700.

Schwarzenbach, S.A. 2003. Women and Constitutional Interpretation: The Forgotten Value of Civic Friendship. In *Women and the United States Constitution: History, Interpretation, and Practice*. S.A. Schwarzenbach and P. Smith (Eds.). New York, NY: Columbia University Press, pp. 1–19.

Segal, M.W. 1995. Women's Military Roles Cross-Nationally, Past, Present, and Future. *Gender & Society*, 9, 6, 757–775.

Sheppard, D.L. 1989. Organizations, Power and Sexuality: The Image and Self-Image of Women Managers. In *The Sexuality of Organization*. J. Hearn, D.L. Sheppard, P. Tancred-Sheriff, and G. Burrell (Eds.). London: Sage Publications, pp. 139–157.

Shilts, R. 1993. *Conducting Unbecoming: Gays and Lesbians in the U.S. Military*. New York, NY: St Martin's Press.

Siegel, R.B. 2002. She the People: The Nineteenth Amendment, Sex Equality, Federalism, and the Family. *Harvard Law Review*, 115, 58, 947–1045.

Smith-Rosenberg, C. 1992. Discovering the Subject of the 'Great Constitutional Discussion,' 1786–1789. *Journal of American History*, 79, 3, 841–873.

Snitow, A. 1990. A Gender Diary. In *Conflicts in Feminism*. M. Hirsch and E.F. Keller (Eds.). New York, NY: Routledge Press, pp. 9–43.

Snyder, R.C. 2003. The Citizen-Soldier Tradition and Gender Integration of the U.S. Military. *Armed Forces & Society*, 29, 2, 185–204.

Stewart, L.P., Stewart, A.D., Friedley, S.A., and Cooper, P.J. 1990. *Communication between the Sexes: Sex Differences and Sex-Role Stereotypes* (2nd Edition). Scottsdale, AZ: Gorsuch Scarisbrick Publishers.

Titunik, R.F. 2000. The First Wave: Gender Integration and Military Culture. *Armed Forces & Society*, 26, 2, 229–257.

U.S. Census Bureau. 2010. Demographic Profile. http://www.census.gov/popfinder/. Retrieved January 29, 2013.
West, C., and Zimmerman, D.H. 1987. Doing Gender. *Gender & Society*, 1, 125–151.
Young, I.M. 2005. The Logic of Masculine Protection: Reflections on the Current Security State. In *Women and Citizenship*. M. Friedman (Ed.). New York, NY: Oxford University Press, pp. 15–34.

Chapter 11

American Civil Liberties Union (ACLU). Combat Exclusion Policy for Women. https://www.aclu.org/combat-exclusion-policy-women. Retrieved September 8, 2013.
Associated Press. 2013. Infantry Skeptical about Women in Combat Units, Says Marine Commandant. February 1. http://www.foxnews.com/us/2013/02/01/infantry-skeptical-about-women-in-combat-units-says-marine-commandant/. Retrieved April 22, 2013.
Defense Advisory Committee on Women in the Services (DACOWITS). 2012. Status Report. http://dacowits.defense.gov/Portals/48/Documents/Reports/2012/Annual%20Report/dacowits2012report.pdf. Retrieved January 26, 2013.
Evans, B. 2013. Defense Department to Remove Female Combat Exclusion Policy. *Brandpoint Online Journalism*, Ohio University. January 28. http://www.ivn.us/2013/01/28/military-to-remove-female-combat-exclusion-policy/. Retrieved January 29, 2013.
Friedrich, E. 2012. Navy Pins First Nuclear-Qualified Female Submariners. December 5. http://www.kitsapsun.com/news/2012/dec/05/navy-pins-first-nuclear-qualified-female/#axzz21.ay2FBLh. Retrieved February 21, 2013.
Harrell, M.C., Beckett, M.K., Chien, C.S., and Sollinger, J.M. 2002. *The Status of Gender Integration in the Military: Analysis of Selected Occupations*. Santa Monica, CA: RAND Publications.
Harrell, M.C., and Miller, L. 1997. *New Opportunities for Military: Effects upon Readiness, Cohesion, and Morale*. Santa Monica, CA: National Defense Research Institute (NDRI), RAND Publications.
Harris, G.L.A. 2009. The Multifaceted Nature of White Female Attrition in the Military. *Journal of Public Management & Social Policy*, 15, 1, 71–93.
Holm, J. 1992. *Women in the Military: An Unfinished Revolution*. Revised Edition. Novato, CA: Presidio Press.
Kredo, A. 2013. Women in Combat Could Hurt Retention, Marines Study Suggest. *The Washington Free Beacon*. February 14. http://freebeacon.com/women-in-combat-could-hurt-retention-marines-study-suggests/. Retrieved April 21, 2013.
Migdal, A., and Leveille, V. 2013. Military Reveals Plans for Integrating Women into Combat Units, But Many Questions Remain. June 19. https://www.aclu.org/blog/womens-rights/military-reveals-plans-integrating-women-combat-units-many-questions-remain. Retrieved July 2, 2013.
Military Leadership Diversity Commission (MLDC). 2011. From Representation to Inclusion: Diversity Leadership for the 21st-Century. March 15. http://www.hsdl.org/?view&did=715693. Retrieved January 26, 2013.
Mount, M. 2010. Women to Begin Serving on Navy Submarines, *Officials Say*. April 29. http://www.cnn.com/2010/US/04/29/women.submarines/index.html. Retrieved August 22, 2010.

Sutton, J. 2013. Ending U.S. Combat Ban Will Even Career Playing Field, Servicewomen Say. January 23. *Reuters* and the *Chicago Tribune*. http://www.chicatribune.com/news/politics/sns-rt-us-usa-military-women-reactionbre90n046-20130123,0,6408329.story. Retrieved January 24.

U.S. Army. 2002. Women in the Army: An Annotated Bibliography. U.S. Army Research Institute for the Behavioral and Social Science. Special Report 48. May.

U.S. Secretary of Defense Chuck Hagel's Memorandum for Proposed Implementation Plans in Response to the January 24, 2013. Secretary of Defense Memorandum Regarding the Elimination of the 1994 Direct Ground Combat Definition and Assignment Rule. 2013. May 21. http://www.defense.gov/news/SecDefWISRMemo.pdf. Retrieved September 8, 2013.

U.S. Secretary of the Air Force Michael Donley's Memorandum on the Air Force's Implementation Plan for Integrating Women into Career Fields Engaged in Direct Ground Combat. 2013. April 24. http://www.defense.gov/news/Air_ForceWISRImplementationPlan.pdf. Retrieved September 12, 2013.

U.S. Secretary of the Army John McHugh's Memorandum Plan for Integration of Female Leaders and Soldiers Based on the Elimination of the 1994 Direct Ground Combat Definition and Assignment Rule (DGCDAR). 2013. April 19. http://www.defense.gov/news/ArmyWISRImplementationPlan.pdf. Retrieved September 12, 2013.

U.S. Secretary of the Navy Ray Maybus' Memorandum on the Department of the Navy Women in the Service Review Implementation Plan. 2013. May 2. http://www.defense.gov/news/NavyWISRImplementationPlan.pdf. Retrieved September 12, 2013.

U.S. Secretary of the Navy Ray Maybus' Memorandum on the Department of the Navy Women in the Service Review Implementation Plan for the Marine Corps. 2013. May 2. http://www.defense.gov/news/MarineCorpsWISRImplementationPlan.pdf. Retrieved September 12, 2013.

U.S. Special Operations Command (SOCOM) Commander Admiral William McRaven's Memorandum for the Army, Marine Corps, Navy and Air Force on the Implementation Plan for the Elimination of Direct Combat Assignment Rule. 2013. March 22. http://www.defense.gov/news/SOCOMWISRImplementationPlan.pdf. Retrieved September 12, 2013.

Watson, J. 2013. Marines Survey Lists Concerns on Women in Combat. February 1. http://bigstory.ap.org/article/marines-head-shares-skepticism-women-combat. Retrieved June 22, 2013.

Weber, C. 2010. Women to Begin Serving on Navy Submarines for the First Time. April 29. http://www.politicsdaily.com/2010/04/29/women-to-begin-serving-on-navy-submarines-for-the-first-time/. Retrieved August 22, 2010.

Women in the Military Services of America (WIMSA). 2011. Statistics on Women in the Military. As of November 30. http://www.womensmemorial.org/PDFs/StatsonWIM.pdf. Retrieved December 18, 2012.

Chapter 12

Asch, B.J., Miller, T., and Malchiodi, A. 2012. *A New Look at Gender and Minority Differences in Officer Career Progression in the Military*. Santa Monica, CA: RAND Publications.

Baldwin, J.N. 1996. Female Promotions in Male-dominated Organizations: The Case of the United States Military. *The Journal of Politics*, 58, 4, 1184–1197.

Burns, R. 2007. Bush Hears about Strain on Troops. *Associated Press*, August 31.

Burrell, L., Briley, D.D., and Fortado, J. 2003. Military Community Integration and Its Effect on Well-being and Retention. *Armed Forces & Society*, 30, 1, 7–24.

Defense Advisory Committee on Women in the Services (DACOWITS). 2003. Women in the Services Status Report. http://www.dacowits.defense.gov/Portals/48/Documents/Reports/2003/Annual/Report/dacowits2003report.pdf. Retrieved May 12, 2004.

Defense Advisory Committee on Women in the Services (DACOWITS). 2005. Annual Report. http://www.dacowits.defense.gov/portals/48/Documents/Reports/2005/AnnualReport/dacowits2005report.pdf.

Defense Advisory Committee on Women in the Services (DACOWITS). 2006. Status Report. http://www.dacowits.defense.gov/portals/48/Documents/Reports/2006/AnnualReport/dacowits2006report.pdf.

Defense Advisory Committee on Women in the Services (DACOWITS). 2012. Status Report. http://dacowits.defense.gov/Portals/48/Documents/Reports/2012/Annual%20Report/dacowits2012report.pdf. Retrieved January 26, 2013.

Department of Defense. 2004. Report on the Status of Female Members of the Armed Forces. Office of the Under Secretary of Defense for Personnel and Readiness. June.

Ellefson, K.G. 1998. *Advancing Army Women as Senior Leaders—Understanding the Obstacles*. Carlisle, PA: Army War College. (AD A344 984).

Harrell, M.C., Beckett, M.K., Chien, C.S., and Sollinger, J.M. 2002. *The Status of Gender Integration in the Military: Analysis of Selected Occupations*. Santa Monica, CA: RAND Publications.

Harrell, M.C., and Miller, L.L. 1997. *New Opportunities for Military Women: Effects upon Readiness, Cohesion, and Morale*. Santa Monica, CA: National Defense Research Institute, RAND Publications.

Harris, G.L.A. 2009a. The Multifaceted Nature of White Female Attrition in the Military. *Journal of Public Management & Social Policy*, 15, 1, 71–93.

Harris, G.L.A. 2009b. Recruiting, Retention and Race in the Military. *International Journal of Public Administration*, 32, 10, 803–828.

Harris, G.L.A. 2012. Multiple Marginality: How the Disproportionate Assignment of Women and Minorities to Manage Diversity Programs Reinforces and Multiplies Their Marginality. *Administration & Society*, 2012, 20, 10, 1–34.

Holm, J. 1992. *Women in the Military: An Unfinished Revolution*. Novato, CA: Presidio Press.

Hosek, S.D., Tiemeyer, P., Kilburn, R., Strong, D.A., Ducksworth, S., and Ray, R. 2001. *Minority and Gender Differences in Officer Career Progression*. Santa Monica, CA: RAND Publications.

Joint Economic Committee. 2007. Helping Military Moms Balance Family and Longer Deployments. Senator Charles Schumer (Chair) and Congresswoman Carolyn Maloney (Vice Chair). May 11.

Military Leadership Diversity Commission (MLDC). 2011. From Representation to Inclusion: Diversity Leadership for the 21st-Century. March 15. http://www.hsdl.org/?view&did=715693. Retrieved January 26, 2013.

Moore, B.L. 2002. The Propensity of Junior Enlisted Personnel to Remain in Today's Military. *Armed Forces & Society*, 28, 2, 257–278.

Moskos, C. 2005. Communication via e-mail. January 7.

Nataraj-Kirby, S., and Naftel, S. 2000. The Impact of Deployments on the Retention of Military Reservists. *Armed Forces & Society*, 26, 2, 259–284.

National Military Family Services (NMFS). 2005. Report on the Cycles of Deployment: An Analysis of Survey Responses from April through September 2005.

National Security Advisory Group. 2006. The U.S. Military: Under Strain and at Risk. January.
Population Representation in the Military Services. 2011. Office of the Undersecretary of Defense, Personnel and Readiness. http://prhome.defense.gov/portals/52/Documents/POPREP/poprep2011/contents/contents.html. Retrieved February 27, 2013.
Smith, S.D. 2006. Committee Examines Issue of Women Separating from Military. *Armed Forces Press Service*. August 28.
Tilley, J.A. 2013. A History of Women in the Coast Guard. http://www.uscg.mil/history/articles/WomeninCG.pdf. Retrieved September 14, 2013.
U.S. General Accountability Office (GAO). 1994. Military Academy: Gender and Racial Disparities. GAO/NSIAD-94-95. March.
U.S. General Accountability Office (GAO). 2001. Military Personnel: First-term Personnel Less Satisfied with Military Life than those in the Mid-career. GAO-02-200, December.
U.S. General Accountability Office (GAO). 2007. Military Personnel: Strategic Plan Needed to Address Army's Emerging Officer Accession and Retention Challenges. GAO-07-224. January.

Chapter 13

Baker, H. 2006. Women in Combat: A Culture Issue? U.S. Army War College. March. No. ADA 4439305.
Baum, C.L. 2002. The Effect of Work Interruptions on Women's Wages. *Labour*, 16, 1, 1–37.
Berger, M.C., Black, D.A., Amitabh, C., and Scott, F.A. 2003. Children, Non-Discriminatory Provision of Fringe Benefits, and Household Labor Market Decisions. In *Work, Well-Being and Public Policy*. S.W. Polachek and K. Tatsiramos (Eds.). Oxford, UK: Oxford University Press, pp. 309–349.
Bhagwati, A. 2013. Why the Military Needs to Recruit and Promote More Women. *Washington Post*. May 24. http://articles.washingtonpost.com/2013-05-24/opinions/39492232_1_two-women-more-women-anu-bhagwati. Retrieved May 27, 2013.
Blalock, H.M. 1967. *Toward a Theory of Minority Group Relations*. New York, NY: John Wiley Publishing.
Blau, F.D., Brinton, M.C., and Grusky, D.B. 2009. The Declining Significance of Gender? In *The Declining Significance of Gender?* F.D. Blau, M.C. Brinton and D.B. Grusky (Eds.). New York, NY: Russell Sage Foundation, pp. 3–34.
Budwig, M., and England, P. 2001. The Wage Penalty for Motherhood. *American Sociological Review*, 66, 2, 204–225.
Catalyst. 2013. Women CEOs of the Fortune 1000. http://www.catalyst.org/knowledge/women-ceos-fortune-1000. Retrieved September 18, 2013.
Chang, M.L. 2012. *Shortchanged: Why Women Have Less Wealth and What Can Be Done about It*. New York, NY: Oxford University Press.
Cooney, R.T., Weschler, S.M., Segal, D.R., and Falk, W.W. 2003. Racial Differences in the Impact of Military Service on the Socioeconomic Status of Women Veterans. *Armed Forces & Society*, 30, 1, 53–86.
Defense Advisory Committee on Women in the Services (DACOWITS). 2012. Status Report. http://dacowits.defense.gov/Portals/48/Documents/Reports/2012/Annual%20Report/dacowits2012report.pdf. Retrieved January 26, 2013.

DeGruy Leary, J. 2005. *Post Traumatic Slave Syndrome: America's Legacy of Enduring Injury and Healing*. Milwaukie, OR: Uptone Press.

Ellefson, K.G. 1998. *Advancing Army Women as Senior Leaders—Understanding the Obstacles*. Carlisle, PA: Army War College.

England, P. 2009. Toward Gender Equality: Progress and Bottlenecks. In *The Declining Significance of Gender?* F.D. Blau, M.C. Brinton and D.B. Grusky (Eds.). New York, NY: Russell Sage Foundation, pp. 245–264.

Fenner, L.M. 2001. Moving Targets: Women's Roles in the U.S. Military in the 21st Century. In *Women in Combat: Civic Duty or Military Liability?* L.M. Fenner and M.E. deYoung (Eds.). Washington, DC: Georgetown University Press, pp. 3–104.

Frederico, C.M., and Sidanius, J. 2002a. Racism, Ideology, and Affirmative Action, Revisited: The Antecedents and Consequences of "Principled Objections" to Affirmative Action. *Journal of Personality and Social Psychology*, 82, 488–502.

Frederico, C.M., and Sidanius, J. 2002b. Sophistication and the Antecedents of White's Racial Policy Attitudes: Racism, Ideology and Affirmative Action in America. *Public Opinion Quarterly*, 66, 145–176.

Friesbie, W.P., and Neidert, L. 1977. Inequality and the Relative Size of Minority Populations: A Comparative Analysis. *American Journal of Sociology*, 82, 1007–1030.

Goldin, C. 2009. The Rising (and Then Declining) Significance of Gender. In *The Declining Significance of Gender?* F.D. Blau, M.C. Brinton and D.B. Grusky (Eds.). New York, NY: Russell Sage Foundation, pp. 67–101.

Grimes, D.S. 2002. Challenging the Status Quo? Whiteness in the Diversity Management Literature. *Management Communication Quarterly*, 15, 381–409.

Harris, G.L.A. 2009. The Multifaceted Nature of White Female Attrition in the Military. *Journal of Public Management & Social Policy*, 2009, 15, 1, 71–93.

Harris, G.L.A. 2011. The Quest for Gender Equity. *Public Administration Review*, 71, 1, 123–126.

Hartmann, H., Rose, S.J., and Lovell, V. 2009. How Much Progress in Closing the Long Term Earnings Gap? In *The Declining Significance of Gender?* F.D. Blau, M.C. Brinton and D.B. Grusky (Eds.). New York, NY: Russell Sage Foundation, pp. 125–155.

Holm, J. 1992. *Women in the Military: An Unfinished Revolution* (Revised Edition). Novato, CA: Presidio Press.

Insight. 2010. Lifting as We Climb: Women of Color, Wealth and America's Future. Center for Community Economic Development. Spring. http://www.insightcced.org/uploads/CRWG/LiftingAsWeClimb-WomenWealth-Report-InsightCenter-Spring2010.pdf. Retrieved September 9, 2013.

Jackson, R.M. 2009. Opposing Forces: How, Why, and When Will Gender Inequality Disappear? In *The Declining Significance of Gender?* F.D. Blau, M.C. Brinton and D.B. Grusky (Eds.). New York, NY: Russell Sage Foundation, pp. 215–244.

Kanter, R.M. 1977. *Men and Women of the Corporation*. New York, NY: Basic Books.

Kanter, R.M. 1979. Power Failure in Management Circuits. *Harvard Business Review*, 57, 4, 65–75.

Kennedy-Pipe, C. 2000. Women and the Military. *Journal of Strategic Studies*, 23, 4, 32–50.

Kravitz, D.A., Klineberg, S.L., Avery, D.R., Nguyen, A.K., Lund, C., and Fu, E.J. 2000. Attitudes toward Affirmative Action: Correlations with Demographic Variables and with Beliefs about Targets, Actions, and Economic Effects. *Journal of Applied Social Psychology*, 30, 1109–1136.

Law, S.A. 1999. White Privilege and Affirmative Action. *Akron Law Review*, 32, 603–621.

Mazur, D.H. 1998. Women, Responsibility, and the Military. *Notre Dame Law Review*, 74, 1, 1–45.

Mehay, S.L., and Hirsch, B.T. 1996. The Post Military Earnings of Female Veterans. *Industrial Relations*, 35, 2, 197–217.

Military Leadership Diversity Commission (MLDC). 2011. From Representation to Inclusion: Diversity Leadership for the 21st-Century. March 15. http://www.hsdl.org/?view&did=715693. Retrieved January 26, 2013.

Patterson, M.B.D. 2000. America's Racial Unconscious: The Invisibility of Whiteness. In J.L. Kincheloe, S.R. Steinberg, N.M. Rodriguez, and R.E. Chennault (Eds.). *White Reign: Deploying Whiteness in America* (pp. 103–122). New York, NY: St. Martin's Press.

Polachek, S.W. 2009. How the Life-Cycle Human-Capital Model Explains Why the Gender Wage Gap Narrowed. In *The Declining Significance of Gender?* F.D. Blau, M.C. Brinton and D.B. Grusky (Eds.). New York, NY: Russell Sage Foundation, pp. 102–124.

Putko, M. 2008. The Combat Exclusion Policy in the Modern Security Environment. In *Women in Combat Compendium*. M. Putko and D.V. Johnson III (Eds.). Carlisle, PA: U.S. Army War College. January, pp. 1–20.

Renfro, C.L., Duran, A., Stephan, W.G., and Clason, D.L. 2006. The Role of Threat in Attitudes toward Affirmative Action and Its Beneficiaries. *Journal of Applied Social Psychology*, 36, 41–74.

Reskin, B.F., McBrier, D.B., and Kmec, J.A. 1999. The Determinants and Consequences of Workplace Sex and Race Composition. *American Review of Sociology*, 25, 335–361.

Ridgeway, C.L. 2009. Gender as an Organizing Force in Social Relations: Implications for the Future of Inequality. In *The Declining Significance of Gender?* F.D. Blau, M.C. Brinton and D.B. Grusky (Eds.). New York, NY: Russell Sage Foundation, pp. 265–288.

Ridgeway, C.L., and Correll, S.J. 2004. Motherhood as a Status Characteristic. *Journal of Social Issues*, 60, 4, 683–700.

Rosen, L.N., Durand, D.B., Blieses, P.D., Halverson, R.R., Rothberg, J.M., and Harrison, N.L. 1996. Cohesion and Readiness in Gender-Integrated Combat Service Support Units: The Impact of Acceptance of Women and Gender Ratio. *Armed Forces & Society*, 22, 537–553.

Schneider, B. 1987. The People Make the Place. *Personnel Psychology*, 40, 437–453.

Segal, D.R., and Segal, M.W. 2004. American Military Population. *Population Bulletin*, 59, 4, 1–44.

U.S. Bureau of Labor Statistics. 2013. Women in the Labor Force: A Databook. February. http://www.bls.gov/cps/wlf-databook-2012.pdf. Retrieved September 9, 2013.

U.S. Census Bureau. n.d. Age and Sex Composition: 2010. 2010 Census Briefs. http://www.census.gov/prod/cen2010/briefs/c2010br-03.pdf. Retrieved September 8, 2013.

U.S. General Accountability Office (GAO) 2007. Retirement Security: Women Face Challenges in Ensuring Financial Security in Retirement. GAO-08-105. Washington, DC: U.S. Government Printing Office.

U.S. Secret Service. n.d. Julia Pierson, Director, United States Secret Service. http://www.secretservice.gov/director.shtml. Retrieved May 20, 2013.

West, M., and Curtis, J.W. 2006. AAUP Faculty Gender Equity Indicators 2006. American Association of University Professors (AAUP). http://www.aaup.org/reports-publications/publications/see-all/aaup-faculty-gender-equity-indicators-2006. Retrieved September 15, 2013.

White House Council on Women and Girls. 2011. Women in America: Indicators of Social and Economic Well-Being. March. Prepared by the U.S. Department of Commerce and the Executive Office of the President of the United States, Office of Management and Budget. http://www.whitehouse.gov/sites/default/files/rss_viewer/Women_in_America.pdf. Retrieved September 9, 2013.

Yoder, J.D. 1991. Rethinking Tokenism: Looking Beyond Numbers. *Gender & Society*, 5, 178–192.

Chapter 14

Defense Advisory Committee on Women in the Services (DACOWITS). 2012. Status Report. http://dacowits.defense.gov/Portals/48/Documents/Reports/2012/Annual%20Report/dacowits2012report.pdf. Retrieved January 26, 2013.

Dockterman, E. 2013. Here's How Much Money the Government Shutdown Cost the Economy. *Time Swampland*. October 17. http://swampland.time.com/2013/10/17/heres-what-the-government-shutdown-cost-the-economy/. Retrieved October 24, 2013.

Fenner, L.M. 2001. Moving Targets: Women's Roles in the U.S. Military in the 21st Century. In *Women in Combat: Civic Duty or Military Liability?* L.M. Fenner and M.E. deYoung (Eds.). Washington, DC: Georgetown University Press, pp. 3–104.

Francke, L.B. 1997. *Ground Zero: The Gender Wars in the Military*. New York, NY: Simon & Schuster.

Harris, G.L.A. 2009. The Multifaceted Nature of White Female Attrition in the Military. *Journal of Public Management & Social Policy*, 15, 1, 71–93.

Holm, J. 1992. *Women in the Military: An Unfinished Revolution* (Revised Edition). Novato, CA: Presidio Press.

Jamieson, D. 2013. Shutdown Deal Gives Federal Workers First Raise in Three Years, Unless Congress Changes Its Mind. *Huffington Post Politics*. October 17. http://www.huffingtonpost.com/2013/10/17/government-shutdown-over_n_4116368.html. Retrieved October 24, 2013.

McCarthy, T., and Newell, J. 2013. Congress Passes Bill to Raise U.S. Debt Ceiling and End Shutdown. *The Guardian*. October 16. http://www.theguardian.com/world/2013/oct/16/us-debt-limit-brink-shutdown-senate-deal-live. Retrieved October 24, 2013.

Mead, M. 1949. *Male and Female. A Study of the Sexes in a Changing World*. New York: W. Morrow Publishing.

Peters, G., and Woolley, J.T. n.d. The American Presidency Project. Citation of Franklin D. Roosevelt, "Address at Los Angeles, California," October 1, 1935. http://www.presidency.ucsb.edu/ws/?pid=14953#axzz2jNiBa6tT. Retrieved October 1, 2013.

Serbu, J. 2013. Pentagon Says Shutdown Wasted at Least $600 Million. October 18. *Federal News Radio*. http://www.federalnewsradio.com/394/3484997/Pentagon-says-shutdown-wasted-at-least-600-million. Retrieved October 19, 2013.

Snyder, R.C. 2003. The Citizen-Soldier Tradition and Gender Integration of the U.S. Military. *Armed Forces & Society*, 29, 2, 185–204.

Index

Note: Locators followed by "*t*" denote tables in the text

A

Abu Ghraib prison scandal, 102
Active Component (AC), 259
Active guard reservist (AGR), 164
Aethelflaed, 32
AGR (Active guard reservist), 164
Air Defense Artillery, 204–206
Air Education and Training Command (AETC), 94
Air Force Academy, 190
Air Force Base (AFB), 69, 138
Air Force Institute of Technology (AFIT), 174
Air Force Officer Qualifying Test (AFOQT), 81
Air Force Qualifying Test (AFQT), 274
Air Force Special Operations Command (AFSOC), 265
Air Force Specialty Codes (AFSCs), 139, 170, 261
Air-land Battle Doctrine, 156
Air National Guard (ANG), 261, 272
Alexander II, Pope, 32
Amazons, 28, 30
American
    Civil War, 38
    experience, 37–56
    Legion, 184
    military, 37
    Red Cross, 38
American Civil Liberties Union (ACLU), 5, 175, 200, 255, 257, 268
Aquino, Corazon
    assassination attempts, 57
    feminine phrases of Tagalog, 58
Areas of concentration (AOC), 259
Arizona Air National Guard (AZANG), 169
Arizona Army National Guard (AZARNG), 155
Armed Forces Vocational Aptitude Battery (AFSVAB), 274
Armed Services Vocational Aptitude Battery (ASVAB), 217, 224
Army Air Corps, 184
Army Air Force Exchange Services (AAFES), 132
Army National Guard (ARNG), 155
ARNG (Army National Guard), 155
Arninatu, queen
    controlled Hausa empire, 29
    forged trade route agreement, 29
Aspin, Les, 71
AV-8B Harrier, 68
AZARNG (Arizona Army National Guard), 155

B

Barrow, Robert, 59
Barton, Clara (first president of American Red Cross), 38
Basic Officer Course (BOC), 264
Battle dress uniform (BDU), 107
Battle of Badr, 34
Battle of Bull Run, 38
Battle of Monmouth (1778), 39
Battle of the Bulge, 156
Battle of the Camels, 34
BCT (Brigade Combat Team), 259
Book of the Deeds of Arms and Chivalry, 34
Borginis, Sarah, 38
Boxer, Barbara (D-CA), 7

331

Bray, Linda
 female lead troops, 60
 Operation Urgent Fury, 60
Brennan, Justice, 253
Brewer, Lucy (first female marine), 38
Brigade Combat Team (BCT), 259
Bronze Star Medal, 222
Brown, Harold, 196, 199
Bureau of Naval Personnel, 181

C

Candace, Queen of Ethiopia
 encountered by Alexander, 29
 war plan, 29
Captain Mac. *See* McAfee, Mildred
Career Intermission Pilot Program (CIPP), 270
Care for Newborn Children (CNC), 271
Center for Military Readiness (CMR), 72
Central Intelligence Agency (CIA), 96, 164–165
Chief of Naval Operations (CNO), 59, 93
Chief Warrant Officer (CWO), 163
Cicoca v. Rumsfeld et al. (2013), 97–98
Citizenship, 182, 193–194, 200
 second-class, 251–252, 255
 woman's definition, 251
Citizen-soldier, 159
426th Civil Affairs Battalion, 80
Civil Rights Act (CRA) of 1964, 119, 252, 256
Clarke, Mary, 61
 practice of coeducational training, 62
Clarke, Mary (Major General), 288
Cleopatra VII of Egypt, 31
Clinton, Bill, 186–188
Clinton, Hillary Rodham, 252
COANG (Colorado Army National Guard), 164
Coast Guard, 67
Cochran, Jacqueline, 153
Cohen, Sharron Frontiero (second lieutenant), 173–178
Cohen, William (R-ME), 58
Cold War, 204
Collins, Susan (R-ME), 116
Colorado Army National Guard (COANG), 164
Combat exclusion policy, 11, 57–85, 183, 190–191, 194–195, 199–201, 206, 210–211, 215–216, 221–222, 225–226, 228, 236–238, 294–295
 Air Force
  not prevent women from aircraft, 59
  recruitment of women increased, 67
  women assigned to remote locations, 60

Congress, 70
DoD, 294–295
expanding female force, Marine Corps, 66
federal employees, 293–294
Holm, 60
less contentious Navy, 62
McPeak's judgement, 59
motherhood penalty, 284
obstructing advancement of women, Army, 61
participation in labor force, 284–285
path to full agency, 296
repealing, 295–296
 Air Force, 261
 army, 259–260
 BCT, 259
 impact, 269–272
 implementation to adhere, army, 260
 marine corps, 263–264
 navy, 261–263
 recruitment based on gender, 258
 retention programs, 271
 U.S. Special Operations Command, 265–266
 women in military, retention, 272, 275
revolution continues, 293–297
sexual assault against women, 289–290
women
 in combat, 60
 integration, 279
 and men earnings, 284
 in military, 296
Combat support force (CSF), 64
Command Sergeant Major (CSM), 208–209
Congressional Research Service (CRS), 15
Continental United States (CONUS), 76, 140, 152, 200, 213
Critical Skills Retention Bonus, 272
Cruz, Ted (R-TX), 7
CSM (Command Sergeant Major), 208–209
Cushman, Pauline, 38
CWO (Chief Warrant Officer), 163

D

DACOWITS. *See* Defense Advisory Committee on Women in the Services (DACOWITS)
Dahia, Queen of Carthage and Mauritania, 29
Defense Advisory Committee on Women in the Services (DACOWITS), 7, 41, 62, 131, 146, 210, 268, 287–288, 294

Defense Equal Opportunity Management
    Institute (DEOMI), 71
Defense Manpower Data Center (DMDC), 56
Democratic Republic of Congo, 29
Department of Defense (DoD), 5, 45, 63,
    183–185, 195, 196, 257, 268, 294
De Pisan, Christine (1390–1429), 33
Direct Combat Probability Coding (DCPC), 60
DoD (Department of Defense), 5, 45, 63,
    183–185, 195, 196, 257, 268, 294
Don't Ask, Don't Tell, and Don't Pursue policy,
    183–184, 187–188, 191, 246
Drill Sergeant/instructor, 209–210, 217–218
Dumbing down effect, 82
Dunning, Maria "Zoe," 183–192

E

Edmonds, Sarah Emma, 38
Eleanor of Aquitaine, 33
Enforcement of heterosexual gender role, 119
Equal Rights Amendment (ERA), 252, 254
Explosive Ordnance Demolition (EOD), 180

F

Fait accompli, 222
Feats of Arms and Chivalry, 33
Federal Bureau of Investigation (FBI), 43
Female engagement teams (FETs), 55
Female warriors. *See* Amazons
First attack land force. *See* Ground Combat
    Element (GCE)
Fly Girls. *See* Monkiewicz, Anna Flynn
Forgotten War. *See* Korean conflict
Forward operating base (FOB), 218
Foster, Jane, 68
Fourteenth Amendment to the U.S.
    Constitution, 252–256, 296
Free-fire zone, 244
Frontiero v. Laird (1970), 175
Frontiero v. Richardson (1973), 174–175

G

Gay/lesbian person, 184, 191
    ban on military service, 184, 186–189
Gender
    in military, 244–256
    polarization, 244
    in workplace, 243
General Accountability Office (GAO), 11

G forces (gravitational forces), 59
Gillibrand, Kirsten (D-NY), 7, 89
*Girls Come Marching Home: Stories of Women
    Warriors Returning from the War in
    Iraq, The*, 232
Glass Ceiling Act of 1991, 252
Greek art, 30
Greenhow, Rose O'Neal
    Confederate Army, 38
    passing intelligence, 38
Gross national product (GNP), 111
Ground Combat Element (GCE), 263
Gulf War, 60

H

Hagel, Chuck, 7, 259
Hamozyn, 30
Harpalykos, King of Thrace, 30
Harris, Marcelite, J. (retired Major General), 251
    African Americans, 138
    aircraft maintenance officer course, 139
    avionics squadron commander, 139
    combat exclusion policy, 143
    first women
        in aircraft maintenance officer, 138–139
        on Board of Directors of USAA, 142
        in Director of Maintenace, 138, 140
        in Director of Training, 138
        in field maintenance squadron
            commander, 139
        in Major General, 138
        in Vice Commander military aircraft, 138
    received Bronze Star for Vietnam era
        conflict, 140
    TDY, 140
    U.S. Air Force, 138
    Vice Commander for Oklahoma City Air
        Logistics Center, 140
Hatch, Judith (retired MSG), 168–173
    Air National Guard/U.S. Military Reserve,
        168–169
    combat exclusion policy, 172–173
    first woman challenge the National Guard
        and Reserve's policy, 169–170
Hatshepsut, Queen of Egypt, 28
Hausa empire, 29
Herodotus, 28
Hobby, Oveta Culp, 42, 245
Holcomb, Thomas, 44
Holloway, James, 199
Holm, Jeanne, 139, 256

Holmstedt, Kirsten, 232
House Armed Services Committee (HASC), 89
Huey, 164

I

Illinois Air National Guard (ILANG), 169
Inactive ready reservist (IRR), 192
Individual Ready Reserve (IRR), 270
Infantry Officer Development (IOD), 264
Intercontinental ballistic missiles (ICBMs), 59–60
Internal Revenue Service (IRS), 123
Intorre, Sandra, 211–216
    early life, 210
    first uniformed women at Camp Zama, 211
Invisible War, The, 6, 88
Iraq and Afghanistan Veterans of America (IAVA), 55
Iskra, Darlene
    first woman commander in the U.S. Navy, 179–183
    supported in Operation Desert Shield/Storm, 180

J

Jackson, Rose Marie, 192–195
    first female Cohort of Surface Warfare Officers in the U.S. Navy, 192
    held various positions, 193
    supported in combat zone (Operations Desert Shield/Storm), 193
Jacksonville Naval Air Station, 224, 228
Jebel Sahaba, 27
Judge advocate general (JAG), 67, 96, 184, 187, 231
Judith, Queen of Falashes, 29

K

Kansas Army National Guard (KSARNG), 155
Kime, William, 68
King, Martin Luther, Jr., 251
Klay and Hellmer v. Panetta et al. (2013), 98
Korean conflict, 54, 204, 214, 222
Kravec-Kelly, Tiffany, 216–222
    Combat Action Badge recipient, 216
    early life, 217
    first female PSYOP Team Chief (U.S. Army Reserve), 216
    first woman unofficially served in *37F "I"* Indicator position, 216
    marriage conflict, 220
Krusinski, Jeffrey, 89
KSARNG (Kansas Army National Guard), 155
Ku Klux Klan, 229
Kumaratunga, Chandrika Bandaranaike, 57

L

Lady of the Mercians. *See* Aethelflaed
Lieutenant colonel (LTC), 156
Lioness. See Operation Iraqi Freedom
Lott, Trent, 204
Louis VII, King of France, 34
LTC (lieutenant colonel), 156

M

Malady, 278
Maloney, Carolyn (D-NY), 104
M16A1 rifle, 209
Marine corps, 263–264
Marine Gazette, 12
Mariners
    assignment, 180–181, 185, 193–196, 198–200
    women, 179–202
Marquet and Kendzior v. Gates et al. (2012), 98
Masculinity, 244, 246–247, 249–250
Master Sergeant (MSG), 168
Mazur, Anne, 204
Mbandi, Zinga, 30
McAfee, Mildred, 42
McCain, John (R-AZ), 116
McCaskill, Claire (D-MO), 114
McHugh, John (R-NY), 91
McKeon, Howard (R-CA), 89
McPeak, Merrill, 59
    combat exclusion policy judgment, 60
    women disqualified from combat, 59
Mead, Margaret, 295
Middle East, 31
Military
    advertising campaigns, 245
    ban on gay/lesbian/homosexuals, 246
    role of men, 243
    service
        ban on gays/lesbians, 186–189
        to bar women, 183
        use of gender, 189–190, 194, 201

training in, 244, 246
woman's
   difficulties, 250
   experience, 251
   integration, 245
   role, 243–244
Military Leadership Diversity Commission (MLDC), 7, 84, 268, 287
Military occupational specialties (MOSs), 62, 166, 217–219, 224, 260, 268
Military Personnel Center, 139
Military Sealift Command, 199
Military sexual trauma/assault (MST), 91
Military Students' Services, 222
Monkiewicz, Anna Flynn, 151–155, 251
   first women to fly for WASP, 152
   served as reserve police officer, 154
   served in WWI, 152
   U.S. Air Force, 152
Moses of Her People, The, 39
MSG (Master Sergeant), 168

N

National Cemetery in Arlington, 38
National Defense Authorization Act (NDAA), 66, 192, 200, 263, 268
National Gay and Lesbian Task Force, 187
National Military Command Center, 200
National Military Family Services (NMFS), 269
National Public Radio's (NPR's), 88
Naval Air Station (NAS), 224, 228
Naval Criminal Investigative Service (NCIS), 93
Naval War College, 181
Navy School of Diving and Salvage, 180
NCO in charge (NCOIC), 228
Negishi Microwave site, 198–199
Nineteenth Amendment to the United States Constitution, 251–252
Noncommissioned officer (NCO), 209, 223–225, 228, 234
Nontraditional occupations, 280
North Atlantic Treaty Organization (NATO), 68
Nurse corps, 40

O

Observation helicopters (OH), 164
Octavian, 31

Office of the Secretary of Defense (OSD), 66
Officer candidate school (OCS), 180, 184, 192
Officer Training School (OTS), 138
On-the-jobtraining (OJT), 170
Operation Enduring Freedom, 55, 75, 186
Operation Iraqi Freedom, 55–56, 186
Operation Just Cause, 54–55
Operation New Dawn, 56
Operations Desert Shield/Storm, 55, 61, 71, 84, 180, 182, 186, 193–194, 205
Operations Enduring and Iraqi Freedom, 210, 217–218, 221, 223–234
Operations tempo (ops tempo), 228, 269
Operation Urgent Fury, 54–55
   Bray, Linda, 60
   female lead troops into combat, 60
Owens v. Brown, 196, 199
Owens, Yona, 196–202

P

Pacific Air Force (PACAF), 140
Panamanian Defense Force (PDF), 49
Panetta, Leon, 5
Paul, Rand (R-KY), 7
Pearl Harbor (1941), attack on, 41
Pentagon
   annual report on sexual assault, 88
   sexual assault prevention program, 89
Pentagon rhetoric, 288–289
Permanent change of station (PCS), 161
Petronio, Katie, 237
PFC (Private First Class), 157, 218
Pitcher, Molly, 39
Playboy magazine, 92
Pollution theory, 284
Polygraph, 189
Posttraumatic slavery syndrome (PTSS), 278
Posttraumatic stress disorder (PTSD), 104
Prisoners of war (POWs), 12, 20–21, 40, 71, 213
Pritchett, Cynthia (CSM), 207–211
   early career field, 207
   first female CSM
      Combined Armed Center (Ft. Leavenworth, Kansas), 207
      with Command and Coalition enlisted troops in Afghanistan, 207
      Ft. Belvoir, Virginia, 207
      Subunified Combatant Command at Times of War, 207
   first female Senior Enlisted Advisor, 207
   first female Sergeant, 207

Private First Class (PFC), 157, 218
Pro bono, 187
Psychological operations (PSYOP), 216–220
Public Broadcasting System (PBS), 104
Pumping Iron II: The Women, 247

Q

Quicksand in Southeast Asia, 46

R

Re-orgy. *See* U.S. Military Academy
Reserve component (RC), 262
Reserve Officer Training Corps (ROTC), 157, 193, 204–205, 214, 222
Risk rule, 70
Rodriguez, Pamela (retired Colonel), 155–160
    Army National Guard, 155
    combat exclusion policy, 159
    first female
        aviator in KSARNG, 155–156
            Battalion Commander of AZARNG, 155
            Commander of ARNG WAATS, 155
            Company Commander, 155
    LTC/Tank Battalion, 156
    PFC, 157
    ROTC program, 157
    second women to fly Skycrane helicopter, 155
Rogers, Edith Nourse (R-MA), 40
Roman Empire
    Chiristianity to Europe, 32
    rule, 31
Roosevelt, Eleanor, 210
Roosevelt, Franklin, 296
Rosenberg, Anna, 44
ROTC (Reserve Officer Training Corps). *See* Reserve Officer Training Corps (ROTC)

S

Scholastic Aptitude Test (SAT), 185
Schroeder, Patricia (D-CO), 13, 50
Scythian Amazons/Sarmatians, 28
Segal, David, 181
Segal, Mady Wechsler, 181
Selective Reenlistment Bonus, 272
Service Women's Action Network (SWAN), 5, 116, 268

Sex role orientation, 244
Sexual assault, 89–132
    investigation of Air Force instructors, 94
    in military, 91, 104
    military information theft by prostitue spies, 112
    penalties, 249
    Task Force report, 105–106
    against women, 104
Sexual Assault and Prevention Response Office (SAPRO), 88
Sexual harassment, 90, 121, 180, 183, 190–191, 197, 201
Sexual orientation, 184, 186, 188–189
Shammuramat, Assyrian Queen, 28
Sirica, John, 200
Snyder, Vic (D-AK), 91
Solomon, Queen of Sheba, 30
Southeast Asia (SEA), 48
Special Operation Forces (SOF), 265
Special Operations Community, 180
Speier, Jackie (D-CA), 115
Status quo, 196
Stipe, Beverly "Sam," 203–207
    commanded mission support functions
        in Ronald Reagan Ballistic Missile Test Center (Marshall Islands), 205
        in Space and Missile Defense Command (U.S. Army Kwajalein Atoll), 205
    first woman
        in Nike Hercules Battery Missile Unit, 203
        in Patriot Battery Missile Unit, 203
    in Operations Desert Shield/Storm, 205
    various assignments, 205
    various business/services, 207
Strategic Air Command (SAC), 161
Sudan, 27
Summer, Rita, F., 160–163
    C-130 navigator, 160
    combat exclusion policy, 162
    first women
        coherts of navigators, 160
        to complete navigator training, 161
    served in 917th Air Refueling Squadron, 161
    U.S. Air Force, 160
Sumner, Charles, 253
Super grades, 212
Survival, escape, resistance, and evasion (SERE), 81

SWCC (special warfare combatant-craft crewmen), 262
Symbol of America's independence, 39

T

Tailhook scandal, 94
TDY (Temporary duty), 161
  assignments, 140
Team Lioness, 223, 225–227, 232, 235, 237
Temporary duty (TDY), 161
  assignments, 140
Temporary Separation Policy, 271–272
Thompson, Trish (retired CWO5), 163–167
  AGR in COANG, 164
  combat exclusion policy, 166–167
  discovered gadgetry in C-141, 165
  first cohert of women warrent officers, 163–164
  first women CWO5, 163
  flew in UH-1, 164
  rank E-5, 164
  U.S. Army, 163
TRADOC Analysis Center (TRAC), 260
Training and Doctrine Command (TRADOC), 260
Treasure of the City of Ladies, 33
Tubman, Harriet, 39

U

UH-1, 164
Underground Railroad, 39
Uniform Code of Military Justice (UCMJ), 88
United Arab Emirates, 186
United Service Organizations (USOs), 138
United Services Automobile Association (USAA), 142
USAA (United Services Automobile Association), 142
U.S. Air Force, 68, 138, 261
  Cohen, Sharron Frontiero. *See* Cohen, Sharron Frontiero (second lieutenant)
  Harris, Marcelite, J. (retired Major General). *See* Harris, Marcelite, J. (retired Major General)
  Monkiewicz, Anna Flynn. *See* Monkiewicz, Anna Flynn
  not prevent women from aircraft, 59
  recruitment of women increased, 67
  Sumner, Rita, F. *See* Sumner, Rita, F.
  Vaught, Wilma, L. (retired Brigadier General). *See* Vaught, Wilma, L. (retired Brigadier General)
U.S. Army, 259–260
  compensation, 239
  drawbacks, 236
  female recruitment proportion, 249
  Intorre, Sandra. *See* Intorre, Sandra
  Kravec-Kelly, Tiffany. *See* Kravec-Kelly, Tiffany
  male sexual relations
    military information theft, 112
    with prostitue spies, 112
  Pritchett, Cynthia (CSM). *See* Pritchett, Cynthia (CSM)
  Rodriguez, Pamela. *See* Rodriguez, Pamela (retired Colonel)
  sexual assault, 90
  Stipe, Beverly "Sam." *See* Stipe, Beverly "Sam"
  Thompson, Trish. *See* Thompson, Trish (retired CWO5)
  Wilmot, Michelle. *See* Wilmot, Michelle
U.S. Army Research Institute for Environmental Medicine (USARIEM), 260
U.S. Army Special Operations Command (USASOC), 260
U.S. Bureau of Labor Statistics (U.S. BLS), 282
U.S. Central Command (CENTCOM), 209
U.S. Department of Homeland Security (DHS), 271
U.S. Department of Transportation, 67
U.S. General Accountability Office (GAO), 45, 61, 282
U.S. Marine Corps, 184, 187, 192
U.S. Merit Systems Board Protection (USMSBP), 120
U.S. Military Academy, 204
U.S. Naval Academy, 183–185, 190, 198
U.S. Navy, 179, 183–184, 192, 196, 261–263
  Coast Guard subordinated to, 67
  combat exclusion policy
    expanding female force, Marine Corps, 66
    less contentious, 62
  decision points, 261–263
  Dunning, Maria "Zoe," 183–192

U.S. Navy (*Continued*)
    Don't Ask, Don't Tell, and Don't Pursue policy, 183
    sixth class of woman entered, 183
  Iskra, Darlene
    first woman commander, 179–183
    supported in Operation Desert Shield/Storm, 180
  Jackson, Rose Marie
    first female Cohort of Surface Warfare Officers, 192
    held various positions, 193
    supported in combat zone (Operations Desert Shield/Storm), 193
  Owens, Yona, 196–202
  Tailhook scandal, 94
USS *Abraham Lincoln*, 72
USS *Acadia* (AD-42), 182
USS *Constitution*, 38
USS *Dwight Eisenhower*, 73
USS *Hector* (AR-7), 180
USS *Hoist* (ARS-40), 181
USS *Lexington*, 69
USS *Opportune*, 180–182
U.S. Special Operations Command (USSOCOM), 259, 268, 280–281
U.S. Supreme Court, 110, 252
Utility helicopter (UH), 158

V

Vaught, Wilma, L. (retired Brigadier General), 88, 144–149
  career officer, 146
  chaired NATO Committee on Women, 146
  commander of U.S. Military Entrance Processing Command, 145–146
  commander of WAF squadron, 145
  discharge due to eyesight problems, 145
  Dupont Company, 145
  first women
    to attain rank of general officer, 144
    to deploy with bomber wing, 144, 146
    Industrial College graduate, 146
    line officers, 146
  management analyst in Wing Commander, 146
  U.S. Air Force, 144
Veterans Administration (VA), 167, 207, 237, 239, 279
Viet Cong, 49
Vietnam conflict, 54
Vietnam syndrome, 49
Vinson, Carl (R-GA), 62
Voting Rights Act of 1965, 256

W

War
  of 1812, 38
  and peace, 57
  against Tamil separatists, 57
WASPs (Women's Airforce Service Pilots), 42, 152
WAVES (Women Accepted for Voluntary Emergency Services), 41, 197
Webb, James, Jr., 64
Western Army Aviation Training Site (WAATS), 155
Wilmot, Michelle, 223–239
  first embedding female Soldiers and Marines (Operations Enduring and Iraqi Freedom), 223
  member of All Woman Combat Force (Team Lioness), 223
  misidentified race, 227
  promotion withdrawn, 233
  served as NCO, 228
WINS (Women in the Naval Services), 197
Wolfenbarger, Janet, 10
Women
  in Air Force, 48
  Amazon army, 28, 35
  assigned duties
    of Air Force to remorte locations, 60
    for noncombat ships, 63
  austere working conditions, 63
  Coast Guard, 67
  combat cockpits assignment, 68
  femininity, 244–250
  in military, 83
  myths, 74–83
  opponents, 12–15
  pilots, 59
  pollution theory, 88
  proponents, 15–20
  represented within occupation
    active duty commissioned officer by military, 25*t*
    of active force by military, 23*t*
    of reserve commissioned officer by military, 26*t*
    of reserve force by military, 24*t*
  roles in combat, 60

sacrifice and wounded in military campaign, 22t
served in military campaigns, 21t
sex crimes in military, 89
soldier raped and killed, 88
total military force, 21t
in war. *See* Women in war
warrior, 30
Women Accepted for Volunteer Emergency Services (WAVES), 41, 197
Women Airforce Service Pilots (WASPs), 42, 152
Women Armed Services Integration Act of 1948, 67, 202
Women in Military Service for America (WIMSA), 12, 144, 263
Women in the Air Force (WAF), 48, 139, 152–153
Women in war, 27
    American experience, 37–56
    disguised themselves as men, 38
    educated, 44
    health problems, 41
    memorial statue, 39
    military recruits, 44
    served as spy, 40
    wounded avoided going to hospital, 38
Women Marines Organization, 271
Women on ships, performance, 271

Women's Army Auxiliary Corps (WAAC), 40
Women's Army Corps (WAC), 40–42, 153, 184, 212–213, 245
Women's Integration Act of 1948, 58
Women's Research and Education Institute (WREI), 58
Women's Rights Project, 200
World War I (WWI), 53
    women's experience, 40
    yoeman, 53
World War II (WWII), 8–9, 53–54, 184, 196–197, 211–214, 245, 258

X

Xena: Warrior Princess, 28

Y

Yoemanettes, 53
Yoruba people (West Africa), 29

Z

Zaire. *See* Democratic Republic of Congo
Zenobia, Queen of Palmyra, 31–32
Zumwalt, Elmo, 198–199